Dragoons in Apacheland

Dragoons in Apacheland

Conquest and Resistance in Southern New Mexico, 1846–1861

William S. Kiser

University of Oklahoma Press : Norman

Also by William S. Kiser
Turmoil on the Rio Grande: The Territorial History of the Mesilla Valley, 1846–1865
(College Station, Texas)

This book is published with the generous assistance of The McCasland Foundation, Duncan, Oklahoma.

Library of Congress Cataloging-in-Publication Data

Kiser, William S., 1986–
　Dragoons in Apacheland : conquest and resistance in southern New Mexico, 1846–1861 / William S. Kiser.
　　　pages　cm
　Includes bibliographical references and index.
　ISBN 978-0-8061-4314-9 (cloth)
　ISBN 978-0-8061-4650-8 (paper)
　1. Apache Indians—Wars—New Mexico. 2. United States. Army. Cavalry, 1st—History—19th century. 3. United States. Army. Dragoons Regiment, 2nd—History—19th century. 4. Apache Indians—New Mexico—Government relations. I. Title.
　E99.A6K54 2012
　978.9'03—dc23

2012024000

The paper in this book meets the guidelines for permanence and durability of the Committee on Production Guidelines for Book Longevity of the Council on Library Resources, Inc. ∞

Copyright © 2013 by the University of Oklahoma Press, Norman, Publishing Division of the University. Manufactured in the U.S.A. Paperback published in 2014.

All rights reserved. No part of this publication may be reproduced, stored in a retrieval system, or transmitted, in any form or by any means, electronic, mechanical, photocopying, recording, or otherwise—except as permitted under Section 107 or 108 of the United States Copyright Act—without the prior permission of the University of Oklahoma Press.

For Donald Fixico,
my adviser and academic mentor at Arizona State University,
for showing me the way

And for my friends
Chase Kane, Justin O'Connell, and Justin Pribble

Contents

List of Illustrations	ix
Preface and Acknowledgments	xi
Introduction	3
Prologue: Duplicitous Proclamations	13
1. The Soldiers	19
2. The Apaches	37
3. The Early Years of Military Occupation	54
4. The Department under Sumner	89
5. The Woes Continue	124
6. One Regime to the Next	152
7. Events Foreshadowed	174
8. "Campaign of Clowns"	203
9. The Mescaleros	232
10. The Dragoons' Final Years	272
Conclusion	284
Notes	293
Bibliography	331
Index	345

Illustrations

Figures

Dragoon buttons excavated in New Mexico	23
Dragoon martingales and rosettes excavated in New Mexico	23
Apache knives and iron arrowheads	44
Colonel Edwin Vose Sumner	98
Governor James S. Calhoun	99
Present-day site of Fort Conrad	103
Fort Fillmore, 1854	109
Fort Webster, 1851 or 1852	114
Territorial Governor William Carr Lane	130
Cuentas Azules	135
Indian agent Michael Steck	150
Territorial Governor David Meriwether	154
Brigadier General John Garland	157
Fort Thorn, 1856	160
Mowry Mine, c. 1864	190
Colonel Benjamin Bonneville	206
Present-day site of Fort Stanton	257

Maps

Chiricahua Apache homelands, mid-nineteenth century	40
Mescalero Apache country, c. 1830	233

Preface and Acknowledgments

By the time I was in middle school, my dad and I had visited most of the 1850s forts in southern New Mexico dozens of times and had metal-detected at several of them, finding old dragoon buttons, insignia, belt buckles, and other relics that serve as some of the last remaining physical vestiges of the history contained in this book. Those trips sparked my interest in this topic.

I started reading everything I could find on Apache and U.S. military history and began taking notes; I also made many trips to the university library, during which time I learned how to operate a microfilm machine and read seemingly archaic nineteenth-century handwriting. At that period in my life, this was nothing more than a hobby to fill free time, and I gradually moved on to other projects throughout my high school years. When I began college at New Mexico State University, I returned to my dragoon and Apache research with more seriousness and resolve. What began as simply a history of the dragoons became far more than that as I started looking into additional source materials. I came to realize that the story involved a number of different groups, not just the dragoons, and the tale could not be told without including all of those peoples.

While I was an undergraduate student at NMSU, several individuals assisted me and provided support. I wish to thank Jeffrey Brown, Charles Harris, Jon Hunner, Mark Milliorn, and Louis R. Sadler—all members of the History Department who collaborated with me during my four years at the university. At the NMSU library and archives, Stephen Hussman and Larry Creider were particularly helpful.

Several small portions of this work became my M.A. thesis at Arizona State University. The process of converting my amateurish research and writing into a more scholarly, academically acceptable narrative took a lot of time and patience; with the help of my committee, this book as a whole truly matured. First and foremost I wish to thank my committee chair and academic mentor, Donald Fixico, for his tireless efforts in helping me improve all aspects of my writing and research. I also extend my gratitude to my committee members, Christine Szuter and Jannelle Warren-Findley, for their advice and assistance throughout the process. This final product is a book that is twice as long as and bears very little resemblance to the first draft that I wrote as an undergraduate. More than anybody else, these three persons deserve credit for helping me grow as an historian.

Other faculty and staff at Arizona State University who deserve my appreciation include Nancy Dallett, Peter Iverson, Joe Lockard, Brooks Simpson, Philip VanderMeer, Mark von Hagen, and Kent Wright. I specifically wish to thank John Southard, my friend and fellow graduate student, for reviewing and editing much of my work; John's gracious efforts have saved me many mistakes and have improved my publications as a whole.

My friend Edwin R. Sweeney, the preeminent historian of Apache history, has also helped me with this project—no work on the Apaches would be complete without consulting Ed Sweeney. He graciously helped me with research and provided information from his own files. Ed also read a preliminary draft of the manuscript and provided invaluable advice and commentary, which helped improve the work as a whole, and for that I am most grateful.

I enjoyed the benefit of conversations with several individuals with knowledge in this particular subject area. Mark Stegmaier reviewed two chapters of this work and provided commentary as did Bob Sproull, Bob Spude, and Terry Humble. Their consultation was most helpful in shaping the structure of this book. Additionally, during the course of my studies, I have benefited from conversations with many scholars, including Dan Aranda, Durwood Ball, Ned Blackhawk, Brian DeLay, Alan Gallay, Pekka Hämäläinen, Martha Sandweiss, Rachel St. John, Samuel Truett, and Richard White.

Numerous research institutions proved helpful in preparing this manuscript. At the Missouri Historical Society, Dennis Northcott provided copies of the files in the William Carr Lane Papers. At Arizona State University, Ed Oetting obtained important microfilm materials for my use. Susan Irwin and the staff at the Arizona Historical Foundation assisted with research, as did the staff at the Arizona State Archives and the University of Arizona. In Santa Fe, archivists at the New Mexico State Records Center and Archives aided my research, as did staff at the Center for Southwest Research at the University of New Mexico. I also wish to thank John Pierce for assistance with photographs.

At the University of Oklahoma Press, Editor in Chief Charles Rankin has been a pleasure to work with throughout the process and showed a remarkable amount of patience in helping me improve this book prior to publication. I extend to him my most sincere gratitude for his efforts.

No acknowledgement section would be complete without mentioning family and friends. I am blessed with a loving family who supports me in all that I do, including my parents, Dan and Jerine, and my sister Christine. I have been fortunate to have many great friends who support and encourage me in all of my academic endeavors.

Dragoons in Apacheland

Introduction

Herein lies the tale of a brutish, mostly regional conflict between two disparate groups of people vying over the same land and resources and struggling to understand each other's motivations. This war, fought between Anglo-American and Indian forces, is bookended by two colossal conflicts with far-reaching national and international implications, the Mexican-American War and the Civil War. The conflict that erupted between Americans and Apaches in the Southwest Borderlands traces its roots to the U.S. victory over Mexico in 1848, which enabled the United States to take political and legal possession of New Mexico Territory—a somewhat synthetic ownership from the indigenous perspective, and one the Apaches opposed violently throughout the ensuing decades. The fighting proceeded unabated in New Mexico for fifteen years until being punctuated by another, mostly unrelated event two thousand miles to the East, a clash that pitted father against son and brother against brother. That conflict, the American Civil War, forever altered the intercultural melee transpiring in New Mexico's parched desert terrain.

Although neither the Mexican-American War nor the Civil War was fought for the purpose of affecting Indian relations, both represent turning points in Anglo-Apache interactions. The Mexican-American War helped instigate Anglo-Apache conflict, bringing

American troops and Apache warriors into constant contact with each other and also necessitating the implementation of U.S. policy and administration in the newly acquired territory. The Civil War enlarged the scale of that conflict as more U.S. troops arrived in the territory after 1861. It also initiated a more rapid influx of settlers to New Mexico and the arrival of new technologies, including the telegraph and the railroad. The fifteen years between these wars, a period with its own distinctive political, military, and cultural characteristics, is the subject of the following narrative.

As the Apaches actively resisted American encroachment, violence became a defining characteristic of the antebellum southwestern frontier and deeply affected the lives of all who ventured into the region. Engulfed by perpetual warfare, entire southwestern communities and societies were shaped and then reshaped by patterns of reciprocal animosity that ultimately enabled Anglo-Americans to exert considerable levels of influence over both Indians and the natural landscape: the relationship between Anglo-Americans and Apaches epitomizes this phenomenon.[1] Dominion over New Mexico's land and people would not come easily for American imperialists, however, as the fifteen-year period of conflict antecedent to the Civil War clearly demonstrates.

This work places events in southern New Mexico in the larger context of mid-nineteenth-century American nation-building and economic expansion. It emphasizes the functions of individuals within the civil and military areas of government and examines the contentiousness between them; it analyzes the role of military force at both an individual and local level, involving both Apache warriors and American soldiers; and perhaps most significantly, it highlights the evolving dynamics of relationships and interactions—within differing cultural and geographical boundaries—in shaping the southwestern landscape and the people inhabiting it.

Two separate conflicts are fleshed out in this book. The first involves that outlined above, pitting Apache Indians against Anglo-American soldiers, pioneers, and bureaucrats in a fierce competition for domination of space and resources. The second is the story of white men fighting each other, not with firearms or weapons, but with carefully aimed wit and bureaucratic maneuvering. Just as Apaches fought foreign invaders to retain control of the land, so too did white men fight each other over their preferred outcomes for that land and the ultimate disposition of the Indians. Thus, this narrative entails two simultaneous conflicts transpiring in New Mexico, neither of which would be satisfactorily resolved during the interwar period, but both of which would have severe ramifications for the respective actors involved.

In 1849 the federal government transferred the Bureau of Indian Affairs to the Department of the Interior, marking the first time that jurisdiction over Indian affairs fell to any entity outside the War Department.[2] This division of authority at the highest level signified the beginning of a seemingly interminable contention between factionalized federal and territorial bureaucrats regarding proper policies in the western territories, their implementation by civil officials, and their enforcement by military forces.[3] A resulting struggle for power and prestige emerged between civil authorities and military officers, inevitably trickling down to affect almost every occupant of New Mexico: not only the longtime Hispanic inhabitants, who suffered the hamstringing effects of endemic Indian depredations, but also the Indians themselves, who endured civilian reprisals and full-fledged military actions.

The conflict between Apaches and Anglo-Americans in the pre–Civil War era can be attributed to several basic causes that, when considered in tandem, represent a broad range of difficulties that defined human interactions across much of the interwar western frontier. Cultural misunderstandings, political corruption in Santa Fe and Washington, anti-Indian ideologies, recalcitrant troublemongers within the Apache tribe and among American settlers, irresponsible army officers and troops, unscrupulous American and Mexican traders, and a general inability of civil and military officials to coalesce on a single policy all undermined an everlasting effort to arrive at a mutually acceptable coexistence in the Southwest Borderlands. Personal motivations underlying all of the above-mentioned factors contributed to both individual behaviors and mutual interactions at the local, territorial, and national levels.

A thorough understanding of these motivations through modern interpretive frameworks is crucial to arriving at an adequate comprehension of Anglo-Apache conflict in the Southwest during the antebellum years. If we can come to appreciate these fundamental characteristics of New Mexico's pre–Civil War frontier, we can better understand why these peoples' descendants and successors—Cochise, Victorio, and Geronimo on the Apache side, and James H. Carleton, George Crook, and Nelson A. Miles on the American side—came to wage the violent struggle that they did beginning in the 1860s.

The administration and enforcement of federal Indian policy in New Mexico during the territory's antebellum years, as relating specifically to the Apache tribes, has commonly been given short shrift among historians in favor of subsequent policies and events spanning the 1860s through the 1880s. Yet it is during the years preceding the Civil War, with New Mexico in its infancy as a U.S. possession, that the roots of later Anglo-Apache struggles can be found. The vicious interactions that defined the well-known Cochise, Victorio, and Geronimo conflicts had as their predecessors the 1850s Apache Wars, a struggle that lasted many years, claimed many lives, and produced little aside from increased animosity and suffering. Indeed, New Mexico's federal and local Indian policies during this formative prewar period, including the role of the Apaches themselves in continually reshaping U.S. policy and redirecting military activities through their own actions, deserve a more detailed analysis.

Scholarship since the 1920s has forced historians to rethink intercultural exchanges occurring in the West. Academics once interpreted western history as a unilateral movement from the East that culminated, according to Frederick Jackson Turner, with the 1890 census as a symbolic "closing" of the frontier. Many historians in recent years, however, have challenged such simplistic and ethnocentric notions. Turner's conception of the frontier came under direct opposition when his former student, Herbert Eugene Bolton, proposed the "borderlands" theory as an interpretive counterpoint.

Bolton's vision involved a more broad-ranging conceptualization of history, one that accounted for multiple actors and perceived human interactions as occurring in various directions rather than according to the linear progression of Turnerian thought.[4]

While Turner and Bolton represented pioneering methodological approaches to American and western history in general, not until the early- to mid-twentieth century did military historians begin focusing on army complicity in U.S. westward expansion. The works of Averam B. Bender, Robert M. Utley, and Robert W. Frazer revolutionized scholarly thought on the military's role in the Southwest and have continued to influence historians. Bender and Utley produced far-reaching studies covering the military's involvement across the vast western domain, while Frazer's several publications focused on events in antebellum New Mexico specifically and shed light on the military's participation in economic development. Still others, including Durwood Ball and Robert Wooster, have built upon previous military historians' arguments and modernized those earlier narratives, fleshing out historical events through broader analyses that take into account transnational perspectives.[5]

Another important methodological approach deployed in this study is that of scholars of American Indian history, many of whom have essentially written military history but with a bilateral approach incorporating both American and indigenous armed forces. Among the Apache historiography specifically, Morris E. Opler, Angie Debo, and Dan L. Thrapp emerged early on as influential scholars, with Opler representing a pioneering ethnohistorical approach. Edwin R. Sweeney has greatly increased our knowledge of, and broadened our perspectives on, Apache history in his excellent works, all of which have irrefutably influenced scholarly thought regarding the Chiricahua Apaches and their influence on the evolution of the Southwest Borderlands. In his pivotal monograph *Mangas Coloradas,* Sweeney mined Spanish-language sources and archives south of the border in order to vividly portray the ongoing collision between Apaches and Mexicans, allowing historians to more thoroughly comprehend the nature of preexisting intercultural conflict in this porous transnational region.[6]

The emergence of the so-called new western history movement in the early 1990s, with Richard White, William Cronon, and Patricia Limerick as three of its best-known progenitors, once again caused a shift in analytical interpretations and allowed historians to ponder the true complexity of a multidimensional frontier where numerous ethnic groups clashed violently in defense of geographic, communal, and spiritual space.[7] Most recently, revisionist scholars such as Ned Blackhawk, Brian DeLay, and Pekka Hämäläinen have catapulted new western history and indigenous-history movements to entirely new levels, ones that see human interactions and movements in the Southwest as less simplistically linear and more complexly amorphous. These authors have provided readers with thoughtfully construed inversed narratives that place previously marginalized actors at the center of the story, bringing to light heretofore untold tales of human struggle and survival in a frontier plagued by violence on multiple levels of political and cultural hierarchies. In so doing, they have highlighted indigenous power and agency as a primary determining factor in relations with Anglo-Americans, in essence filling in the puzzle using previously underappreciated components of borderlands history.[8]

The aforementioned authors and theoretical approaches represent not a comprehensive overview of interpretive strategies for American frontier history, but rather a general synopsis of the progressive evolution of historical thought with an emphasis on selected sources that have influenced this book. My research and interpretations attempt to mesh certain elements of these approaches in consideration of their applicability to the micro-narrative of Anglo-Apache conflict in southern New Mexico. Although I attempt to account for the Apache role as much as possible, I make no claim to write ethnohistory, nor should this work be considered a component of the "new Indian history" movement.[9] While continuing to consider many of the more antiquated approaches to western history, I endeavor to employ some of the modern frameworks in hopes of encouraging readers to rethink historical events, and even more specifically military history, in the Southwest. I have set out to portray military and Apache history as it transpired in a relatively short timeframe, 1846–61, and across a comparatively diminutive geographic area, southern New Mexico.

Ultimately the struggle between Apaches and U.S. dragoons can be summarized as a clash of competing cultural imaginations of the landscape that originated in vastly differing pasts, presents, and desired futures. The Apaches viewed the surrounding environment as the center of their community, their own spatial construct that formed a crucial component of both individual and tribal identity, providing the ingredients necessary not only for existence but also for prosperity. Through a combination of raiding-induced pastoralism, harvesting naturally growing mescal, and hunting wild animals, Apaches sustained themselves for generations in moderated hegemony over the land and developed, over the course of many years, a staunch sense of nationalistic pride comparable to that of Anglo-Americans.[10]

Apaches styled themselves as being intimately linked, both physically and spiritually, with the natural world and utilized resources and animals only sparingly as a means of coexisting with the environment. Their god, Ussen (Creator of Life), "put the Apache on the land which He had created for us." Certain persons within the tribe possessed a specific *power*, defined by one Apache as "a mysterious, intangible attribute difficult to explain." Epitomizing this reverence for the landscape and the tribes' own providential beliefs, one Apache, Ace Daklugie, exercised his power by chanting:

> Ussen gave us this land,
> Through our forefathers
> It has come to us.
> It was our land
> Before the White Eyes came;
> It is still our land.[11]

Although Apaches rarely spoke of their traditional faith and power, the few accounts that they related to early ethnologists indicate a unique relationship to the land through their creator,

Ussen.[12] Apache myths and folktales include references to lightning, thunder, rain, and water as natural phenomena emanating from one and the same divine force.[13] As he surrendered to U.S. troops in 1886, Geronimo nostalgically stated, "Once I moved about like the wind," a reference not simply to the stealthy celerity of movement for which he and other Apaches had become famous among non-Indians but also to the Apache perception of the natural environment, forming a mutual give-take relationship based on necessity, not excess.[14]

The antithesis to the Apaches' imagined landscape came first in the form of early Spanish colonists, then agrarian and pastoral Mexicans, and finally with Brigadier General Stephen Watts Kearny and his command on an autumn day in October 1846 (see prologue). All of these newcomers to Apachería collided violently with indigenous peoples, imagining the landscape in a different way consistent with their own cultures and almost invariably ambivalent to those already inhabiting the region. In the eyes of these imperialists, the Apaches' conservative utilization of resources and veneration for the landscape did not constitute optimum use. An 1850s *Santa Fe Weekly Gazette* editorial epitomized the American perspective, proclaiming that New Mexico possessed "great dormant resources . . . , and the Indian incubus keeps them dormant."[15] Sylvester Mowry, a dominant political and entrepreneurial fixture in southern New Mexico and Arizona, echoed the *Gazette*'s attitude when he wrote in 1857, "The Apache is the generic name for the whole race of Indians which have been for more than a century the scourge of northern Mexico, and which are today the great obstacle to the settlement of Arizona, to the transportation of the mails overland to the Pacific, and to the development of the immense mineral wealth of the Territory."[16]

Such statements exemplified Americans' insatiable desire for complete dominion over land and resources, and their supposition of providential design caused them to believe that the Southwest beckoned for "civilized" occupation through the installation of their own political and economic infrastructures. To them the landscape represented a region destined for the development of a capitalist economy, one where exploitation and extraction of natural resources could be strategically combined with improving technologies and transportation to advance their mid-nineteenth-century dreams of nation building and Manifest Destiny.[17]

In this rapidly evolving southwestern world, events and circumstances were oftentimes manipulated from thousands of miles away by individuals with little or no firsthand experience of the region, continuously affecting both intracultural and intercultural relationships in New Mexico. Thrust into the middle of this complex power struggle were the U.S. dragoons, mounted troops charged with garrisoning frontier outposts and enforcing Indian policy in a militarized landscape. These soldiers, many of them young men newly immigrated from Europe who merely sought a paying job—and perhaps an adventure—also personally affected the surrounding landscape and its people. While such men might have possessed little authority in formulating policy or issuing orders, their day-to-day interactions with the Apaches became a primary dictating factor in the diplomatic, or sometimes undiplomatic, paths that their superiors pursued.

The chapters that follow highlight the role of empowered politicians and military officers in the context of everyday frontier life as experienced by the dragoons. This work attempts to elevate the average soldiers, whose roles have been shrouded by 150 years of history, to a level of importance comparable to that of more-prominent public officials. Serving as low-paid privates at secluded posts, most of these men had no vested personal economic or political interest in the landscape, and so, contrary to the more transparent officers and politicians, their motivations are sometimes difficult to determine. Yet their collective efforts had an undeniable influence on Anglo-Apache conflict as it played out among bureaucrats at the higher territorial and national stratum.

Americans sought to conquer and control—to exert authority and power—over all components of the western landscape in order that they might realize its full economic potential. The Apaches composed an axiomatic facet of that landscape much the same as lofty mountain ranges, raging rivers, and desiccated deserts. All of these natural and human elements required conquering and subjugation before U.S. supremacy could be fully imbued in the Southwest, and over the several decades following Kearny's arrival, countless individuals streamed westward intent on accomplishing just that. The Apaches, like most western tribes, became a critical force of resistance in a cycle of conquest driven by an American obsession with exercising hegemony over land and people. Just as swarthy lawyers challenged preexisting claims in order to gain legal dominion over western lands; just as engineers constructed dams and sought ways to manipulate streams and rivers; just as the plow tilled millions of acres of virgin soil; and just as the miner's pick slowly chipped away at formidable mountain peaks, so too did the U.S. Army set out to subdue the Apaches, all of these being a means toward a common desired end for the western frontier. The pages that follow will show that the government—both civil and military authorities—materially failed in these attempts throughout the post-1846 period.

Unrelenting in their aspirations, civil and military officials advanced American designs on the southwestern landscape throughout the antebellum era by vigorously pursuing their goals through different strategic approaches, essentially seeking to subjugate, remove, or even exterminate any Apache occupants who would not relent and using the dragoons as a tool to help achieve those objectives. Two opposing cultures with vastly differing goals for their own futures were thus pitted against one another in a war that would endure for the better part of four decades, commencing in the late 1840s and not ending until the surrender of Geronimo and his followers at the aptly named Skeleton Canyon in September 1886. In the process, countless persons would come to see the anomaly enshrouding General Kearny's irrational vision of a benign coexistence in New Mexico, one where raiding and reprisals never occurred and where Americans slept free from fear in the company of their Indian brethren.[18]

PROLOGUE

Duplicitous Proclamations

The inception of U.S. Indian policy in New Mexico occurred in June 1846, when Stephen Watts Kearny departed Fort Leavenworth, Kansas, en route to Santa Fe with a command of 1,586 troops comprising the Army of the West.[1] This military force acted in conjunction with two additional large commands, the Army of the Center and the Army of Occupation. Together, the three armies marched toward Mexico—the former through Texas and the latter from Vera Cruz to Mexico City—in a war that would perpetuate the American philosophy of Manifest Destiny. Under orders from the secretary of war, Kearny's army marched into New Mexico intent on taking possession of that province in the name of the United States.

A man of temperate demeanor emanating from a prominent eastern family, Kearny enlisted in the New York militia prior to the War of 1812 and spent the rest of his life serving in the U.S. Army. By the time he led the Army of the West, Kearny already could boast more than three decades of military experience.[2] His troops followed him westward along the Santa Fe Trail, entering New Mexico in August 1846. As the command approached the New Mexican settlements from the northeast, it remained wary of a possible attack; after all, the two nations were at war and many of the locals, as Mexican nationals, perceived the army as a hostile invader. The general alluded to the cultural disparities that his troops would experience in orders issued on August 17, just days before entering Santa Fe. "We are taking possession of a country and extending the laws of the United States over a population who have hitherto lived under widely different ones," he acknowledged, reminding his subordinates, "humanity as well as policy requires that we should conciliate the inhabitants by kind and courteous treatment."[3]

Entering Las Vegas, Kearny climbed atop an adobe roof and delivered the first of several speeches to the Mexican residents. Through an interpreter he informed them of his mission to conquer New Mexico, stressing that he hoped to do so without bloodshed but would use force if necessary. With the American occupation, he told them, the U.S. government would provide New Mexicans with greater protection from hostile Indians than had been previously afforded under Mexican administrations. Perhaps underestimating the difficulty entailed in keeping such a bold pledge, Kearny promised complete security from Indian raiding. "From the Mexican government," the general proclaimed, "you have never received protection. The Apaches and Navajos come down from the mountains and carry off your sheep, and even your women, whenever they please. My government will correct all this."[4]

President James K. Polk backed Kearny in this pledge, seeking leverage over a weak Mexican government and believing that, by assuming responsibility for preventing Indian forays, the United States could more easily induce the negotiation of a favorable treaty—one ceding to it vast amounts of Mexican territory—in order to end the war.[5] Previous Mexican administrations had invariably exerted insufficient effort and resources toward defending settlements in New Mexico, Chihuahua, and Sonora from Apache raiding, owing in large part to a wholesale neglect of and widespread ambivalence toward these northernmost provinces. Indeed, the widespread devastation across northern Mexico, inflicted by both Apaches and Comanches in the decades preceding Kearny's arrival, precipitated a relatively straightforward American victory during the war.[6] Looking to capitalize on the peoples' desperation and gain their allegiance, the U.S. government aimed to reverse these precedents of unhindered Indian incursions through a combination of diplomacy and military force, although events in the ensuing fifteen years would prove that most American officials had little notion of how to achieve an effective balance.

Kearny might have imagined how difficult it would be for his countrymen to uphold his promises, but the responsibility would fall on the shoulders of his successors, for his orders instructed him not to remain in New Mexico but to continue marching toward the California coast. Indeed, numerous federal and territorial officials would grapple with Indian affairs in upcoming years, burdened with the task of enforcing ill-conceived guarantees. Several years later Superintendent of Indian Affairs James L. Collins lamented that "Kearny . . . did not remain long enough in the Territory to find out his mistake, for mistake it certainly was," blatantly begrudging his predecessor's assurances of complete protection for the people.[7] Had the general understood the calamitous responsibilities entailed in preventing Indian depredations, he might not have uttered his fateful words to the New Mexicans.

Kearny pressed onward toward Santa Fe, where Governor Manuel Armijo awaited his arrival with a sizable body of troops and contemplated the outcome of a potential clash between the two forces. One might have reasoned, and in fact Kearny expected, that the New Mexicans would resist the invading army, yet Governor Armijo had difficulty making the decision whether to stand and fight or to turn and run. Knowing that his adversaries possessed greater determination and superior firepower, and also being persuaded by his American acquaintances in Santa Fe to avoid resistance, the governor made the last-minute decision to surrender New Mexico. Thus, the Army of the West occupied Santa Fe without firing a single shot; scarcely in all of U.S. history had such a bloodless conquest occurred. Kearny departed Santa Fe for California on September 25, leaving behind the majority of his 1,500 men under the command of Colonel Alexander W. Doniphan. He did, however, take with him one hundred dragoons, along with Lieutenant William H. Emory's 14-man topographical engineering unit to record and map the route across southern New Mexico to the Pacific coast.[8]

The march to California took Kearny directly through the heart of Apache country, making his expedition the first large American military force to come into contact with members of that tribe. Dispatching an advance party to meet with the Indians, the general hoped to dissuade them from fleeing at the sight of a sizable body of foreign invaders.[9] By October 19 the troops had reached the Gila River, where they met Mangas Coloradas, principal chief of the Chiricahua Apaches. Despite the intense apprehension that he must have felt in making such a bold commitment to total strangers, Mangas swore "eternal friendship to the whites," assuring Kearny that his Apache followers would allow Americans to pass peacefully through their country, sleeping among his people in safety and without fear of attack. Furthermore, the venerable Apache chief offered to furnish the Americans with guides to ensure their safe passage through the region. Had Mangas known what the future held, he likely would not have made such gracious gestures.[10]

General Kearny displayed a sense of respect for the Apaches, who could have contested his march westward had they chosen a course of hostility rather than friendship. In his chronicle of the campaign, Lieutenant Emory nostalgically recollected that "several [Apaches] wore beautiful helmets, decked with black feathers, which, with the short skirt, waist belt, bare legs and buskins, gave them the look of pictures of antique Greek warriors." Such a description invokes images of the "noble savage" popular in contemporary literary works and indicates the culturally misinformed manner in which these early Americans viewed their Indian counterparts. Further describing the encounter, Emory noted: "The Mexican dress and saddles predominated, showing where they had chiefly made up their wardrobe. One had a jacket made of a Henry Clay flag, which aroused unpleasant sensations, for the acquisition, no doubt, cost one of our countrymen his life."[11] Even at this early juncture, evidence of the Apaches' victims and the extent of their raiding could clearly be seen manifested in their wardrobes and other possessions, an omen of encounters to come.

At this informal initiation of Anglo-Apache relations, no open hostility occurred. Indeed, the two sides professed friendship toward one another and pledged to shun future violence. Having had little previous interaction with Americans aside from a few fur trappers and traders passing through during the previous two decades, the Apaches had little reason to act aggressively and therefore exhibited an affable disposition toward the visiting white men. At that time the two shared a common enemy in Mexico and might have perceived each other as potential allies in future military offensives against that country; one Apache chief purportedly told Kearny's command: "You have taken New Mexico, and will soon take California; go, then, and take Chihuahua, Durango, and Sonora. We will help you. . . . The Mexicans are rascals; we hate and will kill them all."[12] It would not take long, however, for these feelings of benevolence to dissipate and be replaced with open distrust and hostility, largely as a result of unwarranted treachery and malevolent reprisals by members of both sides.[13]

The story of Kearny's occupation of New Mexico has been retold innumerable times by historians as a tale exemplifying President Polk's imperialistic aspirations and America's overt aggression toward Mexico. But on a deeper level, Kearny's actions during his brief one-month passage through New Mexico illustrate far more than that. In that short timeframe, he initiated two very distinct intercultural relationships, both bearing some unique characteristics while simultaneously epitomizing the unsympathetic American attitude toward preexisting occupants of the Southwest. As a leading general in a time of war, Kearny acted in a capacity that allowed him both civil and military authority, and therefore his behavior during encounters first with the Mexicans in Las Vegas and Santa Fe, and later with the Apaches near the Gila River, initiated a series of blunders that defined antebellum New Mexico Indian affairs. In his capacity as a military officer, Kearny promised the Mexican inhabitants that his government, through troops provided by the War Department and funds from Congress, would protect them from hostile Indian raiding. A month later, meeting with the Apaches in a diplomatic capacity, he and Mangas Coloradas professed eternal friendship toward one another. Kearny thus upheld his obligations to federal officials, but after being immersed in New

Mexico for more than a month and having become familiar with the existing state of hostilities between the Indians and Mexicans, he must have realized the contradiction of his words. As Kearny might have guessed, it would prove impossible for the U.S. government to achieve both of his professed outcomes.

CHAPTER 1

The Soldiers

Anglo-Apache conflict in southern New Mexico prior to the Civil War involved two groups that found themselves vying for power and control over a shared southwestern landscape. Vast cultural differences separated the two, and each group struggled to understand the other. Beyond the difficulties of coexisting with their neighboring Native inhabitants, Anglo-Americans also had trouble coping with the unforgiving environment and sundry other unfamiliar characteristics of the Desert Southwest. The troops stationed in New Mexico experienced innumerable hardships resulting from poor equipment, dilapidated living quarters, and grueling campaigns in the field, among other challenges.[1] Throughout the decade of the 1850s, three types of U.S. troops operated against the Apaches: dragoons, mounted riflemen, and infantry. Each regiment bore distinctions in composition and tactical training, but all served the shared purpose of fighting Indians.

The rigors of frontier army life in antebellum New Mexico are sometimes overlooked because much of the extant primary-source material emanated from higher-ranking officers who enjoyed advantages not available to enlisted men.[2] While junior officers typically did not fare much better than their subordinates, the higher-ranking men who reported on troop conditions often did so from a skewed perspective because their elevated status allowed them privileges and amenities otherwise unavailable to the bulk of the soldiers.

In the diary that he kept from 1850 to 1856, Private James A. Bennett of Company I, First Dragoons provides a rare glimpse of daily life for soldiers during this time period. Bennett arrived in Santa Fe at the age of eighteen and enlisted in the army, perhaps underestimating the hardships that he would face. During his six years with the First Dragoons, Bennett would be stationed at more than a half-dozen different southwestern posts. He saw action against the Navajos, Utes, Jicarilla Apaches, and Mescalero Apaches, traveling thousands of miles on horseback while enduring scorching hot summers and brutally cold winters with only limited provisions, typifying the arduous duties of an 1850s dragoon.

On March 30, 1854, during a skirmish with hostile Apaches, Bennett received a gunshot wound through both thighs, the ball ultimately lodging itself two inches below his groin. "The horses dragged me one half mile [before] I managed to mount my horse ... blood flowed freely," he later recalled. Arriving back at his post, he "was taken off [the] horse, having ridden 25 miles after being wounded." Bennett spent the next several months in the hospital recovering from his painful wounds, the healing process being significantly impeded by rudimentary medical equipment and technology. "The doctor we have here knows nothing," Bennett complained. "I asked him to extract the ball last night but it was not done until today."[3] Many of the casualties discussed hereafter, soldier and Indian alike, doubtless shared Bennett's excruciating medical experience during this primitive antebellum era. The fact that these men readily thrust themselves into a conflict so brutal and ruthless is evidence of the importance that Anglo-Americans placed on quelling Indian raids and opening the frontier for safe settlement.

The U.S. Regiment of Dragoons (the predecessor to the cavalry) was organized pursuant to an act of Congress dated March 2, 1833. In May 1836 this outfit became the First Regiment of Dragoons after the raising of another regiment, designated the Second

Dragoons.⁴ Following the Mexican-American War, these two units served throughout the western territories, with many of their component companies being stationed at New Mexico's posts. Together with the infantry and the Regiment of Mounted Rifles, the dragoons undertook the unenviable task of thwarting Apache, Ute, Comanche, and Navajo raiding in New Mexico up until the onset of the Civil War.

Each of the two dragoon regiments contained a maximum of 652 men, substantially less than the 802 allotted to the Mounted Rifles. A congressional act of June 17, 1850, mandated that dragoon companies contain a maximum of 50 enlisted men per company, with ten companies in each of the two regiments.⁵ But the tactical nature of Indian warfare on the western frontier, coupled with the vast domain requiring protection, ultimately induced an executive order increasing each company's allowable manpower to 74 in certain regions, New Mexico being one of them.⁶ In 1855 the secretary of war reported that each regiment contained 615 enlisted men, indicating that company strength had indeed been augmented, though not to the maximum capacity.⁷

For the most part, dragoon companies never boasted full strength. Secretary of War Charles M. Conrad, in his annual report of 1850, noted, "It rarely happens . . . that a company is complete, for, while on the one hand the enlistments can never exceed the limit prescribed by law, deaths, discharges, and desertions must always cause the number of men actually enrolled and in pay to fall far short of it." Conrad pointed out that this characteristic held especially true on the western frontier, estimating that the number of men "fit for duty" typically fell 30–40 percent short of the legal organization of the army.⁸

The Regiment of Mounted Rifles (commonly abbreviated "RMR") could best be described as another dragoon regiment, only under a different name. Congress, recognizing the need for additional cavalry troops on the western frontier but hesitant to raise a new regiment at the higher pay grade of dragoons, created the Regiment of Mounted Rifles in 1846. The four-company unit would receive the "pay of infantry, and forage of dragoons," which reduced War Department expenditures on the regiment by roughly 10 percent annually.[9] Riflemen were trained to fight as infantrymen but rode horses for speed during the chase. How strictly this tactical ideology was followed in New Mexico is questionable, for tracking and fighting the elusive Apaches as infantrymen seldom proved successful. Each company contained a maximum of sixty-four privates. Riflemen did not generally receive assignments in New Mexico until 1851; from that point on they routinely participated alongside dragoons and infantry in military maneuvers against the Apaches, especially after 1856, when the War Department transferred all Mounted Rifle companies remaining in Texas to New Mexico.[10]

Finally, the infantry actively partook in Indian affairs during these years as well. Of the army's 1855 aggregate total of 12,703 troops, almost half of them—5,582—belonged to infantry regiments.[11] In 1850s New Mexico, the vast majority of foot soldiers belonged to the Third Infantry Regiment.[12] While these troops often performed thankless duties as laborers at their respective posts, they nevertheless did receive occasional exposure to the rigors of campaigning, especially after Colonel Edwin V. Sumner assumed command in 1851. Unfortunately, the unique characteristics of Apache warfare often rendered the infantry useless in the field. The Apaches "stand in little awe of troops on foot," Secretary of War Conrad admitted, "but a light and active cavalry could pursue and chastise them, or recapture their plunder, whereby their depredations would be rendered more dangerous and less profitable."[13] As Conrad and many others knew, mounted dragoons and riflemen held a distinct advantage over infantry in that they could be mobilized for pursuit at a moment's notice and move rapidly.

In theory, the 1850s dragoon would have an impressive physical appearance, wearing uniforms ornamented with gilded buttons and insignia and laced with the standard yellow pennons adorning trousers and blouse alike. According to army regulations, they would ride perfectly fit horses similarly decorated in shiny regalia, including rosettes and martingales featuring the identifying markings of both the company and the regiment. In actuality, as will

Dragoon uniform buttons excavated in New Mexico. Photograph by the author.

Dragoon martingales and rosettes (horse accoutrements) excavated in New Mexico. The letters correspond to the respective dragoon companies. Photograph by the author.

be seen throughout these pages, most dragoons rarely maintained such an appearance; to be sure, the harsh southwestern environment, reverberating from numbing cold to extreme heat, did not prove conducive to such pomp and show.[14] Soldiers partaking in burdensome post duties and difficult marches through treacherous terrain hardly concerned themselves with ensuring a striking physical appearance in a region where scarcely anybody would see them anyway. While post quartermasters retained a significant amount of army-issue accoutrements in storage, most soldiers only donned them when on parade, preferring instead to dress more casually and comfortably when on the march.[15] Indeed, many officers continually submitted requisitions to replace obsolete, worn-out government-issue uniforms and equipment, a reality hardly befitting the oft-painted image of an ideal dragoon.

Life on the frontier could be daunting, perhaps more so for soldiers than for any others who ventured westward.[16] They performed unrewarding tasks under unfavorable conditions for minimal pay. One can scarcely imagine the seclusion and isolation these men experienced in a territory situated thousands of miles from what they considered to be civilization. As attested to in numerous diaries and journals, the Southwest's sparsely populated, predominantly Mexican villages did not constitute civilized life in the eyes of newly arrived soldiers from the East.

Private Josiah M. Rice, who saw a considerable amount of military service in New Mexico, frequently bemoaned the repulsive tendencies exhibited by some of the residents he encountered. "[Mexicans] are the meanest and most contemptible set of swarthy thieves and liars to be found anywhere," he wrote in a scathing, ethnocentric indictment of Hispanic character. "The rich ones will cheat and swindle and the poor [will] sneakingly pilfer anything." Even worse, according to Rice, were the clergy: "The priests are high in position and always rich, but in morals and character they are, with few exceptions, even below their followers."[17] Rice's superior, Colonel Sumner, shared these sentiments. In 1852, as commander of the military department, he excoriated New Mexicans as being "thoroughly debased and totally incapable of self-government, and there is no latent quality about them that can ever make them respectable.... [T]hey have more Indian blood than Spanish, and in some respects are below the Pueblo Indians, for they are not as honest or as industrious."[18] Another officer complained, "The population [of New Mexico] at this time with individual exceptions was not half civilized."[19] While these racially skewed observations certainly did not apply to all persons in the territory, they provide a fairly accurate overview of the prejudiced outlook shared by many Anglo-American soldiers of that time.

Yet another difficulty the troops faced in their daily encounters with New Mexicans arose from linguistic differences, as communication between the two cultures oftentimes proved overly toilsome. Many of the army's antebellum enlistees came directly from Europe, having recently immigrated from the British Isles and Germany, and joined the military as a means of travel, adventure, and economic subsistence. In the 1860 census, for example, Company D, First Dragoons at Fort Buchanan contained fifty-one men between the ages of eighteen and forty-seven. Of those, twenty-seven were born in the United States, while twenty-four listed their place of birth as somewhere in Europe (sixteen being from Ireland). Company G, First Dragoons (also at Fort Buchanan) listed forty-one men, of whom twenty-five (61 percent) were immigrants.[20] Because of their diverse cultural and dialectal backgrounds, several languages were spoken among the soldiers, Spanish seldom being one of them. Many of the hired Mexican laborers who worked at southwestern military posts spoke only Spanish and therefore struggled to understand instructions from soldiers, which served only to exacerbate tensions. With few exceptions, neither the Anglo-American troops nor the Mexican-American inhabitants could effectively speak the other's language, and interpreters were few and far between.

Ironically, soldiers sometimes found themselves victimized by the federal government just as the Indians did. Most troops in the West received poor clothing and inadequate provisions from a cash-strapped War Department. Eastern bureaucrats devoted little attention to the necessities of soldiers stationed in a territory so far removed from the bulk of the nation's population. In terms of expenditures, Washington officials concerned themselves more with fortifying posts in the East, especially with monumental Mexican-American War costs still to be repaid and the threat of sectional conflict looming on the horizon. For most politicians, more important things demanded their attention than equipping troops to fight hostile bands of "savages," especially when New Mexico already bore the distinction of being the country's most expensive military department to maintain.[21]

In 1852 Colonel Sumner recommended that the War Department abandon New Mexico altogether, a suggestion that Secretary of War Conrad likewise advocated. Citing imperfect peace accords and interminable Indian warfare, the colonel believed that the government should "withdraw all the troops and federal officers, and let the people elect their own civil officers . . . under the general supervision of our government. . . . With regard to their protection from the Indians, they would have the same that was extended to them by the Mexican government—that is to say, permission to defend themselves."[22] An unapologetic Mexican-American War veteran, Sumner evinced little sympathy for the territory's Mexican inhabitants, who he viewed as an inferior race, and often felt that his assignment in Santa Fe represented nothing more than a waste of his time and taxpayer funds. Sumner's letter found publication in the *Santa Fe Weekly Gazette* and incited considerable controversy, given the harmful nature of his rhetoric. "All classes of our citizens," retorted the newspaper's editor, "Americans and Mexicans, males and females, old and young, will find themselves gratuitously and maliciously assailed" upon reading the colonel's recommendation to withdraw the troops.[23]

Secretary of War Conrad ventured a step further and suggested that all civilians be compensated for their property and relocated elsewhere, thereby eliminating the necessity for troops altogether. "Even if the government paid for the property quintuple its value," he hypothesized, "it would still, merely on the score of economy, be largely the gainer by the transaction, and the troops now stationed in New Mexico would be available for the protection of other portions of our own and of the Mexican territory."[24] These suggestions emanated from a profound level of frustration among military and civil authorities following more than six years of failed attempts to control New Mexico's nomadic tribes. Many of these men, exhibiting Anglo-centric ideals common to that era, did not believe that protecting the mestizo population warranted excessive expenditures and political hardships.

In an attempt to mitigate these concerns, officials such as Sumner and Conrad sought exit strategies that would allow the citizens to govern and defend themselves while the United States retained legal possession of the territory. Naturally, the civilian population condemned their point of view. The *Santa Fe Weekly Gazette* reprinted Conrad's statement and offered a terse rebuttal: "a proposition of this kind . . . [excites] in our minds nothing but cool contempt for its folly and absurdity." It also satirized Sumner as "the Big Bug of Albuquerque" and all but criminalized the military commander for both his policies and his ambivalence toward the territory's citizens.[25]

A dragoon private could expect to receive a paltry salary of $8 per month, while an officer's pay exponentially exceeded that amount. In 1851, lieutenants in the First Dragoons earned from $169 to $600 annually, with higher-ranking officers receiving considerably more. Infantry lieutenants accrued a comparable salary, averaging between $360 and $690. In addition to this base income, officers received allowances for rations and servants, often in amounts exceeding $1,000.[26] In 1854, under the administration of President Franklin Pierce, Congress passed legislation allowing a $4 wage increase for military personnel, bringing a dragoon private's earnings to $12 per month.[27] Miniscule stipends and infrequent visits from the paymaster created widespread discontent and worsened an already woeful level of morale.[28] The massive disparity between enlisted-men and officer salaries only exacerbated the situation.

To their credit, officers continuously pressured army paymasters to ensure that their troops got paid. In May 1852 Colonel Dixon S. Miles reported that a portion of his Fort Fillmore garrison had not received any pay in more than six months, despite military regulations requiring that the paymaster visit each fort bimonthly.[29] This six-month waiting period was not atypical of frontier military posts. Transporting specie hundreds of miles across the plains and through hostile Indian territories to distant New Mexico often proved difficult and time consuming. Miles called the situation at his post "burdensome" and requested that headquarters send a paymaster to Fort Fillmore without any further delay.[30] Others suffered similar shortcomings: Major Enoch Steen, in command at Fort Buchanan in 1857, championed his troops' cause when he complained to the paymaster that his men had not been paid in over ten months. "This long non-payment has caused a great deal of inconvenience," Steen lamented, "and no little grumbling among the soldiers."[31]

Such long delays between payments might have been a blessing in disguise in some instances. When the paymaster did make his rare appearance at a frontier fort, the soldiers could almost immediately be found gambling away their earnings. In March 1851 Private James Bennett recorded: "[The] paymaster arrived yesterday. Paid off the troops . . . all were interested in playing cards. Money exchanged hands as fast as possible. Up jumped one cursing himself, his parents, his God, his evil fortune. Another that fiendish smile exhibited because he had won his fellows' money. . . . [M]orning found many still gambling. Lost their sleep and their money. This is a practice followed very much by soldiers."[32] The proclivity of some men to wager hard-earned salaries speaks to the immense boredom prevalent at many of the frontier posts.

The majority of western forts rarely received adequate supplies or provisions from the quartermaster department, a reality that compounded dilemmas arising from infrequent pay and arduous duties and only further depleted troop morale. Each installation required four distinct types of supplies: ordnance, clothing and equipment, medicines, and subsistence stores.[33] With the exception of subsistence materials, such as forage and grain for horses, most of these items were manufactured in eastern factories and shipped to Fort Leavenworth, Kansas. From there wagon trains freighted supplies across the plains to regional depots, such as Fort

Union, from which location items were distributed to the smaller forts.

Not surprisingly, the cost of transporting these goods gravely concerned federal officials. Prior to the Mexican-American War, most military establishments in the East could be reached via navigable waterways, thus limiting freight expenditures. Following the addition of the 525,000 square miles of Mexican Cession lands in 1848, however, the army transferred the bulk of its troops to the western frontier. The area's vastness, coupled with the isolation of many military posts, initiated a drastic increase in spending.[34] In 1844, prior to the addition of the Mexican Cession lands, War Department expenditures totaled only $870,999. Six years later, for the fiscal year ending June 30, 1850, costs had multiplied more than ten-fold to $9,687,024.[35] In his 1850 annual report, Commissary General George Gibson ominously predicted that this trend would only worsen over time. "Every effort has been made to lessen the immense quantity of transportation required," Gibson explained, "by procuring in those [frontier] countries every part of the ration they could furnish—so far, however, with but little success. The distance of a large portion of the army from the sources of supply and the perishable nature of the ration have greatly increased the expense of subsisting the army; nor can it reasonably be expected this expense will be materially diminished for many years."[36]

Needless to say, some shipments of goods never arrived at their destinations, falling victim to the countless perils faced en route to New Mexico. As a result the military regularly issued contracts to local civilians in order to keep the forts supplied. The regional quartermaster's office at Paso del Norte frequently purchased locally grown subsistence stores to supply the three posts in that vicinity, including Doña Ana. Regimental Quartermaster R. W. Bowman noted in 1850 that the price of these contracts, "although high compared with that of the States, is less than half the cost of transportation from [the East]."[37] The frequency with which the army issued civilian contracts continued to rise correspondingly with the increasing number of troops stationed in the territory. In 1855 the War Department awarded 237 contracts for forage, fuel, subsistence, and transportation within New Mexico.[38] Even so, the basic necessities always remained in short supply, and many military campaigns floundered due to the fact that troops simply lacked adequate provisions.

Soldiers on the frontier often were housed in deplorable quarters. Most early New Mexico posts consisted of adobe brick buildings topped with leaky wooden roofs and dusty (or muddy) dirt floors. Lydia Spencer Lane, the wife of an officer with the Regiment of Mounted Rifles, recorded her homemaking inconveniences during a brief stay at Fort Craig in 1856. As an officer's spouse, she and her infant son were permitted to occupy the best room the post had to offer. Even so, she recalled, "the rain streamed through the roof like a shower-bath, and, though everything was saturated in the room . . . , we took it."[39] This woeful description applied twofold to enlisted men's barracks, which received only moderate upkeep. Modern amenities such as plumbing and running water simply did not exist at antebellum frontier military posts, nor did the structural components of adobe buildings adequately protect the inhabitants from inclement weather.

Family life was virtually nonexistent among enlisted men, and even among the officers, only a select few brought their loved ones to live with them.[40] The aforementioned Mrs. Lane, who spent the majority of her time traveling in the West with her rifleman husband, represents a rare exception to this rule. Another such example, Dixon S. Miles, relocated his family from Baltimore to Fort Fillmore in 1854. As a military man his entire adult life, Colonel Miles's family became well acquainted with frontier hardships. Of his eight children, three of them had been born at military posts; four of them died before reaching the age of two.[41]

New Mexico's unforgiving desert climate further menaced the soldiers. In the summers the southwestern sun bore down on the men and made them miserable in the heat. Water and whiskey often were the only drinks available; those who chose whiskey frequently found themselves under arrest by the following morning. Indeed, many soldiers spent weeks confined in filthy post guardhouses awaiting trial for alcohol-related offenses. In 1852 a total of eighty-one courts-martial occurred among the First and Second Dragoons.[42] Conduct at each post directly mirrored the commanding officer's enforcement of discipline. Some, such as Colonel Miles at Fort Fillmore, operated as strict disciplinarians and staunchly adhered to military protocol. Others, including Colonel Charles A. May and Captain Reuben Campbell, who intermittently held command at the Socorro post, exerted minimal effort toward disciplinary endeavors. An 1850 inspection of the post revealed: "Those of the Infantry are well instructed. The Dragoons are less perfect."[43]

Communication between posts presented a dilemma unimaginable in today's world. The telegraph, though invented in 1844, remained a mere figment of the imagination in isolated New Mexico until after the Civil War. All correspondence took place either by mail or in person; written communications had to be carried by dispatch riders for many miles over treacherous trails and rough wagon roads. Rarely did any message reach its destination in under a few days, and depending on weather conditions, it could take much longer. The inability to quickly spread notice of Apache depredations severely hamstrung the army's attempts to overtake the raiders and recover pilfered livestock.

One serious shortcoming in military effectiveness stemmed from the fact that the War Department exerted little effort toward adapting to the unique fighting and living conditions on the frontier. The overwhelming success of U.S. troops during the Mexican-American War created a sense of complacency among military leaders and civilian inventors; indeed, as one military historian has noted, "few innovations marked the history of the Army from the Mexican War to 1861."[44] Military strategy, as well as general equipment and technology, remained in a relatively antiquated state up until the 1860s.

Although the soldiers possessed relatively modern firearms, they remained inadequate for fighting frontier Indians in guerrilla-like warfare. When the dragoons arrived in New Mexico in the late 1840s, the metallic cartridge had not yet been adopted. The military's regulation-issue ammunition consisted of a .69-caliber round lead ball and gunpowder, all contained inside a paper cartridge.

Muskets, the most common firearms issued to the troops, had been a regulation firearm since 1842, but these highly inaccurate smoothbore weapons were ineffective at long ranges. Furthermore, if water penetrated the paper cartridges and moistened the gunpowder, or if the cartridge was dropped and broke open, the entire round became useless.

Even worse than the standard-issue musket, the Model 1847 musketoon was a sawed-off version of the same weapon issued to infantrymen. One soldier who had the misfortune of carrying one lamented, "[The musketoon] kicked like blazes, had neither range nor accuracy, and was not near as good as the musket, and was only used because it could be more conveniently carried on horseback."[45] Colonel Joseph K. F. Mansfield, while inspecting the department in 1853, further denounced these weapons for their uselessness: "The musketoon as an arm for the dragoon or mounted man in any way is almost worthless. . . . [T]here is no probable certainty of hitting the object aimed at, and the recoil [is] too great to be fired with ease." In contrast, Mansfield noted that the carbine and Sharps rifles "can be fired with rapidity and with suitable practice with great certainty."[46]

In November 1853, experimental models of the Sharps carbine underwent a six-month trial period with Captain Richard S. Ewell's dragoons at Los Lunas, New Mexico.[47] Ewell's report held nothing but praise for the new firearms. "[They] are fired far more rapidly than Hall's carbine or the service rifle," he affirmed, "with equal accuracy below two hundred yards, and rapidly increasing superiority ahead of that distance." He claimed that his company would be rendered "doubly efficient with the Sharps carbine than the present arm."[48] Colonel Daniel Chandler, commanding at Fort Conrad in 1854, likewise received a sampling of these new carbines for experimental use in the field. On an expedition against the Mescalero Apaches, Chandler selected several of his dragoons to carry the weapons. He praised the firearms overall, albeit less so than Ewell. Several faults could be found, including the lack of a shoulder strap for ease of transport. Without this feature, troops experienced difficulty holding on to the gun while riding, a problem clearly manifested during a running fight that took place between the colonel's troops and the Apaches. It proved nearly impossible to control the horse, aim, and shoot during mounted combat situations. Regardless of such shortcomings, Chandler reported that the Sharps carbine would be a much more effective armament for his dragoons than the muskets they currently used.[49]

Despite positive overall results during these field trials, it would be several years before the army adopted the Sharps carbine; not until 1858 did it become standard issue for dragoons.[50] Another major advancement came in 1855, when the army began using newly devised .58-caliber conical projectiles. Offering an appealing alternative to the obsolete and inaccurate .69-caliber smoothbore musket balls, this new innovation by Frenchman Claude Etienne Minié revolutionized firearm technology. Despite the paramount importance of this invention to nineteenth-century warfare, the Minié ball arrived too late to assist most dragoons in the Southwest.

The hardships faced during everyday life at New Mexico's forts paled in comparison to the difficulties troops endured when campaigning. Some of the more active dragoon companies traveled between 2,000 and 3,000 miles each year in pursuit of Indians. These excursions placed tremendous strain on men and animals alike. Rations consisted of bread (hardtack), coffee, beans, and either salt beef or pork and comprised the principal diet when in the field, but the quartermaster seldom issued these items liberally enough to fulfill the soldiers' daily needs.[51] Not infrequently did dragoons and infantrymen endure month-long scouts carrying rations meant to last only a week or two. In the summers especially, water became scarce; soldiers often had to camp without it, sometimes for two or three nights in a row. And where there was no water, there would also be no grass for the animals. During one expedition, Private Josiah Rice vividly recalled, "Our poor mules and horses were screaming and howling in want of grass all night long, which made our lieutenant so angry that he swore he would gag the whole of them."[52]

On most campaigns the weather would almost invariably present hardships. New Mexico's climate undergoes drastic changes from one season to the next: in winter it can be unbearably cold, and in summer hellishly hot. Summer rains, although providing a temporary respite from the heat, brought with them considerable misery for the soldiers in the field. Private Rice, accompanying an expedition in the early 1850s, recalled these unenviable circumstances: "At night, it rained tremendously hard, and [having] no tent, we crawled under the limber of our gun, to preserve ourselves from the rain. . . . [T]he water came running into us like a river, and in the morning, wrapped in a soaking blanket, were our men crawling around the fire to warm themselves; a more woe-begone set of men you never saw."[53] Standard government-issue winter clothing, especially boots and shoes, nearly always lacked in quality and durability. Infantrymen oftentimes returned to their posts barefoot, the soles of their shoes quickly succumbing to the rocky, mountainous terrain.

Such poor living conditions severely hampered the morale of most frontier soldiers, and justifiably so. But the men sought relief with various entertainments, including the occasional joke. On April 1, 1853, Private James Bennett provided himself with a laugh at the expense of his comrades. He recalled that he "sent over 20 men to the Commanding Officer for various pretexts, where they were informed that they were 'April Fools.'" His unfortunate victims probably failed to view the incident with as much humor as Bennett.[54] Besides the jokes they played on each other, the only other pastimes available to the men came in the form of saloons and brothels in the small New Mexican towns. These provided a temptation that many simply could not resist, despite the severe consequences that came with such behavior if caught. James Bennett, while stationed at Albuquerque, wrote: "The soldiers will be out of camps nights in spite of orders of officers. Four fandangoes [Spanish dances] every night in town and the camp is full of women."[55] The military kept strict orders in place at every post prohibiting soldiers from departing without first being granted a leave of absence, but any attempt to keep men away from the towns generally failed. Those caught absent from the post might be charged with desertion, a criminal act for which severe punishment could be expected. One dragoon private, after being arrested while attending a fandango in Albuquerque, received the typical punishment for deserters: a court-martial ordered that he be drummed out of the service, forfeit all of his pay, have his head shaved, receive fifty lashes on the back, and be branded on the hip with the letter "D" for deserter.[56]

Despite the severe repercussions if caught deserting, many soldiers joined the army for that very reason. A significant number of men enlisted for the sole purpose of traveling westward free of charge under the protection of the military, deserting immediately upon arrival and continuing west to try their luck in the California gold fields. This happened frequently at Forts Bliss, Fillmore, and Webster, the three southernmost posts in New Mexico during the early 1850s.[57] The road to California went directly through Forts Fillmore and Bliss and passed a mere half-day ride south of Fort Webster. In 1852 alone, twenty-five men of the First and Second Dragoons deserted from Fort Fillmore, a significant percentage of the 174 total regimental desertions that year across the entire Southwest, including Texas.[58] The ease with which soldiers could sneak away and quickly be en route to California increased the frequency of desertions. In October 1852, for example, seven soldiers (six dragoons and one infantryman) deserted from Fort Webster.[59] Following this incident, Colonel Miles, commanding at Fort Fillmore, acknowledged the heightened rate of desertion at his post as well, saying that "California Fever" had set in among his men. Not surprisingly, a pattern began to develop: every time the soldiers were paid, post commanders would invariably find one or two men missing from the ranks the next morning.[60] The many immigrant parties traveling to California always welcomed these men into their groups, realizing that when passing through Indian country, safety could be found in numbers.

The life of the 1850s frontier soldier posed innumerable hardships. Equipment and provisions seldom met the troops' expectations; several months often passed between visits from the paymaster; sickness and disease haunted many of the posts; discipline remained mediocre because of prostitution, gambling, and alcohol available at nearby civilian settlements; and morale thus proved difficult to maintain. The life of the frontier soldier in southern New Mexico can truly be described as one of extreme privation, exposing them to countless perils in addition to skirmishes with hostile Indians.

Officers in Santa Fe and Washington, D.C., who had not personally experienced these hardships often did not fully appreciate the daily struggles that troops faced. Many of the orders being carried out in frontier New Mexico emanated from men sitting in offices far removed from the scene of action. Their physical absence resulted in directives that simply could not be satisfactorily fulfilled. Superior officers expected to see definitive results from their troops in the field, not understanding the shortcomings they faced when operating against Apaches in their own homelands. Because they possessed only a nominal knowledge of frontier operations, higher-ranking officials did not adequately equip their troops and therefore detracted from their ability to act effectively in the field. Many of the hardships the dragoons suffered can therefore be attributed not only to the Apaches whom they fought and the rough environment in which they operated, but also to the military chain of command and its failure to adequately prepare and provision its troops. These three components of antebellum New Mexico military operations coalesced in the frequent failure of campaigns against nomadic tribes.

CHAPTER 2

The Apaches

To Anglo-Americans in the mid-nineteenth-century Southwest, the Apaches represented perhaps the most formidable of all challenges. While the soldiers struggled in the region's difficult climate and terrain, the Apaches thrived in it and revered the landscape for the physical and spiritual sustenance it provided them. Southwestern New Mexico had been their home for countless generations, and Apaches knew every tactic necessary to ensure their survival under even the most adverse conditions. The retention of their homeland and its surrounding environs, comprising a crucial component of Apache identity, formed the primary motivation for patterns of tribal life and inspired their staunch resistance to intrusions during the antebellum era.

Unfortunately, the Apaches kept no written records during the mid-1800s, providing a serious obstacle to historians wishing to uncover their perspectives and motivations. Most extant primary-source materials come in the form of memory, tradition, and oral histories passed down from one generation to the next. As those Apaches who experienced antebellum intercultural conflict in New Mexico died over the passage of many years, so too did much of their side of the story become lost or verbally altered by their descendants.

There are two important types of categories into which published Apache accounts fall: oral traditions that entail stories being passed down through multiple generations, and oral histories involving one individual recounting an event that he or she personally experienced. Oral traditions are the most problematic because stories of historical events often change when they are remembered and retold by a nonparticipant. For the purposes of this work, I have relied only on a select few oral histories that come from Apaches who partook in actual antebellum events, all of which have been authenticated or corroborated through comparison to Anglo-American documentary evidence. Even these sources are few and far between, however, as most Apaches who experienced the turmoil of the 1850s did not survive into the twentieth century, when ethnographers began recording their stories.[1]

Most surviving accounts of Anglo-Apache relations in the 1850s come from whites who lived in New Mexico. Consequently, many extant records are biased in favor of the Americans and represent the anti-Indian parlance common to that era. Some persons embellished their experiences in order to appeal to a popular audience and to align with prevailing ethnocentric ideologies. One scholar has compared the disparate nature of Apache oral histories and Anglo-American military and government reports to the literary device of cacophony, an apt metaphor in many instances.[2] Care has been taken herein to avoid usage of those Anglo-American primary sources on Apaches that are known to have been embellished or fabricated. Indeed, had the Apaches maintained written records, they would reveal a startlingly different tale than those of the soldiers, politicians, and settlers who recorded their experiences as seen through their own eyes.

The Chiricahua Apache tribe of southwestern New Mexico and southeastern Arizona called themselves *tinneh*, or *indeh*, meaning "man" or "people." The aggregate tribe consisted of several separate, often autonomous subgroups that were recognized internally among themselves and, to a lesser extent, externally by American officials as well. Each band typically claimed its own specific homeland, although they recognized no predetermined geopolitical boundaries and often joined forces for defensive purposes and seasonal raiding into northern Mexico. Additionally, disparate bands often coalesced during ceremonial gatherings and harvesting periods.[3]

The vast desert region over which the Apaches exerted power—today comprising southwestern New Mexico, southeastern Arizona, northwestern Chihuahua, and northeastern Sonora—is distinguished by extreme aridity and basin-and-range topography. The Apaches utilized the drastic changes in altitude between the basins and ranges to their advantage depending on the changing seasons. During cold winter months, they moved their villages, or rancherías, to lower elevations, and during the hot summers, they returned to the higher elevations. Thus the topographical and meteorological characteristics of the desert landscape often determined Apache settlement and migration patterns throughout the year. The harvesting of mescal also influenced tribal movement: at certain times entire bands would return to specific regions to gather this important staple.[4] After the mescal harvest had been fully consumed, the tribe often resorted to raiding in northern Mexico and along the Rio Grande for the remainder of the year. These incursions instigated a bitter conflict between the Apaches and Mexicans, one that raged simultaneously with the Anglo-Apache violence during the 1850s and therefore pitted the tribe against two separate foes, dividing their forces and resources and rendering it more difficult to effectively resist both American encroachment and Mexican reprisals.

These patterns defining the Apache ethos remained mostly unchanged for centuries until the mid-1800s, when Americans arrived in New Mexico and forever altered tribal lifeways. The influx of settlers—ranchers, farmers, miners, and soldiers—after 1846 drastically affected the Apaches' ability to move freely and unmolested throughout their homelands and challenged their traditional beliefs about the land. "At first the lure was minerals in our mountains; later the land itself was wanted for grazing," recalled Apache James Kaywaykla. "It was the prospectors and miners whom we considered most objectionable, for they groveled in the earth and

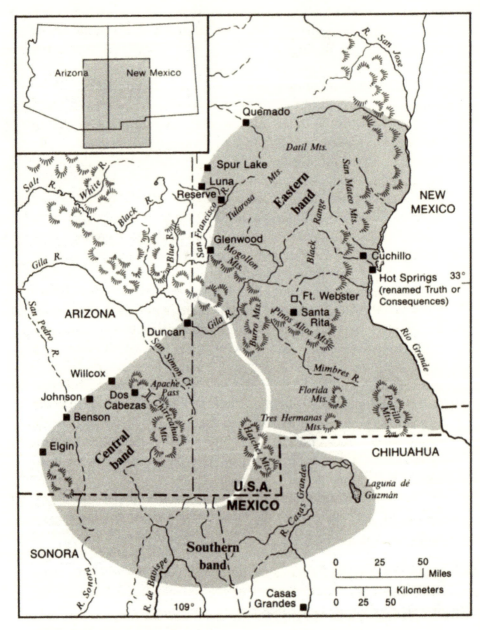

Chiricahua Apache homelands, mid-nineteenth century. Reproduced, with permission, from *Handbook of North American Indians*, ed. William C. Sturtevant, vol. 10, *Southwest*, ed. Alfonso Ortiz (Washington, D.C.: Smithsonian Institution, 1983), 402 (fig. 1).

invoked the wrath of the Mountain Gods by seeking gold, the metal forbidden to man. It is a symbol of the Sun, of Ussen Himself, and sacred to Him."[5] Ace Daklugie reiterated this aversion toward physically altering the landscape: "Apaches believed that . . . grubbing into Mother Earth caused earthquakes, and Apaches feared earthquakes. . . . [T]hey saw the effects of the shaking earth and thought that the Mountain Spirits, who are the servants of Ussen, caused the shaking to avenge the desecration of the mountains."[6]

The arrival of Americans had other consequences as well. Important water sources often became the site of a cattle ranch or military post, rendering vital resources unavailable to the nomadic Apaches as they migrated from one location to another. Tribal sacred sites sometimes became the locations of small towns. Settlers decimated wild-game populations, especially deer and elk, forcing the Indians to rely more heavily upon plundered livestock and government-issued rations for subsistence. Unscrupulous American and Mexican merchants provided a market for stolen articles and, worse, distributed debilitating liquors among the tribes that in turn sparked violent outbreaks—some of which would have never occurred. Self-proclaimed civilian militias attacked peaceful Apache camps and indiscriminately slaughtered defenseless women and children. South of the border, Mexican citizens did the same. Widespread encroachment thus had innumerable negative effects upon the Apaches and their fluidity of movement. From these forced fundamental alterations to traditional lifeways grew a violent conflict between Apaches and Americans that claimed the lives of countless men, women, and children on both sides and that did not dissipate for decades.

The three most prominent Apache bands, or subgroups, were the Chiricahua (who called themselves the Chokonen), the Mogollon and Gila/Mimbres (calling themselves the Chihenne), and the Janeros or Carrizaleños, who resided almost exclusively in the northern Mexican states of Chihuahua and Sonora and were known as the Nednhi.[7] In modern east-central Arizona, the Western Apaches—which the late Grenville Goodwin identified as consisting of five subgroupings, the White Mountain, Cibecue, San Carlos, Southern Tonto, and Northern Tonto—lived mostly independent of the New Mexico subgroups and rarely came into contact with American forces before the Civil War era.[8] Within each band there might be several smaller "local groups," described by one ethnologist as "a number of extended families who lived in the same general area and together exploited its resources. . . . [I]n most Apache tribes local groups that were in loose contact and could call upon one another for ambitious undertakings and emergencies constituted named bands."[9] The present study, though, pertains primarily to the Chiricahua Apaches, including the Mogollon and Gila/Mimbres bands and local groups of southwestern New Mexico.

Apache kinship and community structures made it difficult for American officials to properly identify and estimate subgroup populations. "The Apache embrace so many bands, and are so widely scattered, that it is extremely difficult to enumerate them," Boundary Commissioner John Russell Bartlett observed in 1850. "It is unusual to find 200 of them together," he continued, estimating that the total Apache population did not exceed 5,000 at that time.[10] Indian agents continued to grapple with this numerical ambiguity for years to come, continually struggling in their attempts to accurately portray the size of the tribe. Seasonal raiding and individual visits between family members of different bands meant that an entire subgroup contingent rarely convened for any length of time.

The profound importance of each band to Apache culture and identity cannot be overstated. These subgroups represented the basic structural component of the tribe, upon which all community and kinship revolved.[11] Only when necessary would several bands unite for a common purpose, sometimes forming warrior alliances for raiding or defense. The complex configuration of the Apache tribe and the relatively small size of individual bands made it difficult for those unfamiliar with them to distinguish one subgroup from another; as a consequence, many raids during the 1850s were attributed to innocent groups and resulted in punitive expeditions that targeted the wrong band. This frequent misidentification of groups within the larger tribe had its beginnings in the early American occupation period and would remain a characteristic element of Apache-Anglo struggles for decades to come.

The army's inability to understand Apache tribal organization is manifest in an 1859 report issued by department commander Colonel Benjamin L. E. Bonneville, noting, "the name Apaches is a general one . . . ; [the] Mogollon Apaches, Gila Apaches, Mimbres Apaches, Chiricahua Apaches, and Pinal Apaches merely designate their locality."[12] While Bonneville did distinguish between groups, his ascribed identities erroneously and simplistically asserted that all five of these contingents comprised one and the same "general" tribe and that the only discernible difference between them was the region in which they lived. Contrarily, all five lived and operated mostly autonomous of one another, due in some part to the geographic disparities that Bonneville noted but in larger part to their own tribal community structure, which many federal and territorial officials failed to understand. Bonneville's five bands might be likened to modern residents of five different U.S. states: all might share a common heritage as Americans, and some might even claim the same ancestors, yet none of the five may ever even meet or affiliate with one another during their lifetimes.

Because one band of Apaches committed robberies along the Rio Grande did not mean that every Apache had committed or even abetted the crime. In fact, it meant that every Apache *not* associated with the guilty party was completely innocent. The simple concept of guilty versus innocent, a cornerstone of the American judicial system, went widely ignored in a frontier environment where haughty soldiers, miners, Indian agents, and legislators placed personal ambition and economic gain above the moral principles upon which their own nation had been founded. In countless instances soldiers and civilians failed to make any distinction between Apache subgroups and simply pursued and attacked any Indians they encountered. When one small band embarked on a marauding expedition, the army often sought to punish *all* Indians, paying little attention to the fact that those upon whom they wreaked havoc were in many cases innocent of the crimes perpetrated. Much of the "success" that officers reported came at the expense of peaceful Indians; rarely did they manage to punish those tribesmen guilty of a particular atrocity. Inherent misunderstandings of tribal

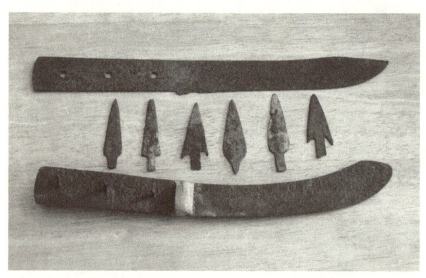

Apache knives and iron arrowheads dating to the antebellum era. Photograph by the author.

structure continued virtually unabated into the post–Civil War era and exacerbated the tension between the two cultures in the years to come.

Countless tales of incredible endurance can be found in nearly every account written about Apaches. By the time a male child reached the age of five, he had learned all he needed to know to fight and survive in the harsh desert environment.[13] Well trained by their elders in the arts of military strategy, Apache warriors could be counted among the most cunning and fierce enemies the army ever faced in the West. Under every circumstance in which an average white man would have succumbed to the elements, an Apache could find a way to survive. He or she could walk or ride with little or no rest for days—or nights—and where a wandering American explorer might have perished from thirst under the scorching summer sun, an Apache could locate vital water sources invisible to the naked eye.[14]

Despite this remarkable propensity for survival, the Apaches were overwhelmed by the torrents of settlers flooding into their region in the years following the Mexican-American War. The Anglo-Americans numbered in the millions, the Apaches in the thousands.[15] As more foreign interlopers entered the territory in search of their personal manifest destinies, especially in the years during and after the Civil War, it became exceedingly difficult for the Apaches to execute subsistence raids. During the antebellum period, however, with the territory's population still relatively small, raiding the Rio Grande settlements provided the tribe's principal means of sustenance. As a nomadic people, the Apaches essentially raided as a form of artificial agriculture; for warriors, the livelihood of their wives and children often depended upon the success of such strikes. "Raiding approaches hunting in economic significance," observed one Apache ethnologist; "in fact, these two pursuits may be said to be rival industries. . . . [T]he raid is recognized as an integral aspect of the economy." An overarching interest in the spoils of war provided the determination for most Apache raiding parties, as "glory and enhanced status were [only] by-products of the raid."[16] In this singular characteristic the Apaches differed substantially from men of contemporary Plains Indian tribes, many of whom partook in raids and warfare as a form of masculine expression through the exhibition of martial valor.[17]

Between the years 1846 and 1850, John Russell Bartlett claimed that Indians (including Navajos, Comanches, Utes, and Apaches) despoiled New Mexico's ranches and haciendas of 12,887 mules, 7,050 horses, 31,581 cattle, and 453,293 sheep.[18] These numbers, astounding as they seem, likely still fall short of the actual total, which is impossible to ascertain. In 1857–58 Secretary of the Interior Jacob Thompson compiled a detailed report of indemnity claims filed by New Mexico's citizens for stolen livestock. This included claims dating as far back as 1847, although most of the ones prior to 1854 (121 of 244) were ruled invalid since the 1834 Indian Intercourse Act required that a claim be filed within three years of the incident.[19] In the eight-year period 1847–55, citizens filed 244 claims totaling $502,986.68, although Thompson acknowledged that "the department is informally advised that claims to a much larger amount will eventually be presented."[20] These remained unsatisfied at the time of the secretary's report in 1858, and many of the claimants never received any type of remuneration. Seventy-two of the claims (or roughly 30 percent) specifically cited the Apaches as the depredators; the remaining 172 attributed blame to Utes, Comanches, Jicarilla Apaches, or Navajos.[21] These numbers also fail to reflect the number of Apache depredations in Chihuahua and Sonora, where the majority of their attacks actually occurred.[22]

Raiding villages along the Rio Grande and in northern Mexico was a practice in which the various Apache bands had indulged for generations and upon which they depended for survival when other food sources became scarce.[23] Two distinct types of strikes occurred: one intended solely for subsistence through the theft of livestock; the other characterized by a vengeful bellicosity utilizing seek-and-destroy tactics against anything in their path. Each raid originated from a specific motivation, and individual warriors within the tribe would often organize and lead parties depending on the purpose. On most subsistence raids, violence and death came only incidentally as victims attempted to defend their families and property. To ensure success, these parties consisted of only between five and fifteen warriors (women never accompanied a raiding party) because they could travel more stealthily and swiftly in small groups.[24]

On vengeance raids, war parties might consist of over one hundred warriors, organized by a specific individual with an avowed purpose.[25] In 1851 a young warrior of about thirty years of age named Goyahkla accompanied his band to the Mexican village of Kas-Ki-Yeh (Janos, Chihuahua) to barter with the inhabitants, with whom the tribe had recently been on peaceful terms. Learning that the Indians had encamped near the town, Colonel José María Carrasco, commanding general of military forces at Fronteras in the neighboring state of Sonora, gathered 400 men and marched eastward into Chihuahua. Apaches had killed 298 Sonorans in the preceding two years alone, and Carrasco sensed an opportunity for revenge.[26] The Sonorans attacked the unsuspecting Apache camp, killing twenty-one and seizing fifty-six more as captives, most of whom were transported deep into Mexico with little chance of ever being repatriated.[27] Among the dead were Goyahkla's mother, wife, and three small children. The surviving members of the band returned to southern New Mexico, where an aggrieved Goyahkla began plotting revenge and recruiting warriors from neighboring bands to join him on a massive, brutal strike into Sonora that would make no attempt to differentiate between men, women, and children. He later recalled this raid: "Still covered with the blood of my enemies, still holding my conquering weapon, still hot with the joy of battle, victory, and vengeance, I was surrounded by the Apache braves . . . [and] gave orders for scalping the slain."[28] In later years Anglo-Americans would come to know Goyahkla by his Mexican name, Geronimo.

Geronimo's experience leading this punitive expedition against Sonora typified the tribe's mode of revenge warfare. As the man who suffered the most grievous personal loss during Carrasco's attack, his Apache community expected him to organize the tribe's retribution as a form of self-vindication as well as personal prestige. With each passing raid, the hatred between the Apaches and the Mexicans intensified. Dr. Michael Steck, an Apache agent at Fort Thorn beginning in 1854, attested to this long-standing animosity. "It has from time immemorial been the custom of the Indians to steal from the New Mexicans and then the Mexicans to steal from them," he wrote. "This system of thievery and retaliation has been kept up, and under the Mexican rule organized parties were permitted to make campaigns for the avowed purpose of stealing Indian stock."[29]

Beginning with Mexican independence in 1821, chronic political and economic unrest plagued the infant country and diverted government attention away from protecting the frontier settlements. This held especially true in Sonora and Chihuahua, where secluded residents found themselves virtually ignored by their government and army and suffered the effects of devastating Apache and Comanche raids. Mexico's first ruler, Agustín de Iturbide, enacted a veritable monarchy and quickly fell into disfavor with the population. By 1824 Mexico had a democratic constitution, but rulers continued to come and go at an alarming rate. The 1828 election established a dangerous political precedent for the country when the democratically elected president was overthrown by Vicente Guerrero, who the government recognized as a legitimate ruler despite his coup. Soon afterward, Antonio Lopez de Santa Anna arrived on the scene and would go on to promulgate numerous forced changes in leadership during upcoming years. The turmoil surrounding the Texan rebellion in 1836 only exacerbated Mexico's political unrest. The country found itself with a new leader every couple of years, and policy objectives reverberated accordingly. Under these tumultuous states of affairs, the Apaches enjoyed almost free reign in the northern provinces throughout the 1820s and 1830s and utilized the opportunity to augment their plunder in the form of human captives, livestock, horses, and sundry other trinkets and trade items of Mexican manufacture.[30]

Continuously terrorized by Apaches, Mexico's oft-looted northern provinces did take independent action at the local level of government in an attempt to curb the Indian raids. Sonora passed legislation in 1835 encouraging its residents to hunt Apaches, offering to pay bounty hunters 100 pesos for each warrior scalp. The neighboring state of Chihuahua quickly followed suit, passing a similar law in 1837.[31] These decrees had a noticeable effect, with untold numbers of Apaches falling victim to the treachery of shrewd scalp hunters, the most notorious being the American James Kirker. Other Indian tribes, including the Comanches, began to target the more-easterly bands of Apaches (mainly the Mescaleros) after realizing that profits could be gained more easily from them.[32]

But this endorsement of scalp hunting also had an effect opposite of that intended. In 1841, for example, a mere four years after Chihuahua passed its law, 168 Mexican deaths occurred at the hands of Apaches amid 2,730 animals being stolen.[33] By the time U.S. troops arrived in 1846, the irreconcilable enmity existing between the Mexicans and Apaches had reached unprecedented levels. Sonoran officials acknowledged in 1849 that "very few pueblos in the state [of Sonora] have not experienced some form of devastation."[34] Reiterating this observation, Indian Agent Edmund A. Graves aptly explained in 1854: "They [the Apaches] live mainly by plundering and robbing both Old and New Mexicans. . . . [T]hey generally extend their peregrinations into the Mexican States of Coahuila, Chihuahua, [Sonora,] and Durango, from which States they drive off much stock, and take their captives."[35] Between the years 1851 and 1853, Apaches were blamed for more than 500 deaths in Sonora alone.[36] The Mexicans doubtless inflicted heavy casualties upon the Indians during that time as well, although they often embellished reports and no Apache records exist to reflect the precise number. Apache beliefs regarding the afterlife of a deceased person meant that they almost always carried their dead and wounded from the battlefield. Therefore, reports of casualties during combative encounters often represented mere guesswork on the part of their opponents and eyewitnesses. Many officials, Mexican and American alike, exaggerated Apache losses during hostile engagements in order to create a false appearance of victory and illuminate their own reputations.[37]

The nature of engagements between the Apaches and U.S. troops differed drastically from traditional military tactics of the antebellum era.[38] While military officers still clung to strategies learned from their European forefathers of pitched battles in wide-open spaces, the Apaches adopted more practical tactics, ones well suited for the rugged environment in which they lived. Despite inferior technology, their expertise in guerrilla warfare almost invariably gave them the upper hand in skirmishes with enemy forces. Apaches engaged in battle only when they held a major numerical or strategic advantage. Ambushes at vulnerable locations, usually from behind large boulders at elevated positions, represented their traditional mode of fighting. In this, American troops trained in obsolete European warfare techniques had to adapt quickly in order to avoid catastrophic losses. Guerrilla warfare on the Apaches' terms became a defining characteristic of military engagements in southwestern New Mexico and often resulted in minimal Indian casualties.

Despite the implementation of thoughtful military strategy, the Apaches did not always emerge victorious from their raids and battles. Years of continuous conflict, coupled with scalp hunters and epidemic diseases, had a gradual but pronounced effect, resulting in a diminishing population and a corresponding decrease in fighting strength. Writing in the mid-1850s, Indian Agent Michael Steck noted: "[T]here is a great disposition between the number of [Apache] men and women. This may be accounted for from the fact that for at least the last 100 years the tribe has either been at war with Old or New Mexico, sometimes both, and with neighboring tribes, and the men being killed in numerous battles . . . , they cannot bring into the field over half the number of warriors that they could have done 20 years ago."[39] Colonel Sumner similarly observed in 1851, "This predatory war has been carried on for two hundred years, between the Mexicans and Indians, quite time enough to prove, that unless some change is made the war will be interminable." As impetus for the continuing conflict, Sumner explained that "they steal women and children and cattle from each other, and in fact carry on the war, in all respects, like two Indian nations."[40]

As time passed, perpetual warfare with both the Mexicans and the Anglo-Americans continued to weaken the several Apache bands. The silver lining for New Mexico rested in the fact that ongoing Indian conflicts with Chihuahua and Sonora shifted focus away from the American settlements along the Rio Grande. "The facility and impunity with which [Mexico] is plundered and robbed, has measurably saved our own people from like visitations during the last and present years," Governor David Meriwether admitted in 1853.[41] This seething animosity endured for generations, even after the Apaches had been removed from New Mexico and Arizona. Geronimo, well advanced in years and living at the Apache reservation near Fort Sill, Indian Territory, in the early 1900s, proclaimed, "I am old now and shall never go on the warpath again, but if I were young, and followed the warpath, it would lead into Old Mexico."[42]

As countless military officers and Indian agents came to discover, the Apaches were traditionally a nomadic people. Government officials with sparse knowledge of and little concern for this cultural characteristic continually proposed that Apaches be permanently settled in built homes or on reservations. Governor William Carr Lane's 1853 treaty, although never ratified, sought to place the

Gila Apaches in fixed dwellings on a reservation near Fort Webster. So too did Governor Meriwether pursue this outcome in his provisional compact with the Gila and Mescalero Apaches at Fort Thorn in 1855. Many officials, civil and military alike, embraced this immobilizing strategy as the most appropriate disposition for New Mexico's Indian tribes. Writing in 1856, *Santa Fe Weekly Gazette* editor James L. Collins insisted that every Apache band be coerced to reside in "pueblos" on small Gila River reservations in the most remote part of the territory.[43] None of these recommendations were acted upon, and not until the post–Civil War era would the federal government set aside reservations for the Apaches. Even then, forcing the tribe to abandon a wandering way of life firmly established in centuries of tradition proved difficult on a professional level and unreasonable on a human level.

Of all those concerned with Apache affairs throughout the 1850s, Michael Steck no doubt understood the Indians the best. As Indian agent he warned his superiors that the Apaches would never be willing to live in permanent houses because of their superstitious nature. Writing to the Bureau of Indian Affairs, Steck explained: "Their prejudice against houses is founded upon a tradition which is universally believed among them, that they are the descendents of Montezuma, and at the time of his death they were directed by their wise maker, to show their grief by destroying their houses, breaking their crockery, and flying to the mountains to live as they do now . . . in miserable little huts built of willows bent and tied together, and covered with branches and shrubbery."[44] He astutely warned that any attempt to persuade them to construct permanent dwellings would result in failure. This component of Apache culture made it difficult to place them on a reservation where they would be willing to remain for any extended period of time.

Communication presented another barrier in these intercultural relationships. Three languages were spoken in southern New Mexico: English, Spanish, and Apache (Athapaskan). For the most part, the Indians' native dialect could be understood only by them and was seldom used when communicating with the whites. Fortunately, many of the Apaches learned a considerable amount of

Spanish during their lifetimes, as a result both of continuing hostilities with the Mexicans and of their proclivity to adopt Mexican women and children captives into the tribe. Assistant Surgeon E. P. Longworthy commented in 1853 that "nearly all the Indians in this country speak Spanish; a very few, who have been raised with the Mexicans, read, and even write it."[45] Most communication between the Indians and the whites therefore took place in Spanish and required an interpreter; consequently, individuals speaking dual languages were highly sought in New Mexico and became some of the highest-paid men on the frontier, making on average forty-five dollars per month in 1858.[46]

The federal government's most frequent "solution" to Indian problems in New Mexico came in the form of the peace treaty. Officials negotiated hundreds of agreements with Indian tribes over the years, with varying degrees of success. Most were broken by both sides before even reaching Congress for ratification. Writing about this dilemma, Agent John Ward noted that "ten minutes after an Indian makes his mark upon the paper containing a treaty which he has made with you, he is ready to break it, and it cannot be otherwise."[47] Ward failed to mention, however, that the Americans oftentimes deserved an equal share of the blame. The civil government rarely upheld its end of the bargain pertaining to rations and supplies being issued to the Indians, while the military violated treaty provisions by ordering attacks against innocent bands living peaceably near their agencies. James Kaywaykla, an Apache born into Victorio's band in the 1870s, remarked: "There is another custom incomprehensible to the Apache: it is that by which a piece of paper can compel a man whose word is not good to adhere to his promises. Even more is he confused when words can be so twisted that even the paper is worthless."[48]

As the army would eventually learn, the only consistent means by which an Apache could be caught was by another Apache. The Indians possessed an unsurpassed knowledge of their vast homelands, an area covering thousands of square miles across the Southwest Borderlands. Their hiding places, located in the most mountainous and non-traversable terrain imaginable, numbered in the thousands and were situated throughout the region. Were it not for the advent of the Apache scouts in the 1870s, who for various reasons agreed to assist American troops, the last "renegades" may have never been caught. In the 1850s, however, the army had no Apache scouts; instead, the military frequently employed the services of local Mexicans as guides, but often to little avail.

The Chiricahua Apaches, broken down into subgroups and scattered across thousands of square miles of forbidding desert terrain spanning two external political sovereignties (Mexico and the United States), would come to epitomize Indian resistance to Anglo-American intrusion on the western frontier. Perhaps no other tribe became so renowned for their exploits in defending their homelands than the Apaches. Modern usages of the term "Apache" in popular culture corroborate the notion that the tribe struck fear into the hearts of many who dared enter their communal domain attempting to transplant American dreams of hegemony and authority over the landscape. The Apaches, motivated by a reverence for the land and their own desire for survival and prosperity, formed the antithesis to the dreams exhibited by American officials, settlers, and soldiers who sought to implement altogether foreign spatial constructs in reforming the Southwest Borderlands and its inhabitants. These underlying intercultural motivations led to the conflict analyzed henceforth in this book.

CHAPTER 3

The Early Years of Military Occupation

The permanent presence of American troops in New Mexico beginning in 1846 inevitably sparked controversy and disagreement over countless matters, not the least of which was the optimum policy that the U.S. government should pursue regarding the management of the region's several Indian tribes. These tribes did not welcome the presence of U.S. troops and military posts within their homelands, realizing that this imperiled their community structures and hindered their mobility. From the Indians' perspective, this represented a foreign invasion and a gesture of open hostility. In the upcoming years, policies aimed toward mitigating the "Indian problem" in New Mexico would be the dual responsibility of both civil and military officials, whose conflicting visions of a desirable outcome often left them at odds with one another.[1] Thus, fundamental discrepancies in perceptions of the southwestern landscape and its inhabitants created two levels of conflict, the first characterized by open hostilities between Anglo-Americans and Apaches, the second being a bureaucratic power struggle between civil and military authorities emanating from incongruities in policy at both the federal and territorial level.[2]

At the end of the Mexican-American War, New Mexico as claimed by the United States consisted of a vast expanse of barren deserts and nearly impassable mountain ranges, interrupted only by the occasional fertile valley. Entrepreneurial pioneers, their imaginations molded by romantic and providential notions of Manifest Destiny, envisioned the region as a future site of farms, ranches, transportation routes, and even industrialization near the more-reliable water sources. They failed—or refused—to recognize the preexisting Indian and Mexican uses for the land, neither of which fit into the newcomers' conception of proper economic exploitation.[3] Although the full extent of New Mexico's mostly untapped natural resources would not be fully realized until years later, explorations during the 1840s and 1850s initiated a great migration into its borderlands. The inevitable result of this population influx would be a convergence of political, military, social, and kinship forces—involving Anglo Americans, Mexicans, and Indians—with the southern New Mexico landscape serving as the spatial setting for this contest.[4]

The signing of the Treaty of Guadalupe-Hidalgo on February 2, 1848, and its subsequent ratification marked the official end of the Mexican-American War. The agreement proved to be a litigious attempt at diplomacy from the beginning, with severe tension arising from the various stipulations negotiated between the two nations. Several of its articles instigated debate, especially the delineation of the new boundary line separating the two nations. It would take many years and millions of dollars to satisfactorily sort out the treaty's ambiguities. The resultant controversy exemplified the overwrought diplomatic relationship between Mexico and the United States during that time.[5]

To be sure, with the sudden arrival of American civilians and troops in the Apache homelands after the war, conflict between the two groups was nothing short of inevitable. But article 11 of the Treaty of Guadalupe-Hidalgo directly affected Indian affairs and exacerbated intercultural tensions.[6] According to the article's provisions, the U.S. Army would protect Mexican citizens south of the border from Indian raiding and repatriate any Mexican captives recovered from the Indians to their families.[7] In 1850 President Zachary Taylor dispatched agents to both California and New Mexico with instructions to ascertain "the number of Mexicans held as captives there by the savage tribes, whose release and restoration to their own country this government is bound."[8] These agents held innumerable other duties, however, many pertaining to the sectional crisis surrounding the admission of these new territories to the Union, and their task of enumerating Mexican captives went mostly unfulfilled.

A year later Taylor's successor, Millard Fillmore, specifically mentioned these treaty obligations in his State of the Union address, proclaiming: "We are bound to protect the territory of Mexico against the incursions of the savage tribes within our border with equal diligence and energy as if the same were made within our territory or against our citizens. . . . Instructions have also been given to the Indian commissioners and agents among these tribes in all treaties to make the clauses designed for the protection of our own citizens apply also to those of Mexico."[9] Several months later Secretary of State Daniel Webster wrote President Fillmore stressing the dire circumstances along the Rio Grande, noting that "marauding incursions, and the violent seizing of persons to be transported across the [Mexican] line, have taken place, and are very likely to be repeated."[10] As head of the State Department, Webster and his subordinate agents no doubt received the brunt of criticism from Mexican dignitaries regarding Apache captivities and the failure to enforce article 11. Secretary of War Conrad likewise bemoaned the situation, viably noting that enforcement of the article would be impossible unless U.S. troops were stationed in Mexico and further proclaiming that preventing Indian incursions across the border would require "corresponding efforts on [Mexico's] part."[11]

Fillmore and other federal officials failed to appreciate the difficulties entailed in upholding such a pledge. Further evidence that the U.S. government failed to take this obligation seriously can be found in the Indian affairs commissioner's orders to James S. Calhoun upon his appointment as New Mexico's first Indian agent in 1849. The bureau advanced Calhoun a sum of $3,800 for contingent expenses upon his arrival in New Mexico, of which a paltry $300 was to be used for "the release of such Mexican captives as may be found among the Indians."[12] He would have been hard pressed to achieve the liberation of a single captive with such negligible funds.

Boundary Commissioner John Russell Bartlett, following a two-year stead in the Southwest from 1850 to 1851, wrote the secretary of the interior a lengthy report on enforcement of article 11. Bartlett, having spent a considerable amount of time among the Apaches and Mexicans during his tour of the Southwest, offered firsthand accounts of a seemingly hopeless situation. In Sonora especially, Apache incursions had left an unmistakable trail of destruction. "Depopulated towns and villages, deserted haciendas and ranches, elegant and spacious churches fallen to decay . . . show to what extent the country has been overrun," the commissioner wrote. "There is scarcely a family in the frontier towns but has suffered the loss of one or more of its members or friends. In some instances whole families have been cut off; the father murdered, the mother and children carried into captivity. . . . I heard the melancholy tales of afflicted parents whose children had been torn away from them by the Indians." To counteract such widespread devastation and captive taking, and to enforce article 11, he recommended that an expedition consisting of at least two companies of dragoons be dispatched against the Coyotero and Pinal Apaches (Western Apaches), citing these two subgroups as being responsible for a majority of the plundering in northern Sonora.[13]

Bartlett described a trend decades in the making. Long before the first U.S. citizens arrived in New Mexico, the Apaches had frequently raided towns and villages in northern Mexico, taking an incalculable psychological toll upon residents there. Indeed, decades of unfaltering Indian strikes invoked a perpetual state of fear among people in Chihuahua, Sonora, and southern New Mexico to the extent that entire populations were redistributed simply as a precaution for avoiding future attacks.[14] The practice of seizing Mexican women and children and adopting them into the tribe only added to the rampant fear and apprehension prevailing throughout northern Mexico at this time. The complex kinship and communal nature of these captivities, which had become commonplace by 1848, made it difficult for the U.S. Army to uphold article 11.

While most of those taken captive initially fulfilled tribal domestic needs for servants to perform menial chores, many of the women eventually became wedded to Apache men. Similarly, Mexican boys taken into captivity (usually under ten years of age) were raised as kin within each band and trained as warriors as a means not only of assimilation and acculturation but also of replenishing the tribe's fighting strength. Trooper John Reid, a soldier traveling through New Mexico in 1857, observed: "Each of the *wild* bands and tribes hold their captives, regardless of the nation to which they belong, as slaves. If females they take them to wife; if males, on manifesting *merit* and willingness, they are adopted into the tribe. Concerning these an apparently singular fact has often been observed: after remaining with the Indians some months but few of these *slaves* manifest any inclination to escape, or to be released, from their captors."[15]

Perhaps the most well-known example of this coerced acculturation is Mickey Free, born in 1847 as Felix Telles. At the age of thirteen, Apaches raided his father's ranch in the Sonoita Valley of southeastern Arizona (then New Mexico) and carried the boy away. Felix underwent a complete transformation of identity, and in reinventing himself he adopted a new life and culture that afforded him a true sense of belonging. As a symbolic gesture of his transformation, he also took an Apache name during the acculturation process. Mickey Free (as Americans called him) went on to be a warrior in his tribe and later became a famed Apache scout for the U.S. Army. He died in 1914 at Arizona's Fort Apache Indian Reservation, having lived out the duration of his life as an Apache in spirit if not in blood.[16]

Complex kinship bonds and integrative community relationships gradually formed between the Apaches and their Mexican captives, rendering the treaty obligations toilsome for the army to uphold. From the Apache point of view, article 11 required them to surrender family members, not captives. Many Indian agents and army officers quickly discovered that the Apaches would not simply turn over their adopted wives and children for repatriation. Both American and Mexican authorities misunderstood, and sometimes completely overlooked, this complex dynamic of Indian culture. From their perspectives, captive taking was a cruel practice that ripped women and children away from their families and created immense heartache. They and the Apaches held vastly differing views on intercultural captivity and slavery, and indeed both perspectives were wholly valid within their own societies. Yet this only gave rise to increased tensions in the region in the years immediately following the Mexican-American War.[17]

At New Mexico's southernmost military posts, article 11 proved especially burdensome because of their proximity to Mexico. Beginning in 1848, commanding officers at Doña Ana, and later at Fort Fillmore, continuously grappled with this responsibility, often becoming frustrated in their efforts. In their opinion the repatriation of Mexican captives detracted from the ability to perform other more-important duties. Both military and civil officials realized that this legal requirement placed them in a dilemma and sought to have the article abrogated. When Congress ratified the Gadsden Purchase six years later, it included a clause nullifying article 11, although by that time irreparable damage had been done as a result of ill-conceived enforcement attempts.[18] As a direct impetus for intercultural clashes and power struggles, the Treaty of Guadalupe-Hidalgo became one of the earliest premeditators of conflict between the U.S. government and the various Apache bands.

Moreover, the treaty also exacerbated preexisting anxieties between the United States and Mexico immediately following the war because Mexican authorities found it unacceptable that U.S. officials failed to enforce article 11. Alejo García Conde of Chihuahua, describing a recent treaty negotiated between that state and the Apaches in June 1850, denounced this failure on the part of the Americans in a statement published in a Chihuahua City newspaper. "The Apaches have never manifested a desire for peace as they do now," Conde wrote. "We have investigated the cause for their change of heart and we do not believe the Americans had anything to do with it. [After all], the Americans have not complied with the Treaty of Guadalupe Hidalgo."[19] Three years later, writing to Secretary of State William L. Marcy, Envoy Extraordinary and Minister Plenipotentiary Juan N. Almonte reiterated Conde's complaint and admonished the Americans' continued failure to comply with treaty requirements. According to Almonte, the stipulations had been "reduced to a cipher" by the U.S. government, and as a result, "the greatest portion of the frontier of Mexico has been entirely laid waste . . . by a series of [Indian] incursions that have neither been prevented nor checked although coming precisely within the pale of the category to which the stipulations of the 11th article ought to be applied."[20]

Article 11 clearly occupied a prominent position in the center of a three-way struggle for power and prestige involving the United States, Mexico, and the several Apache bands. All three became deadlocked with one another in disputes over the enforcement (and nonenforcement) of the treaty, and it can therefore be used as a lens through which to view the Anglo-Apache violence that proliferated in the Southwest Borderlands after 1848. An analysis of U.S. military operations and Indian policy in southern New Mexico preceding and subsequent to Conde's editorial and Almonte's correspondence offers some insight into the complexity of combating Apache raiding across an international border and an expanse of desert covering thousands of square miles.

In 1848, with the Ninth Military Department (which administered army activities in New Mexico), under the command of Colonel John M. Washington, 885 troops from infantry, dragoon, and the Mounted Rifles regiments garrisoned the region's ten posts and bore responsibility for enforcing article 11 and for protecting citizens from Indian raiding. These men comprised approximately 10 percent of the total regular army at that time.[21] In June 1849 large numbers of reinforcements arrived in the territory, including one company of the Second Dragoons under Captain Croghan Ker, four companies of the Third Infantry under Lieutenant Colonel

Edmund B. Alexander, and two companies of the Second Artillery.[22] Six additional companies of the Third Infantry, consisting of 257 men under Major Jefferson Van Horne, arrived at El Paso (Franklin) on September 28, making that the strongest post in the department.[23] With the arrival of these troops, nineteen companies garrisoned New Mexico's posts, a substantial show of force and seemingly sufficient to afford protection to civilians.

Secretary of War Conrad reported in November 1850 that the regular army totaled 12,927 officers and men, of whom 7,796— roughly 60 percent—occupied stations on the western frontier.[24] The vastness of the territory annexed through the Mexican Cession diverted the military's focus from the Southeast, where troops previously fought Seminoles and other Indian tribes, to these newly acquired western possessions. According to Conrad, the military's most important duty would be "the protection of Texas and New Mexico against the Indian tribes in their vicinity . . . , [an] object [that] has engaged the anxious attention of the department, and all the means at its disposal have been employed to effect [sic] it."[25]

In the early years of military occupation, U.S. troops did not inhabit forts or permanent encampments but instead resided in rented quarters among New Mexico's civilian settlements. Owing to the territory's immense geographic area, the large distances separating these towns deeply concerned military officers attempting to discourage Indian raiding. "As the frontier is many hundred miles in extent, these posts are necessarily a considerable distance apart," Conrad lamented. Despite the fact that almost one thousand troops occupied New Mexico's ten posts, he admitted that "the utmost vigilance and activity on the part of the officers in command cannot prevent small bands of Indians from passing between them and committing depredations on interior settlements."[26]

The effectiveness of locating the troops within the confines of towns became an object of intense debate among military personnel. Without a doubt, the citizens desperately needed military support to prevent the Indians from plundering at will, a protection that had not been afforded previously by a Mexican government distracted with financial insolvency, internal rebellions, and political unrest. The daily presence of troops also invigorated local economies, where merchants came to enjoy a consistent revenue stream and capitalized on opportunities to contract with the army for forage and other essential provisions. A major predicament that arose, however, emanated from the fact that societal vices were readily available to the men. One department commander referred to Santa Fe as a "sink of vice and extravagance" in 1851 and subsequently ordered its garrison removed to the newly constructed Fort Union, some eighty miles distant.[27]

Despite the restrictions that officers implemented, some of the men still snuck away to saloons and brothels and often contracted a wide array of diseases as a result. Aside from the containment of Indian depredations, troop health became a predominant concern for commanding officers on the western frontier, especially with military medical personnel spread thinly across that immense realm.[28] During the six-year period from 1848 to 1853, the Medical Department treated an astounding 134,708 cases of illness in an army averaging only about 10,000 men.[29] Not just in New Mexico but all across the frontier, soldiers found themselves hospitalized due to illness on an average of three times each year. The ratio of deaths to the number of troops between 1849 and 1855 was 1 in 33, or almost exactly 3 percent. This percentage increased during the immediate prewar years: the Ninth Military Department boasted a mean strength of 1,579 troops during the five years preceding the Civil War, with 114 recorded deaths due to illness. An average of 1 in 121 medical cases proved fatal during the period spanning 1849 through 1860, with an overall mortality rate of just over 2 percent during that same time span.[30]

While locating the soldiers within town limits served as a deterrent for Apache incursions, it did not discourage the practice altogether. In most cases, increasing the number of troops proved to be nothing more than a minor setback for the Indians. Raiding parties could easily target more-remote locations in order to avoid the troops. The entirety of the Rio Grande valley south of Albuquerque, with farms and ranches spread miles apart, was settled by Mexicans who relied upon the water and vegetation to sustain their sheep and cattle herds. Accordingly, raiding warriors simply diverted their focus to these more-isolated haciendas.

The town of Socorro, long a target of Apache spoliations, would be among the first in the territory to come under the protection of U.S. troops. Socorro was founded as a Spanish mission along the Rio Grande in 1626 "in a recess of the hills and mountains, which . . . form a grand amphitheatre here on its north, west, and south sides. On the N.N.W. a chain of mountains has been pierced by the river, and its south wing, rising into scattered and gloomy peaks, descends southwardly in two broken ridges."[31] Socorro's surrounding landscape epitomized the rough terrain in which the Apaches thrived. In October 1848 Companies D and E of the Second Dragoons replaced the battalion of mounted volunteers that formerly garrisoned the village. In addition to Socorro, other New Mexico towns occupied by troops included Taos, Santa Fe, Abiquiú, Galisteo, Las Vegas, Albuquerque, Los Lunas, and Doña Ana. Three of these towns (Los Lunas, Socorro, and Doña Ana) existed within the boundaries of Apache country; consequently, the posts at these three locations would be among the busiest in the territory.

In 1848, troops also took station at Doña Ana, a farming village hugging the east bank of the Rio Grande sixty miles north of El Paso. Founded in 1843 on a Mexican land grant, it was the first town established in the Mesilla Valley, followed shortly afterward by nearby Las Cruces and Mesilla in 1849 and 1850, respectively.[32] By all accounts Doña Ana was a dirty, haphazardly constructed place. Boundary Commissioner Bartlett passed through in 1850 and observed it to be "a small town of five or six hundred inhabitants [situated] upon a spur of the plateau, fifty or sixty feet above the bottomlands, thereby commanding a wide prospect of the adjacent country. It has been settled but a few years. . . . [I]ts houses are mostly of a class called *jacals*, i.e. built of upright sticks . . . filled with mud, though a better class of adobe buildings have just been erected along the main street, for the occupation of the military, and for places of business. The central position of Dona Ana, and its fine lands, led to its selection for a military post."[33] Passing through the village in June 1851, only two months before the military abandoned their post there, Dr. S. W. Woodhouse observed an equally unbecoming scene. Describing the forlorn atmosphere surrounding him, Woodhouse penned in his journal that he "arrived at Don Anna [sic].... [H]ere ... the houses are miserable, even those occupied by the troops.... Maj. Sheppard [sic], who commands, Dr. Tenbrook, who is Surgeon of the post, & Lieut. O'Banion [sic] of the Infantry are the only officers at the post."[34] The living conditions at secluded Doña Ana clearly did not compare favorably to those that wayfaring visitors knew in the East.

Companies D, F, and H, First Dragoons as well as Company B, Third Infantry called Doña Ana home at various times throughout its use as a military post. Company H, First Dragoons, under the command of Lieutenant Delos B. Sackett, arrived there first and quartered themselves in rented adobe quarters on the town's southeastern fringe.[35] Lieutenant Sackett, who surveyed and plotted the Las Cruces town site in 1849, served as the temporary post commander until the arrival of Major Enoch Steen in July. Steen, a prominent military figure in New Mexico throughout the 1850s, would serve at Doña Ana intermittently from 1849 until just prior to its permanent abandonment by the military in 1851. One contemporary described the major as being "a man of splendid physique, of the most temperate habits, [with] the endurance of old Daniel Boone himself."[36] The territorial newspaper further lauded the veteran commander, proclaiming that "although well advanced in years he still exhibits the enthusiasm of youth."[37]

Doña Ana immediately became a pivotal location for Apache relations and remained so for over two years. Numerous military campaigns emanated from that post, and any Indians wishing to discuss peace or negotiate a treaty had to travel there to do so. On October 10, 1850, Doña Ana underwent the periodic inspection customary for all military installations. Army inspector George A. McCall noted the presence of 54 men of Company H, First Dragoons and 43 men of Company B, Third Infantry, bringing the aggregate force to 97 men, including officers.[38] The garrison boasted slightly less than one-tenth of the total military force in New Mexico, which in 1850 consisted of twenty-one companies numbering 1,188 men in all.[39]

McCall praised Steen as an officer who "has shown much zeal in the performance of his duties, particularly in several expeditions against Apache Indians in the Sacramento Mountains and on the River Gila, in which he had several engagements with them, and was once severely wounded." In addition, McCall remarked, "Taken all together . . . it affords me pleasure to say that this company [H, First Dragoons] is in better order than any I have seen in this department."[40] Company H's horses appeared to be in the most serviceable condition of any encountered during his tour. Dragoon mounts commonly became unfit for service, suffering immensely from the many rigors and hardships involved in pursuing the Apaches on a regular basis. The good condition of these animals aided the men in the many chases upon which they embarked.

While McCall considered the Doña Ana post to be in excellent condition, Major Steen felt otherwise. Only one month before the inspection, Steen had complained to the adjutant general in Santa Fe that his troops lacked the proper clothing and provisions typically issued to soldiers, claiming to have placed a requisition with the department quartermaster almost two years earlier that remained unfulfilled. A similar situation existed sixty miles south of Doña Ana, where the post at Paso del Norte (current day El Paso and Juárez) also lacked the necessary supplies and provisions. McCall made no allusion to this in his reports for either place. In fact, his report for Doña Ana noted, "Clothing and equipments are of good quality and sufficient for present wants," a statement directly contradicting that of Steen.[41] Either McCall overlooked the issue during his inspection, or the officers had differing opinions on what constituted adequate equipment. A general shortage of supplies haunted troops in New Mexico throughout the antebellum era and made it all the more difficult for them to effectively counteract Apache hostilities.

Like most other troops in southern New Mexico, those stationed in Socorro would not have to wait long before seeing action against the Apaches. On March 6, 1849, Apaches stampeded twenty mules belonging to Don Antonio Constante's herd in the nearby Rio Grande valley. Upon learning of the incident, 1st Lieutenant Abraham Buford immediately left Socorro with twenty men of the Second Dragoons and eventually struck the Indians' trail leading westward into the precipitous Mogollon Mountains.[42] The pursuit was a short one, however; in the excitement Buford left Socorro in such haste that he failed to take any rations for his men. After this debacle Buford contacted headquarters requesting a force of between eighty and one hundred dragoons and cited the need to enlist local Mexicans familiar with the landscape to serve as guides. He suggested that an expedition take the field sometime in late April or early May, taking advantage of the moderate temperatures then. The lieutenant also voiced his frustration with the frequency of Apache depredations and his inability to keep them in check: "The majority of [the Apache] nation has no other occupation than that of stealing, and until they can be taught . . . a lesson to respect the rights of another nation, I consider any treaty with them as worthless."[43] Other officers would come to share Buford's feelings after enduring identical circumstances. This communication, citing the need to "teach the Apaches a lesson," would be echoed innumerable times across the department in upcoming years.

Major Steen, experiencing similar aggravation near Doña Ana, had seen enough. After less than a year at that post, numerous Apache raids had drawn his troops into the field, but they had always returned unsuccessful. Steen also shared Buford's view of the Indians as an inferior form of humanity; in a written communication with headquarters in August 1849, he suggested a large-scale campaign in hopes of eradicating the Apaches' unhindered pillaging. "In my opinion," he declared, "nothing short of a good whipping will do any good. The [Apaches] will break [a] treaty faster than [we] can make them. . . . 200 mounted men can leave Secora [*sic*] and in five days be in the heart of their country just about the copper mines; there is a good wagon road all the way. . . . [After] 4–5 weeks in their country with a good force they will be glad to make a peace treaty." According to the major, in order to be successful the operation must involve troops from several different posts converging from multiple directions and should last for at least four to six weeks, during which time "all their women, children and horses may be taken [and their warriors killed]."[44] His suggestion represented the beginning of the army's destructive-warfare strategy in southern New Mexico, an approach that many of his military colleagues likewise advocated throughout the antebellum years.

The Ninth Military Department never authorized Steen's proposed campaign, primarily because resources and manpower were stretched extremely thin across New Mexico at that time. Indeed, for the first five years after Kearny's 1846 conquest, the army focused its efforts toward the Navajos and dedicated only minimal resources to troops in New Mexico's southerly regions. The first Navajo campaign occurred in November 1846, when Colonel Alexander W. Doniphan and his Missouri Volunteers marched into the orange-hued mesalands of northwestern New Mexico and negotiated a treaty with several tribal headmen at Ojo del Oso (Bear Springs). Two years later Colonel John M. Washington led a major expedition into Navajo country and met with mixed results, killing a principal chief but failing to broker any meaningful peace agreements. A third campaign, this one under Colonel Sumner, took the field in August 1851 and resulted in the establishment of Fort Defiance, the first post in Navajo country. All three operations mobilized hundreds of troops who remained in the field for several weeks at a time, the unintended consequence being that supplies and reinforcements could not be spared for campaigns against the Apaches to the south.

The department's refusal to authorize Steen's multifaceted, prolonged Apache campaigns resulted from the focus on Navajos. For this reason, operations against the Apaches during the period 1846–51 consisted of localized efforts on the part of a single post commander, usually Major Steen at Doña Ana and his colleagues at Socorro. Much of this fighting must therefore be viewed in the larger context of Indian affairs across the entire territory. The reason that Steen's proposals so often failed to materialize owed more to inadequate military resources in southern New Mexico rather than to any negligence or ambivalence on the part of officials in Santa Fe.[45] Indeed, this would hold true to a certain extent throughout the antebellum era, with large campaigns taking the field against the Navajos up until their incarceration at Bosque Redondo beginning in 1863.

By December 1849 Colonel Charles A. May, who Steen recommended to lead the campaign into Apache country, had assumed command at Socorro in place of Lieutenant Buford. On December 19 a small band of Apaches, consisting of approximately thirteen warriors and two chiefs, congregated in the small community of Lemitar a few miles north of Socorro, presumably to trade with the inhabitants. Further investigation revealed that several of these Indians had previously been detained in the Socorro guardhouse for unspecified offenses. Colonel May ordered that they be arrested and escorted back to the post, where he hoped to coerce them into signing a treaty. Both chiefs resisted confinement and declined May's proposal, pointing out that several of their men were drunk and wisely prophesying that, because of this, trouble might ensue. The colonel nevertheless dispatched a detachment of dragoons to apprehend the Indians, who once again found themselves in the Socorro jail, their inebriation no doubt enabling the troops to capture them with relative ease. While the Indians remained in confinement, May awaited instructions from headquarters as to their ultimate disposition.[46]

To be sure, this small group of Apaches had committed no crimes and did nothing to provoke the townspeople. Their purpose in Lemitar appears to have been solely for bartering, and in the course of their dealings with the locals, they obtained liquor and became intoxicated, a testament to the tactics of Mexican traders there more than anything. Such incidents, while resulting in no loss of property or life, gradually fostered a contempt between Apaches, New Mexicans, and the military, which promulgated deteriorating relations between all three. Many of the territory's residents enticed the Indians into their towns for trading but then, once they became intoxicated and unruly, hurriedly called upon the troops to defuse the situation. In later years officers came to view this contradictory behavior as hypocritical, and their sympathy for the residents diminished accordingly.

In December 1849, four months after Steen offered his plan of campaign, the Apaches reappeared along the Jornada del Muerto (Journey of the Dead), an old Spanish wagon road connecting central New Mexico with the Mesilla Valley. Travelers feared this perilous route because of an absence of water and the frequent Apache raids to which the barren landscape made them vulnerable.[47] Learning of the recent depredations on the Jornada, Steen left Doña Ana with Company H, First Dragoons and rode northward to the site of the attacks. He then divided his command, with half of the men remaining on the Jornada and the other half probing westward until striking the Rio Grande near the San Diego crossing. By the time news of the raids had reached Doña Ana, however, the Indians already had a one-day head start on the soldiers. Both columns traveled over sixty miles in different directions without locating the Indians' trail.[48]

Emboldened by their success on the Jornada, a band of Gila Apaches raided even closer to Doña Ana on February 2, 1850. This time they drove off one of the town's livestock herds, in the process wounding four Mexican herders and characteristically taking a young boy captive.[49] Steen's dragoons immediately rode in pursuit, accompanied by 2nd Lieutenant Laurence W. O'Bannon and a detachment of Company B, Third Infantry. Fifteen miles into the chase, Steen dispatched O'Bannon with an advance party of twenty-five of his best-mounted dragoons, who followed the Apache trail while the larger body of troops, remaining with Steen, attempted to intercept the Indians' retreat route into the mountains. Once again, the major underestimated his enemy's ability to elude capture. After a chase exceeding forty miles, the dragoons' horses broke down, preventing further pursuit.[50]

On their return to Doña Ana, the dragoons spied two men standing atop a distant hill, who they at first supposed to be Mexican herders. Upon closer investigation, they proved to be Indians, perhaps members of the raiding party who had detached themselves from the larger group to avoid capture. They immediately fled at Steen's approach, driving a small herd of stolen livestock in front of them. The dragoons mounted their already broken-down horses and renewed their pursuit. A short distance farther they realized that they in fact had come upon a much larger group of Indians, consisting of between thirty and forty warriors, who had remained hidden until the troops approached. The Apaches atop the hill had merely been a decoy to draw Steen into a fight that his men had little chance of winning. According to Steen, the Indians began "cursing us in bad Spanish and calling us to come over and fight them."[51] A force of that size could have offered a difficult challenge to the small detachment of dragoons, who remained separated from O'Bannon's men. Recognizing the perilous situation he faced, Steen started a fire in hopes that the smoke would draw the other detachment to his position. When O'Bannon failed to join him, Steen was forced to return to Doña Ana, simultaneously denying the Apaches the fight they desired and allowing them to return to their mountain camps safely with their plunder.

Meanwhile, O'Bannon's twenty-five-man detachment succeeded in overtaking a second, smaller band of Indians, whereupon one of the dragoons, a Private Teagarden, wounded one raider in a brief skirmish. In response, the intrepid Apaches charged directly at the soldiers with lances leveled, although their tactic failed to inflict any injury. "I must take this opportunity," Steen subsequently reported, "to urge upon the commanding officer of the department the necessity of arming Company H with Colt revolvers; had this man [Teagarden] had one of these weapons he would probably have killed several of these Indians."[52] Following the brief encounter, O'Bannon pursued for another thirty miles, the entire time a mere half mile behind the Apaches. As the dragoons closed the gap, the Apaches discarded all surplus items, including blankets and personal belongings, in order to relieve their horses of excess weight. Ultimately the lieutenant abandoned the chase; the fleet Apache ponies, superior to those the troops rode, persevered long enough to carry their riders to safety.

An unpleasant surprise awaited Steen as his detachment trotted back into Doña Ana. When he departed, the major took his entire available military force and left the town unprotected, a blunder of foresight that the Apaches had anticipated. No sooner had the soldiers passed from view than another raiding party descended upon the town, stealing mules and horses with little opposition. The first strike had merely been a decoy to draw the troops away from town, ensuring the success of this even larger raid. If Major Steen had been frustrated by Apache tactics before this incident, this ruse must have left him nothing short of infuriated. He angrily penned a letter to headquarters begging permission to lead an aggressive campaign against the Gila Apaches:

> I [urge] upon the commanding officer of the department the necessity of a campaign against these Indians, especially when Indians become so bold [they] will come in broad daylight within a mile of a U.S. garrison where dragoons are stationed and drive off stock and murder the defenseless herders.... I think it becomes necessary to chastise them and this can only be done by a regular organized campaign against them.... [W]hen these Indians start on a marauding expedition they come mounted on their best horses ... and at the same time have relays waiting for them at 25 or 30 miles distant ... and thus are mounted on fresh animals and can snap their fingers at us whose animals are broken down by the long chase; thus it is nearly impossible for any dragoons to overtake them and for this I urge the necessity of an expedition against them.... I would suggest that a depot be selected at or near the copper mines and that it be established as the base of operations.[53]

On March 6 Steen left Doña Ana to reconnoiter the area surrounding the old Santa Rita copper mines, hoping to ascertain the most economical means of conducting an unrestricted punitive expedition into that country. He returned on March 23, having spent over two weeks inspecting the region and declaring it to be "decidedly the best location for a post."[54] Santa Rita offered a strategic point from which to direct a campaign for several reasons, not the least of which being its proximity to the Apache homelands. Furthermore, the location already boasted living quarters built by

Mexican miners, although the buildings had become severely dilapidated due to long-term abandonment and exposure to the elements. Even so, Steen believed that they could be restored in less than a month and immediately thereafter occupied by three companies of troops. The natural resources necessary to sustain such a post, most notably timber, water, and forage, abounded throughout the vicinity. In fact, the major proclaimed these three critical elements to be "as good if not better than can be found in any portion of New Mexico." As a final persuasive argument, he pointed out that the military could save as much as $15,000 annually if the department relocated his Doña Ana garrison to Santa Rita.[55]

Steen also recommended that a column comprised of no less than 150 troops advance on the upper Gila River from the north as soon as possible. This would prevent the Apaches from utilizing a northerly escape route into the impregnable Mogollon Mountains. The northern force would then continue sweeping southward toward the copper mines, where they would unite with a detachment from Doña Ana to be led by Steen himself. The veteran commander met with disappointment, however, when his superiors in Santa Fe explained that the department lacked the resources necessary for an Apache campaign, adding that troops for such an expedition could not be spared from any of the more northerly posts, where the Navajo conflict continued to rage.

According to Steen, if the department permanently stationed his company of dragoons at the copper mines, such an expedition might not be necessary. Placing a large garrison of troops in the heart of the Apache country had not yet been attempted and would have been a bold act, hindering the Indians' ability to emerge unscathed from raids and doubtless having a psychological effect as well. This appears to be the first time an army officer alluded to the possibility of posting troops in such a location and removing them from the Rio Grande settlements. In conceiving this strategy, Steen prophesied the future military framework in New Mexico, one that would be implemented upon the arrival of a new department commander in 1851. The visionary officer thus emerged as one of the first in southern New Mexico to suggest not only a destructive-warfare strategy but also the placement of troops closer to the Apaches' women and children, thus posing a more imminent threat to their community structures.

Moreover, the major contended that the morale of his troops could be significantly improved by transferring them to a more healthful and secluded mountainous region. Living among the Mexican population at Doña Ana placed tremendous strain upon the Anglo-American soldiers. According to Steen's reports, his troops quarreled with the townspeople on an almost daily basis. Some of these intercultural struggles doubtless arose from differing perceptions of power and authority. The soldiers, although relative newcomers to southern New Mexico, saw themselves as racially superior to the Mexicans around them and entertained their own aspirations for the surrounding landscape. Having been born into an agrarian society and raised in the region, most New Mexicans felt a strong personal bond with the land and resources and were reluctant to surrender their well-earned hegemony to pretentious whites speaking a different language and operating under different belief systems. Indeed, some of the residents still felt an allegiance to the Mexican government and did not appreciate receiving orders from the same troops who had just recently defeated their native country in war. But two more years would pass before department headquarters acted upon Steen's recommendation.

Meanwhile, an almost nonexistent civil government in the newly created territory, coupled with ambiguity over the application of laws and authority, further exacerbated the lack of cooperation among officials. Indeed, for the first three years of American occupation, the military commander also served as civil governor, vesting one man with the authority normally divided between two separate arms of government. Not until 1850 would the military and civil powers be divided between two men, although the separation would have little effect on preexisting internal animosities.[56]

While Steen busied himself on a reconnaissance of Apache country, troops in Socorro continued to experience problems of their own. Rumors began circulating of a supposed conspiracy between the Indians and local residents, an uncommon occurrence because of interracial acrimony but not an altogether unheard-of phenomenon when sufficient incentives existed. In April 1850 news reached Socorro that a nearby grazing camp, where the post herd of nearly 1,000 animals was kept, guarded by an eleven-man detachment, might be attacked. Colonel May, commanding at Socorro, became especially concerned because his garrison had been severely depleted by transfers and illnesses during the preceding months. If an attack did occur, May feared that "it [would be] impossible for me at any moment to mount over 25 men, as the remainder of the company is required to the post duties." He pleaded for a company of infantry to be stationed there "to perform the garrison duties, that I may at any moment place every dragoon at the post in the saddle, and should the enemy make his appearance, be in a position to administer proper chastisement."[57]

Although Apache and Mexican conspirators never targeted the grazing camp, tensions arose again in July when a party of "suspicious-looking" Mexicans appeared twelve miles south of town and initiated trade relationships with the Indians. When news of this reached Socorro, May frantically dispatched a detachment of Second Dragoons under Captain Reuben Campbell with orders to detain the men. But the suspects spied the troops' approach and fled, leaving behind nine animals bearing army brands.[58] The stolen stock likely had been traded to them by Apaches prior to the dragoons' arrival, evidence of an ongoing commerce in contraband.

As evidenced by the situation at Socorro, the depletion of military garrisons became a common problem befalling every post in the territory. In 1850 seven companies of dragoons operated in New Mexico; of those seven, not a single one boasted full strength. During McCall's inspections, he specifically noted, "either the military force at present in New Mexico is idle and inefficient, or the extent of frontier entrusted to its protection is out of proportion to its strength and the character of its organization." McCall believed that 2,200 men—double the current number—of which he concluded the majority must be mounted, would be necessary to control New Mexico's Indians. Colonel John Munroe, Ninth Military Department commander at the time, further alluded to the inadequacy of troops in New Mexico, writing in March 1850 that ten companies of dragoons, each with sixty men and fully serviceable horses, "is the minimum . . . required." At the very least, the two officers noted, the conversion of one or two infantry companies into dragoons would lessen the strain.[59]

Secretary of War Winfield Scott partially solved this problem in August 1850 when he dispatched some 750 troops of the First Dragoons and Seventh Infantry to New Mexico. Scott explained the situation to Munroe:

> These reinforcements are deemed necessary to enable you to protect the people of New Mexico. . . . It is known here, that the Legislature of Texas has been summoned, by the Governor of that State, to meet, on the 12th instant, to adopt measures for extending her political and civil jurisdiction over that part of New Mexico, on this side of the Rio Grande, claimed as a part of Texas. It is quite possible, perhaps probable, if the disputed boundary between Texas and New Mexico, be not earlier established by Congress, that a large body of troops may be levied, in all this month, by Texas and sent to New Mexico, to effect, by force of arms, the object stated. Accordingly, you are hereby instructed, in the case of any military invasion of New Mexico, from Texas, or by armed men from any other State or States, for the purpose of overturning the order of civil government that may exist in New Mexico at the time, or of subjugating New Mexico or Texas, to interpose, as far as practicable, the troops under your command against any such act of violence.[60]

No Texan invasion ever transpired, the dispute being resolved on September 9 in what became known as the Compromise of 1850. This congressional action eased the political tension between Texas and New Mexico surrounding the boundary issue, simultaneously making New Mexico an official U.S. territory under the guise of popular sovereignty. The confusion surrounding Texas boundary claims and coinciding ambiguities in jurisdiction did, however, provide opportunities for swarthy American businessmen to exert dominion over the land. The Texas claim of the Rio Grande as its western boundary would have placed Doña Ana in that state rather than in New Mexico. Land speculators seized the opportunity, sending emissaries to New Mexico "in determined efforts to despoil [New Mexicans] of their land and property" by issuing head-right claims (usually in one-square-mile parcels) "to persons who had served in wars . . . and also to original settlers."[61] One of these 640-acre head-right claims contained the entire village of Doña Ana, despite the fact that the town had been a part of an earlier Mexican land grant and many citizens already owned private property there.

While Major Steen operated first and foremost as a military officer adhering to protocol, he, like many others, saw this crisis as an opportunity to capitalize on the vulnerability of the New Mexican population. In 1850 assistant Texas commissioner William Cockburn, under the authority of Commissioner Robert S. Neighbors, sold the claim—including the entire town of Doña Ana—to Steen, who remained stationed there with his troops.[62] Outraged residents promptly addressed a petition to his superior, Colonel Munroe, deriding the major for taking "a league of land including the houses of the town and the cultivated lands and a grand portion of the adjoining lands. . . . [I]t is contrary to all natural right and to that of the people."[63] A controversy erupted surrounding Steen's unscrupulous actions, with department headquarters scorning him for becoming involved in such "analogous claims" and reminding him that the Treaty of Guadalupe-Hidalgo provided inhabitants "the most ample guarantee that they shall be maintained & protected in the full enjoyment of their property."[64] Ultimately the department transferred the major elsewhere to ease tensions; he lost title to the nefarious land claim and, presumably, the entire sum that he paid the Texans as well.[65]

On the surface Steen's actions merely represent another attempt by Americans to exploit New Mexican people and resources. But his temporary dabbling in Mesilla Valley land speculation doubtless influenced his approach to dealing with the Apaches in his capacity as a military officer. Located as it were at the single largest southern New Mexico town at that time (prior to Mesilla's founding), Steen's head-right claim would have been worth a substantial pecuniary sum if Indian raiding could be subdued and more people induced to settle there. His indefatigable zeal toward pursuing and chastising the Apaches and his proposal to establish a satellite post at Santa Rita del Cobre must have been influenced at least partially by his status as a property owner in the Mesilla Valley, for he would have stood to gain financially from the defeat or removal of the Indians.[66]

Indeed, Steen emerged as one of southern New Mexico's early advocates for economic expansion and frequently alluded to vast mineral deposits in the surrounding mountains as evidence that the region would undergo a rapid increase in population if only the Apaches could be constrained. On his campaigns in the copper mine region, the major often collected ore specimens and submitted them to higher authorities, requesting that they be professionally assayed.[67] In 1854 he showed several specimens around St. Louis in hopes of sparking greater interest among potential settlers and investors. He exhibited copper, silver, and gold samples from the headwaters of the Gila River to the staff at the *St. Louis Daily Missouri Republican,* which printed a summary of the region: "[Steen] represents the whole country is abounding in mines ... and only requiring the aid of capital and enterprise to make it the most productive section of the continent."[68] A week later the same newspaper praised the productivity of silver mines near Las Cruces, claiming that "they have done very well so far, and pay well with such rude machinery as has been used."[69] As the gateway to New Mexico via the Santa Fe Trail, St. Louis offered the perfect location for Steen to promote migration into the territory in furtherance of his own and other Anglo-Americans' economic interests. The Apaches remained the primary obstacle to white hegemony over the southwestern landscape, though, and by the time the region did undergo a substantial population increase in the 1860s, Steen would no longer be present to reap the benefits.

Others at Doña Ana also viewed the region as one with strong potential for growth and expansion. Louis William Geck, a private serving with Company H, First Dragoons beginning in 1846, mustered out of the service at Doña Ana on February 6, 1851, after completing his five-year enlistment. A native of Poland, Geck opted against returning to the eastern states and instead made the Mesilla Valley his permanent home. He took advantage of an option for honorably discharged soldiers to file a claim for bounty land with the U.S. Pension Office, requesting a parcel just southeast of the Doña Ana plaza and church. Upon approval of his claim in June 1851, the thirty-two-year-old established a general store in preexisting buildings that sat on his newly acquired land and shortly thereafter underwent the naturalization process in the district court to become a bona fide U.S. citizen. Over the next several years, Geck secured land conveyances from no less than a dozen local citizens for various lots throughout the village as well as at nearby Mesilla, and in so doing the ex-dragoon became a prominent landholder in the burgeoning Mesilla Valley.

Geck's actions are representative of the rapid process of Americanization that befell many previous Mexican land grants in the valley once U.S. soldiers and merchants arrived and began settling the region.[70] Geck, like Steen, recognized the economic potential existing in southern New Mexico; unlike Steen, however, he obtained his landholdings through legitimate means that allowed him undisputed legal ownership of the property. The War Department's issuance of bounty claims was, in essence, an early prototype for what would become the Homestead Act of 1862. By nonchalantly awarding parcels of land to honorably discharged soldiers in the Southwest, the U.S. government ensured that settlement would continue to increase. The department, through its encouragement for former soldiers to remain on the frontier after their terms of enlistment, helped perpetuate, and even intensify, the continually flowing stream of westward migration. This would become even more evident during and immediately following the Civil War, when dozens of discharged Union troops remained in New Mexico and became a driving force politically, economically, and socially.

Although not the initial intention, political apprehension emanating from the Texas–New Mexico boundary crisis also had the effect of bolstering military forces in the territory and relieved some strain from the soldiers already stationed there. Infantry troops throughout the department received much-needed reinforcements when General Scott dispatched several companies there in 1850. Infantrymen primarily performed various maintenance labors in and around the military posts. In most cases it was impractical for them to chase Indians; after all, mounted troops could rarely keep up with them, much less foot soldiers. For this reason many infantrymen became envious of their dragoon counterparts, whose duties they imagined to be far more exciting. Lieutenant George R. Gibson, Third Infantry, admitted, "In the infantry we could not enjoy the excitement of the chase or see the face of the country . . . that the mounted troops did, who were continually scouring the country for amusement as well as provisions."[71]

Meanwhile, Major Steen accosted the department commander to sanction a campaign into the Gila country. On August 2 Colonel Munroe, acknowledging the potential knowledge of the country to be gained from such an expedition, authorized Steen's march to the headwaters of the Gila River.[72] Two days later, less than six months after scouting the copper mines, Steen left Doña Ana and struck northwestward in compliance with orders, taking with him sixty men of Company H, First Dragoons. Upon arriving at the mines, he held a parley with several prominent Apache chiefs (including Mangas Coloradas) whose bands, collectively composing the Gila Apaches, had taken refuge in the vicinity.[73] This was the first time Steen actually met face-to-face with any Apaches in a diplomatic capacity; prior to this incident, his views were predicated upon preconceived notions of their culture and character, which he soon found to be mistaken.

Among his purposes in this expedition, Steen sought to enforce article 11 of the Treaty of Guadalupe-Hidalgo by coercing the Indians to surrender two Mexican boys, aged twelve and thirteen, who they had taken captive during a raid at Doña Ana in December 1849. Through interpreters the Apache headmen, including Delgadito and Josecito, assured Steen that the two boys had already been traded as peons to the Pueblo Indians, a false claim meant to dissuade further inquest. In actuality the two boys, Teofilo and Mateo

Jaramillo, had been ransomed in Sonora four months earlier on April 12, 1850, by Chief Josecito and his followers, who admitted to Sonoran authorities at the time that their band held seventeen more captives, mostly young children.[74] Perhaps more important than recovering the two captives, however, were the numerous talks Steen held with the Apache chiefs. Mangas Coloradas, the most notable of those present, would participate in nearly all future peace negotiations with the U.S. government. More than any other tribal leader, he endeavored to maintain a harmonious relationship with the Americans. A decade later it would lead to his downfall.

Entering the dragoon camp with a small escort of about twenty warriors, the six-foot-five, broad-framed Mangas Coloradas spoke extensively with Steen, who summarized their conversation in his subsequent report. "I had quite a long talk with them, in which I explained as clearly as possible the views and wishes of our government," he explained. "They replied that they were very desirous of being and remaining at peace with the Americans—but at the same time would swear eternal hatred to the Mexicans; that while the Americans could pass where they wished through their country, and could eat and sleep with them as safely as if he was by his own friends; with the Mexicans it was and ever would be 'War to the Knife.'"[75] This long-standing Apache bellicosity toward Mexicans seemed apparent to anybody familiar with the two races. "The fact is," wrote Private Josiah Rice in his diary, "they so heartily despise Mexicans that they say they would kill them all were it not that they serve as herdsmen to them."[76] This traditional enmity would make it difficult to uphold the various stipulations of the Treaty of Guadalupe-Hidalgo, for U.S. officials simply could not appeal to both groups without compromising American neutrality in the ongoing conflict. Here again, four years after General Kearny's meeting with the Apaches in 1846, can be seen the unintended duplicity of his professions of faith and friendship toward both the Indians and the territory's Mexican inhabitants.

Steen emerged from the conference with some sense of accomplishment. Mangas Coloradas's profession of friendship toward Americans had been reassuring; whereas beforehand the officer felt strongly that no treaty could be effective, he now entertained some hope that peace might be brokered in the future. "An agent with a few thousand dollars' worth of presents," he wrote afterward, "can without doubt conclude a lasting peace with this powerful band who have hitherto given us so much trouble."[77]

If headquarters had acted quickly upon the opportunity, a lasting truce with the Apaches might have been achieved. At that time, however, Santa Fe officials acknowledged, "there is not a dollar in the hands of the Indian Agent [James S. Calhoun] or any government officer which could be appropriated for the purchase of any goods, for any tribe."[78] Unfortunately, as frequently occurred, civil authorities dithered away too much time contemplating the proper procedural approach, and the moment of opportunity passed before they took any decisive action. The recent transfer of the Bureau of Indian Affairs to its new Department of the Interior overseers also meant that no specific agent had yet been appointed to serve the Apaches (Calhoun had only recently received the appointment as superintendent of Indian affairs, overseeing all New Mexico tribes), and Indian policy in the region therefore remained in its developmental infancy.

Not long after Steen's visit to the copper mines, the patience and good will of the Apaches would be put to the test. In addition to the problematic article 11, the Treaty of Guadalupe-Hidalgo contained other troublesome provisions as well. As originally written, the document left many pertinent questions unanswered regarding the proper placement of the international boundary separating Mexico and the United States. Although the Rio Grande demarcated Texas and Mexico, the east-west line between New Mexico and the northern Mexican states remained to be determined. To mitigate this legal ambiguity, both countries created commissions charged with mutually determining the proper placement of the boundary. The work of these two contingents was to be carried out in a harmonious manner that, in theory, would deter any further disputes between the two nations.[79]

Having already surveyed several portions of the border, both commissioners planned to meet at El Paso on November 30, 1850;

from there they would continue conducting their surveys westward.[80] Up until this time, the U.S. Boundary Commission had been headed by Commissioner John B. Weller of Ohio and Chief Surveyor Andrew B. Gray. Although temporarily disbanded in December 1849 when Weller submitted his letter of resignation, work resumed after President Taylor appointed John Russell Bartlett to serve as Weller's replacement. Bartlett accepted the appointment on June 19, 1850, and arrived at El Paso in November.[81]

In May 1851, after languishing for five months in El Paso collaborating with the seventy-man Commission for the Limits of the Mexican Republic, headed by Pedro García Conde, Bartlett and his assistants finally marched westward. Recognizing the location's benefits, he chose the copper mines at Santa Rita del Cobre as his temporary headquarters. Captain Louis S. Craig, with eighty-five men of the Third Infantry, served as the military escort. Bartlett expressed grave concerns with the fact that he was to be accompanied solely by infantry. For the duration of his time at Santa Rita, he continually pressured authorities in Santa Fe for a force of dragoons to protect the commissioners, but his pleas went unfulfilled. Indeed, the department commander explicitly stated before Bartlett even took the field that "not more than one company will be required to give protection to the commissioner and his party," clearly underestimating the difficulties that would later arise with Apaches in the area.[82]

Difficulties quickly arose with the local tribes following Bartlett's arrival at Santa Rita. Initially the two groups coexisted with minimal tension, the Apaches being "daily visitors to our quarters, entering the houses and tents of the Commission with perfect freedom and the most entire confidence."[83] Surveying parties departed from the copper mines almost daily and always returned safely, and the Apaches refrained from stealing the expedition's animals and supplies. But the presence of a large body of Americans for such a lengthy period of time inevitably caused distress among the Indians, and relations began to deteriorate. The Apaches had no way of knowing the ultimate intention of these men and no doubt feared that they intended to stay indefinitely. The longer they remained, the more pronounced their mark on the surrounding landscape and resources, something that the Indians doubtless noticed and increasingly resented.

Bartlett sparked dormant anxieties when he unexpectedly wrested two captives from the Apaches and repatriated them to their Mexican families in accordance with treaty requirements. One of the boys, José Trinfan, had been captured six years earlier at Fronteras, Sonora; the other, thirteen-year-old Saverro Heradia, had been with the tribe for five months since his capture at Bacoachi, also in Sonora. Bartlett's subsequent promise to compensate them in the amount of $250 worth of presents failed to appease the Apaches. The paltry offer offended several of them, including Mangas Coloradas, who did not appreciate being bribed through an uneven exchange of cheap trinkets for humans that tribal families had adopted as their own kin. Bartlett later repatriated a third Mexican captive, a young girl named Inez González, to her home in Santa Cruz, Sonora. She arrived at Santa Rita in the possession of Mexican traders who obtained her directly from a band of Western Apaches (probably either Coyoteros or Pinals) in modern-day southeastern Arizona. Much to the traders' chagrin, the commissioner took the girl from them in accordance with the treaty. Bartlett would nostalgically recall "the peculiar gratification to me to be enabled to restore to their parents . . . two boys [and a girl] who had long been in captivity."[84]

The Apaches' discontent soon became obvious. Animals began disappearing on an almost daily basis, inconveniencing soldiers and surveyors alike. In total, Apache raids resulted in the loss of some 150 horses and mules belonging to the boundary commission.[85] Enraged over the loss of property, Captain Craig wrote to General Scott, insisting that "these Indians must be well-flogged, and be made to return all the property they have stolen, or this country can never be settled. . . . [M]y opinion is that the government ought to send two mounted regiments to this country."[86]

On July 25, 1851, a disquieted Bartlett wrote to Colonel Sumner in Santa Fe stressing the urgent necessity of a larger military escort and practically begging him to dispatch a company of dragoons to the copper mines. He hoped that Sumner would send Major Steen's company at Doña Ana, a mere two days away from Santa

Rita. "I have from the beginning been of the opinion that a single company of infantry was totally inadequate," Bartlett lamented. "Still more inadequate would even a *full* company be under existing circumstances, and far more so is the one now stationed here under Brevet Colonel Craig, which doesn't number more than about 40 effective men."[87] Augmenting the commission's already mounting fears, the Apaches proceeded to attack a small group of Californians on the nearby Janos Trail into Mexico, killing one and wounding several others. Despite this telling incident, Bartlett's and Craig's multiple pleas for reinforcements proved ineffective, and Sumner remained unwilling to dispatch a dragoon escort.[88]

The boundary commission's presence soon encouraged other hearty pioneers to enter the area. By September 1851 a group of between fifteen and twenty American settlers had arrived near Santa Rita and commenced gold-mining operations.[89] Their arrival signaled the beginning of a trend that increased exponentially in upcoming years as more and more white miners ventured into the region. Despite the army's powerful presence, emboldened Indians continued to steal from miners and soldiers alike. The popularity of this location for goldseekers ultimately would be among the reasons for which the department succumbed to Steen's and Craig's wishes and build a post there in 1851. Initially named Cantonment Dawson, it occupied the old buildings at the copper mines after the commission's departure.[90]

In his published *Personal Narrative,* Bartlett recalled numerous encounters, both friendly and hostile, with the Apaches. Among his reminiscences is a lighthearted tale illustrative of the vast differences in culture between the Indians and Anglo-Americans. According to Bartlett, a group of Apaches visiting the copper mines inquired about the presence of whiskey. Himself committed to temperance, the commissioner "positively refused, denying that I had any. Although this was the simple truth, they did not believe it.... [T]hey were constantly on the look-out for it, and when they saw a bottle they asked if it did not contain the coveted liquor. I one day handed them a bottle of catsup and another of vinegar, and told them to ascertain for themselves. A taste put a stop to their investigations, and they were afterwards less inquisitive." In self-exoneration he further stated: "In all my intercourse with the Indians, during the two and a half years I was in their country, I never gave them a drop of ardent spirits. I also prohibited others from doing so; but on a few occasions, had reason to believe that my orders were disobeyed."[91]

Having completed the boundary survey in that vicinity, Bartlett and his crew departed Santa Rita del Cobre in August 1851 and continued trekking westward. Their further work would be short lived, however. In early 1852 California senator John B. Weller opened a debate in Congress that ultimately led to the suspension of all surveying activities. Less than a year later, on December 22, 1852, the federal government officially disbanded the commission despite the fact that some surveys remained unfinished.[92] Notwithstanding its premature dispersal, the boundary commission served one important regional purpose beyond that of geographical surveys: it proved to the authorities in Santa Fe that prior reports advocating a post at Santa Rita had been justified.

The military post at El Paso, despite being in Texas, remained under the jurisdiction of the Ninth Military Department during this time. In January 1851 Apaches descended upon the El Paso area on three consecutive nights, each time running off several mules from Sam Magoffin's ranch north of town. Magoffin immediately blamed the Gila Apaches, although no one positively proved that accusation; the guilty parties could have been Mescalero Apaches from east of the Rio Grande, a tribe notorious for raiding that area. Major Jefferson Van Horn, commanding at El Paso, found his garrison too depleted to pursue the Indians and also lacked enough horses fit for service. He did, however, send an express rider to Lieutenant Buford at Doña Ana, who also decided against pursuit. Indeed, Buford's troops suffered from similar shortcomings. Post returns almost invariably cited a shortage of mounts at Doña Ana; in June 1850, for example, the seventy-six men of Company H, First Dragoons had only fifty-five serviceable horses.[93] The fact that troops at El Paso could not pursue them must have influenced the Apaches' decision to raid there. Indeed, local haciendas experienced a high frequency of livestock thefts at the hands of the Apaches, partially because the area was midway between the homelands of both the Gila and the Mescalero tribes and therefore highly accessible to both groups.

Van Horn's report on the poor condition of his horses brought to light a common circumstance in antebellum New Mexico. Difficulties surrounding the quality and durability of mounts prompted considerable attention from officers and inspectors, a limitation partially resulting from the War Department's continuing struggle to minimize expenditures in the western territories.[94] In 1838 the quartermaster general estimated that in providing forage and "mounting and keeping each dragoon mounted," the army incurred an annual expense of $100.33 per soldier, or $54,360 annually across both regiments. Furthermore, this figure represented expenditures during the Seminole Wars in Florida, where easier transportation of forage reduced costs.[95] In New Mexico the cost of maintenance far exceeded this amount, and with military officials desperately attempting to reduce costs, many dragoon mounts suffered from inadequate care. Troops frequently failed to catch raiders simply because their horses gave out, forcing the men to walk back to their posts while leading their broken-down mounts behind them.

According to one 1850 report, the vast majority of dragoon horses came from Missouri and Illinois. Upon arriving in New Mexico, these animals endured a monumental change in climate. It typically required at least twelve months for a horse to become fully acclimated to the arid desert environment, assuming it even survived the long journey across the Santa Fe Trail. The army usually pressed these animals into service immediately rather than slowly breaking them in, and as a result, "a very large percentage of the American horses sent to the country die during the first year."[96] In reference to the mounts at the Socorro post, one inspector noted, "[they have] been well selected for size and strength, but, either from the influence of climate, or from hard usage or want of proper forage, have much degenerated since their arrival in New Mexico."[97] Dragoon mounts had an average life span of a mere three years, a testament to the hard and tedious service expected of them. The weight of a dragoon soldier with full provisions added to the burdensome life of a horse. Inspector McCall wrote a separate report for every military post in the Ninth Military Department, and not once did he encounter one with enough serviceable horses to accommodate the entire garrison.[98]

McCall's observations were not unique to his own inspections. Secretary of War Conrad alluded to similar characteristics of Indian warfare in his 1850 annual report: "The only description of troops that can effectually put a stop to these forays," he explained, "is cavalry." New Mexico's Indians—and especially the Apaches—challenged the military inasmuch as "whether for war or for the chase, they are invariably mounted, and are well skilled in the management of the horse."[99] Two years later Agent John Greiner assumed command of Indian affairs in New Mexico and observed:

> There are [an estimated] 92,000 Indians in this territory. . . . [W]e have not 1000 troops here under Colonel Sumner to manage them. Out troops are of no earthly account. They cannot catch a single Indian. A dragoon mounted will weigh 225 pounds. Their horses are all poor as carrion. The Indians have nothing but their bows and arrows, and their ponies are fleet as deer. Cipher it up. Heavy dragoons on poor horses, who know nothing of the country, sent after Indians who are at home anywhere and who always have some hours start, how long will it take to catch them? So far, although several expeditions have started after them, not a single Indian has been caught![100]

The situation across the entire western frontier was perhaps best summarized by Thomas Fitzpatrick, an agent to several of the Plains tribes. Like Greiner, he fully recognized the futility of controlling hostile Indians in order to encourage civilian settlement and economic expansion: "It must be apparent that a skeleton company of infantry or dragoons can add but little to the security of five hundred miles square of territory; nor can the great highways of Utah and New Mexico be properly protected by a wandering squadron that parades them once a year." Fitzpatrick proposed that the government choose one path, either peace or war, and adhere to it. "The policy must be either an army or an annuity. Either an inducement must be offered to them greater than the gains of plunder, or a force must be at hand able to restrain and check their depredations. Any compromise between the two systems will only be productive of mischief. . . . It will beget confidence, without providing safety; it will neither create fear, nor satisfy avarice; and, adding nothing to the protection of trade and emigration, will add everything to the responsibilities of government."[101]

In pursuance of the annuity alternative, Congress passed the controversial Indian Appropriation Act on February 27, 1851, which affected all Indian agents and the manner in which they dealt with the tribes. With Commissioner of Indian Affairs Luke Lea (a staunch assimilationist) as its chief advocate, the law outlined the government's moral obligation to care for the Indians and ensure their well-being.[102] While some officials in fact did keep this in mind during their dealings with New Mexico's tribes, the majority of them conveniently forgot.

Significant changes in policy objectives and their implementation loomed on New Mexico's immediate horizon. In 1851 a visionary new territorial governor and a replacement commander of the Ninth Department brought with them innovative yet contrasting visions. James S. Calhoun became New Mexico's first appointed civil governor and superintendent of Indian affairs, roles that afforded him authority over Indian policy throughout the entire territory. His objectives differed tremendously from those of his newly arrived counterpart in the military department, Colonel Edwin V. Sumner. As a result of continuous disagreements over New Mexico's future development and conflicting conceptions of what the disposition of the Indian tribes should be, many things would change from a military and political standpoint during the incumbencies of Calhoun and Sumner, whose contentious relationship and divergent visions effectively undermined hospitable relations with New Mexico's Indian tribes.

CHAPTER 4

The Department under Sumner

While policy initiatives and treaty negotiations in New Mexico would fall to civil officials within the Bureau of Indian Affairs, the Ninth Military Department retained responsibility for actually enforcing those policies. This systematic dispersal of authority between two government entities had only recently been instituted when Indian affairs were removed from War Department jurisdiction in 1849. The division of power between autonomous departments of government did not, however, prevent military officials from meddling in Indian policy whenever possible, and this interagency conflict became highly debilitating in early territorial New Mexico. In an alarming trend that did not fully dissipate for many years, individuals within both departments vied for supremacy and sought to advance their own policy notions according to how they perceived the Apache conflict. During the early part of the decade, officials administered Indian affairs in view of maintaining strategic viability on multiple fronts. New Mexico's leaders, therefore, were influenced in their actions by several responsibilities, including the need to protect citizens from Apache raiding, repatriate captives, maintain financial solvency, encourage continuing American settlement, and perpetuate economic exploitation of the landscape. The fulfillment of these objectives, most recognized, would require a mixture of diplomacy and force in subduing the Apaches.

During the first five years of U.S. military presence, from 1848 to 1853, the federal government doled out over $12 million solely on defending New Mexico's inhabitants from marauding Indian tribes; the War Department incurred much of this expense in order to maintain forts and equip the soldiers.[1] With congressional allocations at a minimum, cost-conscious politicians at both the local and national levels invariably took this into consideration when pondering policy objectives. In many instances politicians concerned with sectional debates and the astronomical costs of waging the war with Mexico sought to trim appropriations by contending that it would be cheaper to negotiate treaties and distribute tribal annuities rather than pay the excessive costs of equipping military expeditions, freighting supplies cross-country, and paying troop salaries.[2] Additionally, the American public generally opposed a large standing army, and therefore military commanders sought to improve the efficiency of existing forces rather than enlisting more men to disperse their duties. In New Mexico especially, this inhibited the army's overall effectiveness inasmuch as the number of soldiers available simply could not adequately defend the territory's vast domain.

While the military maintained a pronounced presence in New Mexico beginning in 1846, the civil government proved to be much slower in developing. Many of the shortcomings that army officers experienced during the period 1846–50 arose due to an absence of strong leadership in the regional government. Because New Mexico had yet to achieve official recognition as a U.S. territory, a civil governor and superintendent of Indian affairs had yet to be named, and much ambiguity remained as to its political future. Not until the arrival of James Calhoun in 1849 to serve as Indian agent, coupled with congressional approval of the Compromise of 1850, did New Mexico's civil authority reach a state of relative stability, at which point the territorial legislature became operational.

By the time New Mexico became a territory in September 1850, the United States had been attempting to govern Indian affairs there for four years, but little had been achieved. Military leaders rarely reached a consensus on policy objectives within their own district, much less across disparate bureaucracies. Many officials in the War Department and the Bureau of Indian Affairs received their appointments as a result of political loyalty, not because of personal expertise in their respective fields. As a result, officials often served only briefly and changed with each new presidential administration.[3] The preliminary step toward consistency came with the appointment of Calhoun as New Mexico's first territorial governor and superintendent of Indian affairs. Initially appointed as an agent by Commissioner of Indian Affairs William Medill, Calhoun would play a crucial role in the development and implementation of Indian policy during his three-year stint in office.[4] He accepted the position underestimating the extreme hardships and headaches that it would entail.

Calhoun arrived in New Mexico on July 22, 1849, to assume the post of Indian agent; less than a year later, on March 3, 1850, he was appointed governor and served thereafter in both capacities. He entered into a difficult situation, Commissioner Medill ominously informing him, "So little is known here [in Washington] of the condition and situation of the Indians of that region [New Mexico] that no specific instructions relative to them can be given at present." Calhoun recognized that his primary undertaking would be that of controlling the territory's Indian tribes, who had raided the settlements with impunity during previous Spanish and Mexican administrations. "The Indians generally are in a bad temper," he lamented, "[and] the number of troops is not sufficient here to keep upon them a proper check; infantry are useful only to protect posts, stations, and property. Mounted troops are the only arm of this country that can be effectively used against the Indian tribes of this remote region."[5] Lacking military authority, Calhoun depended on the troops and their commanding officers to enforce his policy initiatives, a reliance that continually burdened him as he attempted to promulgate a mutual understanding on Indian policy with his military counterparts.

A nearly bankrupt territorial treasury and a woefully insufficient line of communication between Santa Fe and Washington,

D.C., severely inhibited the governor's ability to act effectively. Correspondence with federal authorities took months to reach its intended destination. "I am yet without the slightest intelligence from the States," Calhoun wrote after taking office, "and I must repeat, the mail facilities are not such as we are entitled to, and that it is, infinitely, of more importance to the Government at Washington than to us—the controlling powers should be advised more promptly in reference to the various sinuosities daily perpetrated in this far off region."[6] Oftentimes responses to Indian raids, as well as peace overtures proffered by Indian chiefs, required quick and decisive action on the part of civil and military leaders in order to have any hope of success. Receiving authorization from Washington officials could take months, by which time the opportunity had almost invariably dissipated.

By continuously failing to send the supplies and ammunition necessary to carry on an effective Indian campaign, the federal government further undermined Calhoun's efforts. Writing to Secretary of War William L. Marcy prior to arriving in New Mexico, Calhoun pleaded his case and requested permission to raise a militia to augment the regular forces already stationed in the territory: "A Mounted Regiment of Dragoons will be required, at no distant day, for service in New Mexico. . . . [I]n sixty days, if not in *less* time, I can raise a regiment, one thousand strong. . . . [I]f it can be so organized, we are ready to enlist for two, three, four, or five years."[7] To his chagrin, Marcy succinctly replied that "the Executive has no authority to accept the services of the regiment which you offer to raise."[8] Contrarily, Marcy's successor, Charles M. Conrad, openly advocated such a strategy. He believed that "if properly armed and organized into a kind of militia, under direction of officers of the army, [citizens would] render essential aid in protecting [New Mexico] against the sudden inroads of the more savage tribes. . . . [T]he experiment is well worth making."[9] Conrad and Calhoun thus agreed on the issue and might have pursued a working relationship between the civil and military authorities had their terms of office more directly coincided.

Unable to issue an executive order himself, Calhoun appealed to civilians to take matters into their own hands, encouraging "all able-bodied male citizens of the Territory, capable of bearing arms, [to organize] volunteer corps to protect their families, property, and homes."[10] He envisioned the development of a safe and prosperous territory through the active participation of the people themselves; the approximately one thousand soldiers stationed there simply could not quell all of the Indians on their own.

In his first inaugural address to the new territorial legislature, the governor denounced the Indians for "their butcheries and devastation and desecrations" and called upon lawmakers to condone the raising of a militia "in order to be able to defend our firesides."[11] Ultimately, Calhoun's hopes of mobilizing an armed citizenry went unrealized; both Colonel Munroe, commanding the Ninth Military Department, and President Fillmore refused to provide weapons for civilians, many of whom simply could not afford to purchase their own. A lack of funds in the treasury rendered Calhoun helpless to provide arms, and the task of chastising the Indians remained the sole responsibility of the army.[12] A frustrated governor summarized his predicament:

> The Indians, presuming upon their knowledge of safe retreats in the mountains, and our entire ignorance of all avenues, except established military roads and well known trails, are not to be subjected to just restraints until they are properly chastised. When they shall feel themselves so chastised, they will sue for peace.... The very gravest subject connected with our Indian affairs in New Mexico relates to the wandering tribes, who have never cultivated the soil, and have supported themselves by depredations alone. This is the only labor known to them. The thought of annihilating these Indians cannot be entertained by an American public—nor can the Indians abandon their predatory incursions.... [T]his subject, I humbly conceive, should engage the earnest attention and early consideration of the Congress of the United States..., for no earthly power can prevent robberies and murders, unless the hungry wants of these people are provided for, both physically and mentally.[13]

Calhoun tried in earnest to understand the full scope of the Indian situation. He realized that Apaches typically raided New Mexico's settlements not so much for pleasure or to inflict heartache upon their victims. Rather, the majority of depredations north of the Mexican border resulted from sheer necessity; one could not expect the Indians to cease this practice as long as their families remained impoverished and starving. The governor also concluded that constant warfare with the Indians would be ineffectual, resulting in unnecessary bloodshed and loss of life. Although he did not favor a policy of annihilation, many of his counterparts exhibited less humanitarian ideologies, giving rise to contentious relationships not only with the Indians but with other U.S. authorities as well.[14]

In 1850 Calhoun contacted Commissioner of Indian Affairs Orlando Brown to suggest that New Mexico be divided into sections for policy purposes, one for each major tribe whose homelands fell within territorial boundaries. He recommended selecting "four districts of [the] country, the districts not to be within one hundred miles of each other, defining and marking distinctly, the boundaries of each district; and into these limits, the Apaches, Comanches, Navajoes, and Utahs, with their straggling bands . . . , should be forced to enter and remain, under penalties that would secure submission."[15] Clearly frustrated by the task of controlling four separate tribes, Calhoun sought to resolve these issues with one stroke of Commissioner Brown's pen. This would have allowed the governor to devise individual policies designed specifically to fit the needs of each of the four tribes, whose community and kinship structures differed substantially and made it impractical to apply a universal Indian policy. Territorial politicians similarly recognized the potential benefits of a subsystem within the region. New Mexico congressional representative Hugh N. Smith recommended splitting the territory into five, rather than four, districts and suggested that a separate Indian agent be appointed to each one.[16] Ultimately these requests fell on deaf ears in Washington, and Calhoun would be forced to carry on with what few resources he had available.

The governor's remarks concerning the Indian tribes showed signs of a differing point of view when juxtaposed with other 1850s officials. While Calhoun generally pursued a humanitarian agenda, John Munroe, Ninth Military Department commander from October 1849 until July 1851, remained somewhat indifferent toward New Mexico and the Indians living there, adhering to his duties as an army officer but doing little more beyond that. One observer wrote that the colonel "would brew his pitcher of toddy at night, and take the first drink of it at noon the next day, after which hour he would not attend to any official business."[17] Indeed, Munroe achieved little aside from promoting the status quo during his time as department commander. Ineffective though he proved to be, Munroe at least fostered only minimal contention with his government counterparts. In contrast, his successor would prove much less amenable to civil authority.[18]

Not long after Calhoun took office as governor, Edwin Vose Sumner replaced Munroe as military commander.[19] A staunch, authoritative figure, the fifty-four-year-old Sumner would incite controversy throughout his time in New Mexico. The colonel had earned the sobriquet "Bull Head" during the Mexican-American War when a bullet supposedly glanced off his skull without doing any damage. He became best known for his sweeping reforms and complete reorganization of the Ninth Military Department, undertaken with a direct view toward Indian affairs and fiscal solvency. Despite these changes, Sumner's own sentiments toward the indigenous tribes remained fundamentally at odds with those of Calhoun, resulting in multiple points of contention between civil and military leadership and marginalizing the role of diplomacy in any Indian negotiations.[20]

Regarding Indian affairs specifically, Sumner's preferred approach mirrored Major Steen's recommendations a year earlier when he outlined the tactical maneuvers necessary to carry on a destructive war of attrition. Writing in 1853, the colonel delineated his stance on warfare with the Indians, regardless of specific tribal or subgroup affiliation: "If I could think that a war could be carried on against the Indians, as against Whites—in other words, that private property could be spared, non-combatants protected . . . the subject would be divested of most of its difficulties. . . . The Indians will never stand to receive personal punishment at our hands, and consequently the only possible way to chastise them is to destroy their growing crops, and it will be impossible to make any distinctions between the friendly and unfriendly. They would all profess friendship, of course, to save their property."[21] Sumner's comments, intended to inform civil officials of his preferred strategy, reveals much about his approach to Indian affairs while in office. Indeed, he exacted a heavy toll on some of the territory's tribes, especially the Navajos, through his policy of targeting all Indians—women and children, young and old, guilty and innocent—in their camps and crushing their means of subsistence in order to force them into submission.

When he took office as commander of the Ninth Military Department, Colonel Sumner received explicit orders from Secretary of War Conrad pertaining to the redistribution of New Mexico's military forces. "There is reason to believe," Conrad wrote, "that the stations occupied by the troops in the Ninth Department are not the best for the protection of the frontier against the inroads of the Indians. Accordingly . . . you will use sound discretion in making such changes . . . you may deem necessary and proper." He reiterated the importance of this strategy when explaining that "the [War] Department is induced to believe, that both economy and efficiency of the service would be promoted by removing the troops out of the towns where they are now stationed, and stationing them more towards the frontier and nearer to the Indians." Accordingly, Sumner would "immediately, on assuming command, revise the whole system of defense . . . , scrutinize the administration of [the quartermaster and commissary] departments, and rigidly enforce all regulations having reference to the economy of the service."[22]

Inspector George A. McCall, while conducting overviews of each post in 1850, also recognized the necessity for widespread strategic change. "The only way in which a military force can be advantageously and effectively employed to put an end to Indian spoliations in New Mexico," he believed, "is to post them, not in our settlements or on our borders but in the heart of the Indians, to punish them in their strongholds for the offences they commit beyond their own boundaries."[23] In this opinion both Conrad and McCall echoed Major Steen's recommendations from more than a year earlier to relocate his garrison at Doña Ana to the copper mine region in placing them closer to the Gila Apache homelands.

Boundary Commissioner Bartlett also commented on military strategy in the territory, but he took an antipathetic view toward Sumner's farming and subsistence operations, which he believed hindered the army's ability to protect the citizens. "A change should be made in the system pursued at the frontier posts," Bartlett professed. "Soldiers should not go into quarters, and then remain quietly devoting themselves to agriculture . . . , for the consequence of the present system is, that by their attending to the fields, they . . . neglect their proper duty as soldiers." He went on to suggest that "the soldiers should leave their quarters, and be kept moving from one point to another. Let them be a few days in a mountain pass, next at some oasis in the desert . . . , and again in some beautiful valleys. . . . [T]his active life . . . would tend more to overawe and subdue the Indians."[24]

Pursuant to official orders and his own personal preferences, Colonel Sumner promptly relocated many of his military posts upon assuming command of the department. In the months that followed, he laid out the design for an entirely different military framework in New Mexico, one that would remain mostly unchanged for years to come. Immediately after arriving in the territory, Sumner proclaimed the withdrawal of troops from the settlements to be "a matter of vital importance, both as it regards discipline and economy. . . . It is unquestionably true that most of the troops . . . have become demoralized, and it can only be accounted for, by the vicious associations in these towns."[25] The colonel's words and actions proved to be highly controversial among the people, who feared that the removal of troops from towns would directly compromise their safety and livelihood. At Doña Ana indignant citizens quickly drew up a petition to Governor Calhoun, who although sympathizing with them, lacked the authority to abrogate

Colonel Edwin Vose Sumner, pictured here as a major general in the Union Army during the Civil War, sometime between 1861 and 1863. Courtesy National Archives and Records Administration, Washington, D.C.

any military decisions. The petition read, in part: "[We] have heard from good and trustworthy sources from persons in this circuit that there is rumor that the Cavalry and Infantry, now attached to this colony will be removed in a few months, and, knowing and realizing that the execution of such a movement would bring imminent peril to us, to the extent that our lives and families might be sacrificed and the little we have to live upon will be exposed to the fury of the bloody hands of the Apaches, just as we have been in past years."[26]

Governor James S. Calhoun. Used by permission, Utah State Historical Society, all rights reserved.

In directly challenging the military's (and more specifically Sumner's) authority, these residents voiced the sentiments of people throughout the territory, many of whom depended upon the presence of troops for both protection and economic sustenance. South of Doña Ana, Simeon Hart, owner of a mill near El Paso, likewise protested Sumner's removal of troops from nearby San Elizario, Texas, to newly established Fort Fillmore. Hart first began contracting with the military to supply the southernmost posts in 1850, and relocating troops from the El Paso region meant that Hart would likely lose his contracts.[27] The pragmatic Sumner, being a staunch authoritarian, did not budge on his intentions. All civilian protestations, he assured the secretary of war, were entirely unfounded and emanated "directly or indirectly from those who have hitherto managed to live, in some way, from the extravagant expenditures of the Government." Any petitions or protests, the colonel advised, must be summarily rejected.[28]

In late 1851, not long after Sumner's changes had taken effect, Major Thomas Swords bore witness to the reorganization of the department and, echoing Governor Calhoun, called upon the citizens to defend themselves against raiders when necessary:

> Colonel Sumner has now adopted the true policy by occupying positions beyond the present settlements, where ... by their presence in their country, they can take control of the wild Indian tribes more effectually, than when at a distance from them. The inhabitants of the towns and large settlements should be taught to depend upon themselves as did the first settlers in the western states. By the distribution of arms and ammunition to them under proper restrictions ... [the civilians] would soon be made valuable partizan [sic] soldiers, and after overcoming their terror of the Indian, be ever anxious and ready to meet him, instead of, as now, fleeing in terror at his approach.[29]

In contrast, Governor Calhoun believed that "the lives of the citizens of the Territory are in imminent danger if Colonel Sumner insists in carrying out his views to withdraw his main force from the settlements." Despite the intense public outcry and the support of the governor, the citizens did not succeed in reversing Sumner's decision. As a civil official, Calhoun could do little to countermand the colonel's orders, nor could he have exerted much influence upon the stubborn department commander even if he had tried.

Sumner had multiple motivations in relocating his forces, some of which extended beyond his orders from the secretary of war. Aside from distancing the soldiers from the societal vices offered at the Mexican settlements, the colonel also sought to avoid the exorbitant prices being paid to rent living quarters for the troops and to transport subsistence stores to secluded settlements. Captain Thomas L. Brent, serving as assistant quartermaster in 1850, toured New Mexico and concluded that the most viable strategy for reducing expenditures would be to move the territory's posts in view of implementing farming operations. He pointed out the "great expense with supplying the troops with forage," owing partially to the "profuse and extravagant manner in which [grain and corn] was used."[30] Indeed, throughout the 1850s the department spent more money annually on grain and forage than all other locally grown goods combined.[31]

Based on his observations, Captain Brent believed that "the remedy for this [overspending] will . . . be the establishment of posts in the heart of the Indian country at such points that supplies can be raised in the vicinity on government farms." He noted that similar experiments had proven successful elsewhere, namely at Council Bluffs and Fort Leavenworth, and believed that the same strategy for increasing troop self-sufficiency might work in New Mexico.[32] Sumner therefore had two important points to consider when selecting locations for new military posts. First, the new location had to be such that it allowed for easy troop deployment and remained easily defensible. Second, it needed to contain ample natural resources for the maintenance and self-sufficiency of the troops. If new posts could be constructed in locations that facilitated large-scale farming operations, then the immense quantities of forage being imported from outside the territory could be reduced and, by default, expenditures could be minimized.

Sumner also aimed to build on the cheapest land available that could still be considered practicable for a military establishment. He occasionally utilized the citizens' desperation to his advantage, offering to place small detachments in certain locations within the settlements, though only if the price was suitable.[33] With no alternative course of action, citizens in several instances succumbed to Sumner's demands for cheap rent. This proved especially true in the more southerly towns of Doña Ana and El Paso. The colonel placed Fort Fillmore nearly equidistant between the two locations on a tract of private land owned by Hugh Stephenson, a local miner and rancher.[34] Doubtless under pressure from local residents, Stephenson struck a deal with Sumner that essentially allowed the military free use of the land, leasing the tract to the government for a mere ten cents *per year* for twenty years, an arrangement that must have pleased Sumner.[35] A competing offer came from El Paso merchant James W. Magoffin, who proposed selling the army a 320-acre tract of land for $15,000, pointing out that the department currently paid over $1,500 annually to lease quarters nearby and could thus avoid further rent payments while simultaneously owning the property.[36] In light of Stephenson's offer, it comes as no surprise that Sumner declined Magoffin. The lease agreement ensured military protection for settlers in the Mesilla Valley for years to come and minimized government expenditures, although Fort Fillmore would be abandoned long before the twenty-year term expired.

Pursuant to Colonel Sumner's reorganization, Fort Conrad was established on September 8, 1851, on the west bank of the Rio Grande twenty-four miles south of Socorro. The army situated the post "on a sandy, gravelly *mesa,* or table-land, which rises abruptly from the grassy bottoms of the river about half a mile west of the Rio Grande." In the nearby river bottoms could be found "a light-yellowish sand . . . that covers the surface of the ground in patches like snow." Although the army did not realize it at the time, the location of the post near these "alluvial low lands" would result in a high rate of sickness as malarial diseases quickly set in among the men.[37]

The troops stationed at Socorro, under the command of Major Marshall S. Howe, immediately transferred to the newly selected site and began construction of the new fort. Built on the privately owned Pedro Armendariz land grant, the location of Fort Conrad would incite legal controversy when the American owners of the property, Hugh Smith and Thomas Biggs, claimed that the post was located on their holdings and that the military therefore owed them rent. Certainly this notion did not sit well with Colonel Sumner. Eventually the matter came to a resolution in a Socorro courtroom, where a judge ruled in favor of Smith and Biggs. Not surprisingly, this led to the relocation of Fort Conrad to a site just beyond the Smith and Biggs claim.[38] Still, despite the close attention that this issue demanded, Fort Conrad would remain in service from September 1851 until its abandonment in March 1854. During that time, an array of different companies garrisoned the post, including Company I, First Dragoons and Companies D, E, and K, Second Dragoons.[39]

The considerable distance of twenty-four miles separating Fort Conrad and Socorro effectively discouraged most soldiers from indulging themselves in the sexual promiscuity available at the town's brothels. Still, a few of the men occasionally made the journey without being caught. The fact that some contact between

Site of Fort Conrad as it appears today, looking northeast, with the Rio Grande Valley in the background. The windmill on the left-hand side of the picture marks the location of the fort, now private property. Nothing is left but a few scattered glass fragments and nails to suggest the fort's former presence. The structure sat atop a low-lying mesa rising fifteen to twenty feet above the river bottom. Photograph by the author.

the soldiers and Socorro's female population continued to occur seemed obvious to Assistant Surgeon E. P. Longworthy, who oversaw Fort Conrad's post hospital. In his annual report, Longworthy remarked extensively on the poor health of the garrison. While he described the majority of the illnesses as malarial fevers emanating from nearby mosquito-infested lowlands, other types of diseases appeared as well. "The whole number of diseases treated in eighteen months, in a command averaging 479 men, was 562," the doctor reported. "Five deaths occurred at Fort Conrad, three from diarrhea, one from emphysema, and one from acute pneumonia." He also noticed a prevalence of syphilis and gonorrhea owing to "the shocking low state of morals here."[40] Removing the troops from Socorro, though helpful, had not been entirely effective in eliminating all illnesses among the soldiers. The fact that the number of cases treated exceeded the number of men at the fort by eighty-three served as an unmistakable testament to the harsh realities of frontier military life. The boredom and seclusion that the troops endured no doubt contributed to the "shocking low state of morals" Longworthy mentioned.

Continuing his reorganization of the department, Sumner ordered the construction of Fort Fillmore midway between Doña Ana and El Paso on the eastern bank of the Rio Grande, only a stones' throw from Mexico at that time. Prior to the 1854 Gadsden Purchase, the Rio Grande still delineated the international boundary as far north as Doña Ana, although the exact placement of the line remained hotly debated at that time. Therefore, the construction of Fort Fillmore on the eastern bank of the river placed it directly on the border and in close proximity to the 3,000 Mexican citizens residing at Mesilla, several miles upstream on the western bank. During the post's first three years, this situation detrimentally affected the maneuverability of its troops, for they could not legally cross the river onto foreign soil ("the disputed area") without it being perceived as a hostile act toward Mexico and threatening to undermine the tenuous peace existing between the two nations. Not until the ratification of the Gadsden Purchase in June 1854 would soldiers at Fort Fillmore be able to cross the Rio Grande, whether it be to visit Mesilla or to chase Indians.

The garrison from Doña Ana, under the command of Lieutenant Abraham Buford, encamped at the selected site for Fort Fillmore on September 15, 1851. Dixon S. Miles of Company K, Third Infantry arrived shortly thereafter to assume the role of post commander and oversee construction. The garrisons from El Paso and San Elizario also removed to the new site, and by October 1853 eight officers and 269 troops called Fort Fillmore home.[41] Throughout its ten years as a military installation, the fort boasted one of the largest garrisons in the territory; furthermore, when Colonel Mansfield inspected the post in 1853, he reported the quarters there to be the best he had seen.[42]

Like all southwestern posts of its day, Fort Fillmore was constructed of adobe, a building material with which the Americans had little familiarity. Consequently, the military hired resident laborers from nearby Mesilla Valley communities to manufacture the bricks. They also hauled timber for the roofs from Soledad Canyon on the western slope of the nearby Organ Mountains. The post developed slowly, as attested to by John Russell Bartlett, who spent several days there shortly after construction commenced. "The barracks at Fort Fillmore are as yet quite crude," he wrote, "being mere *jackals* [*sic*], that is, built of upright sticks filled in with mud. They were hastily put up; but it is the intention of Colonel Miles to have more substantial buildings of adobe erected forthwith."[43]

Fort Fillmore utilized the hired labor of local New Mexicans on a regular basis throughout its existence. These civilians not only helped build the post and maintain its gardens but performed other basic duties as well. Ten Mexicans worked full time there in March 1852, helping make adobes and construct wooden flooring and roofing for some of the buildings, receiving compensation in the amount of seventy-five cents per day "and a part of the soldiers ration."[44] Other instances periodically arose requiring civilian labor as well. In August 1855 the fort suffered from a severe shortage of soldiers to perform general post duties, to the extent that only one man at a time could be spared for sentinel duty. "There is of necessity, as at all posts, certain labor required," Colonel Miles wrote, and "this can be avoided and [would] permit me to mount additional guard, if the quartermaster is permitted to hire but a few Mexicans, not over 5 or 6, who can be obtained at 5 or 6 bits per day.... [T]his is decidedly cheaper to the government than the employment of soldiers."[45] Indeed many New Mexico forts depended heavily on civilian labor during the 1850s, but while the availability of such workers eased the tasks of the troops, it also created tension throughout the post as interracial misunderstandings cropped up. Ethnocentric mentalities led officers and troops alike to bark irreverent orders at the laborers, causing considerable resentment throughout the local communities.

Colonel Miles arrived at Fort Fillmore on September 28, 1851, to assume the role of post commander, a responsibility that he would hold periodically for a number of years. Miles, who played a critical role in New Mexico Indian affairs throughout the 1850s, was described by one contemporary as being "surprisingly vigorous in action. With grizzled hair and beard he displayed the social habits of a man of forty. He was a great talker and sometimes gave his vivid imagination a loose rein. Undaunted in the face of hardships and privations and ready to accept any responsibility, he was nevertheless a strict constructionist of orders."[46] Lieutenant Henry Lazelle, who made the colonel's acquaintance in 1857, wrote in his diary, "I found him to be a person of very brilliant imagination, accompanied with great facility of composition, which enabled him to converse upon all topics . . . but as he seemed to possess an unfortunate memory, or carelessness of agreement of his thoughts; it was sometimes painfully unpleasant to compare his statements, particularly when he was under the least excitement from liquor."[47] Others found Miles much less pleasant. During a visit to the post in 1853, Governor William Carr Lane remarked that he "was obliged, unwillingly, to quarter with Col. Miles, a walking sponge, martinet, and a——."[48]

A post the size of Fort Fillmore required a large amount of subsistence stores to remain operational. Miles and his fellow officers maintained a sizable garden to provide provisions for the garrison. These agrarian pursuits complied with orders received directly from Secretary of War Conrad outlining a new plan for farming operations at posts all across the western frontier.[49] Colonel Sumner, in view of his goals to reduce War Department expenditures, advocated for this plan as well and ordered officers throughout his command to comply. Like many other military experiments in New Mexico, this one proved to be a dismal failure for a variety of reasons.

Pursuant to Conrad's orders, Miles wrote to Colonel Sumner requesting permission to hire Mexicans from Mesilla as farm laborers. Much like the manufacturing of adobes, the soldiers knew little about effective farming methods in the arid Southwest and relied upon the knowledge of those more familiar with the country. Still, a stubborn Sumner refused to adopt local techniques, opting instead to employ the processes used in the East. He ordered Miles not to allow the implementation of "the [locals'] miserable method of cultivation except in irrigating, about which they know more than we do."⁵⁰ Although he disagreed with Sumner about hiring residents to manage these efforts, Miles concurred with him regarding irrigation. "The making and management of acequias [irrigation ditches], all important to the raising of any vegetable or grain, is only understood by those raised in this country," he admitted.⁵¹

As a traditionally agrarian society, the inhabitants of the lower Rio Grande valley had generations of experience with appropriate farming techniques and would be an asset to any military farming operation. Although Sumner stubbornly opposed utilizing local labor and techniques (aside from irrigation), he ultimately conceded and granted Miles permission to hire several local workers at Fort Fillmore, although he expected unreasonably productive results. "The farming operations have not been as successful at all the posts as I expected," Sumner grumbled, "but I think that all the difficulties will vanish when it is known and felt that no officer will be continued in command of a post who does not exert himself to carry out the orders of the government in relation to this matter."⁵²

Miles could scarcely be blamed for the failure of certain crops in the Mesilla Valley. Sumner typically denied requests to hire civilian laborers, and the soldiers at Fort Fillmore put little if any effort into maintaining the farms. "I regret that I cannot approve the hiring of Mexican laborers," the colonel had notified Miles. "I cannot subscribe to the doctrine that soldiers can do nothing. To the contrary, I believe *they can be made to do anything* that others can do."⁵³ Ultimately, despite Sumner's protestations, local residents performed most of the hard labor at Fort Fillmore, at extra expense to the army. The fact that the soldiers failed to manage their own gardens became obvious to their officers. In 1852 Major Steen enlightened his superiors that "soldiers are but bad farmers at best, even in countries better adapted to cultivation than New Mexico."⁵⁴ During his inspection of the department in 1853, Colonel Mansfield likewise noticed this dilemma: "This [farming] duty of the troops seems to have proved a failure generally. The mode of cultivation in this territory is necessarily so different from that to which the American and European, who constitute the rank and file of our army, have been accustomed, and the business so entirely different from the pursuits of an officer and soldier, that it is not at all astonishing it did not succeed."[55]

Miles's efforts, however well intentioned they may have been, were ill fated from the beginning. By 1852, less than a year after Fort Fillmore's establishment, the farming experiment had proven to be a complete failure. At Fort Conrad, 150 miles to the north, these operations likewise failed.[56] Numerous reasons were cited, not the least of which being the unpredictability of the Rio Grande, which often overflowed its banks and inundated the fields. According to one army observer in 1852, the river's width ranged from two hundred to six hundred yards at various points, "and its current sweeps along with a force that undermines and destroys hundreds of acres of cultivated land in a single season. . . . [I]t changes its channel, on an average, once per annum."[57] Regional aridity also affected military farming operations: only 9.86 inches of rain fell in southern New Mexico during the eighteen-month period spanning September 1851 and March 1853.[58]

Despite operational failures at Fort Fillmore, it remained one of the most pivotal posts in New Mexico for nearly ten years. Its location near the crossroads of the Camino Real and the road to California rendered it indispensable to travelers seeking a safe stopping place. Additionally, its proximity to several small towns, including Las Cruces, Doña Ana, and Mesilla, increased the fort's level of importance to the civilian population. A plethora of regiments passed through Fort Fillmore, including Companies B, D, and H of the First Dragoons and Companies D and K of the Second Dragoons as well as several companies of Colonel Miles's omnipresent Third Infantry.[59]

While Colonel Sumner remains best known for his redeployment of forces and pursuit of cost efficiencies in New Mexico, he did propose several fundamental changes to military tactics in the field. Whereas previous observers had continually insisted that only mounted dragoons could have any hope of success on Indian campaigns and wrote off infantrymen as useless, Sumner felt otherwise. Shortly after assuming command in July 1851, he outlined a

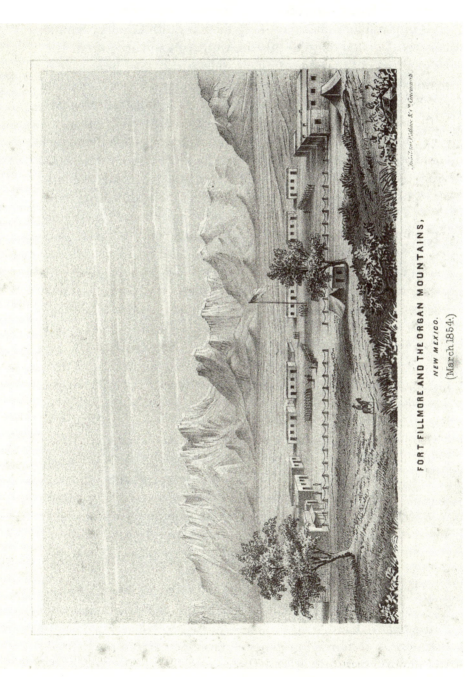

Fort Fillmore, 1854, in a view looking east. Courtesy New Mexico State University Library, Archives and Special Collections (03390019).

strategy for future campaigns, one contrary to all previous policies. "It is impossible to make any long marches with Cavalry," Sumner believed, "loaded down as they are with arms and accoutrements." He pointed out that most Indians rode astride fleet horses far superior to those the army possessed. Therefore, when they finally reached the scene of action, the troops could not "act offensively in the saddle, and their broken down horses, are a great embarrassment, requiring a large part of the command to protect them, such could otherwise be used offensively on foot." To remedy this tactical shortcoming, he proposed that all future Indian campaigns consist almost exclusively of infantrymen, although he acknowledged that "there should always be a small body of *very select horse*" accompanying them. Even then, the colonel claimed that any mounts must be led on foot until required for action.[60]

Sumner's plan for employing infantry on extensive field campaigns had both its pros and cons. Indeed, dragoons continually suffered from equestrian difficulties, with forage often inadequate and water scarce during expeditions. Yet two distinct types of military action occurred throughout southern New Mexico. The first came in the form of a spontaneous reaction to an Apache raid, requiring troops to chase the marauders at full speed in order to have any hope of immediately overtaking them. In such circumstances, infantrymen had no chance of catching the well-mounted Apaches. The other type of military action involved long campaigns in the field that often required weeks of planning. In these instances troops sought to locate the Apaches in their homelands and attack them at their campsites, making quickness of travel less important than perseverance in the field. Therefore, Sumner's proposal to conduct campaigns with infantrymen could only be successfully implemented in certain instances when extensive planning preceded military action.

The troops at Forts Conrad and Fillmore immediately saw action against the Apaches. On November 13, 1851, Lieutenant Buford left Fort Fillmore with fifty-eight men of Company H, First Dragoons in response to reports of a raiding party in the Robledo Mountains northwest of Doña Ana. Arriving at the scene, the dragoons discovered the corpse of a herder who had been lanced and scalped by the Indians. Following the trail southward, the troops finally abandoned the chase after arriving at the Mexican border. Buford and his company had witnessed a favorite strategy of Apache raiding parties, that of crossing the border into Mexico when being chased by American troops. Doing so accorded well with Apache geopolitical spatial constructs, which were indifferent to an arbitrary line separating the United States and Mexico. Although they certainly understood that Mexicans and Americans owed allegiance to different leaders and governments, the Indians did not differentiate between them in a precise geographic manner. Indeed, the Apaches recognized the entire region—identified on cartographers' maps as northern Sonora and Chihuahua and southern Arizona and New Mexico—as their singular homeland, long before it became internationally divided after the Mexican-American War. For Americans and Mexicans to suggest that Apaches must recognize the same imagined boundary contradicted Indian notions of land use and dominion. Therefore, the perception of Apaches crossing the Mexican border as a swarthy tactic can only be applied when viewed from the U.S. Army's perspective, but it changes when seen from the Indians' traditional geopolitical standpoint. The Apaches' construct of spatial surroundings is an important factor when considering their imagined landscape as it contrasted with that of Anglo-Americans.

As noted, the Indians quickly realized that American troops could not chase them into Mexico following the Treaty of Guadalupe-Hidalgo. Because they recognized no such boundary themselves, raiders identified this opportunity as a convenient means for escape and frequently used it to their advantage. John Russell Bartlett alluded to this inadvertent sanctuary in his *Personal Narrative*, writing, "a difficulty arises when the Indians, on being pursued, take refuge in Mexico, where our troops cannot follow them." He recommended that federal officials seek some type of diplomatic arrangement with the Mexican government that would allow "small bodies of U.S. soldiers . . . to enter Mexican territory. This plan would be agreeable to the Mexican authorities, as they informed me."[61] Not until July 29, 1882, would the United States and Mexico negotiate a diplomatic pact allowing U.S. troops to operate on Mexican soil in pursuit of hostile Apaches.[62]

Indian raiding continued in earnest throughout December 1851. In that month alone eight claims were filed with the government for livestock thefts at several southern New Mexico locations.[63] The most shocking outrage of the month, however, claimed the life of Robert T. Brent, a member of the territorial legislature. Brent was traveling on the Jornada del Muerto when a band of Apaches attacked his party and killed the lawmaker. Learning of his death, a grieving but enraged legislature declared that "since the entrance of the American army under General Kearny this Territory has been a continual scene of outrage, robbery and violence carried on by the savage nations by which it is surrounded." New Mexico's congressional delegate presented a bill that would mandate the organization of at least two new volunteer regiments in the territory to be armed, equipped, and paid by the U.S. government. Such a plan, however, never received approval, owing in part to widespread dissent among other territorial officials at that time.[64]

Unabated depredations in southern New Mexico eventually led to the establishment of another military post, the first to be constructed in the heart of the Apache homelands. On December 28 Brevet Major Israel B. Richardson led sixty-seven men of Company K, Third Infantry to Cantonment Dawson at the old Spanish copper mines, some eighty miles northwest of Fort Fillmore. Here he established Fort Webster (named for Secretary of State Daniel Webster) on January 23, 1852.[65] Sumner's correspondence suggests that the colonel fully expected this new post to curb Apache raiding and hoped to negotiate a treaty with the Gila band soon afterward. If the Indians desired peace, Sumner instructed Richardson, they must agree to "abstain, at once, from all depredations upon the Mexicans," in which case Sumner and Governor Calhoun would meet with them at Fort Conrad pursuant to a peace agreement.[66] Subsequent events at Fort Webster would prove this expectation ill founded, and many months would pass before any such negotiations began.

Forts Webster, Conrad, and Fillmore would serve as the backbone of the U.S. Army's presence in southern New Mexico in the early 1850s. They thus became important nodes of federal power, from which dragoons and infantrymen embarked on campaigns into Indian country. Writing to superiors in Washington, D.C., Sumner stressed the practicality of his deployments. "It is unquestionably true," he wrote, "that the most certain way to subdue Indians, is to establish posts in the heart of their country." Located nearer the Indians' cherished homelands, the forts would "confine them [the Apaches] at home—they will never venture to make distant hostile expeditions, and have their families and property within striking distance of vigilant garrisons."[67] Though no definitive results had yet been achieved, the colonel remained optimistic that this constituted the proper course of action. "The new posts in the Indian country [will have] the happiest effect," he prophesied. "Indeed it is plain that this is the only certain way of controlling the Indians."[68]

Major Richardson and his infantry company would remain stationed at Fort Webster for almost a year, and conflict arose with nearby Indians immediately after the troops arrived. One afternoon a small band of Gila Apaches approached the post, displaying no signs of hostility. Nevertheless, a skirmish ensued, provoked by the infantrymen, who began firing indiscriminately at the Indians as they drew near. Several Apaches were wounded in the initial volley, and those who remained uninjured fled frantically into the hills. Even the formidable Apaches could not lay siege to the heavily fortified positions held by the troops, barricaded inside the protective adobe walls of the fort where they could fight without fear of sustaining injuries.

The soldiers' brash action would not go unchecked; rarely did the Apaches allow such an outrage to pass without seeking retribution. Only two days later, on January 26, some two hundred Apache warriors led by Chiefs Delgadito and Ponce descended upon Fort Webster, outnumbering the garrison almost four to one.[69] In the desperate fight that followed, three soldiers lost their lives: Sergeant Bernard O'Daugherty, Sergeant Nicholas Wade, and Private John Croty. The body of Sergeant Wade was discovered some distance

Fort Webster, at the Santa Rita del Cobre mines, 1851 or 1852. Bainbridge Bunting Papers, MSS-385 BC, Box 2, Folder 21, Center for Southwest Research, University Libraries, University of New Mexico, Albuquerque.

from the post; he had been captured, tortured, and mutilated. Another soldier involved in the fight, Private Matson, vividly recalled the scene that followed: "A funeral at a lonely frontier fort, after a skirmish in which the comrades who are buried have been killed and one tortured by savages, is a sorrowful affair."[70]

While these events unfolded at Fort Webster, a detachment of troops from Fort Conrad also found themselves exposed to Apache hostilities. On January 25, 1852, a mail escort consisting of ten privates and one noncommissioned officer came under attack at Laguna, a camping place near the northern end of the Jornada del Muerto. Three soldiers were killed and another fell wounded, while the Indians suffered at least two of their number killed and one injured. Upon hearing of the engagement, Major Marshall S. Howe, commanding at Fort Conrad, dispatched Companies D and H, Second Dragoons under the command of Lieutenant Evans, who managed to locate the Indians' trail but arrived too late to have any hope of catching them. According to those present during the attack, however, the perpetrators may not have been Apaches. "The corporal [accompanying the mail escort] is sure that there were white men among the number, as they had large whiskers and curly hair that he was so well satisfied that [they were whites] that he cursed them in English," Howe reported.[71] It is not altogether improbable that a small group of renegades, posing as Apaches, attacked the escort. Though rare, this type of deceptive action was occasionally perpetrated not only by white men but by Mexicans as well.

Major Howe entertained a belief common among many military men of his day that all Apaches should be punished, whether guilty of a crime or not. His upbringing and training as an army officer shaped his perceptions of Indians, and his imagined western frontier held no place for people he viewed as savages. Such ideologies, common among officers and enlisted men alike, inevitably resulted in numerous engagements in which troops knowingly attacked innocent Indians simply for the sake of having something to report to higher authority and to further their reputations. Howe, riled by the incident on the Jornada and anxious to leave Fort Conrad on an expedition into Apache country, seized the opportunity, informing his superiors, "I learn unofficially that at a distance of some 80 to 100 miles west of this [Fort Conrad] is a large camp of Indians, which if troops could be spared [from other posts] for the purpose, it might be well to make them a visit."[72]

Recent Apache depredations soon induced the military to take action in southern New Mexico. Raids continued to occur in the vicinity of Socorro and San Antonio, attributed to Gila Apaches who had begun to retaliate for the murder of two Indians at San Antonio the previous fall.[73] On February 3, 1852, a mere one week after the attack on the mail escort, Colonel Sumner authorized a month-long campaign into Apache country to consist of 300 troops from both dragoon and infantry companies, with Major Howe in overall command. Howe would march in a westerly direction to Fort Webster, where Sumner instructed him to "proceed to the camp of the Gila Apaches, and if possible inflict upon them a signal chastisement."[74] When it left Fort Conrad, however, the actual column boasted only 175 men, slightly over half the intended number. Still, as the largest military force that had yet been mustered against the Gila Apaches, it represented an early manifestation of Sumner's militant Indian policy and would be the first of many such expeditions to come. Significantly, the colonel dispatched three dragoon companies as part of this campaign, a direct contradiction to his earlier statements that only foot soldiers should be utilized for such expeditions.

Three weeks passed before Howe's campaign took the field. On February 12 Major George A. H. Blake of the First Dragoons arrived at Fort Conrad with fifty-two men of Company I and twenty men of Company F; they brought only fifty-nine horses, though, leaving thirteen dragoons without mounts. The two majors awaited the arrival of Captain Richard S. Ewell from Los Lunas with Company G, First Dragoons, before departing. Two civilian guides accompanied the expedition, including a Mexican who had escaped Apache captivity after almost twenty years. The army frequently employed both Mexican and Pueblo Indian guides on treks into unknown regions, hoping that their familiarity with the landscape would lead them to the Indians and eliminate unnecessary hardships. In most instances, however, officers wound up cursing their guides as incompetent after wandering aimlessly through the arid mountains.

Only five days into the campaign, a small band of Apaches surprised the advance scouting party, wounding one of the guides through the hip. The attackers apparently numbered only about fifteen, but Major Howe opted not to pursue, rationalizing that it might have merely been a ploy to lead the soldiers into a larger ambush. Still, the incident proved sufficient to unnerve the officers. The troops camped that night along the Mimbres River, where a sardonic James Bennett scribbled in his diary: "We were all, every man, to be on post during the night. Only think of it! [175] men to watch and guard [a few] officers! Oh, that our government only knew the courage of some of her officers!"[75]

On February 27 Howe and his command arrived at Fort Webster. Only one month having elapsed since the skirmish there that claimed the lives of three soldiers, the remaining men understandably feared another attack. Private Bennett wrote of Fort Webster: "There are 50 men here, all frightened out of their wits. They have old wagons, logs, barrels, rocks, and other articles too numerous to mention, piled around their fort, making it almost impossible to get to it. . . . [T]hey expect momentarily to be attacked by the Indians."[76] The Fort Webster garrison must have been relieved at the sight of Howe's large column as it approached from the east. But on March 1 the major left the post with his entire contingent and marched northwest toward the Gila River. Less than a day later, he encountered fresh signs of Indians and, for reasons his men never fully understood, sent a rider back to request reinforcements. The 175-man force Howe commanded was more than sufficient to discourage any hostilities the Indians might have been planning. At any rate Major Richardson and 31 men of Company K, Third Infantry joined the column, leaving only 25 men to garrison the post. One disgruntled officer complained, "[Howe's] expedition thus far has been a total failure. I am well informed that he did not go over twenty or twenty-five miles from [Fort Webster], and never saw an Indian during the period he was absent. He cannot however state that there are none in the country, for on his march to this place his command was fired upon by the Indians and his guide severely wounded."[77]

The irrational request for additional troops infuriated Gouverneur Morris, the commanding officer at Fort Webster; Howe had merely seen signs of Indians, not the Indians themselves. Major Morris replied that any additional troops should have accompanied the column when it left the fort. If Morris's observations were correct, then Howe made little attempt to locate the Indians, instead leading his command on an aimless trek through the mountains. Immediately after reaching the Gila River, Howe ordered a countermarch and returned posthaste to Fort Webster, not even bothering to send out scouting parties en route. His deliberate avoidance of the Apaches received further corroboration in the journal of a dragoon under his command. According to Private Bennett, while marching back to Fort Webster, the troops spotted rising smoke and grazing cattle in the distance, both certain signs of a nearby Indian camp: "After a moment's consideration, [Howe] turned and gave the command, 'Countermarch!' Oh! What feelings arose within the breast of each soldier that had a spark of courage in him! To endure a long journey, get in sight of the Indians, have a spirited action in anticipation, and then our cowardly old Major from mere personal fear orders a 'countermarch!' The shouts of the men should have caused his cheek to have flushed with shame . . . shame on him who boasts of being an American and an officer in the army and is guilty of such cowardice."[78] Having traveled so far, the troops might have found a fighting pursuit to be a welcome respite from the monotony they had endured. On its march to and from the Gila River, the column traversed such rough terrain that by the time the weary men of the Third Infantry finally returned to Fort Webster, their shoes were completely worn out; some were even barefoot. One soldier called the expedition "the greatest piece of humbuggery I have encountered since I joined the Army."[79]

By March 23 the troops had returned to Fort Conrad, having encountered no other Indians than those that ambushed the advance scouting party more than three weeks earlier. Perhaps a fitting end to the expedition occurred on the night before returning to the post, when a grass fire broke out in the camp and destroyed almost all of the property belonging to Company K, Second Dragoons. Bennett later recalled: "It was an exciting time. 300 guns and several pistols, lying promiscuously on the ground, discharged their deadly contents in all directions. . . . [T]he Major didn't seem to enjoy it."[80] With this culminating event, Howe's campaign had proven to be a calamity in almost every sense. The wide range of hardships experienced by the troops illustrated the extreme difficulty of locating the Apaches and operating in the treacherous terrain of their homelands with only minimal equipment and rations. Large campaigns proved difficult to equip and maneuver once in the field, making it tactically challenging for troops to operate against the more mobile Apaches. The most beneficial effect, although not apparent at the time, was likely the psychological effect such a large body of soldiers had on the Apaches. Although never openly confronting the Americans, they doubtless lay concealed in the hills observing the column's movements. As the first campaign of this magnitude to traverse the Gila Apache country, it must have been a revelation to the Indians that U.S. military manpower would be difficult to oppose in open fighting.

Howe's failure prompted Major Morris to consider embarking on a similar expedition but with a different strategic approach. Being stationed at Fort Webster, Morris had a much shorter distance to ride in order to reach Apachería and could lead a scout without Howe's counterproductive oversight. Having previously conversed with some of the Gila Apaches at his post, Morris possessed a better understanding of their way of life. "They live in the saddle, are perhaps the best mounted of any Indian on the continent, subsist on plunder, and have no habitations . . . that the command under Major Howe is able to reach or destroy," he wrote. He suggested detailing a body of troops much smaller in number than Howe's campaign, which had proven the impracticality of sending two hundred men as a single unit into Apache country. The Indians, who had scouts watching every movement of the army, would flee before any sign of them could be found; in a sense the soldiers were chasing phantoms that only appeared if and when they wanted.

Morris understood that employing a smaller force would reduce his visibility while increasing maneuverability, thus improving the likelihood of finding and engaging the Indians. He also correctly surmised that Sumner would be unlikely to support another campaign of such a large and costly nature. Consequently, Morris requested permission to enlist local miners, for a period of thirty days, to serve in place of soldiers at Fort Webster in the event that Sumner was unwilling to dispatch replacements.[81] The colonel authorized the major to take whatever independent action he might deem necessary, "with the means that you have," but expressed his regret that reinforcements could not be spared at that time.[82] Ultimately the entire campaign became unnecessary when several Apache leaders rode into Fort Webster seeking to negotiate a peace treaty.[83] Nevertheless, Morris's astute observations did offer an alternative tactical approach for future military campaigns, and Colonel Sumner seemed to realize its value.

While these field operations played out, a rift continued to develop between Governor Calhoun and Colonel Sumner back in Santa Fe. Both men enjoyed a substantial amount of power and influence in their respective administrations, but in following their own personal convictions regarding Indian policy, they traversed divergent paths. An order from Washington in 1851 stating that Indian agents, who worked under the Interior Department as civil officials, must be allowed to accompany military expeditions provided the impetus for further fractiousness in the territorial government. Congressional representative Hugh Smith alluded to this a year earlier when he wrote, "neither superintendents, agents, nor formal contractors or commissioners, can be effective without the presence and co-operation, for some time, of a strong and active military force."[84]

Governor Calhoun learned of the order in a communication from Commissioner of Indian Affairs Luke Lea in April 1851, who wrote: "I have been informed that it is contemplated to increase the military force of New Mexico, with a view to the prosecution of hostilities against the Indians. In that event it will be necessary that one or more of the officers of this department shall accompany each detachment of troops sent against the Indians, so as to be in readiness to act in that capacity as occasion may require."[85] The instructions Colonel Sumner received from Secretary of War Conrad in July differed little: "In all negotiations and pacific arrangements with the Indians you will act in concert with the superintendent of Indian Affairs in New Mexico, whom you will allow to accompany you in the expeditions into the Indian Territory, if he should deem it proper to do so, and to whom you [will] afford every facility for the discharge of his duties."[86]

Sumner ardently opposed the direct involvement of civil officials in any military action. While this partially owed to his disdain for shared authority, the fact that the Quartermaster Department covered all expenses for civil officials when accompanying military campaigns also influenced the colonel's noncompliance. Although he could do nothing to countermand an order from the secretary of war, Sumner frequently circumvented the mandate by refusing to provide the necessary escorts and traveling amenities for agents accompanying expeditions. On other occasions the troops hurriedly took the field before an Indian agent could arrive to accompany them.[87] After assuming command in New Mexico, Sumner wasted little time in penning a letter to Calhoun outlining the extent to which he would comply with these orders, effectively warning the governor (and Indian agent) to expect little cooperation from the military.[88]

In 1852 Calhoun began planning a trip to Fort Webster in hopes of negotiating a treaty with the various Apache bands in that vicinity. The governor cancelled his plans, however, when Sumner informed him that there would be no military escort available.[89] Calhoun's frustration was manifested in a letter to the commissioner of Indian affairs, to whom he complained: "It is now clear, I shall not be able to visit the Gila Apaches, as I intended, and deemed absolutely necessary, because Col. Sumner declines affording this Superintendency escorts for my purpose—If this course is in pursuance of instructions from Washington, our Indian affairs must be conducted by the officers of the Army, or they must be neglected."[90] Having thus been openly rebuffed by Sumner, Calhoun began to realize the futility of challenging the unwavering commander.

In October 1851, just a few months prior to this contentious exchange between Sumner and Calhoun, Indian Agent John Greiner called attention to the dire circumstances existing in the territory. "Everybody and everything in this country appears at cross purposes," he observed, citing severe Indian problems and a lack of harmony among territorial officials:

> Between the savage Indians, the treacherous Mexicans and the outlawed Americans, a man has to run the gauntlet in this country. Three governors within twelve years have lost their heads and there are men here at present who talk as flippantly of taking Governor Calhoun's head as though it were of no consequence whatsoever. . . . [I]n the first place the civil and military authorities are at war. Colonel Sumner refuses to acknowledge the right of the Governor to send Indian agents with him to the Indian country—and will not afford the proper facilities for them to go—and the governor refuses to send them. . . . The American troops are at war with the Indians, and if they could only catch them would give them fits, but Colonel Sumner is on his way back from their country without even seeing one of them.[91]

Sumner remained unwilling to allow Indian agents to accompany military expeditions, and Calhoun seemed reluctant to force the issue. Indeed, by this time the governor had become highly exasperated in his dealings with military authorities.

In addition to advocating peace treaties as a preferable alternative to hostilities, Calhoun advanced other policy objectives as well. He emerged as one of the first territorial leaders to propose the creation of an Apache reservation, something that would not become a reality until long after his death.[92] In 1852 he wrote that "every Indian difficulty in this territory should be settled, and fixed, during the ensuing twelve months," but he predicted that, if the status quo were maintained, "our troubles and difficulties with these Indians will not end in twelve years." The governor acknowledged the necessity of establishing additional military posts and also noted that "commerce with the Indians must be restricted," a direct shot aimed at unscrupulous traders operating throughout the territory. Finally, he once again stressed that the Indians "should be required to remain within certain fixed and well defined limits, under pain and penalties, that would secure the end, or prevent its repetition."[93]

Had Calhoun's immediate successors shared some of his thoughts regarding New Mexico's Indians, especially the establishment of reservations within traditional tribal homelands, many bloody encounters might have been averted. This, coupled with the issuance of rations at regular intervals, would have led to a pronounced decrease in depredations since the Apaches typically raided not as a declaration of hostility, but as a form of economic subsistence. Although for the most part inadvertently, future New Mexico civil and military leaders condemned countless Indians, American soldiers, and civilians to an early grave because of their own failures to come to an agreement on Indian policy. The difficulties experienced by Calhoun and Sumner, as well as the agents and troops under their respective authority, would not subside for years to come. In the meantime the hardships that troops endured in the field and the petty quarrels over policy matters in Santa Fe would continue virtually unabated.

CHAPTER 5

The Woes Continue

Repeated failures to overtake and chastise the Apaches in the early months of 1852 left Colonel Sumner indignant and searching for answers. Since taking command of the Ninth Military Department in 1851, Sumner had achieved his desired restructuring of military posts but had accomplished little in the way of Indian affairs. The Apaches continued to raid haciendas and settlements with impunity, on most occasions retreating unmolested to the safety of their mountainous haunts. Despite looming changes in civil leadership, these failures in both Indian policy and military enforcement continued throughout the spring of 1852. Sumner fell into disfavor not only with territorial leaders but also among citizens, whose patience began to founder as they saw no definitive results in minimizing Indian depredations. Although some of these failures resulted from the unprovoked actions of troops and their commanders in the field, as well as incapable and unmotivated Indian agents, Sumner usually stood the one to blame.

In 1852 a disillusioned Sumner wrote to his superiors in Washington, D.C., recommending that the government abandon New Mexico altogether, leaving it to the Mexicans and Indians. Pegging the people of New Mexico as "idle and worthless," the colonel believed that the removal of all U.S. troops would be in the government's best economic interest. The Mexicans and Indians, he stated, could then be left alone to fight among themselves as they had before 1846. Sumner obviously failed to envision the landscape with the same thoughtful intuition as others. Whereas Major Steen, during his time at Doña Ana, had seen the potential for vast growth in the Southwest once Indian threats could be mitigated, Sumner could perceive nothing more than an immense, barren desert wasteland unfit for habitation by any "civilized" race of people. The colonel's opinion must have been shared by numerous others at that time, especially among the enlisted men, many of whom would have had no objections to abandoning the territory completely.[1]

While soldiers exposed to the rigors of everyday life in New Mexico's most secluded regions may have shared these views, abandonment remained politically impractical, and most federal officials ignored Sumner's suggestion. The idea did, however, invoke the contempt of the territory's citizens, who voiced outrage at Sumner's outlandish, racist statements. Irate residents, already infuriated over the colonel's redistribution of troops away from the settlements, berated the commander through anonymous newspaper editorials, one person spurning him as "too stupid and dishonest to acknowledge himself wrong" while another openly declared his command a total failure: "his every official act, for the two years that he has been at the head of this department, has been one series of blunders and absurdities."[2] Some of these comments doubtless emanated from frustrated merchants, who lost considerable amounts of business and lucrative government contracts when Sumner removed the troops from town limits and attempted to institute a system of self-sufficient farming at the isolated forts.[3]

While Sumner endured the wrath of implacable Santa Fe journalists, the Apaches continued their forays in the southern half of the territory. The Indians had developed a habit of raiding government mail escorts traveling on the Jornada del Muerto, recognizing the vulnerability of these small parties traversing the flat, indefensible terrain. On the same day that Major Howe had departed from Fort Conrad on his Gila River campaign, the Apaches ambushed a ten-man mail escort four miles from Point of Rocks near the southern end of the Jornada. As the startled troops desperately sought defensive positions, Private Collins of the Second Dragoons was killed and another man fell wounded, both while instinctively exiting one of the wagons. In the ensuing skirmish the escort killed one Apache and wounded two others, but the outnumbered troops soon retreated southward to the Mesilla Valley, losing most of their animals to the marauders in the process. The detachment remained at Doña Ana while awaiting orders from Dixon S. Miles at nearby Fort Fillmore. The following day Captain Barnard E. Bee and ten additional dragoons departed that post to reinforce the mail escort on the remainder of its journey.[4]

From this point forward, Colonel Miles would continuously urge the department to increase the number of troops detailed to escort the mail; the ten men traditionally allotted were simply inadequate to discourage Indian attacks, especially on the Jornada del Muerto. "I am convinced," he wrote, "[that] no party of ten men can now travel the Jornada in safety, and I shall until otherwise directed send for the future 20 men with the mail."[5] Another practical course of action might have been to dispatch a second detachment from Fort Conrad to travel south on the Jornada and meet the mail halfway, but the garrison at that post numbered only eighteen effective men at that time (the majority of the garrison being in the field with Major Howe's campaign) and none could be spared for that purpose. Major Lawrence P. Graham of the Second Dragoons, placed in temporary command of Fort Conrad during Howe's absence, notified Colonel Miles that it would be impossible to send troops to meet the mail escort, for doing so would leave only eight men at the fort, rendering it and its supply stores vulnerable to a possible attack. Problems associated with depleted garrisons would continue to haunt the department for years to come, with inadequate troop strength often enabling Apache raiders to escape unscathed.

By May 1852 Gouverneur Morris at Fort Webster still had not been granted permission to carry out his proposed campaign, which he had hoped would be more successful than Major Howe's expedition two months earlier. That same month Cuchillo Negro

(Baishan), leader of a sizable band of Gila Apaches who lived primarily between the Santa Rita copper mines and the Rio Grande, visited a Fort Webster picket camp on the Mimbres River with approximately fifty of his followers. A rider set out to inform Major Morris of Cuchillo Negro's pacific overtures; Morris arrived the following morning with a detachment of Company E, Second Dragoons to meet with the chief. Realizing that he lacked the authority to conduct treaty negotiations, the major informed Cuchillo Negro that "the U.S. would not enter any treaty of peace with one portion of the Apaches and be at war with the next."[6] In making such a statement, Morris exhibited a rare quality among early New Mexico military officers, that of differentiating between bands and recognizing the importance of Apache tribal structure in treaty negotiations. Seemingly desirous of entering into peaceful terms with the whites, Cuchillo Negro dispatched several of his warriors to locate the other headmen, most notably Mangas Coloradas, and ask them to gather at Fort Webster. Morris sent an express rider to Santa Fe notifying the governor of the circumstances, hoping to receive direction on how to proceed.

Unfortunately for Cuchillo Negro and his followers, he chose an inopportune time to seek peace. Before news of their intentions could reach Santa Fe, a very ill Governor Calhoun departed for Missouri on May 6, 1852. Not expecting to finish the trip alive, Calhoun arranged for a coffin to be constructed beforehand and took it with him on his journey home. His foresight had not been ill founded; Calhoun died en route and was buried along the Santa Fe Trail, a most unceremonious end for a man who the territorial legislature posthumously lauded as their "beloved governor."[7] Calhoun's biographer, Annie H. Abel, summarized his tenure as governor and commissioner of Indian affairs in New Mexico: "He had no especial fitness for the position except moderate familiarity with the region where his duties were to lie; but he proved himself a thoroughly capable and honest official."[8] Indeed, had he been alive, Calhoun likely would have followed through with Cuchillo Negro's wishes, recognizing it as an opportunity to advance his proposed policy of creating reservations that otherwise never materialized.

James S. Calhoun left New Mexico for the last time on May 6, 1852, and died later that summer, having conceived many of New Mexico's first Indian policies in the American era, and he had endeavored to see them carried out to the best of his ability. Conflict and contention within his own government circles continuously undermined Calhoun's efforts. In Colonel Sumner he found a colleague with whom he could seldom cooperate and vice versa, resulting in confusion and mayhem in Santa Fe that in turn affected the entire territory. Calhoun's successor, William Carr Lane, arrived in September 1852 and would continue to implement many of his predecessor's humanitarian policies, preferring whenever possible to extend the olive branch rather than counter violence with violence. Yet as with Calhoun, Lane would find it difficult to work harmoniously with the military and therefore perpetuated an already discordant interdepartmental relationship.

The rift that developed between New Mexico's civil and military authorities during Calhoun's incumbency continued long after his untimely death, the greatest losers through it all being the Indians. What started as petty squabbles over differing opinions regarding policy matters quickly mushroomed into a competition of egos between Calhoun and Sumner, whose competing visions for the future of New Mexico clashed at every turn. Plagued with tunnel vision, neither official was willing to sway from his intended path, and both men stubbornly refused to compromise in order to arrive at a coalescence of Indian-policy objectives. Calhoun supported the negotiation of peace treaties and advocated the establishment of permanent reservations within the Indians' traditional homelands as a preferable alternative to removal or assimilation. Meanwhile, Sumner adhered to his vision of quick, decisive military action to quell Indian raiding, despite the fact that such campaigns typically punished only innocent bands within the larger Apache tribe. Military operations as antecedent to treaty negotiations also encouraged violent reciprocity, exacerbating the human toll inflicted by the Apaches during raids that otherwise would have been strictly for subsistence.

A more practical course for these two commanders to take would have been to set egos aside and cooperate with one another, mixing Interior Department diplomacy with War Department force. A proper, thoughtfully devised plan would have taken into account cultural differences, tribal structure, economic and personal objectives, and other vital considerations. Certain components of both Calhoun's and Sumner's strategies proved beneficial, but those components needed to be meshed together in order to form an effective, long-lasting policy that would avoid unnecessary bloodshed and suffering. This did not occur during Calhoun's tenure as head of New Mexico's civil government, and the arrival of his successor resulted in a mere continuance of this interdepartmental conflict.

Named governor of New Mexico by President Fillmore on July 17, 1852, William Carr Lane would prove to be another important figure in early territorial Indian affairs. A well-educated physician from Missouri, Lane married into a prominent family at the age of twenty-nine and had three children. At the time of his appointment to New Mexico, he already boasted considerable political experience, having served numerous terms as mayor of St. Louis. A renowned surgeon who once declined an opportunity to become a U.S. senator, Lane reluctantly accepted the post as New Mexico's governor, which would place him in the center of Indian-policy debates. But none of Lane's previous political experience could have prepared him for the situation that awaited at the western end of the Santa Fe Trail.

Lane did not arrive in New Mexico's capital for his inauguration until September, leaving a significant period during which the territory had no officially appointed governor. Colonel Sumner, still in command of the Ninth Military Department, immediately seized the opportunity and declared himself acting governor until Lane made his appearance. Perhaps anticipating the ensuing controversy, Sumner issued a circular prior to Calhoun's departure, claiming that the former governor had given his blessing that "the military authority of this Department will so far take charge of the Executive Office as to make the preservation of law and order absolutely certain."[9] The colonel felt wholly justified in taking this action, writing to Secretary of State Webster that "efforts are being made at this time by some designing Mexicans to throw off our government." Consequently, Sumner "felt it [his] duty, in which

Territorial Governor William Carr Lane. Courtesy Palace of the Governors Photo Archives, New Mexico History Museum/DCA, Santa Fe (negative no. 9999).

Governor Calhoun fully concurred . . . , to assume the duties of the executive office so far as to ensure the maintainance [*sic*] of law and order."[10] The revolutionary sentiments among "designing Mexicans" did not permeate territorial affairs to the extent that the paranoid Sumner believed, yet the possibility provided ample justification for his assumption of civil authority and temporarily silenced his critics at the national level.[11]

Sumner assumed authority as governor on May 8, 1852. For the brief period of three months, he acted as the supreme commander of the territory, controlling both military and civil affairs, during which time he proclaimed himself de facto superintendent of Indian affairs as well. His actions drew the ire of many inhabitants, and by October complaints about Sumner's "interference . . . in civil affairs" had reached the president, although no official action occurred owing to Lane having already arrived to assume the governorship.[12]

On May 31, during the gap between appointed governors, Gouverneur Morris wrote to department headquarters regarding his isolated Fort Webster garrison. He made no allusion to his previously requested Apache campaign, nor did he mention pending treaty negotiations with Cuchillo Negro. Instead, Major Morris asked permission to abandon the current Fort Webster and reestablish it at a new location several miles east of the copper mines on a bluff overlooking the Mimbres River. The few remaining miners who had been working near Santa Rita del Cobre had all moved elsewhere, many of them becoming weary of constantly peering over their shoulder, wondering when the next Apache attack might come. Consequently, according to the major, Fort Webster no longer needed to protect the mines. He cited numerous additional reasons for requesting the move, particularly pointing out that the Apaches frequently camped in the Mimbres Valley, making it beneficial from a strategic standpoint to relocate to a place where troops could more easily monitor this activity. Furthermore the valley offered an exceedingly fertile landscape and appeared well adapted for both cultivation and settlement. Its west side featured a precipitous, nearly impassable mountain range, which Morris incorrectly believed would hinder Apache attempts to steal livestock from the post herd. Moreover, the lengthy line of communication between the current site and Forts Fillmore and Conrad, both located on the Rio Grande far to the east of the copper mines, could be shortened by several very mountainous miles by moving the post.[13]

Many of the building materials at Santa Rita del Cobre, with the exception of the adobes, could be easily transported and reused to construct portions of the new compound. Owing to the dilapidated condition of the preexisting structures at the mines, it would be easier to construct living quarters at the new site rather than attempt to repair those already in use. Finally, and perhaps the most critical argument in support of his cause, Morris reminded Colonel Sumner that the department paid rent for the privately owned buildings at Santa Rita. Relocating to the Mimbres Valley would eliminate this expense, and the major well knew that the department commander always sought new ways to cut operating costs.[14] Unfortunately for Morris and his garrison, the tumultuous political situation in Santa Fe arising from Calhoun's departure and contentious transfers of authority proved detrimental to the plan. Several more months would pass before Sumner authorized the relocation of Fort Webster, which finally came in July.[15]

A drastic increase in troop desertions added to the innumerable problems existing throughout the territory during the summer of 1852. Colonel Miles wrote from Fort Fillmore on June 17 that troops continued to desert regularly from the detachment at Magoffinsville, near El Paso; four dragoons and one infantryman had disappeared from there in the first two weeks of that month alone.[16] At Fort Fillmore Company H, First Dragoons had been reduced to only twenty-four privates available for active duty, a testament to the widespread effect of desertions. Miles requested permission to withdraw the detachment of dragoons from Magoffinsville after seven more went missing during the latter half of June. The necessity of a military presence, he argued, did not justify the risk of losing more troops this way. Even Fort Fillmore, the largest post in southern New Mexico, could claim only thirty-seven dragoons available for duty in July.[17] With the army stretched so thin, it became increasingly difficult to prevent Indian depredations along the Rio Grande. Not until early September would Miles receive desperately needed reinforcements at his post: on the sixth, forty-eight privates and eight officers of Company K, Second Dragoons arrived there; a day later Company C, Third Infantry arrived with seventy-one privates and seven officers.[18]

During his brief three months at the helm of civil government, Colonel Sumner, along with Indian Agent John Greiner, traveled to Acoma Pueblo on July 11 to negotiate the first treaty between the United States and the Chiricahua Apaches.[19] Between 1778 and 1868 the federal government arranged hundreds of such compacts with various Indian tribes across the continent. Of the innumerable treaties negotiated and signed, the Senate ratified 374 of them. Arising almost simultaneously with American independence, the concept of Indian treaties emerged as a mechanism of Anglo-American lawmaking to recognize the sovereignty of any tribe entering into such an agreement. The government, however, rarely observed Indian treaties with the same reverence as treaties with other "civilized" nations; the popular perception of Indians as a savage, subordinate race provided ample justification for most officials to denigrate such pacts as inconsequential and to feel no remorse in violating them.[20] The final Indian treaty negotiated in the United States, involving the Navajos, achieved ratification in 1868. Three years later Congress abolished the practice, wary of granting sovereignty to different groups of peoples within the country's borders and likewise apprehensive about the implied powers contained in such agreements.[21]

Sumner's undertaking at Acoma therefore represented the first U.S. recognition of Chiricahua Apache sovereignty and in fact would be the only treaty with that tribe ever ratified. Ironically, Sumner's status as a military official meant that he did not hold the proper authority to negotiate such diplomatic arrangements, a power typically reserved for the civil government, although he would have argued that his status as acting governor gave him this right. New Mexico's new congressional delegate, Richard Weightman, disapproved Sumner's actions in a subsequent letter to Governor Lane: "[He] has assumed to negotiate treaties with the Apaches notwithstanding the law of Congress that hereafter all treaties with Indians should be negotiated by an officer of the Indian Department [sic]." Nevertheless, Weightman admitted that the treaty would likely be approved by the Senate and would therefore "be of advantage to the public interest."[22]

The selection of Acoma as the meeting place seems odd, it being located near Navajo country in northwestern New Mexico, a considerable distance from traditional Apache homelands. Sumner likely chose this location because of its proximity to his headquarters in Santa Fe, therefore lessening the distance he had to travel to meet the Indians. Even before departing Santa Fe, though, tensions arose between the two civil and military representatives of the government. In his diary Greiner complained that "Col. Sumner assumes to be the head of the department, claims that [he] is governor by virtue of necessity and by virtue of his office of governor is [also] supt. of Ind. Affs. I did not know before that he assumed such power and questioned his right very strongly. . . . I offered to leave the question for the judiciary to decide; he objected . . . saying he should act on his own responsibility."[23] Indeed, many persons (in addition to Greiner) questioned the legitimacy of Sumner's authority over civil officials.

Clearly disenchanted with the military commander's actions in the absence of a lawfully appointed territorial governor, Greiner questioned Sumner about the number of troops that would serve as an escort to Acoma. Writing on July 3, the agent cited the fact that "a large body of Indians is expected to be in attendance" and asked the colonel to provide his personnel with "such a force as you may deem necessary for the protection of councilors and for the benefit of the public service."[24] Sumner, true to form, responded in a terse but succinct manner. "I have to inform you," he stated, "that I am going myself to meet and treat with the Gila Apaches at Acoma on the 11th inst. in conjunction . . . with the senior Indian agent in this territory. I shall take such military force as I may deem necessary."[25] In other words, a military escort for Greiner would not be forthcoming unless he intended to travel with Sumner, which he did not. Greiner departed Santa Fe en route to Acoma on July 6; Sumner did likewise a day later, effectively avoiding the agent during the journey.

Despite these initial shortcomings, negotiations went forward as planned. The all-encompassing treaty that resulted instituted numerous restrictions upon the Apaches, both culturally and geographically. Mangas Coloradas, the most influential Apache chief of his time, traveled to Acoma and made his mark upon the agreement—the first and only one he ever signed. Other Apache signatories included Cuentas Azules, Blancito, Negrito, Capitan Simon,

Cuentas Azules. From Rex Strickland, *El Paso in 1854, with a 30-Page Handwritten Newsletter by Frederic Augustus Percy Entitled El Sabio Sembrador,* ed. E. H. Antone and Carl Hertzog (El Paso: Texas Western University Press, 1969).

and Capitan Vuelta.[26] Greiner specifically acknowledged the importance of Mangas Coloradas's presence at the event, writing, "Mangas is . . . their chief captain and councilor and can speak for all his people, [and] promises fair for them."[27] Without the chief's blessing, the treaty would have been meaningless to most Apaches.

Article 5 became the most controversial—and, for that matter, difficult to enforce—aspect of the Acoma Treaty. It stated that the Apaches must thereafter "desist and refrain from making any incursions within the territory of Mexico of a hostile or predatory character . . . and refrain from taking and carrying into captivity any of the people or citizens of Mexico . . . [and] surrender to their agent all captives now in their possession."[28] This stipulation resulted directly from article 11 of the Treaty of Guadalupe-Hidalgo, which held the U.S. government responsible for thwarting all Indian raids into northern Mexico. Not surprisingly, this provision went widely ignored by both sides in the years to come. It proved impractical, if not impossible, for the military to enforce, and Agent Greiner immediately realized the futility of the requirement: "It will be extremely difficult to keep these Indians at peace with the people of Old Mexico.... [T]he people of Sonora & Chihuahua have treated these Indians very badly . . . and I fear it will be almost impossible to prevent hostilities between them." In a letter to newly arrived Governor Lane, Greiner further reiterated his feelings of antipathy toward the people of Old Mexico: "[The Apaches] complain bitterly of the bad faith & treachery of the people of Sonora & Chihuahua, and if half their statements are true, the Indians would be justified in seeking revenge."[29]

Testifying before Congress some years later, Greiner vividly recalled the conversation between Mangas Coloradas and U.S. authorities regarding the topic of Apache raiding into Mexico. The agent had asked the chief about "the cause of the difficulties, with the people in Chihuahua and Sonora," to which the Apache leader replied, "Some time ago my people were invited to a feast; aguardiente or whiskey was there; my people drank and became intoxicated, and were lying asleep, when a party of Mexicans came in and beat out their brains with clubs." The chief then described another incident in which "a trader was sent among us from Chihuahua. While innocently engaged in trading . . . a cannon concealed behind the goods was fired upon my people and quite a number were killed." Also at that time Chihuahua began offering a bounty of one hundred fifty dollars for each Apache scalp, "and we have been hunted down ever since," Mangas lamented. He concluded by asking Greiner a rhetorical but valid question: "How can we make peace with such a people?"[30] Outlining this portion of the treaty negotiations, the Santa Fe newspaper editorialized, "so the probability is, that when they [the Apaches] get home [from Acoma], they will make an inroad upon the settlements of Sonora [and Chihuahua], and our government cannot prevent them."[31]

The treaty's eighth article required the Apaches to allow the military to construct forts and agencies, "at such times and places as the said government may designate," regardless of the proximity to Apache homelands.[32] In a consequence that the Indians perhaps did not foresee, numerous posts soon appeared within what the Apaches considered the heart of their domain. Mangas Coloradas likely did not realize initially the tremendous ramifications for his people from this treaty, which essentially allowed Anglo-American encroachment onto traditional Apache lands and opened the floodgates for future settlement, forever altering the tribe's highly revered landscape and hindering their mobility. Anywhere the army built a fort, civilian settlement almost invariably followed as various frontiersmen sought to exploit the surrounding countryside in any manner that might yield a profit. Without military protection, civilian interlopers often kept their distance from places near the Apaches, but with troops nearby, they could settle with little fear of being attacked.

Congress ratified the treaty on March 23, 1853, and President Franklin Pierce signed it into law two days later. Mangas Coloradas likely granted his approval only because he realized the utter futility of resistance. In the seven years that had passed since his fateful meeting with General Kearny on the Gila River, hundreds if not thousands of Americans had passed through Chiricahua country en route to California. Scores of these individuals decided to forgo the complete journey to the coastal state and simply settled on Apache lands, where they began mining, ranching, and farming at locations of their choosing. The chief noticed this trend and doubtless realized that it did not bode well for his community. He and his immediate followers did their utmost to uphold the treaty's terms. Ultimately, however, Mangas Coloradas could not control small groups of recalcitrant renegades within his own tribe who did not recognize his authority, and conflicts ensued each time they broke the provisions of the treaty. Unfortunately, innocent Apaches typically received the brunt of the military's retributive wrath while the hostile miscreants escaped unscathed.

A frequent oversight of many treaties, including the Acoma Treaty, arose from the difficulty Anglo-Americans had in distinguishing between guilty and innocent bands within the larger tribe. Apaches, as with most other Indian tribes, lived and operated within their own smaller cliques. Local groups often acted entirely independent of one another, converging only for seasonal mescal harvests or for large raids targeting Chihuahua and Sonora. The complex structure of the Apache tribe as a whole made it difficult for the army to distinguish one from another. Oftentimes it remained unclear which bands directly or indirectly participated in the negotiation of a specific treaty, and occasionally one group remained hesitant to implicate another in wrongdoing even if it meant suffering the consequences along with the guilty. Such misunderstandings of Apache tribal structure created intense and sometimes irreconcilable strife between the military and the Indians, a rivalry perpetuated by the treaty's general ambivalence toward differentiating between groups within the larger tribe.

The Acoma negotiations represented the high point of Sumner's tenure as self-appointed territorial governor. Submitting the resulting document to superiors in Washington, D.C., he proudly boasted of his accomplishment and prophesied, "If I can keep the Mexicans from committing depredations on them, I have no doubt the peace will be lasting."[33] The irony lies in the fact that the Senate ratified the agreement reached by Sumner, who as a military officer should have deferred to civil authority during the negotiations, yet in upcoming years Congress summarily rejected treaties made by both Governor Lane and Governor Meriwether. A year later the delicate peace accord remained mostly intact, although many throughout the territory expected it to be broken at any time. Captain John Pope of the Corps of Topographical Engineers wrote in 1853, "the state of comparative peace to which they [the Apaches] have been brought by the Treaty of Acoma in 1852, is well understood to be a very uncertain and precarious arrangement and one liable at any and every moment to be abruptly terminated."[34]

Hoping to capitalize on the opportunity provided by the recent negotiations, Greiner traveled to Fort Webster shortly afterward to meet with several Apache chiefs who had not joined Mangas Coloradas at Acoma. Arriving at the copper mines, the agent summoned the chiefs but found that "these Indians are very wild." After sending runners in every direction, he waited three days before any Apaches appeared at the fort. After Greiner assured one emissary of his benevolent intentions, the warrior left and the next day returned with over two hundred of his tribesmen, including Chiefs Ponce and Llatana (probably Itán). The agent failed to negotiate any formal peace accord, but he did secure assurances from the chiefs that their followers would "not go into Old Mexico to commit depredations" if the U.S. government would "protect them and their families on this side of the [international boundary] line."[35] However well intentioned Greiner's efforts may have been, they proved meaningless, as the Apaches never relented in raiding Mexico for any significant period of time.

Sumner, who savored his additional authority as acting head of the civil government, became embittered when it came time to abdicate his gubernatorial office to Lane in September 1852. "As soon as the Secretary [William Carr Lane] takes his post, Sumner says he will remove the troops from [Santa Fe], for no other reason than to embarrass the civil authorities and to make it apparent that the civil authorities cannot govern," observed Greiner.[36] Before the new governor even reached the territory, Sumner transferred his military headquarters from Santa Fe to Albuquerque, purposely distancing himself from Lane, and from all civil authority for that matter.[37] "The unfortunate and long continued existence of the military government in New Mexico has in that country caused certain persons both civil and military to forget or lose sight of the American ideas of the subordination of the military to the civil power," observed Delegate Weightman.[38] With such intense friction epitomizing the relationship between Lane and Sumner from the start, little would be accomplished while both remained in office.

The new governor and superintendent of Indian affairs proved equally stubborn in cooperating with military leaders, and in fact exacerbated the rift emanating from the previous relationship between Calhoun and Sumner.[39] Lane found himself at odds with the department commander not only over Indian policy but also on international policy (regarding the boundary between Mexico and the United States), a disagreement that inevitably spilled over into Indian affairs. Controversy arising from this dysfunctional relationship ultimately resulted in both Lane and Sumner being ousted from their positions and new officials brought in to replace them.[40]

Colonel Sumner, a lifelong military man who had served honorably in the Mexican-American War, generally advocated the use of force to subdue the manifold bands of depredating Indians throughout the territory. His hawkish concept of an effective policy, shaped by his many years of fighting Indians on the frontier, could appropriately be termed a doctrine of destructive warfare. In contrast, Governor Lane continued in the footsteps of his predecessor, advocating a more humanitarian approach of negotiating peace treaties and issuing rations at the various Indian agencies. Lane would dedicate his efforts toward that end throughout his time as governor and superintendent of Indian affairs. Sumner for his part believed that the Acoma Treaty sufficed for all Apaches and therefore did not support Lane's attempts to negotiate agreements with other bands, perceiving such exertions as redundant and a waste of time.

Tempers flared in the summer of 1852 when Colonel Miles and Major Morris, each serving as commanding officer at their respective stations, began quarrelling over the distribution of supplies. A department order issued a year earlier had provided explicit instructions for the supply of Fort Webster, delegating that duty to the post commander at Fort Fillmore, which thus served as Webster's supply depot. But the remote mountainous location of Fort Webster and the depleted force at Fort Fillmore rendered it difficult to transport essential provisions on a regular basis. Frustrated with Miles's failure to adequately supply his command, Morris submitted a formal complaint to headquarters in July.

Miles took this personally and tendered an immediate rebuttal, igniting a feud between the two men that ultimately led to Morris being transferred to another post. Miles also submitted a formal complaint, charging Morris and his fellow officers at Fort Webster with trading contraband items (including whiskey) to the Gila Apaches and knowingly purchasing stolen livestock from them.

"The Indians have never been as active around here in thieving as at present," the colonel wrote on August 16, "and which will be continued as long as this wholesale trading of mules is permitted at Fort Webster."[41] Such an accusation carried serious implications: it was highly illegal to trade contraband articles of any type with the Indians, and the consequences would have been severe had sufficient evidence existed for indictment at a court-martial.

Before the conflict fully developed, Morris received long-awaited orders from Santa Fe to relocate Fort Webster to the Mimbres Valley.[42] On September 2 the army officially abandoned the original site, although the relocation did little in the way of stifling the contraband trade. Not long afterward, Colonel Sumner ended the controversy by replacing Morris with Major Enoch Steen as the new post commander, effectively distancing the quarrelsome officers from one another.[43] The change in command would be slow to occur; not until November 20 did Steen head for the Mimbres Valley with his Company H, First Dragoons. Sumner's evident refusal to investigate the situation at Fort Webster suggests either an ambivalent attitude toward Morris's actions or a complete lack of evidence. By transferring the major to another post, Sumner brought about an unceremonious finale to a petty controversy, and Miles must have been disappointed that his efforts had resulted only in an informal reprimand.

When the troops moved to the new site of Fort Webster, Company E, Second Dragoons transferred from Fort Fillmore to further reinforce the garrison. Under the command of Lieutenant Nathan G. Evans, Company E consisted of eight officers and fifty-nine privates, all of whom remained at their new post until its permanent closure a year later.[44] Upon leaving Fort Fillmore, Evans transported approximately 10,000 rations to stock the new fort. Additionally, his troops brought several hundred head of beef cattle recently purchased from civilians at Doña Ana. The animals were badly needed; one officer wrote to Fort Fillmore claiming that "the few beeves left at Fort Webster . . . are so poor as not to be fit for issue."[45] The men who had garrisoned the original site must have welcomed the arrival of the much-needed reinforcements and supplies.

Not long before Major Morris received his transfer, he reported that the Indians in his vicinity, presumably those comprising Cuchillo Negro's band of Gila Apaches, had been in continuous violation of the new treaty, though it had not yet been ratified in Congress and therefore neither party held any legal obligations. The Indians, however, entertained not the slightest understanding of the long and drawn-out governmental procedures occurring two thousand miles away. One Apache agent who did understand their confusion appropriately pointed out, "you might as well talk Greek to [the Apaches] as try to explain the delays and that Congress must appropriate the money."[46] Military and civil officials rarely attempted to explain such circumstances to the Indians, however, perhaps recognizing that it provided an excuse to operate under the favorable provisions of the treaty.

On July 25 Morris reported the theft of fifteen head of cattle from the Fort Webster post herd, all of which had been the property of the U.S. government. Three days later the Apaches stole a yoke of oxen belonging to Lieutenant O'Bannon of the Third Infantry. In September, only a few days after the establishment of the new Fort Webster in the Mimbres Valley, the Apaches struck again. On one occasion they drove off a small herd of beef cattle, and in another instance they stampeded fourteen mules, several of which belonged to the officers.[47] Morris quickly filed a $175 indemnity claim on two of the stolen mules that belonged to him.[48] A seven-man guard watched over the post herd at all times, but this clearly proved ineffective, the Indians having little trouble avoiding that obstacle.

Concerns at Fort Webster were partially relieved on October 12, when Chief Ponce came to the fort and returned the majority of the stolen stock in an attempt to uphold the treaty obligations. The delight of the officers would prove to be brief, however, because the animals disappeared again the very next night along with all of the horses belonging to Company E, Second Dragoons.[49] These thefts left much of the Fort Webster garrison temporarily dismounted. In early 1853 the number of dragoons stationed there, including Companies E and H, numbered 115 total; of those, only 52 had serviceable horses; thus the remaining 63 dragoons became, in essence, infantrymen following this theft.[50] Frustration must have run rampant among the troops, for no matter what precautions the officers took, the Indians managed to steal at their leisure. In an unusual concession Colonel Miles recognized the benign efforts of the chiefs to return the stolen property; even more surprisingly he hypothesized that the thefts were likely the work of a few "vagabond Indians," over whom leaders such as Ponce and Mangas Coloradas exercised little control. Miles recommended that the guilty parties be captured and whipped, something much easier said than done.[51]

Upon his arrival in New Mexico, Governor Lane immediately established an Indian agency at Fort Webster to serve as headquarters for a newly appointed agent, Edward H. Wingfield.[52] In his first report Wingfield noted that only a portion of the buildings had been completed, and many of the soldiers therefore lived in tents. Furthermore, the Apaches to whom he served as agent remained exceedingly impoverished and destitute of provisions, leading him to believe that they had little choice but to steal or starve. Such was the situation at Fort Webster in late 1852.[53]

The office of Indian agent at a frontier military post was a thankless endeavor, and very few men held the position for any considerable length of time. Controversy seemed to go hand-in-hand with the job; many of an agent's actions met with immediate objection by some and yet received the wholehearted endorsement of others. Political, ideological, and moral preferences played no small role in the entire situation. Multiple agents passed through the doors of Fort Webster during its brief one-year existence in the Mimbres Valley; many of them departed with great bitterness toward both the army and the government. The average 1850s Indian agent typically became trapped in the middle of a bureaucratic nightmare and served as a scapegoat for his superiors. Whenever a major raid or uprising occurred, blame frequently shifted to the local agents for not taking preventative measures or for not ensuring that the Indians remained content with their present situation. Similarly, during periods of tranquility, leading army and government officials often took credit and denigrated the more local efforts of the agents in the field. When hostilities arose, the fault oftentimes lay not with the Indian agents, but rather with the military, which indiscriminately attacked women and children at their camps, thus provoking reciprocation.

The first major Indian uprising at the second Fort Webster occurred early in 1853 and resulted from an attack on Chief Ponce's Mimbres River camp by Captain William Steele and a detachment of dragoons. Several Apaches had recently stolen livestock from ranches along the Rio Grande, after which Steele trailed them to the chief's camp. In the skirmish that followed, one Indian was killed and two others wounded, including Ponce himself. Revenge came swiftly. A few days afterward the Apaches attacked the mail escort en route to Fort Webster, killing two soldiers and taking their horses.[54]

The increasing hostility of the Apaches in the region quickly caught the attention of Governor Lane. "Against the miserable, starving, thieving Apaches, complaints are made in every direction," the frustrated governor wrote following one of the skirmishes with U.S. troops.[55] During the month of February, southern New Mexico residents filed numerous indemnity claims, hoping to receive compensation for livestock that Gila Apaches stole.[56] In view of minimizing Apache troubles and appeasing the civilian population, Lane planned a trip to Fort Webster soon after to meet with the principal tribal chiefs. Also influencing his decision was a letter he received a month earlier from Major Steen, commanding at Fort Webster, inviting the governor to visit not only for the purpose of meeting with the Apaches but also to take a tour of the surrounding countryside.[57] Leaving Santa Fe on February 28, Lane proceeded south to Fort Conrad, where a thirty-man dragoon escort joined him for the remainder of his trip.

After stopping briefly at Fort Fillmore, Lane arrived at Fort Webster on April 2 and held meetings with several Apache chiefs of the Mimbres and Gila bands.[58] Following the attack on the mail escort, these chiefs came into Fort Webster regularly and expressed their desire for peaceful relations, perhaps afraid that future military action might erroneously target their innocent followers. On April 7 several of them signed a preliminary compact with the governor containing numerous provisions, the majority of them being rather typical of Indian treaties of that era. The chiefs agreed to locate themselves in permanent camps near the fort, commence cultivating the land, and build permanent dwellings. All of these undertakings found favor with the press in Santa Fe, where editorials lauded Lane's approach to Indian policy. Indeed, several months earlier the *Santa Fe Weekly Gazette* had urged similar strategies: "On the score of humanity, we would urge the policy of settling the Indians in pueblos. . . . [I]t is the only effective means we see of saving them . . . from the shadow of death that has for ages enshrouded them."[59] Such ramblings, of course, typified the popular American sentiment of the time, one that viewed all Indians contemptuously as undeserving occupants of valuable land and resources, exhibiting a staunch ethnocentrism and utter ignorance of Apache culture.

As with Sumner's 1852 treaty, Lane's negotiations hinged upon several false presumptions about Apache lifeways. The most glaring misconception surrounded the placement of the Apaches in permanent dwellings, a practice that tribal spiritual convictions forbade them to do and that no treaty could have induced them to embrace.[60] Similar nonsensical provisions could be found in nearly every article of the treaty. In addition to locating themselves in permanent dwellings, the Mimbres and Gila bands would be expected to enact and enforce laws similar to those of the whites and meant to "prevent their people from doing any manner of evil." (The Apaches had their own set of societal expectations that, they rightfully believed, served them just fine.) Moreover, the Indians would "promise hereafter, never to resort to the ancient custom of retaliation." The peace accord also attempted to criminalize Apache mobility by prohibiting them from traveling routes commonly used by Anglo-Americans, despite the fact that most of these trails ran directly through Apachería. It further stipulated the death penalty for any Apache caught on such trails, the punishment to be enacted "at the hands of the Indians themselves."[61]

The United States, in turn, incentivized the agreement by pledging to supply the Mimbres and Gila bands with rations through the end of 1854 and also promised to hire an overseer to teach them how to farm. The army vowed to protect all Indians who faithfully complied with the treaty, both from hostile military action and from other tribes who might harass them for being on friendly terms with the United States. But neither side remained faithful to their end of the deal for any significant period of time. The government, for its part, failed to defend the Indians who did abide by the terms as attacks on peaceful bands continued to occur. The Interior Department also neglected to provide adequate subsistence provisions in adherence with its obligations. This failure on the part of both the civil and military authorities to uphold Lane's treaty inevitably caused a correlating noncompliance on the part of the Apaches and made the agreement unenforceable.

Adding to the absurdity of this provisional compact, the one chief with the most influence, Mangas Coloradas, had not been present to make his mark upon it. Major Steen, commanding at Fort Webster, clearly understood and appreciated the chief's importance within the tribe, echoing Indian Agent Greiner's remarks at the Acoma conference in 1852 when he admitted, "Mangas has more sense than all the rest of them put together."[62] He did, however, visit Fort Webster a month later, on May 18, at which time Steen explained the contents of the treaty and the chief verbally approved, in a sense solidifying an otherwise imperfect peace.[63] By endorsing Governor Lane's treaty, Mangas Coloradas actually agreed to nothing new; the provisions bore similarities in almost every particular to the Acoma Treaty signed a year earlier and only recently ratified by the Senate.

The detrimental effects of Lane's agreement quickly became noticeable. Within weeks other Apache bands, most notably the Coyoteros and Mogollons (both lived far to the north and west of Fort Webster and had no involvement in the negotiations), began visiting the fort expecting to be issued rations.[64] These hostile bands assumed that the army would supply them in the same manner that it provided for the peaceful followers of Mangas Coloradas. The fact that Agent Wingfield dispensed rations to the Coyoteros and Mogollons infuriated the governor, who wrote to Apache Agent Michael Steck on July 11:

> It was never intended, from the first, to feed any Indian, but those who were employed in raising a crop. Upon what pretense agent Wingfield has collected so many of the wandering Apaches at his agency, and issued food to them, I cannot comprehend. His mismanagement will cause great embarrassment, not only to me, but to you also, and to my successor, by creating expectations amongst the Indians, which must be disappointed, and by exhausting the appropriations for Ind. Affairs in N. Mex. for the current year. . . . [W]hy did Agent Wingfield encourage Mangas to bring his own and other bands, from their homes on the Hela [*sic*], to the Mimbres? Has the agent been insane? I am fully aware of the evils that will result from ceasing to feed starving barbarians.[65]

The rapid influx of unwanted Apaches at the Fort Webster agency caused much alarm among the troops there, prompting Major Steen to contact headquarters to request that reinforcements be sent as soon as practicable. If the Indian agent continued to turn away the Coyotero and Mogollon bands, violent uprisings would inevitably occur. "It was not considered safe for a man to go over 200 yards from the post," Wingfield wrote in reference to Fort Webster, "without being armed to the teeth."[66] The garrison, consisting of only thirty-five troops at that time, would not have been sufficient to quell a disturbance if indeed one did occur.[67]

Despite these strenuous circumstances arising as a direct result of the treaty negotiations, Governor Lane continued his circuit of the territory in pursuit of additional objectives. Having completed the peace accord at Fort Webster (which Congress never ratified), he embarked on an exploration of the Gila River and Santa Lucia Springs (about three miles south of the river, and flowing into it) regions, taking with him a small escort of sixteen dragoons.[68] He considered allotting a portion of that area as a permanent reservation for the Gila Apaches, an idea that had originated with Governor Calhoun in 1851. "My visit to the Gila," Lane wrote, "was for the purpose of ascertaining its fitness for a future location for the Apaches. It will do well for that purpose."[69] At this early period, however, federal officials in Washington shunned the idea of delineating permanent reservations in New Mexico, and it would be years before any such Indian reserves came into existence. Nevertheless, the idea served as a harbinger of thoughtful foresight on the part of Lane, who held the Indians' best interests in mind while pondering such policy objectives.

Had Lane's vision of a reservation along the Gila River been enacted, many future troubles with the Indians might have been averted. The region comprised the heart of the Chiricahua Apache homeland—each year Mangas Coloradas and his followers, often numbering in the hundreds, returned there after conducting seasonal raids into Sonora and Chihuahua. As one of their favorite long-term camping places, the entire tribe might have been willing to live peacefully near Santa Lucia for an extended period of time. Unfortunately, Lane's proposed Gila River reservation met with disapproval when submitted to the commissioner of Indian affairs, who had to consider potential political ramifications and therefore remained unwilling to establish a permanent Apache reserve in New Mexico. To justify such decisions, federal officials often alluded to the fact that the prospective mineral wealth had yet to be determined, perceiving it as folly to place the Indians upon land that might be rich in gold or silver. Others reasoned that these areas had already been legally obtained from Mexico through the Treaty of Guadalupe-Hidalgo and the Gadsden Purchase; thus, by moving the Apaches onto a reservation and issuing annual indemnity payments to them, the United States would be paying for the same land twice. Lane returned to Santa Fe unaware that his treaty and reservation proposals, the two high points of his governorship regarding Apache affairs, would both be rejected by his superiors in Washington.

Ironically, despite the egotism and staunch intragovernmental opposition that defined the Lane-Sumner relationship, some good did emerge from their shared incumbency with the selection of Michael Steck to serve as temporary Indian agent at Fort Webster in 1853. While it might have seemed like another insignificant appointment at the time, the decision turned out to be among the single-most-important events in the history of antebellum Apache relations. The office of Indian agent had traditionally been a controversial one, and civil leaders in New Mexico struggled to find able and willing men to fill such positions. In the first five years of the U.S. territory's existence, several agents had come and gone, and the office desperately needed to be filled by a reliable individual.

A native of Pennsylvania and a medical doctor by training, Steck proved to be equal to this monumental challenge.[70] With his wife suffering from tuberculosis, Steck accepted the position as Indian agent in New Mexico partially as a means of easing her suffering in the dry southwestern climate. In a world where the Apaches could trust almost nobody, they found a friend in Michael Steck. Throughout the several years in which he served as their agent, the doctor remained steadfastly dedicated to the unpopular ideology of fair, equitable treatment for the Indians of southern New Mexico. Gradually, through countless acts of kindness and forbearance, he earned the trust of nearly every chief. Acquiring the Apaches' confidence became a building block for peaceful relations, and Steck emerged as the department's most indispensable resource in the successful implementation of Indian policies.

The garrison at Fort Fillmore had been reduced in size on May 21, 1853, when Sumner relocated Colonel Miles and his Third Infantry to Albuquerque. The only infantry regiment stationed in New Mexico, the Third Infantry boasted an aggregate strength of 798 men dispersed throughout the territory. That number would dwindle over time; two years later Miles reported that his regiment consisted of only 493 men, with 103 being eligible for discharge at the expiration of their enlistment and no new recruits scheduled to arrive.[71]

The relocation of Miles's headquarters would only be temporary and proved to be among Colonel Sumner's last acts as military commander in New Mexico. Before these orders even reached Fort Fillmore, Sumner departed the territory on a leave of absence from

Michael Steck, agent at the Southern Apache Agency. Keleher Collection (ZIM CSWR PICT 000-742-0143), Center for Southwest Research, University Libraries, University of New Mexico, Albuquerque.

which he would not return. His reforms over the previous two years had made him extremely unpopular among civil officials and the general population alike. By December 1852, doubtless exasperated with the continuous criticism of his policies, Sumner began requesting a transfer.[72] His removal of troops from the settlements and implementation of agriculturally self-sustaining military posts successfully reduced department expenditures but incurred the wrath of the territory's merchants and businessmen, who lost their lucrative government supply contracts in the process.[73]

While Lane worked toward negotiating ultimately unsuccessful treaties with various Indian tribes, Sumner had achieved an almost complete reorganization of the Ninth Military Department, and he had done so in only two years. The command forever changed under Sumner's leadership, although the effects were not necessarily benevolent in all respects. The negative consequences of this reorganization would be a great burden for his successor. A simultaneous change in command in the offices of both the governor and the department commander occurred in August 1853. William Carr Lane's term as territorial governor ended in scandal, and Edwin Sumner transferred to another department due to negative public opinion and tensions within the military chain of command.

David Meriwether succeeded Lane as governor and superintendent of Indian affairs, while Brigadier General John Garland replaced Sumner as department commander. A Santa Fe newspaper hinted of improvements to come when on August 13, 1853—immediately following Meriwether's inauguration ceremony and Garland's first remarks to the citizens—the editor wrote, "It was gratifying to behold for the first time in this territory that mutual respect which should have always prevailed between the civil and military authorities."[74] Indeed, Meriwether, Garland, and Steck would collaborate more harmoniously than had their predecessors, promulgating new ideologies and policy objectives along with modified visions for the future of both southern New Mexico and the Apache tribe.

CHAPTER 6

One Regime to the Next

Michael Steck, appointed temporary Apache agent by William Carr Lane in one of his final acts as governor, arrived at Fort Webster to replace Agent Wingfield on July 8, 1853. The doctor had only six months' prior experience, having begun his career in Indian affairs immediately upon his arrival in Santa Fe on December 11, 1852.[1] At the time of Lane's departure, matters remained at a standstill at the Southern Apache Agency. In May 1853, a mere two months before his transfer to Fort Webster, Steck had warned Wingfield to exercise caution when dealing with the Apaches. "My scheme for treating and feeding the Indians is disapproved by Mr. Commissioner of Indian Affairs G. W. Manypenny," he acknowledged, "and I am ordered to stop. . . . [Y]ou are therefore requested to refuse to receive all persons hereafter that you can refuse, without a sacrifice to humanity, into your camp."[2] In this single statement Steck summarized his overall vision for Apache policy, treating each band separately and issuing monthly rations in view of promoting a humanitarian agenda. He also alluded to the continuing discrepancies in policy objectives between individual agents and their superiors.

Steck's primary partner in the implementation of Indian affairs would be his immediate superior, David Meriwether, a fifty-two-year-old native of Kentucky who assumed the office of governor and superintendent of Indian affairs on August 8, 1853. In contrast to Lane, who as a former physician and mayor spent much of his life indoors, Meriwether's hardened physique and stern complexion reflected a lifetime of experience on the frontier. The Kentuckian boasted an impressive political background and, significantly, had already become acquainted with New Mexico some thirty-five years earlier. In 1819, Spanish officials in New Mexico captured the eighteen-year-old Meriwether and held him in confinement at the Palace of the Governors in Santa Fe, accusing him of being an American spy.[3] Indeed, his selection as Lane's successor owed partially to his previous knowledge of and familiarity with the territory, as few eastern politicians could claim a better understanding of its complexities than him. When offered the job, Meriwether admitted that he had no desire to return to the distant Southwest, perhaps remembering his unpleasant incarceration there three decades earlier, but he accepted the appointment nonetheless.

As governor, Meriwether inherited a territory in which the administration of Indian policies by prior officials—civil and military alike—had often been nonsensical. Conditions had deteriorated under the leadership of Governor Lane, whose seemingly redundant treaties never achieved congressional ratification. In his first annual report to the commissioner of Indian affairs, dated September 1, 1854, Meriwether openly criticized Lane's policies. "I entered upon the discharge of the duties of this office . . . and soon found that my predecessor had made a compact with several bands of the Apache tribe . . . which has caused much embarrassment and difficulty," he wrote, referring to the Fort Webster treaty that, although never ratified, led to provisions and rations being issued to hostile bands.[4] This unfortunate misstep on the part of Lane and Wingfield instigated the new governor's primary point of contention with previous Apache policies and doubtless influenced the local newspaper editor, who wrote in December 1853 that all present Indian troubles were "the result of the ruinous policy Governor Lane . . . pursued towards the Indians within our limits."[5]

Nor did Meriwether inherit a territory that could be considered financially solvent. Upon his arrival in Santa Fe, he noted that "the entire amount of money appropriated for contingent expenses of

Territorial Governor David Meriwether. Keleher Collection (ZIM CSWR PICT 742-0109), Center for Southwest Research, University Libraries, University of New Mexico, Albuquerque.

Indian affairs in New Mexico had been expended, except about three thousand dollars, and there were also outstanding claims pending against this [Indian] office amounting to about ten thousand dollars." Additionally, "provisions had been issued [at Fort Webster] to from five hundred to one thousand Indians, at a cost to the government of between fifteen and twenty thousand dollars." Meriwether therefore informed the Apaches, through their agent, "of the disapproval of [Lane's] compact" and ordered a moratorium on the issuance of rations. The end result, as he acknowledged, came in the form of the Indians "resorting to theft and robbery upon the citizens of this Territory for a subsistence."[6] The former governor's peace negotiations thus came to an abrupt end at the hands of new leadership in Santa Fe.

The Department of the Interior exacerbated these problems by habitually failing to provide Indian-affairs personnel with ample resources for such a geographically extensive and ethnically diverse territory. Meriwether estimated New Mexico's Indian population to be "from forty to fifty thousand souls, scattered over a surface of more than two hundred thousand square miles," and informed the commissioner of Indian affairs that "four agents are insufficient for their proper management. Take the Apaches, and the two most remote bands are more than three hundred miles distant from each other."[7] These two "remote bands" had between them but one agent, Michael Steck, whose duties were therefore double those of many of his colleagues.

Meriwether summarized his views toward the issue in a statement he made shortly after becoming governor. He observed that federal Indian policy invariably took two forms, either to "feed them or whip them," and further pointed out that "the former has been the policy of my predecessors, the latter has not been effectually tried."[8] These two generalizations reflect the rival stances of the Interior Department and the War Department, neither of which had coalesced in their objectives prior to Meriwether's incumbency. Thus, the new governor intended to implement a policy almost opposite the conciliatory one that Calhoun and Lane had pursued during the previous three years, an ideology that manifested itself clearly in his immediate renunciation of Lane's 1853 agreement. Apache Agent Edmund Graves likewise condoned, albeit reluctantly, a militaristic approach to Indian policy. "The question arises," he conceded in a letter to the commissioner of Indian affairs, "what line of policy is best calculated for the management of these Indians? It is a question not easily answered, but is pregnant with embarrassment and fraught with difficulty." Even so, Graves recognized the futility of the situation and believed that no course of action, besides that of "whipping them," could ultimately ensure a permanent peace:

> These Indians must live, and when the mountains and forest cease to supply them with food, they will doubtless seek it from those who have it, and if not to be had peaceably, they will attempt to obtain it by force. No creature, whether civilized or not, will perish for the want of food when the means of subsistence is within his reach. . . . To feed and

clothe these Indians . . . is an expensive operation. . . . It is a policy that promises no results beyond the simple fact of keeping them quiet for the time being. As long as this policy is continued, their peace can doubtless be purchased, and they will be kept quiet, but it only postpones the evil day.[9]

With many leading officials entertaining such similar ideologies, it appeared as though rougher times awaited the Apaches. Their only saving grace in the upcoming years would be the dedicated service of Agent Steck. Despite fundamental differences in their desired approach to dealing with the Apaches, Meriwether and Steck collaborated closely in the implementation of Indian policy. This working relationship received further support with the arrival of General Garland as commander of the Ninth Military Department, who proved much more amenable to cooperating with civil officials than had Colonel Sumner.

By the time he took command of the department in 1853, Garland possessed an impressive military résumé with several decades of prior experience.[10] The territorial legislature invited him to attend a session prior to its adjournment, whereupon the new commander received a welcoming ovation from both chambers. The editor of the *Santa Fe Weekly Gazette* referred to Garland as "a veteran of forty-one years standing in the army; and the great services he has rendered his country, and the unflinching patriotism he has always exhibited in the hour of trial, entitle him to the thanks of every American."[11] Upon his departure from New Mexico in 1856, a large gathering convened to show their respect and ensure their former military commander that he held "the regard of every good citizen of this Territory."[12] Indeed, nothing like this transpired when the embattled and unpopular Sumner departed in 1853.

Garland assumed command of an unenviable situation in New Mexico. Sumner's sudden transfer left many things unfinished, especially regarding the destitute condition of the troops resulting from the colonel's tightfisted economic policies. In October 1853, only a few months after taking charge, Garland openly criticized Sumner for leaving the department in a beleaguered state:

Brigadier General John Garland in his Civil War–era officer's uniform. Courtesy National Archives and Records Administration, Washington, D.C.

"My predecessor is an old friend and acknowledged throughout the army to be one of our most efficient and gallant officers in the field . . . but his energies have been misapplied, and he has left the department in an impoverished and crippled condition. . . . [H]is sole aim appears to have been to win reputation from an economical administration of his Department; in this, he will be found to have signally failed, if all his acts are closely looked into."[13] Garland similarly denounced Sumner's implementation of military-run farms, noting that, "with one inconsiderable exception," the entire operation had been a failure.[14]

Sumner's fiscally conservative policies, while they appeared great on paper and won him acclaim with his superiors in the War Department, had in actuality taken a toll on the effectiveness of the soldiers, who oftentimes lacked the supplies and provisions necessary to carry out successful campaigns. The confused state of Indian affairs throughout the territory exacerbated this problem, with agents having been appointed and then abruptly removed just prior to the arrival of Garland and Meriwether. The only agency in New Mexico that remained little changed during this transitional period was that of Michael Steck. Much like it had been while Agent Wingfield resided there in 1852, Fort Webster remained in a woebegone and dilapidated condition, hardly suitable for administrating Indian affairs. In October 1853 army inspector Joseph K. F. Mansfield visited there and reported: "Fort Webster . . . was commenced in October 1852, under the command of Major G. Morris of the Third Infantry, but in November, Brevet Major E. Steen of the First Dragoons was in command. . . . [I]t is among the Apache Indians . . . and dependent for supplies on Fort Fillmore, 135 miles [distant], and Fort Conrad, 150 miles [distant]. . . . The buildings of this post are made of logs and mud and quite indifferent and not sufficient for the command."[15]

Mansfield believed Fort Webster to be improperly situated and suggested that it be moved northwest to a location on the Gila River, closer to the Apaches' homelands and within striking distance of the hostile Mogollon band. After relocating the fort, the remaining buildings on site could be used as an agency for Steck, where he would monitor Apache farming operations along the Mimbres River and issue "presents" to the Indians as a gesture of good faith. Furthermore, it might prove beneficial to station U.S. forces away from the agency in order to avoid tension between the army and the Indians congregating there. The Apaches perceived the continued presence of soldiers as a sign of distrust by the whites and preferred to remain at a distance from them if at all possible. Besides, Steck had already proven his ability to work harmoniously with the Indians without the presence of troops for protection.

The inspector's astute suggestions received only partial consideration. General Garland agreed about the post's continued deterioration, notifying the assistant adjutant general in October that Fort Webster "is not in position for any useful purpose, and very difficult, as well as expensive to maintain." Owing to the fact that "the huts constructed there are expected to tumble down before the spring of the year," he saw no plausible alternative aside from abandoning the site.[16] Pursuant to Garland's orders, Fort Webster would indeed be moved to a new location only two months after Mansfield's visit. The new compound, however, would be built nowhere near the suggested Gila River site.

On November 7 Garland issued an order for the abandonment of Fort Webster, which had served as the Apache agency for over two years; the troops departed five weeks later.[17] As the dragoons trailed off into the distance on a crisp December morning, they looked back and saw the remaining buildings ablaze—no sooner had the last soldier left than the Apaches descended upon the fort and burned it to the ground. They seemed not the least bit remorseful to see the troops depart and expressed their exuberance through this unmistakable, highly visible gesture of defiance. The post that would replace it, to be constructed on the west bank of the Rio Grande some fifty miles to the east, would be named Fort Thorn in honor of 1st Lieutenant Herman Thorn of the Second Infantry, who had drowned while crossing the Colorado River on October 16, 1849.[18]

Like Fort Fillmore to the south, Fort Thorn was constructed mainly of handmade adobes manufactured by local residents at a cost of eight dollars per one thousand bricks. The same hired laborers also constructed an *acequia* that, when finally completed, measured three-and-a-half miles long and carried water from the Rio Grande to the post farms in accordance with Sumner's subsistence program.[19] One visitor in 1857 noted that all of the buildings, "save the hospital, are enclosed in a substantial adobe wall" and further observed that "the citizens, in equal numbers of American and Mexican, reside a few hundred yards from the post, and were generally engaged in vending '*sperits*' [*sic*] and other groceries to, and gambling with, the soldiers."[20] The army built Fort Thorn midway between the small village of Santa Barbara and the wagon road striking westward from the Rio Grande toward the Santa Rita

Fort Thorn, 1856, in a view looking eastward. This sketch, likely drawn by Col. J. H. Eaton, commanding officer at Fort Thorn, appeared in W. W. H. Davis's *El Gringo; or, New Mexico and Her People*, first published in 1856. From this view, the Rio Grande would have been directly behind the fort. From the Harper 1857 edition.

copper mines; according to one officer, this portion of the valley had long been a thoroughfare for Apache raiders.[21] In addition to being more centrally located, the site could also be more easily supplied. At Fort Webster problems frequently arose with the transportation of provisions due largely to its remote location. In view of economic feasibility, Garland deliberately located Fort Thorn along the Rio Grande, only a few miles west of the Camino Real and a mere thirty miles north of Doña Ana; consequently, shipping supplies there would be less laborious. With troops already in place at Los Lunas, Fort Conrad, Fort Fillmore, and Fort Bliss, the establishment of Fort Thorn filled the only major gap in the military's line of defense along the Rio Grande between Albuquerque and El Paso.

On May 9, 1854, President Pierce reappointed Michael Steck to serve as the permanent Apache agent at newly established Fort Thorn; up until that time he had been only a temporary agent, replacing James Smith following his untimely death on December 15, 1853.[22] A contingent of military officers stationed in New Mexico, recognizing Steck as a colleague with whom they could harmoniously collaborate, had written directly to the president three months earlier recommending his formal appointment. Pointing out Steck's "knowledge of the country, and of the Indians, their language, and habits," they assured Pierce that "his appointment would give entire satisfaction to the military authorities."[23]

Steck first proceeded to Doña Ana, where all public stores belonging to the previous agent were to be turned over to him. His orders then instructed him to transfer the agency to Fort Thorn, "provided quarters for yourself can possibly be obtained and no other valid objection arises"; it would remain there until the military abandoned the post in 1859.[24] After transferring his headquarters, Steck wrote to the governor outlining his vision for future Apache relations. He asked for authorization to issue presents worth $1,500 to the Mimbres band, in which case, he insisted, "we need have no fears of further depredations; on the contrary, if not furnished . . . they will be again reduced to the extremity of choosing between stealing or starvation." Steck encouraged Meriwether to consider visiting Fort Thorn and issuing these presents himself as "a means of establishing confidence."[25] By that time, the Apaches' condition had worsened significantly, and civil authorities desperately needed to foster feelings of mutual benevolence to avoid unnecessary bloodshed.

Adhering to the post-Sumner trend of relocating military posts, the department abandoned Fort Conrad in 1854 and reestablished it as Fort Craig nine miles to the south at the foot of Mesa del Contadero, an unmistakable landmark rising abruptly from the immediate eastern bank of the Rio Grande and denoting the northern terminus of the dreaded Jornada del Muerto.[26] Several factors influenced this decision, including the dispute surrounding legal ownership of the land upon which Fort Conrad had been built. The dilapidated condition of the buildings there posed another consideration. During his 1853 tour, Colonel Mansfield reported unenthusiastically on Fort Conrad, noting that "the quarters of both officers and soldiers are falling to pieces. The timbers had rotted away—some of the troops were in tents."[27] Once again, Garland agreed with the inspector's advice: "Fort Conrad is in a state of decay . . . [and] a lawsuit has been decided which gives title to two citizens of this territory; in consequence I have determined to abandon the place and construct temporary buildings some few miles lower down from Valverde where there is a better site."[28] Dr. Longworthy's ominous report on rampant sickness at Fort Conrad reassured Garland in his decision and sealed the post's fate.

Fort Conrad thus came to an end after a mere three years. Its replacement, Fort Craig, would become one of the largest and most strategically important military posts in the Southwest and played a role in Apache affairs well into the 1880s. An officer temporarily stationed there in 1857 described the fort as "an imposing object in this country of small houses. It was simply an enclosure of a rectangular area of about six acres with a massive adobe wall ten feet high, and occupied a high table land which on the east terminated at a short distance on the Rio Grande in a precipitous bluff a hundred feet above the river."[29] The new post's name honored Louis S. Craig, an infantry officer who had accompanied John

Russell Bartlett's boundary commission several years earlier; Craig had been murdered by deserters on June 6, 1852, near Fort Yuma.[30] "Thus is lost one of the Army's most gallant and meritorious officers," remarked Colonel Miles upon learning of the killing.[31]

Perhaps motivated by the relocation of the Fort Conrad garrison, the citizens of Socorro wrote General Garland in March 1854 requesting that a company of dragoons be permanently stationed within the town's limits. They claimed that a recent increase in Indian depredations had caused much alarm and necessitated a military presence nearer the town than Fort Craig. In a tone of desperation, the people even offered to provide forage and water for the dragoons' horses.[32] Apparently, the citizenry's pleas fell upon deaf ears at department headquarters, for there is no record of a company of dragoons ever being stationed at Socorro any time after its garrison left in September 1851.

Troops at Fort Craig immediately began experiencing problems with Apache raiding in the vicinity. On June 5, 1855, a band of Gila Apaches attacked the post's mule herd while grazing twenty miles northwest of the fort. Interestingly, only one soldier had been detailed to oversee the animals, leaving them highly vulnerable to theft; the remainder of the guard detachment had camped some distance away, reportedly working to repair a wagon road in the vicinity. At first sight of the oncoming Indians, the lone soldier instinctively ran to find his comrades. When he did, the raiders drove away the livestock uncontested. Four of the dragoons, mounted on mules, pursued the Apaches westward toward the Mogollon Mountains and kept up the chase until sunset, at which time the Indians scattered in all directions, making it impossible to follow them. Of the twenty-five mules taken, the soldiers did manage to recover eighteen that the Apaches abandoned during the chase. When news reached Fort Craig, the post commander dispatched a small punitive detachment, but their foray did not last long; the next morning the soldiers returned and reported that heavy rains had obliterated the Indians' trail.[33]

By the mid-1850s, many Apaches had become almost entirely dependent on government rations issued from the Fort Thorn agency. This provided both Steck and the military with an important bargaining device: whenever Apaches committed depredations, their rations could be withheld until they returned the stolen property. The tactic became a convenient means for officials to regain pilfered livestock, particularly during the cold winter months when other food sources became scarce. With the Apaches in such a state of desperation and with Steck having established a sense of trust during his two years on the job, conditions seemed optimal for the negotiation of a new treaty.

In April 1855 Governor Meriwether notified Steck that he had received congressional approval to negotiate terms with the Apaches, hoping to build upon the 1852 Acoma treaty.[34] Steck immediately began making preparations for the governor's planned visit to the agency later that spring, summoning the chiefs of several Apache bands that frequented his post to ensure that they planned to participate. But any resulting accord from the negotiations—the first and only one to involve both the Mescalero and Chiricahua Apaches in the same set of stipulations—would be difficult to enforce because the two tribes traditionally lived far apart from one another and seldom commingled. The proposed inclusion of both groups in a single treaty exhibited the naiveté of Meriwether and other officials, who should have approached the two tribes on separate terms. In May, Steck received word from an Apache messenger that Mangas Coloradas would be unable to attend due to illness. His absence, coupled with the Mescaleros' intense dissatisfaction after hearing of the military's intent to construct a new fort along the banks of the Rio Bonito, darkened the skies on what Steck and Meriwether had hoped would be the dawn of a new era in cordial Apache relations.[35]

On June 9 Meriwether reached Fort Thorn, where large groups of Apaches had gathered in anticipation of his arrival. The resulting treaty began innocently enough: "Peace, friendship and amity shall forever hereafter exist between the United States of America and the Mimbres & Gila bands of the Apache tribe." The Gila Apaches relinquished claim to all of their lands in the territory, "except so much as is hereafter reserved to them," and agreed to vacate those lands within nine months and move onto a reservation, the precise boundaries of which remained to be determined. The government planned to establish the Indians on or near the Mimbres River, not far from the abandoned site of Fort Webster, making this the first treaty calling for the cession of a portion of the Apaches' homelands.[36] In hindsight, Meriwether's treaty commenced a domino effect that lasted for thirty years. Gradually, the domain that the Apaches once called their own diminished, falling slowly but surely into the permanent possession of miners and settlers, whose visions hinged upon pecuniary gain through economic exploitation and left no place for a "savage" race of people who might hinder such development. In upcoming years the Apaches continued to find themselves being relegated to small reservations, comprising only a fraction of their original homelands, on the periphery of Anglo-American settlement.

The treaty became problematic before it even reached Washington for congressional approval. As an enticement for Apache consent, the governor had included a provision allowing for the periodic distribution of rations and gifts at Doña Ana, giving rise to unforeseen expectations on the part of the Indians and scaring the unsuspecting townspeople into a frenzy. Colonel Miles, in command at Fort Fillmore, wrote Steck shortly afterward informing him that it had been "a great mistake by the Governor to place any town in the treaty where the Indians could trade—the Mescaleros now believe Doña Ana belongs to them and I cannot by persuasion make them leave it, my force here [at Fort Fillmore], two reduced companies, too small . . . to force them to depart."[37] After learning that unwelcome Indians continued to congregate around the town, Meriwether responded by telling Steck, "I regret to learn that the people of Doña Ana are disposed to gamble with and sell openly to the Indians, and I can see no other way to prevent it than to select some other place for the purchase and distribution of presents."[38] Judging from this statement, the governor sought to shift blame toward the Mexicans, speculating that they brought the annoyance upon themselves by their own interactions with the Apaches. To be sure, no official investigation into Meriwether's accusation took place, and the contraband trade at Doña Ana was never confirmed, but similar incidents occurred throughout New Mexico in the 1850s, lending credence to the governor's claim.

An additional provision of the treaty allowed the president, at his own discretion, to grant twenty-acre parcels within the proposed reservation to each family head over the age of twenty-one in hopes of encouraging the Indians to create permanent settlements and begin farming for their own sustenance. The government would pay the collective Gila Apache bands $6,000 per year from 1856 to 1858, $4,000 per year from 1859 to 1861, and $2,000 annually beginning in 1862 and lasting for twenty years thereafter. The president retained the authority to decide whether this money would be paid directly to the Indians to be used as they wished or if it would be spent on provisions and supplies to be distributed by their agents; none of the funds were to be given directly to the chiefs. In the end all of this would prove inconsequential. As occurred with Lane's Fort Webster treaty two years earlier, the 1855 Fort Thorn accord never achieved ratification, a trend that, according to historian Edwin R. Sweeney, owed partially to the fact that Congress "felt the government should not have to pay the Indians for land lawfully acquired from Mexico, at least by white man's logic and law."[39]

In Santa Fe the editor of the *Weekly Gazette,* James L. Collins, criticized Meriwether's inability to secure a binding agreement with the Apaches and failure to remove them to a permanent reservation somewhere off the map. The newspaper informed its readers that these treaties had been "very justly repudiated by the United States Senate," citing the need to place all nomadic tribes onto small reservations and noting that the Fort Thorn accord would have only relocated two subgroups, not the entire Apache tribe. Collins supported those provisions relocating the Apaches onto lands near the Gila River but suggested that it allowed the Indians too much leniency. His paper took the stance that, "whether they agree to it or not, they should be *compelled* to submit to it. . . . [W]e hold that governments are created to *protect their citizens,* and if the safety of the citizens demands that the Indians should be settled, and restrained to civilized pursuits, then it is not only the right but the *duty* of the government to adopt this policy."[40]

Another reason why many antebellum treaties involving the establishment of reservations failed in New Mexico is revealed in a communication between Steck and Surveyor General William Pelham. In October, before Congress rejected the 1855 treaty, the stipulations of the document caught the surveyor's attention. As a federal official concerned primarily with future settlement patterns and land use, Pelham became curious about the presence of mineral wealth in lands set aside for the Gila and Mescalero tribes, specifically those near the old Santa Rita copper mines.[41] He doubtless foresaw the violent struggles that would ensue if deposits of gold or silver were later found on reservations and sought to avoid such a scenario if at all possible. Steck explained that the mines had been worked as late as 1838 or 1839, admitting that, "South and West of the copper mines, and also within the limits of the contemplated Mimbres reserve, there are gold mines, which, while the copper mines were being worked and the Mexican government had troops stationed there for their protection, were extensively worked."[42] Both men agreed that the governor's chosen site for the reservation could have been better, specifically noting locations along the Gila River as preferable. The Senate's rejection of this treaty thus can be directly linked to the era's fundamental American imperialist ideologies: had the proposed site been a valueless, barren tract of land somewhere in the desert where mineral deposits did not exist, the treaty might have been ratified and the reservation established.

The rejection of Meriwether's treaty could not have come at a more inopportune time. The Apaches remained desperately indigent, almost completely reliant on government-issued rations and subsistence raiding. The treaty would have placed them on a permanent reservation in their homelands and allowed not only for an increased allotment of supplies but also for the distribution of annuity payments that, through Agent Steck, could have been used to improve their livelihood. As it was, the Indians' starving condition worsened throughout 1855, resulting in noticeably amplified subsistence raiding and a corresponding intensification of armed violence.

In November, despite the continued issuance of food at Fort Thorn, troops caught several Apaches stealing from civilian-owned cornfields a mile and a half to the north. A civilian laborer shot and killed one of the Indians, but the others managed to escape. Captain Joseph H. Eaton, commanding at Fort Thorn, reported a week later that there had been no apparent signs of retaliation for this death. Unfortunately, Eaton wrote prematurely: later that month a band of Gila Apaches attacked Mesilla, killing two residents and stealing several head of beef cattle before retreating westward.

To prevent further bloodshed, Steck assembled several influential chiefs at his agency in hopes of discouraging any further retaliatory actions. Often more effective than officially sanctioned treaty negotiations, Steck's individual meetings with Apache leaders became a trademark of his years in service. While he persisted in his attempts to foster tranquility, military leaders continued to act in a haphazard manner that contradicted the Indian agent's efforts. In defiance of Steck's exertions, Captain Eaton advised headquarters that "war with the whole Apache race west of the river should be declared, and they should be made to understand that it will never end. A state of well understood hostility is better than flimsy treaties of peace, which only serve to lull the people of the territory into a false security."[43] Such incompatible objectives between two government officials at the same location inadvertently sent a mixed message to the Apaches, who were being attacked on one front while simultaneously encouraged to seek peace on the other front. The resulting confusion resulted in a wholesale failure by both the military and the Indian bureau to minimize Apache depredations. Eaton's military campaigning caused a heightened level of distrust among the chiefs, who in turn responded to Steck's well-intentioned overtures of friendship with instinctive apprehension and doubt.

Almost in direct contradiction to Captain Eaton's statement was another comment that he made shortly afterward, informing headquarters that most of the recent livestock thefts by Indians could be attributed to the negligence of their victims. He believed that if the citizens exercised more diligence in guarding their property, many such incidents could be avoided altogether. Some Mexican herders neglected to corral their livestock at night and left them to graze unguarded. This being the case, it was not at all surprising that the Indians stole with such impunity. Eaton believed that the army generally, and his troops at Fort Thorn particularly, should not be burdened with the responsibility of recapturing stolen stock lost due to the laziness and carelessness of the victims. Although he made a valid point, it went widely ignored among higher authorities in Santa Fe. One could also question which course of action the captain actually preferred. In one instance he professed contempt for the Apaches and a desire to disseminate a "state of well understood hostility," yet in the next moment he blamed Mexican laziness for Indian outrages and expressed no desire to chase them or recover the stolen property.

November 1855 saw a pronounced increase in Apache raiding. During the first week of that month, 2nd Lieutenant Isaiah N. Moore of the First Dragoons returned to his post at Los Lunas after pursuing a band of Mogollon Apaches who had robbed the hacienda of Juan Padilla along the Rio Grande. The raiders had pilfered some 160 horses and mules, presumably to provide sustenance during the upcoming winter months. In a pursuit that covered almost seventy miles, Moore and his dragoons recovered all but twenty of the stolen animals, and the chase might have continued had it not been for their guide professing "utter ignorance of the country ahead in the direction of the [raiders'] trail."[44]

Lieutenant Moore hardly had time to write his report before he found himself deployed once again. On November 15, Apaches stole 150 mules from the Bernalillo County ranch of Jose Chaves. Leaving Los Lunas with twenty dragoons, Moore pursued the small band of Indians toward the Mogollon Mountains to the southwest. Once again, the raiders dispersed in all directions and left the dragoons no chance of catching them, although they managed to recover 120 of the mules before abandoning the chase.[45] Indeed, the Rio Grande valley in the vicinity of Socorro and Los Lunas had always been vulnerable to Apache raiding, owing in part to the large amount of livestock raised in that area. In October 1856, for example, ranchers in Valencia County (north of Socorro) purportedly owned 207,000 head of stock with an estimated value of $709,400.[46] During the winter months, many area herders grazed their animals along the Puerco River to the west, making the animals a likely target for the Mogollon Apaches as well as the Navajos. As frequently became the case, many of the thefts could be attributed to negligence on the part of the ranchers and herders, leaving their animals poorly attended and in insecure locations.

Despite his continued efforts, Steck's patience would continually be put to the test. The agent recurrently found himself in a quandary, attempting to maintain peaceful relations and eliminate starvation while simultaneously working to fulfill the unreasonable expectations of his superiors in Santa Fe and Washington, D.C. In early December 1855 he gave the Gila Apaches an ultimatum: stop raiding the settlements and return all stolen livestock or face a complete discontinuance of rations at the Fort Thorn agency.[47] Because so many of the Indians, especially women and children, had become reliant upon these disbursements, Steck's threat carried severe ramifications and had a greater psychological effect than could any military campaign. He ultimately showed his compassion, though, and continued dispensing provisions from his agency, pending the Apaches' good behavior.[48]

Although he continued to feed his charges, Steck also suggested the propriety of establishing a permanent military post in the Mogollon Mountains at or near the headwaters of the Gila River. This would be a perfect location, he argued, because that region contained an abundance of every resource necessary to maintain a large body of troops for an extended period of time. Steck echoed Colonel Mansfield's prior recommendation of 1853, noting that the upper Gila environs offered a more practical location for an Indian agency due to the proximity to the Gila and Mogollon Apaches. But as frequently occurred, this advice went unheeded.[49]

While Steck contented himself with the return of stolen animals and the promises from Apache chiefs that raiding would cease, Captain Eaton felt differently. He began planning a sizable campaign out of Fort Thorn, designed primarily as a scare tactic in hopes of exhibiting military prowess and discouraging the Indians from raiding the settlements. On December 5, 1855, Eaton embarked from Fort Thorn with thirty men of Company F, Third Infantry and thirty-one men of Company I, First Dragoons. Upon arriving at San Diego crossing south of the fort, the soldiers were spotted by a group of Indians who, according to Eaton, nearly always congregated in that vicinity. The captain later insinuated that they must have warned other bands of the coming column, because from that moment forward the expedition saw no Apaches.

Eaton's dragoons eventually reached the Florida Mountains, southeast of present-day Deming, at which point they received a dispatch from Steck informing them that most of the Apaches had fled into Mexico upon learning of the soldiers' advance. Because the Indians trusted Steck, he frequently received this type of privileged information from the chiefs, who informed him of their whereabouts to prevent suspicion of their bands being complicit in any wrongdoing. Despite the evident futility of his expedition and this information from Steck, the captain determined to continue his march. He left the infantrymen encamped at a waterhole on the northern end of the Floridas and circumnavigated the entire mountain chain with his dragoons. Not once during the journey did they encounter any sign of Indians, although Eaton remained convinced that they must have passed through that vicinity en route to Mexico.[50]

After rejoining the remainder of his troops, Eaton marched north to Cooke's Spring, where the column finally struck an Apache trail leading toward Santa Lucia Springs and the Gila River valley to the north. A small band of Indians, including one of Mangas Coloradas's sons, approached the troops and informed Eaton that the depredators had already reached the Gila River some eighty miles away. Although the captain knew that Mangas Coloradas and his immediate followers were innocent in the recent thefts, he advised the warriors that, upon returning to camp, they should tell the chief to visit Steck and clear himself of any wrongdoing. If the information that these Apaches provided was accurate, then the troops had no hope of catching any Indians. This realization, coupled with the sudden illness of Captain Alexander Early Steen (son of Major Steen), induced Eaton to forgo additional hardship and return to Fort Thorn. The entire command arrived back at the post on December 21, woefully short of both provisions and results.[51]

Waiting for Captain Eaton was a letter from Agent Steck, who had been away on a leave of absence when the expedition left and had hoped to deter the campaign from embarking in the first place. While inquiring among the Apaches at his agency, Steck had ascertained which band had committed the recent depredations and sought to pass this information along to Eaton to avoid an attack on any peaceful bands that he might encounter. When the agent returned to the fort and discovered that the expedition had already left, he wrote to General Garland, explaining that he had "left word for Col. J. H. Eaton comdg. Ft. Thorn that I knew the thieves & murderers & requested him to take no steps until I returned [from leave], but from certain information that he received from other sources . . . [he] fitted up an expedition. . . . The unexpected movement of the troops into the Indian country without their knowing the particular objective alarmed the whole tribe, who left the vicinity of the agency to watch the movement of the troops."[52] The fruitless march might have been avoided had Eaton taken Steck's advice and postponed the expedition.[53]

During the mid-1850s the government's efforts toward treaty negotiations continued to be in vain, first in 1853 with Governor Lane's provisional compact at Fort Webster and again in 1855 with Meriwether's talks at Fort Thorn. The Indians were not solely to blame for this; while they continued to execute raids on the Rio Grande settlements, American residents committed a considerable number of similar outrages upon the Apaches. Retribution became the standard during this period, undermining all efforts at diplomacy. To be sure, the government frequently failed to uphold its obligations. Attempted treaty negotiations occurring simultaneously with military campaigns sent a confusing mixed message to the Indians and exacerbated the preexisting distrust between the two sides. Had it not been for the presence of Michael Steck at the Southern Apache Agency, relations would have deteriorated much more rapidly, resulting in even more bloodshed.

Throughout the first half of the decade, government officials, including Indian agents, typically understood Apache raiding as a form of subsistence necessary for the tribe's livelihood. While these men certainly did not condone livestock theft, they often acknowledged that the Indians did this primarily as a traditional tribal economic practice rather than as an outright act of war. To this end Indian-affairs officials proposed placing the Apaches on permanent reservations within their homelands and issuing adequate rations to sustain them during hard times. According to these men, feeding the Indians would alleviate their necessity to raid the settlements, ultimately solving that problem altogether. Many War Department officials, though, maintained a starkly contrasting viewpoint. Army officers viewed Apache depredations as an open gesture of hostility and therefore sought to take the offensive against them, carrying the war into their homelands and attacking them before they even embarked on any raids. In this sense both the civil and military authorities had viable reasons for advancing their respective policies. Unfortunately, neither group liked to include the other as they pursued their goals, with the military often acting autonomously of the Indian agents and thereby reversing attempts at a mutually acceptable, peaceable outcome.

By the end of 1855, officers had begun envisioning a new approach to Indian affairs, and civil leaders joined War Department personnel in advocating a militaristic policy toward the Apaches. Years of failed treaties and continued depredations convinced Governor Meriwether, along with many of his subordinate Indian agents, that military action would have to precede future treaty negotiations. The year 1856 saw this new approach implemented throughout southern New Mexico, resulting in continuous military campaigning and pronounced psychological consequences for the Apaches as they continued to defend their homes and families against American encroachment.

CHAPTER 7

Events Foreshadowed

In 1856 both Apache raiding and military campaigning escalated throughout southern New Mexico, the latter representing a shift away from earlier Indian policies attempting to incorporate peace treaties as antecedents to military action. Continuing depredations in 1855 and 1856 had the result of reversing this tradition, often making military action an antecedent to the treaty-making process. For the first time, the heads of the military and the civil government in New Mexico agreed on a policy objective and took collaborative action to implement it. In corroboration with Governor Meriwether and Indian agents throughout southern New Mexico, Brigadier General Garland ordered the first and largest campaign into the field in February 1856, which would prove to be a sign of things to come in the territory's Indian affairs. Throughout the ensuing two years, large-scale military expeditions would define Indian policy in southern New Mexico.

Apache raiding had reached monumental proportions during the final months of 1855. Attempts to issue rations and provisions to discourage subsistence raids had generally failed. Thus General Garland issued orders on February 24, 1856, for a two-pronged attack on the upper Gila River and Mogollon Mountain regions of southwestern New Mexico. In the planning process he made a poor choice of officers to lead the expedition, an unintentional mistake that unfortunately carried severe ramifications for the Apaches. Specifically, the unmeritorious actions of one officer during the upcoming campaign likely provoked members of the Mogollon band to commit one of their most infamous murders of the 1850s, the killing of Navajo Agent Henry Dodge (see chapter 8). This murder would be among the leading reasons for continued military action against the Apaches in 1857, perpetuating violent reciprocity in antebellum Indian affairs.

Under orders from Garland, Lieutenant Colonel Daniel T. Chandler led one column of troops, including some fifteen Mexicans hired to serve as guides and herders. The command marched from Fort Craig westward to the Tularosa River, then swung south while combing the Mogollon Mountains. Here Chandler planned to meet the second column, which departed the more southerly Fort Thorn under the command of Captain Alexander E. Steen. By March 12 Captain Steen had encamped at the Santa Rita copper mines, still a considerable distance south of his intended destination in the mountains. The two columns finally met at a point north of the Gila River, where the scouts discovered and followed a recent trail and eventually came upon the camp of Apaches led by El Cautívo. Chandler immediately ordered an attack, resulting in one Apache being killed and three more wounded. The troops recovered some 350 stolen sheep as the remainder of the Indians fled frantically into the surrounding hills. According to later testimony from Apaches who participated in the engagement, two of their wounded later succumbed to their injuries, bringing the death toll to three.[1]

On their return to Forts Craig and Thorn, the entire command camped along the Mimbres River. Chandler left the main body of troops at that location, placing Major Oliver L. Shepherd in command, and marched with one company of infantry and a small detachment of dragoons in search of another purported Apache camp nearby. Not long after leaving the river, the soldiers discovered the camp of Chiefs Delgadito and Itán, both of whom remained peacefully disposed and regularly drew rations at Fort Thorn.[2] As members of the Gila Apache band, neither of these men, nor their followers, had been implicated in the recent raiding along the Rio Grande. Indeed, the depredations had been attributed to the Mogollon band, with whom Delgadito and Itán were not on friendly terms at the time. Despite this critical detail, Chandler ordered an attack, whereupon approximately sixty infantrymen and dragoons fired a devastating volley into the camp. According to Agent Steck, the men continued firing for some twenty minutes as the startled Apaches took flight in every direction.[3] One of the guides, realizing that the Indians belonged to the peaceful Gilas, convinced the colonel to cease fire. When the smoke cleared, numerous Apaches lay dead or dying on the hillside, victims of the negligence of an army officer and the continuing inability to distinguish between guilty and innocent subgroups.[4]

Ironically, the entire incident could easily have been avoided. Steck had departed from the Fort Thorn agency and joined Captain Steen's command at the Mimbres River; when Chandler left the main body, Steck made the fateful decision to stay behind, opting not to join him on the scout. Had he been present as the soldiers approached the Indian camp, the agent no doubt would have recognized it as that of Delgadito and Itán, both of whom he knew well as regular visitors at his agency.

Steck, furious upon learning of the incident, wrote a scathing report to department headquarters accusing Chandler of egregious misconduct. According to the agent: "[Chandler] approached [the Indian camp] with his command, about 60 men, within musket range and fired into their camp without knowing or stopping to enquire [sic] who it was he was firing upon. The Indians . . . [fled] scattering in every direction into the mts. with the loss of one woman killed, another wounded, three children wounded and at this date one child still missing." Steck pleaded his case against the colonel, explaining, "to manage an Indian he must have confidence in your kind intentions, and how can he confide in you, if when he had been promised a friendly salutation you greet him with musketry and the shrieks of dying women and children?" He claimed that Chandler "knew he was in the heart of peaceable territory" and demanded that the incident be brought to the attention of the proper authorities in Washington, D.C.[5] The agent then wrote to Commissioner of Indian Affairs George Manypenny, informing him that "a most wanton attack was made by U.S. troops upon friendly and unoffending Indians."[6] Steck had no intention of allowing the incident to pass without bringing negative publicity to Chandler's actions, although he would have preferred to see the officer court-martialed.

Colonel Chandler's official report explained the incident from his point of view, which not surprisingly completely contradicted both Steck's report and another written by an officer present during the attack. According to Chandler, while scouting in the hills near the Mimbres River, his guides discovered a horse bearing the same brand as one the Apaches had previously stolen, whereupon he sent out spies in several directions to determine the location of their camp.[7] Receiving affirmative reports of an Indian camp nearby, he ordered Lieutenant Moore and his dragoons to take a circuitous route around the site in order to intercept the Indians' retreat. Lieutenant Matthew L. Davis and his infantrymen then marched up the canyon directly toward the camp and fired the first volley as the Apaches fled into the hills. After several minutes of action, Chandler noticed one Indian frantically waving a white flag "as if desirous of holding a talk," at which point he ordered his men to stop firing. The colonel allowed the man to approach, who proved to be Costales, a well-known subchief and interpreter who frequently communicated with Steck at Fort Thorn.[8] Costales, eschewing violence, managed to convince him that the troops had attacked a peaceful band of Apaches, whereupon the colonel dispatched a messenger to locate Lieutenant Moore and order him not to attack any Indians he might encounter at his position. Based on this report, the entire incident appeared to have been a terrible accident.[9]

On May 26 Steck received a communication from Governor Meriwether pointing out substantial discrepancies in the various reports of the incident. The governor, however, agreed to transmit both Chandler's and Steck's accounts to Washington for further review and possible disciplinary action, pending a War Department investigation.[10] Not surprisingly, this served only to further agitate Steck, who realized that the attack seriously jeopardized his pacific efforts of the past several years. "In reference to Colonel Chandler's report of the Mimbres affair differing from mine, I have only to say that I stated facts, and in as mild a manner as it could be done—there was no circumstance to justify it," Steck fumed in his response to Meriwether. "We expected the friendly Indians to visit us the night before—smokes were made to notify them of our approach and Colonel Chandler directed the rear guard the night before to kill no more broken down animals, but leave them [for] the very Indians he attacked."[11]

Secretary of War Jefferson Davis investigated the incident but ultimately deemed Chandler's version to be satisfactory, dismissing Steck's account as unreliable and biased because of his compassion for the Apaches, a sentiment that General Garland likewise conveyed in his report.[12] The agent's credibility received much-needed support when Lieutenant Davis, whose detachment had fired the first volley, later admitted that he and his fellow officers, including Chandler, knew prior to the attack that peaceful Gila Apaches occupied the camp. In a letter written directly to Steck, the lieutenant explained that he had been in the rear guard when Chandler ordered the attack, and he knew at the time that they were targeting the wrong band of Apaches.[13] If a junior officer in the rear guard knew this, then it stood to reason that the commanding officer would have known as well.

According to Lieutenant Davis, Colonel Chandler knew that the Indians in the camp had not committed the recent depredations, but he attacked anyway. Why? Perhaps Chandler really did mistake them for members of the hostile Mogollon band and believed himself justified in his actions. But another possible answer can be found in an analysis of the commander's morality. Clearly he exercised poor judgment in this instance, something evidently not atypical of him. Chandler once killed one of his own soldiers while on a campaign; an infantry private had been unable to keep up with the column due to thirst, at which point Chandler cut him down with his saber.[14] If an officer could murder one of his own men, it requires no stretch of the imagination to envision that same man knowingly attacking a peaceful Indian camp.

Not surprisingly, the campaign had done little to quell the raids. If anything, the attack on the Mimbres camp incited further animosity among the Apaches and encouraged additional hostilities. In March 1856, possibly as a result of Chandler's actions, the area between El Paso and Fort Fillmore saw an increase in raiding. In these instances the Gila Apaches became the suspects after an arrow bearing the defining markings of that band was pulled from a murdered Mexican herder. Colonel Miles, commanding at Fort Fillmore, also believed that the Gila Apaches were responsible because the stolen livestock had been driven westward from the Rio Grande toward their homelands along the Mimbres River. Because the Mescaleros ranged exclusively on the east side of the Rio Grande, which at that time could only be crossed by boats, it would have been impossible for them to steal the animals west of the swollen river and drive them across to the east bank.

Lieutenant Davis and a detachment of the First Dragoons left Fort Fillmore following the third Indian attack of the month, in which Apaches killed yet another Mexican herder. Davis lost the trail after several hours and returned to the fort. Meanwhile, the brother of the slain man decided to take matters into his own hands. He rode to nearby Doña Ana, where he killed a Mescalero Apache woman selling wood there. This incident could have easily sparked an outbreak in Mescalero hostilities, which would have only exacerbated an already problematic state of affairs. Territorial officials attributed nearly all depredations occurring along the Rio Grande at that time to the Mogollon and Gila Apaches; bringing the Mescaleros into the conflict would have been disastrous, giving rise to hostilities in two geographic regions and forcing the military to simultaneously direct their efforts in opposite directions. Not long afterward, the man accused of killing the Mescalero woman appeared near Fort Thorn, where Captain Eaton recognized, arrested, and confined him in the guardhouse to await trial for the murder. Eaton's prudent action, coupled with Steck's satisfactory explanation to the Mescaleros, probably prevented a large-scale outbreak. The agent's ability to communicate effectively with the Apaches and pacify their young warriors during such tense situations once again prevented further bloodshed.[15]

In May 1856 a band of friendly Gila Apaches under Chief Cuchillo Negro camped at a spring some five to seven miles west of Fort Thorn and began drawing rations from the agency. Rumors circulated that several renegade Mescaleros, guilty of committing depredations in the preceding months and sought by the military, had taken refuge with them in hopes of evading capture. Steck knew of these rumors, and although he thought the Mescaleros had indeed taken shelter in the camp, he also believed that they had done so against the will of Cuchillo Negro and his followers. Upon learning of this, Captain Eaton immediately dispatched a command of eighty men (forty infantry and forty dragoons) with Captain Steen and Lieutenants Williamson and Pender in command. Eaton explicitly ordered the troops not to attempt to capture the Mescaleros but to shoot them if at all possible. He made clear that the Gila Apaches should be left unmolested.[16]

In the event of a skirmish, the troops would have had great difficulty distinguishing between the two different bands while commingled in camp. If a combat situation had occurred, many of the Gilas would have been harmed as well. Before any hostile action took place, however, Cuchillo Negro's scouts sighted the troops and gave warning, whereupon the Indians abandoned the entire camp and fled. When the chief came to Fort Thorn shortly afterward to collect rations, Steck ordered him to either leave immediately or be imprisoned for harboring the renegade Mescaleros.[17] Although compassionate toward the Apaches, Steck always maintained an equitable sense of justice and was never afraid to exert his authority when necessary. This incident represents a very rare example in which members of the Mescalero and Gila polities coalesced for a common cause during the antebellum era. Seldom did the two tribes cooperate in such a manner; while they rarely acted violently toward one another, they likewise did not typically maintain congenial relations. For the most part they avoided one another as much as possible to prevent being implicated in the other's wrongdoings.

Internal feuds and fractious mentalities within the various Chiricahua subgroups typically involved the Mogollon band. Considered to be the most hostile within the tribe, the Mogollons bore responsibility for the majority of depredations that occurred between Fort Thorn and Albuquerque, a distance of some 200 miles up and down the Rio Grande valley. Delgadito, a chief of the Gila band living in the vicinity of old Fort Webster, once told Agent Steck that the Mogollons frequently antagonized him and his followers by "taunt[ing] them as women for being in treaty and receiving rations."[18] Their gestures of hostility toward others indicates that they may have fragmented from their Gila Apache kin in order to maintain a greater distance from the Americans. All of this would come back to haunt them in the near future: a year later, in the summer of 1857, the Mogollons became the target of the largest military campaign ever to enter Apache country (see chapter 8).

As early as January 1856, recommendations surfaced suggesting the relocation of Fort Thorn. Despite the benefits derived from its placement alongside the Rio Grande, the post had suffered from several severe setbacks. Its commander encouraged abandoning Fort Thorn altogether and building a new post on the Tularosa River, north of the Gila and about one hundred miles west of Fort Craig. The army in fact did build a fort at this proposed site, though not until 1872. When Fort Thorn was established, the department perceived it as an optimal spot from which troops could chase both Mescalero and Chiricahua raiders because of its location midway between the homelands of both tribes. In actuality, Fort Thorn sat far removed from their mountainous haunts. Fort Webster had been situated in the heart of Chiricahua country and served its purpose well, but when Fort Thorn replaced it, the department unwittingly distanced its troops from the Apaches' homelands. Furthermore, the establishment of Fort Stanton in 1855 along the Rio Bonito in the Sacramento Mountains of southeastern New Mexico rendered Fort Thorn mostly irrelevant for Mescalero control. The only practical purpose Fort Thorn continued to serve was as the site of Steck's agency, although he established a subagency at Fort Stanton not long after its founding.

In August 1856 the Rio Grande fell below the level of Fort Thorn's *acequias* (irrigation ditches), making it difficult to water crops and run the sawmill. The army temporarily employed several residents from nearby Las Cruces and Mesilla to remodel the ditches to make them usable at lower river levels. In fact the post's *acequia* had always been an area of concern. As early as the summer of 1854, private landowners in the Rio Grande valley above the fort began diverting water into their own fields, preventing it from reaching the fort and causing numerous complaints. Major Israel Richardson wrote to headquarters on June 27, 1854, explaining that the water had been "cut off by people who threaten a lawsuit if I interfere." He named three individuals involved in this dispute: "Lieut. O'Bannon of the Army whose land is farmed by a civilian, a Mr. [Alexander] Duvall and a Mr. [Frank] Fletcher. . . . [U]nless a guard is kept on the acequia, water on which the entire post depends for sustenance is stopped for a week at a time."[19] Not long after this incident, Garland brought about closure by granting the major an unusually lengthy leave of absence, writing, "Richardson has become too obnoxious to a majority of his regiment for professional pride, and the leave was a step for his tendering his resignation."[20]

The most serious problem facing the Fort Thorn garrison, however, revolved around health issues. Being located near the river bottoms, stagnant water and hot temperatures in the summertime created an ideal breeding ground for mosquitoes. As a consequence, ague (malaria) spread rampantly among the men. Though seldom lethal, it was highly debilitating and often left soldiers bedridden for weeks at a time. These illnesses spread with amazing rapidity; any person passing through the region in the summertime was lucky to do so without contracting the disease.

On August 19, 1856, troops of Companies F, H, and I, First Dragoons established a temporary camp on a high desert bluff overlooking the western bank of the Rio Grande a short distance north of Fort Thorn.[21] Pursuant to orders issued by General Garland on

July 28, the three companies left Fort Union en route to southern California, where they had been permanently reassigned. They joined four additional companies of dragoons near Fort Thorn under Major Steen en route to Tucson to establish a new post; collectively they named the site "Camp Blake" in honor of their commanding officer, Major George A. H. Blake.[22] Company F had been stationed at Fort Thorn and received orders to join Major Blake's command and accompany them to California. At that time the unit consisted of only seventeen effective men; most of the company had contracted malaria and could not make the journey.

Fort Thorn's post surgeon, Dr. T. Charles Henry, described the ominous situation at Camp Blake. "In the latter portion of August, Major Blake, of the first dragoons, encamped near here with one company of recruits and the regimental band, and was in a fortnight subsequently joined by two more companies. Sickness, especially ague, commenced very soon after amongst his men, [along with] cases of camp dysentery and throat infection," the doctor reported.[23] On September 14 Blake wrote to Santa Fe requesting that an army medical officer be sent to accompany his command on their march to the Pacific as well as medical supplies to last the duration of the journey. "There are a great number of troops sick at this camp," he lamented, "and there is scarcely any medicine at Fort Thorn of the proper description."[24] On September 29, over a month after establishing the camp, Blake's emaciated dragoons continued their march to California.

The horrid conditions at Camp Blake mirrored those already existing at Fort Thorn, prompting Dr. Henry to report extensively on the unhealthy surroundings. "About the 10th of September last year," he recalled, "ague appeared and a large portion of the command were victims of its influence." In addition to malaria, he noted the presence of a bilious remittent fever that afflicted a number of the troops. "The month of July last, seventy-eight men out of ninety were sick," the doctor reported, adding that, "were there no surgeon at this sickliest post in the territory, these men would die just like the natives all about them."[25] Henry's comments suggest that many of the Apaches who frequented the agency also contracted the disease, for it likely spread quickly between the soldiers and the Indians.

Dr. Henry urged that Fort Thorn be abandoned immediately, suggesting that the post be relocated "not far from the old station of Fort Webster." If the department would not consider reoccupying that site, then he suggested that the post at least be relocated a few miles west, farther away from the Rio Grande. There several large, dependable springs could provide enough water for a military garrison. The primary issue, the doctor recognized, was getting the men away from the swampy river bottoms. The reoccupation of Fort Webster would have been the easiest and most practical method of ensuring the health of the troops while also keeping Indian affairs in mind.[26] Unfortunately, higher-ranking officers disagreed, and Dr. Henry's pleas went unanswered. Had authorities in Santa Fe actually been subjected to the terrible living conditions at Fort Thorn, they likely would have heeded his advice.

The horrible condition of the Fort Thorn hospital only intensified the urgency of the situation. In September 1855, army officials inspected New Mexico's post hospitals and found the medical facilities at that location to be the most deplorable in the entire territory. According to the report, renovations there had begun, and "the temporary hospital occupied whilst the [main hospital] was being built was a wretched jackal [sic] of upright cottonwood sticks, with a flat dirt roof leaking badly, erected in a plain becoming flooded and marshy with every rain." The original plans for Fort Thorn included a hospital inside the post's walls, but that had never been completed, and instead temporary medical facilities were constructed outside the perimeter near the river bottoms. With conditions like these, observers had good reason to call Fort Thorn the "sickliest post in the territory."[27]

By August 1857 Dr. Henry had seen enough. He requested—in fact almost begged—to be transferred to another post as far away from Fort Thorn as possible. "The climate at Fort Thorn," he protested, "[is] much too warm to suit my constitution."[28] Being constantly surrounded by sick men rendered the doctor vulnerable to the illnesses himself, and he struggled to maintain his own health.

His request for a transfer went unfulfilled, and a year later he again wrote to Santa Fe reminding officials of the dreadful conditions at the fort. For the third straight summer, Henry noted, malaria afflicted the post garrison and, indeed, had become worse with each passing year. Company F, Third Infantry and Company B, Regiment of Mounted Rifles had been stationed at Fort Thorn for over two years, the troops suffering immensely the entire time. It seemed impossible to keep more than half a dozen men on duty as "the least exposure to the sun prostrates them for a week to come."[29] Many of the men remained bedridden all summer—as soon as they recovered from one illness, they oftentimes contracted another. In addition to pleading for his own transfer, the doctor urged that these two companies also be removed to an alternate location simply as a gesture of humanity.

The department finally granted Dr. Henry's transfer in the summer of 1858, appointing Dr. P. A. Quinan to succeed him as post surgeon. Quinan inherited a nightmare, and he knew it as soon as he arrived at the post. He painted a very bleak picture of conditions at Fort Thorn, describing it as being "located upon the immediate edge of an extensive marsh, the river making a considerable bend at this point. . . . [T]he buildings constituting this fort are placed within a stone's throw of the swampiest portion of this flat or bottom . . . [presenting] during the hottest months, a surface of oozy mud, covered with green slime, and interspersed with ponds of stagnating water . . . during the same time, a rank vegetation of weeds and grasses undergoes the process of germination, advancement to maturity, and decay." All of this had a profound effect on the garrison. "Scarcely a man of this command can be considered fit for the performance of ordinary garrison duty, so debilitated are they by disease," Quinan ominously observed.[30]

Fort Thorn was not alone in its battles against malarial fevers. Between 1855 and 1859 malaria became the leading cause of illness among troops stationed throughout New Mexico. Every fort along the Rio Grande suffered to some degree, although Fort Thorn always seemed to be the worst. When Colonel Benjamin Bonneville temporarily assumed command of the military department on

October 11, 1856, he recognized the urgency of the issue and before leaving office wrote orders for the gradual disbandment of the garrison, in effect promulgating the demise of Fort Thorn as a military installation. This abandonment, however, would not be carried out in full until the spring of 1859. In the meantime, soldiers continued to suffer there.[31]

An interesting health situation arose when Lieutenant Colonel Benjamin S. Roberts, commanding the Los Lunas post, brought his family to live with him there. Being located along the Rio Grande, Los Lunas was highly susceptible to malarial illnesses. In October 1856 Roberts requested that an army medical officer be stationed there, pointing out that the nearest physician resided in Santa Fe, some ninety miles to the north. After living there for only one month, two members of the Roberts family became ill and were unable to receive the medical attention the colonel thought they deserved. "It appears to me an extreme and unnecessary hardship upon officers who bring their families to this remote frontier," he complained, "that their health and lives should be periled for want of medical attendance and medicines." Roberts eventually took his family to Santa Fe himself after a military surgeon in nearby Albuquerque refused to help: "It is not required of me by regulations," the post surgeon caustically informed him.[32]

Sickness is blind to societal status or military rank, so officers often suffered along with their men. What the medical reports do not indicate, however, is the extent to which illnesses afflicted the Apaches; indeed, officers were typically so preoccupied with the health of their own troops that they remained either oblivious or indifferent to the Indians' suffering. Regularly exposed to the troops when visiting the agency to receive rations, many Indians no doubt contracted malaria and other diseases. Lacking any remedies besides those administered by tribal medicine men, mortality rates must have been relatively high, although no written records exist to preserve these statistics; this element of Apache history remains clouded in the historical record.

Modern-day southern Arizona, which remained a part of New Mexico Territory until 1863, received its first official attention from the War Department on June 17, 1856, when several companies of troops marched westward from Fort Thorn to Tucson and established the first permanent installation in the region. The founding of that military post marked the commencement of relations with the Western Apache bands, many of which had not previously come into regular contact with U.S. troops. Indeed, General Garland recognized this future necessity as early as January 1854, suggesting that a post be established on the Gila River in modern Arizona to protect "the unfortunate inhabitants of Sonora" as well as California emigrants, recommending that as many as five companies be deployed there. Ultimately, since this proposal came a mere three weeks after the signing of the Gadsden Purchase, Garland was unable to follow through with the plan, having first to wait for treaty ratification and the determination of the new international boundary.[33]

The 1853 Gadsden Purchase resulted in the United States acquiring the entirety of the geographic area south of the Gila River, comprising modern southern Arizona as far west as the Colorado River. This expansion necessitated a military presence in that region "to protect the lives and property of its inhabitants," especially in the Santa Cruz and San Pedro River valleys near Tubac and Tucson.[34] Accordingly, in 1856 General in Chief Winfield Scott ordered four of the seven First Dragoon companies stationed in New Mexico to "take post at Tucson, under the command of Major Enoch Steen."[35] Several months passed, however, before Steen satisfied the order. Not until October 19 did he march westward from Fort Thorn with his battalion to establish a permanent post in the vicinity of Tucson, where the column arrived on November 14. These four companies, along with three others under the command of Major George A. H. Blake that had already departed in September, represented a significant transfer of dragoons out of New Mexico. To fill the void, the War Department reassigned several companies of the Regiment of Mounted Rifles stationed in Texas.[36]

By March 1856 the small garrison of Mexican troops stationed at Tucson had withdrawn to Mexico following ratification of the Gadsden Purchase and the official delineation of the new international boundary, leaving the town's residents without military protection.[37] Several bands of the Western Apaches, most notably the Coyoteros, Aravaipas, and Pinals, lived in that vicinity; up to that point, these groups had rarely come into contact with U.S. troops, but with the arrival of Steen and his dragoons, armed clashes became inevitable.[38]

Evidently, Steen never intended to establish his post at Tucson. He made only a cursory visit to the town and conducted a superficial inspection of its buildings, deeming them "unfit for habitation" by his troops. On November 27 the major chose a site near the Calabasas Ranch overlooking the banks of the Santa Cruz River, some eight miles north of the Mexican border (near modern Nogales, Arizona) and sixty miles south of Tucson, for the location of a new post to be called Camp Moore.[39] But Steen's chosen location met with immediate disfavor at department headquarters, and he received orders to relocate to a new site closer to Tucson.[40] He ultimately stationed his troops at a site near the head of the Sonoita Valley, closer to Tucson than Calabasas, but still some forty miles distant. At this location he established Fort Buchanan, named for President James Buchanan.

Steen's final choice for the site of Fort Buchanan thoroughly displeased Tucson's inhabitants, who rightfully pointed out that the post's distance from the town would render it impossible for the troops to protect them from Indian raids. Residents made their feelings known in a petition to General Garland: "If [Steen] was sent here to protect the lives and property of the citizens of the 'Gadsden Purchase,' then he has gone wide of the mark," they lamented. "Some protection it is sure he affords the state of Sonora, but none whatever to his countrymen."[41] The necessity of a military presence in the area, both as protection for residents and a stimulant for the regional economy, could not be denied. Writing a year earlier, Arizona pioneer Sylvester Mowry pleaded with Washington officials to establish not one but four military posts in the region: one "in the vicinity of Tucson, one on the San Pedro [River], one in the vicinity of the Los Miembres [*sic*], and one on the Gila [River], above the Pimos [*sic*] villages."[42] Ultimately, Arizonans would have to settle for just one post on the Sonoita (Fort Buchanan) and later, in May 1860, another on the San Pedro named Fort Breckenridge. Not until after the Civil War would forts be built at all of Mowry's suggested locations.

The owner and operator of extensive mining interests in the Sonoita Valley, Mowry had good reason to request these forts be built.[43] A staunch advocate of establishing an extractive-based American economy in the region, he delivered an address before the American Geographical and Statistical Society in New York on February 3, 1859, in which he outlined, in remarkable detail, every imaginable feature of the region south of the Gila River and west of the Rio Grande with an emphasis on developing farming, ranching, and mining economies. Such development would, Mowry acknowledged, require the continued presence of U.S. troops for protection from Apache raiding.[44]

Like Mowry, Major Steen might have had personal motivations for locating an army post in the foothills of the Santa Rita Mountains south of Tucson. In the years immediately preceding the Civil War, this region saw the opening by Americans of numerous silver mines, supported financially with funding from entrepreneurial easterners seeking to exploit this borderlands region. It comes as no little irony that Steen himself had envisioned southern New Mexico and Arizona as a potentially valuable mining district as early as 1850 during his stead as commanding officer at Doña Ana (see chapter 3). Now, seven years later and some 250 miles farther west (but still within the Department of New Mexico), Steen once again saw an opportunity to advance American hegemony over a mineral-rich landscape, and so constructed Fort Buchanan accordingly.

Steen's successor as post commander at Fort Buchanan, Captain Richard S. Ewell, also became enamored in regional development, holding personal interests in Mowry's Patagonia Mine, only a few miles from the post. Writing to his niece, Ewell gleamed that the mine's "prospects [are] looking quite bright. I have been offered $1,000 for my interest, having at that time expended about $100; so if we fail, the croakers can't say it was an absurd speculation."[45] Steen and Ewell, both prominent officers, clearly sought

Mowry Mine, c. 1864. From J. Ross Browne, *Adventures in the Apache Country: A Tour through Arizona and Sonora, with Notes on the Silver Regions of Nevada* (New York: Harper & Brothers, 1869).

to promote settlement and economic expansion in the vicinity of their own holdings in Apachería through the use of dragoons and infantrymen to enforce order and subdue Indian raids. Their vested interests in the landscape therefore motivated their actions in ordering troops out on expeditions and enforcing Indian policy at this far-removed army outpost.[46]

While acting as commanding officer at Fort Buchanan, Major Steen saw considerable action in the field against the Indians. Regional bands of Apaches, he noted, subsisted almost entirely by raiding Chihuahua and Sonora and had done so with little opposition from the Mexican troops previously occupying Tucson. The majority of depredations in the region occurred at the hands of Chiricahua Apaches led by Mangas Coloradas and Cochise; for the most part, Arizonans only occasionally clashed with the Coyoteros and Pinals who resided in the surrounding countryside. According to Steen, these Western Apache bands desired peace with the Americans and wanted to have their own Indian agent appointed in hopes that they might begin receiving rations and presents, thus minimizing their reliance on plundering northern Mexico's villages and haciendas.

The first major incident involving the Coyoteros and white settlers did not occur until July 27, 1857. Members of the tribe ambushed a party of Texans en route to California near the Chiricahua Mountains of southeastern Arizona, killing two in the process.[47] Ironically, on this same day some 800 troops under the shared command of Colonels Bonneville and Miles and Captain Ewell massacred a Coyotero ranchería on the Gila River near Mount Turnbull (see chapter 8).

As these events transpired, an international incident began brewing when, in the summer of 1857, twenty Mexican troops crossed into the United States near present-day Nogales and murdered four Americans, purportedly attached to a filibustering party, about one thousand yards inside the border at a store owned by Edward E. Dunbar.[48] Steen described the brutality of the murders to the secretary of war and asked that something be done to discourage such incidents from occurring again, thereby preventing future army officers from being in similarly precarious diplomatic situations. Surprisingly, the incident did not have any significant ramifications on American relations with Mexico.[49]

Steen did not remain long at Fort Buchanan. In January 1858 he requested sick leave and left the post for the last time on April 12, less than two years after establishing the first U.S. military installation in southern Arizona's Apache country. Steen subsequently transferred to the Department of the Pacific, along with two companies of the First Dragoons.[50] His temporary replacement as commander at Fort Buchanan would be Major Edward H. Fitzgerald of Company D, First Dragoons.[51]

Fort Buchanan remained an active military establishment for only four years before the army permanently abandoned it on July 23, 1861, in preparation for the looming Confederate invasion of New Mexico via El Paso and the Mesilla Valley.[52] The garrison must have felt little remorse when abandoning the post. By all accounts Fort Buchanan was among the worst stations in the department, its buildings and tents being haphazardly strewn over more than a half mile of terrain and therefore utterly indefensible. According to department commander Benjamin Bonneville, who toured the site in 1859, Fort Buchanan sat "entirely out of position, it being . . . from 80 to 120 miles from Tucson by the travelled road, and on the opposite side of the [Santa Rita] mountains. The post is built more like a village than a military post." The colonel observed that the compound extended "down a slope of a low ridge even into the valley. . . . [T]here are no store houses except temporary sheds covered with tarpaulins. The men's quarters are *jacals* built of upright poles daubed with mud."[53]

During its four years in existence, Fort Buchanan served to discourage Coyotero and Chiricahua depredations in the area south and east of Tucson, protected miners in the vicinity as well as travelers on the California road, and served as a supply base for military expeditions passing through the region. It represented an important milestone in that it provided the first permanent U.S. military presence in southern Arizona and, as such, persuaded hundreds of Americans to relocate there for the purpose of exploitative settlement of the landscape. Still, despite the fort's symbolic importance, it played a less prominent role in 1850s Apache affairs compared to others in the Rio Grande region. Not until the Civil War years would the army begin to concentrate its efforts wholeheartedly on chastising Apaches in southern Arizona.

Returning to affairs along the Rio Grande, a detachment of twenty dragoons under Lieutenant Randall left Los Lunas on November 23, 1856, in pursuit of Apaches, presumably of the Mogollon band, who had ambushed a party of Mexicans nearby and carried off two women as captives.[54] Although article 11 of the Treaty of Guadalupe-Hidalgo had been abrogated three years earlier with the signing of the Gadsden Treaty, army officers still attempted to regain Mexican captives whenever possible. Lieutenant Colonel Benjamin S. Roberts, commanding at Los Lunas, received information that the Apaches numbered in excess of fifty warriors, a formidable opponent for any military command. The fact that the dragoons carried only three rounds of ammunition per man added to the danger of the expedition; Roberts had submitted a requisition for additional munitions two months earlier, but it had yet to arrive when the detachment set out in pursuit. Fearing for the safety of the dragoons, the colonel sent out an additional ten men as reinforcements in the event of a skirmish, but they never caught up with Lieutenant Randall. They followed his trail for some seventy miles until it became covered with snow, making it impossible to discern, then returned to Los Lunas, leaving the twenty-man force to fend for itself.[55]

Randall lost the Apaches' trail on the first day due to the heavy snow but continued pressing forward in the direction that he supposed they might be traveling. On the third day the dragoons stumbled upon the trail again by mere happenstance. That night the Indians surrounded the soldiers' camp and, according to Randall, "showed a strong disposition to take my little party by storm, but the prompt establishment of a strong picket and extinguishing camp fires sufficed to prevent it." The following day the advance guard reported seeing ahead of them five Indian spies, who fled to their camp once they noticed the dragoons approaching. The column advanced to within 300 yards of the camp, located on a thickly timbered and brushy mountainside near the Mogollon Mountains about one day's march from the headwaters of the Gila River and 200 miles from Los Lunas. Just as Randall presumed, the Indians numbered about fifty, nearly all of whom carried rifles or muskets. They fired upon the Americans as they approached, whereupon the dragoons instinctively returned fire. When the Apaches fled, one warrior lay dead on the hillside, and the troops recovered thirty-one stolen animals.[56]

Lieutenant Randall realized he had been fortunate to avoid a massacre and thereafter chose a more cautious course of action. He reported to headquarters: "Owing to the limited supply of ammunition, my men having scarcely two rounds each, and the smallness of my command, I was forced to make my way to the [Gila] river with as little delay as possible. Indeed had I penetrated further into their country, or remained longer, my command would have been wiped out." Outnumbered, destitute of provisions, and short on ammunition, the dragoons were in a near-helpless situation. After considering his options, the lieutenant countermarched his men toward Los Lunas as quickly as possible. The dragoons had already been in the field for ten days, the entire time exposed to deep snow and freezing temperatures. Only twice had they been able to camp at a location with water, and sometimes they could not build a fire for fear of revealing their location to nearby Apaches.[57]

Frustrated with the entire incident, Randall pinned a considerable amount of blame on the citizens of the Rio Grande settlements. It was no secret that these people unwittingly encouraged many of the Indian depredations by trading contraband articles to them. "I cannot refrain from remarking upon the conduct of the Mexicans at Lemitar [New Mexico]," the lieutenant fumed in his closing remarks. "I am well aware of the fact that they supply these hostile Indians with ammunition as well as other articles which necessarily enables them to carry out their plundering."[58] Randall had every right to be upset. He and his men had endured a miserable ten days in the field chasing a better-armed and equipped enemy for the purpose of preventing depredations upon the very people who traded the guns and ammunition to the Apaches in the first place.

Randall's accusations did not represent an isolated incident; reports arose periodically throughout the 1850s of contraband being traded between American civilians and the Apaches. New Mexico congressional representative Hugh N. Smith informed Commissioner of Indian Affairs Orlando Brown in 1850 that Indian agents were necessary "in regulating the proper intercourse of traders with those Indians, as much of our difficulty with them arises . . . from the misconduct of lawless and improper persons who are allowed to go among them under pretence of trading."[59] In June 1850 Colonel John Munroe had authorized all officers under his departmental command to arrest any persons caught trading without a license, targeting especially "persons ... discovered having contraband articles in possession such as arms or ammunition of any kind or liquor of any sort."[60] Major Steen, while commanding at Fort Webster in 1853, similarly informed Governor Lane that "it would be advisable ... to keep the Mexicans from trading with the Indians as they sell them whisky and when an Indian is half drunk they often give a mule for one cup of whisky."[61]

In a cyclical process, Mexican traders provided a convenient local outlet for plundered livestock, oftentimes accepting the illegally obtained animals in exchange for weapons and other articles of war that in turn further perpetuated Apache raiding. Many of the stolen animals came from ranches in Chihuahua and Sonora and therefore could not be easily traced by American officials, making it relatively safe for merchants to barter with the Indians. Francisco Duran, a Mexican who escaped captivity among the Chiricahuas on June 30, 1849, informed Sonoran officials upon his return that "all the items which the Apaches obtained during the campaigns from Sonora they sold to the New Mexicans.... [T]his happened time and time again." He went on to confirm what most Sonorans and Chihuahuans already knew: U.S. citizens in New Mexico continued to "trade with the Indians arms, gun powder, bullets, and other merchandise, in exchange for which the Indians trade the items which they have gained through the pillaging of Sonora," despite the illegal origin of such goods.[62]

James S. Calhoun, while serving as superintendent of Indian affairs in 1849, complained bitterly of the department's inability to check such offenses and alluded to the division of authority between civil and military officials as directly abetting the ongoing illicit commerce. "The trade and uninterrupted intercourse carried on by Mexicans and others with these Indians, has to a greater extent than anything else contributed to the present deplorable condition of affairs," he wrote to Senator W. C. Dawson.[63] Another observer, speaking on Indian policy, complained bitterly of this questionable economic exchange. "Not much can be accomplished until the strong arm of the law is made to reach the unprincipled persons who are engaged in a traffic, which, if not unlawful, should be made so, by both Mexico and the United States," Quartermaster Thomas Swords lamented in a letter to authorities in Washington. "All along the frontier, both on our own and on the Mexican side of the Rio Grande, there are persons who do not hesitate to purchase from the Indian mules and other property which they well know must have been stolen."[64]

As long as traders continued providing guns and ammunition to the Apaches and accepted stolen livestock in exchange, it would be exceedingly difficult for the army to capture and punish them. This also brings to question the utter hypocrisy of the territory's civilian residents. In one breath they cursed the Apaches for stealing from them and pleaded with the military for assistance and protection, yet in the next they professed friendship toward the Indians and traded them the materials necessary to carry out their raids. This economic and social intercourse between the Mexicans and Apaches remained a continuous concern for military and civil officials throughout the antebellum period.

Several of the Apache bands typically remained on friendly terms with the citizenry and often ventured into the towns to haggle with them. While such encounters generally began with benevolent intentions, tragedy sometimes resulted when traditional animosities ignited dormant passions. Intoxicating liquors, often distributed by unscrupulous Mexican traders, further exacerbated tensions during intercultural social interactions. On September 17, 1851, for example, a detachment of Company E, Second Dragoons rode from Fort Conrad to the small town of San Antonio, a short distance south of Socorro, with orders to investigate the murder of two Apaches. A general panic prevailed in the town, where residents feared that the Indians might descend upon them at any moment and enact their customary revenge. The incident began when a dispute erupted between the two Indians and several residents over a gambling debt. Reports cited the intoxication of both parties as a contributing factor in the melee. Witnesses stated that one of the townspeople stabbed and killed both of the Indians and wounded a third, and civil authorities promptly arrested the perpetrator before the troops arrived.[65] Later reports indicated that the culprit was immediately released once the Apaches left town, giving rise to increased depredations in the months that followed.[66] Such instances served as a stark reminder of the tension that arose whenever Apaches and Mexicans commingled in close quarters.

The final days of 1856 witnessed yet another unfortunate incident emanating from the enmity between the two races. On December 29 two Mexicans from the Mesilla Valley, Manuel Meztas and Dolores Sanches, stole sixteen horses from Delgadito's band of Gila Apaches near Fort Thorn. Agent Steck sent two prominent and trustworthy warriors, Costales and Ratón, to follow the trail in hopes of retrieving the animals. Although twelve of the sixteen horses would eventually be recovered, their retrieval came at a high price.[67]

While encamped at the San Diego river crossing several miles south of Fort Thorn, both Costales and Ratón were gruesomely murdered by two Mexicans, including Martín Corrales, who sought vengeance for his captured brother. Corrales fled to Chihuahua, where he remained in safety as attempts by the U.S. consul to extradite him proved unsuccessful.[68] When Lieutenant Alexander Steen arrived at the site on December 31 to investigate, he encountered a grisly scene. "I commenced an examination [of the premises] which resulted in finding . . . a quantity of blood on the floor, and a butcher and table knife lying on the floor, perfectly filled with gore," he reported. "I concluded the person killed had been thrown into the river, and after searching probably an hour and a half, the body of Costales was fished up; he had evidently been killed while asleep; his head was split open with a blow from an axe, his throat cut and the entire scalp taken off."[69]

Trooper John C. Reid, present at Fort Thorn when the murders took place, further corroborated the incident. He noted that Costales, a Mexican by birth, was about thirty years old at the time of his killing and "had been stolen, when a child, from his parents whilst journeying in [Chihuahua], by a party of Indians, headed by Delgareta [Delgadito]." Years later he became a prominent member of the tribe "by his deeds of daring and cunning."[70] Costales exemplified the Apache custom of adopting captive Mexican children into tribal families, a process whereby such captives underwent a complete transformation in identity and essentially "became" Apache through cultural immersion. This custom had the effect of cultivating warriors from captives, many of whom (like Costales) eventually became indispensable defenders of their surrogate families and communities.

Reiterating the horrific sight Steen encountered at the San Diego crossing, Reid pointed out that "the authorities in Chihuahua offered a handsome reward for the apprehension and delivery to them of Costelles [sic], or of his head." During Reid's stay at Fort Thorn, he recalled the Apache coming into the fort and frantically telling the officers "that a number of his horses had been recently stolen by certain citizens (natives) of the town of Mesilla, and that he intended going after them." Costales hurriedly left the post in pursuit of the thieves, and according to Reid, "two days succeeding this the ferryman at the San Diego crossing came to the fort, and announced, that the second night preceding, he had left the ferry in charge of two Mexicans, and on returning the next day . . . had discovered a quantity of gore in his house, and also in a line thence to the river . . . whereupon, Lieutenant Stein [sic] and a body of soldiers, repaired to the spot where the body was supposed to have been thrown in the river, and soon drew therefrom the headless trunk of Costelles [sic]."[71]

The troops never found Ratón's body, but all logic suggests that he suffered a similar fate; indeed, nobody saw or heard from him again. Delgadito, the chief to whose band both men belonged, arrived at Fort Thorn shortly afterward. As so often happened, Steck had to be the bearer of the bad news. Despite the perpetration of these heinous acts, Delgadito remained dedicated to peaceful relations and assured Steck that he would attempt to prevent his followers from reciprocating.[72] Many officials, including Governor Meriwether, remained skeptical of the promise: "Although Delgadito and the head men of the Mimbres Indians said that no attempt would be made to avenge the death of Costales and his companion, I doubt the ability of the chiefs to restrain their people."[73]

The murders of these prominent Apaches could not have been more unfortunate. Both had been influential among their peers and consistently aided military and civil authorities in curbing depredations. Regardless of Delgadito's efforts, their murders became the impetus for numerous retaliatory attacks on the lower Rio Grande settlements. Costales, widely respected among both his fellow Apache companions as well as army officers, had been the one to approach Colonel Chandler during the attack on the Mimbres Apache camp earlier in 1856, convincing him to cease firing on the Indians. The death of this diplomat-of-sorts, a levelheaded man capable of easing tensions whenever they arose, came as a loss for both sides.

While the troops at Fort Thorn grappled with this incident, they faced additional problems emanating from the continuing failure of the War Department to provide adequate provisions. In January 1857 the commanding officer angrily wrote to headquarters reminding the quartermaster that the yearly subsistence stores and supplies for 1856 had not yet arrived. By army regulations each post was to receive an annual allotment of supplies, a requirement that the department quartermaster seldom met. Provisions remained scarce throughout the territory and had to be dispersed equally among all of the posts. Fort Thorn evidently had not received anything during 1856. With the soldiers there frequently in the field fighting Indians or otherwise stricken ill with malaria during the summers, these supplies were vital to the garrison's welfare. Besides a shortage of medicine to treat diseases, the post also suffered from a severe shortage of other items: "The companies have barely sufficient ammunition to perform guard service," Colonel Miles complained after being transferred there for a brief period in 1857.[74]

During his tenure as post commander, Miles not only dealt with supply issues but also found himself crossways with Major Crittenden, in command at Fort Craig to the north. Indeed, petty disputes between officers occurred frequently throughout the territory. In this instance the disagreement arose over the mail service. Crittenden claimed that military regulations did not require him to send the mail south to Fort Thorn. Rather, he insisted that Fort Thorn troops must ride to Fort Craig—a distance of almost seventy miles—and retrieve their own mail. Apparently, neither officer felt obliged to dispatch their own troops for such duties. With Apache raiders plaguing the entire southern half of the territory and many of the troops bedridden with illnesses, Miles and Crittenden should have had more important matters to address. Unable to resolve the issue between themselves, though, they eventually appealed to the assistant adjutant general in Santa Fe, requesting instructions on army regulations relative to transporting mail.[75] Such incidents reflect the continuing distractions undermining the military's implementation of effective Indian policy.

During the month of February 1857, Agent Steck noticed that the Gila Apaches began behaving strangely. They did not visit Fort Thorn to receive their usual allotment of rations, nor had they been in communication with the agency through their couriers. That month ten Gila Apaches attacked the small village of Los Amoles, twenty-five miles south of Fort Fillmore, driving off a herd of livestock and killing both of the Mexicans tending the animals. Twenty men of Company G, Regiment of Mounted Rifles left Fort Fillmore in pursuit, with Lieutenant Alfred Gibbs commanding. A heavy rainstorm soon obliterated the trail, however, and the column returned to the post.[76]

On February 20 the Apaches struck again, on this occasion targeting a ranch near Mesilla. Once again Lieutenant Gibbs rode from Fort Fillmore with a detachment of riflemen. This time the independent actions of residents from Mesilla hindered Gibbs in his pursuit. Several civilians had chased the Indians, overtaken them, but subsequently allowed them to escape. The lieutenant, believing the story to be merely a concoction of their imaginations, continued in pursuit. After a considerable distance Gibbs realized that the trail he followed was not that of the Indians but rather the Mesilla citizens who had been chasing the raiders. By the time he discovered his mistake, the Indians had escaped. The continued meddling of civilians in military affairs thus had kept the troops from engaging the Indians.

Lieutenant Gibbs would have another opportunity in early March, when he departed with sixteen mounted riflemen in response to yet another Gila Apache foray. In this instance the Indians drove off stock one mile south of Robledo belonging to General Land Office surveyor John W. Garretson, who rode a mule to nearby Fort Fillmore and alerted the garrison, whereupon the troops "were soon in pursuit of our red friends." A few miles from Cooke's Spring, northeast of modern-day Deming, the detachment overtook the Apaches, who numbered seven in all, four mounted and three on foot. The riflemen fired at them as they fled over a hill, wounding three in the process. In the ensuing chase the Indian chief, already wounded several times, turned and confronted his pursuers. The man, thought to be Itán, charged at Lieutenant Gibbs on his horse and "inflicted a severe wound in the abdomen" with his lance before being shot dead by another trooper. Upon later examination the troops discovered that ten musket balls had pierced the chief's body.[77]

Gibbs, severely wounded by Itán's lance, dismounted and offered his horse to Corporal Collins, whose own horse had been shot from under him. The immobilized officer remained lying on the ground while the remainder of his company continued the chase. Half an hour later the soldiers returned and reported that six of the seven Indians had been killed. The seventh warrior, wounded numerous times, had crawled behind a rock, where the soldiers had left him to die. Gibbs's comrades immediately sent a rider to Fort Fillmore to bring the post surgeon to treat the lieutenant's wounds. The doctor arrived the next morning and tended to the officer, who bore the unfortunate distinction of being the only soldier wounded in the affray.[78]

Not long afterward, Delgadito's band, which had remained on peaceful terms for an extended period of time, became implicated in an ambush occurring on March 28, 1857, in the Mimbres River valley. The report of the incident seems somewhat embellished by the commanding officer, who claimed that the attacking force consisted of over one hundred warriors. Delgadito led one of the smaller Gila Apache bands and likely could not have mustered such a large force. At any rate, Apaches ambushed twelve men of Company G, First Dragoons under the command of Sergeant Morris as the troops followed the trail of livestock stolen near Cow Springs. When the men returned fire on their assailants, one warrior was killed and another wounded. That these Indians in fact did belong to Delgadito's band seemed doubtful for several reasons, not the least of which being that his Apaches were believed to be in Mexico at the time. Regardless of the questionable identity of the attacking Indians, Delgadito and his followers became the primary suspects, victims of the military's continuing inability to distinguish between Apache bands.[79]

The post-1855 era had seen a pronounced shift in New Mexico Indian policy. Whereas previous officials, such as Governors Calhoun and Lane, had preferred negotiating treaties and feeding the Indians to discourage raiding, it became standard practice under Governor Meriwether to employ military action first. Years of continuous conflict resulted in numerous failed and forgotten treaties, the end result being a newfound hesitation among civil and military leaders to negotiate with the Apaches. By 1856 Governor Meriwether and General Garland agreed with one another that any peace negotiations must be preceded by strong military operations in order to force the Indians into submission.

In upcoming years this increased level of collaboration between the territory's leading officials would have a stronger effect in discouraging Apache raiding. Conversely, although civil and military personnel finally pursued similar policy objectives, they failed to take into account how their actions would affect the collective Apache tribe. As had been the case during previous administrations, both Garland and Meriwether generally neglected to distinguish between subgroups within the tribe. In addition, they failed to account for traditional Apache lifeways that encouraged raiding not necessarily as an act of warfare but as a form of economic and community subsistence, though one at variance with the capitalistic system to which these American officials were accustomed.

CHAPTER 8

"Campaign of Clowns"

The strategy of dispatching large-scale military campaigns into Apache country, one that both Governor Meriwether and General Garland espoused after 1856, manifested itself in a massive expedition that took the field midway through 1857. Provoked by the heinous murder of an Indian agent and continued depredations, the army prepared to display a level of force and manpower never before seen by the Apaches, one that would have a genuine psychological effect for years to come. The campaign mobilized almost 1,000 troops and involved the implementation of total warfare, victimizing women and children in peaceful bands, scorching the earth, destroying resources, and forcing a wholesale Apache retreat into northern Mexico.

In November 1856 a band of Mogollon Apaches roaming in the Zuñi Mountains of west-central New Mexico captured Henry L. Dodge, a respected Indian Bureau official who had served as the Navajos' agent since 1853. Dodge accompanied a scouting party out of Fort Defiance and had strayed from the main body of troops while hunting. When he failed to return to camp after several hours, the commanding officer, Captain Henry Lane Kendrick, initially thought nothing of it. After all, Kendrick conceded, Dodge was "a good woodsman.... [H]is absence from camp gave ... no other anxiety than the fear that he might suffer from the cold before finding us."[1] Despite the captain's faith in the agent's skills as an outdoorsman, he ordered his men to fire their rifles into the air, hoping that Dodge would hear the shots and instinctively return to camp. When the morning sun dawned and he remained absent, the soldiers began scouring the area looking for him. A Navajo guide accompanying the command succeeded in locating the site of Dodge's capture, but no other trace could be found.[2]

Kendrick assumed that the Navajos would not kill their own agent, as most members of that tribe respected and trusted Dodge. Governor Meriwether, therefore, wrote to Dr. Steck requesting that he inquire among the Apaches at his agency in hopes of obtaining information about his missing colleague. If successful in locating Dodge, the governor authorized Steck to pursue every means necessary to ensure his safe return. Department headquarters ventured so far as to condone the payment of $1,000 to ransom the captured agent, something rarely done except for important government officials.[3]

Steck dispatched several small Apache scouting parties from his Fort Thorn agency to search for Dodge. Almost immediately the preponderance of evidence pointed toward the Mogollon band as the guilty parties.[4] Steck received news from Mangas Coloradas that the Mogollon and Coyotero bands had declared war on the whites and had already attacked two wagon trains on the road to Fort Defiance in Navajo country. Events during the preceding year—continuous military campaigning, the establishment of Fort Buchanan, and a continuing influx of white settlers—had driven them to violence in defense of their families and communities. Writing to the adjutant general in January 1857, Colonel Bonneville acknowledged that "reports from Indians sent out to ascertain the fate of Agent Dodge leave no doubt that he was killed by the Mogollons."[5]

Mangas Coloradas later verified that the Mogollons in fact had taken Agent Dodge into captivity and were responsible for his death.[6] The underlying reason that he so readily divulged this information was probably that he feared blame might incorrectly fall to his own followers. The chief wisely kept Steck informed in order to prevent any hostile military actions from being directed toward his band. Indeed, his cooperation in the matter proved astounding; Mangas Coloradas ventured so far as to send his own brother to locate the Mogollon camp and ascertain the fate of the Indian agent. When his brother returned, he related to him the news that Dodge had, in fact, been slain, reportedly in retaliation for the death of an Apache earlier that month.[7]

On February 3, two months after Dodge went missing, Colonel Bonneville sent out a detachment with orders to locate his body, if possible, and return it to Fort Defiance for burial.[8] Surprisingly the command, led by 1st Lieutenant J. Howard Carlisle of the Second Artillery, succeeded in locating the remains, and on February 16, 1857, a solemn military funeral for the slain Henry L. Dodge took place at Fort Defiance.[9] The Mogollons scarcely could have foreseen the ensuing wrath that would be directed toward them and their fellow Apaches as a result of their rash actions. Dodge's wanton murder directly led to the largest military campaign that had ever marched into Apache country. "The depredations committed by the Mogollons are of too outrageous a character to be passed over," Bonneville fumed, "[and] they must be punished." The department commander immediately began making arrangements "to have in their country all the troops that can be spared from other portions of the territory" and expected to accompany them on an expedition that would remain in the field "until [it] shall have accomplished the objective proposed."[10] Equally infuriated with recent Mogollon hostilities, Major W. A. Nichols swore vengeance: "these Indians may be thoroughly chastised, and their band so broken up that they will not be heard from again as a distinct people."[11] The expedition, commanded by Colonel Bonneville himself, set out in April 1857.

Born in France in the late eighteenth century and a military man his entire adult life, Benjamin L. E. Bonneville was by all accounts an interesting character. Respected by some, mocked by others, and loathed by many under his command, he had passed his prime by the 1850s, and many believed him incapable of leading a

Colonel Benjamin Bonneville. Courtesy Fort Smith Museum of History, Fort Smith, Arkansas.

military campaign. A number of his fellow officers viewed his mannerisms as highly peculiar. One man acquainted with the colonel, Lieutenant William W. Averell, condescendingly described him as "a stout, robust old gentleman inclined to the ready conversation and bonhomie characteristics of his [French] race. Those who ever saw him still remember his colloquial habit of beginning every sentence with the phrase, 'I tell you sir.'"[12] Others who met Bonneville blatantly disliked the man, as evidenced in the many reports submitted to headquarters during the course of the Gila Campaign.

Bonneville's campaign consisted of three autonomous columns, all eventually converging at a predetermined site on the upper Gila River. The three-month campaign involved over 900 troops, nearly half of the total number stationed in the territory at that time. The operation would experience one folly after another due in large part to inadequate planning, poor leadership, and utter negligence on the part of the commanding officers. Bonneville commenced the preparations on February 23, 1857, by ordering that Company B, Third Infantry be detached from service at Fort Defiance and transferred to Albuquerque, where it joined Colonel William Wing Loring prior to marching toward the Gila River. The departure from Albuquerque, however, underwent multiple delays, and more than eight weeks passed before Loring's column finally took the field in mid-April, a full six months after Dodge's murder.

The campaign unofficially began on April 20, when Lieutenants Henry Lazelle and John Van Deusen DuBois left Fort Bliss with forty men of Company K, Regiment of Mounted Rifles and eighty troops from Companies B and I, Eighth Infantry. At Fort Thorn they would join the southern column, to be led by Colonel Miles. Lazelle and DuBois camped two miles above Fort Fillmore on the night of April 22 and arrived at Fort Thorn a week later. Lazelle found himself unimpressed with the condition of the post, observing that "most of the officers [were] in the sutler's store, a filthy hole, drinking or preparing to do so." He also observed, "the entertainments of our Fort Thorn acquaintances cannot compare favorably with the sumptuous hospitality and easy manners of some of our Fort Bliss friends. The former seems constrained, hurried, uneasy, and without style."[13] Fortunately for Lazelle, his stay there would be brief.

An ominous indication of future troubles came on the night of April 30, only hours before the expedition planned to leave Fort Thorn. In the early morning hours, under cover of darkness, the Apaches snuck close to the fort and stole sixty-eight mules from the post herd. Since supply wagons carrying four months' provisions had already left the fort ahead of the main column, the Apaches must have anticipated a major troop movement and decided to strike in order to catch the soldiers off guard. With more than three hundred men occupying the fort, "the mules were considered so safe that the herders had all gone to sleep."[14] Lazelle, who was busily making preparations for his men to march out of Fort Thorn the following morning, chided, "this is indeed a beautiful burlesque upon the dignity of our much talked of great expedition which has been fitted out at so great an expense and which is to freely bleed the plethoric treasury of government—originating in the bombastic folly of a silly old man [Bonneville] already in his dotage, and thus far conducted with a degree of stupidity almost asinine."[15] Clearly the junior officers were less than amused with the negligence of their commanders. This incident foreshadowed the hardships that the men would endure in the upcoming summer campaign.

At 7:30 A.M. on May 1, only a few hours after the Apaches stampeded the post herd, Colonel Miles left Fort Thorn with 269 troops en route for the Gila River valley. Of his command, 160 men belonged to Companies C and F, Third Infantry and Companies B and I, Eighth Infantry; the remainder, numbering 109 troops, belonged to Companies B, G, and K, Regiment of Mounted Rifles. Together these seven companies composed the "Southern Column of the Gila Expedition." Bonneville hired six guides and thirty-five Mexican teamsters to accompany the command, placing them under charge of Lieutenant McCooke.[16] A column of 310 men traveling single and double file across the barren southern New Mexico landscape must have presented a formidable sight, visible for miles in every direction.

On its march to the Gila River, the southern column traversed an unnecessarily long and circuitous route. Choosing to follow a winding Indian trail leading westward out of the Rio Grande valley, Colonel Miles led his men to Cooke's Spring on May 2, where Lieutenant Lazelle, already frustrated with his commanding officers, wrote that he "went to bed with a clear conscience, having cursed but thirty-six times today—[I] find that I am rapidly reforming."[17] Lieutenant Edson and his company left the camp ahead of the main column to scout the Florida Mountains for signs of Indians. The troops failed to encounter any recent evidence of Apaches and also sent back news that no water could be found anywhere in that vicinity. "The guide seems to be lost," quipped a frustrated Lieutenant DuBois in his journal. He "neither know[s] where water is to be found nor how to reach it by the shortest route when . . . [he] can find it."[18] Consequently, the column was forced to cross the Mexican border the following day, May 4, where they obtained water at a lake several miles to the south. In doing so, the troops thus violated treaty stipulations, but their brief incursion evidently went unobserved as nothing ever came of the incident.

Leaving Cooke's Spring on May 3, the main body of Miles's column pursued a more southwesterly course along the base of the Florida Mountains until arriving at Carrizalillo Springs, a reliable water source just north of the Mexican border and a favorite Apache campsite. The country through which the soldiers traveled these first few days failed to impress many of the men, it being a flat, parched desert infested with cacti and intersected only by the occasional deep arroyo. "[The] monotony is like what I imagine to be the thoughts of stupid men entombed forever in the infernal abode, but which is perfectly suitable for Mexican inhabitants, and accords well with their character," Lazelle sardonically recorded in his journal.[19] The troops located several abandoned Apache camps in the hills surrounding Carrizalillo Springs, all of which had been recently vacated. Because the direction of the Indian trail it had followed led directly into Mexico, the column could not pursue it any farther and instead began marching north to its intended destination on the Gila River.

Colonel Miles marched directly up the Janos–Santa Rita trail, which had existed since the establishment of the copper mines in 1803, until reaching Cow Springs, where the column pivoted to the northwest and skirted the eastern base of the Burro Mountains. This roundabout path resulted in the discovery of not a single Apache and more than doubled the distance the men would have traveled had they simply marched directly from Fort Thorn to the Gila River. Miles carefully noted in his report that, throughout the entirety of his trek, he had sent out scouting parties every evening before camping to ensure that no Apaches lurked in the vicinity. The colonel failed to realize that most of the Indians had gotten wind of the expedition well beforehand and had fled to Mexico prior to his departure from Fort Thorn.

Lieutenant DuBois confided his frustrations to his journal, complaining, "from Ft. Thorne [sic] to this place we have followed the trail and road, with no other object, apparently, than to find water and reach the depot by a very long road."[20] On May 7, more than a week into the march, Captain Claiborne's advance column reached a spring on the northwest slopes of the Burro Mountains and sent desperately needed water back to their comrades.[21] Despite his generosity and adherence to duty, Claiborne evidently did not count himself among the more gentlemanly officers. Lazelle in particular wrote critically of his crude personality: "Was somewhat amused, but thoroughly disgusted today, in listening to the ever running tongue of Capt. Claiborne whose vulgar personalities, and fulsome conversation render him, unless he is under restraint, or ladies more refined presence, an object to be loathed and shunned."[22]

The spectacle continued as the troops marched onward, each day becoming more aggravated by the fruitlessness of their journey. With summer fast approaching, the southern New Mexico sun exacted a toll on men and animals alike. "The days are clear and cloudless; the heat intense and the dust as suffocating and stifling as the ashes of a burning Vesuvius," complained Lazelle. "The great fatigue of the men consequent from the heat and sandy soil, required frequent halts."[23] Despite the heat of the day, nighttime temperatures dipped low enough to consistently freeze water to a depth of more than half an inch. One morning, as the mercury rapidly rose in the thermometer, the troops enjoyed a brief moment of excitement. "Our gallant and imaginative Colonel [Miles] was this morning highly excited, upon observing on a distant hill some moving objects which he insisted were Indians," the young lieutenant recorded. "It was indeed a cheering sound and for a few moments, raised our monotonous thoughts ... at least until the more rational, and keener sighted of our party, could pronounce our Indian friends to be a few straggling antelope."[24]

The advance column finally arrived at the Gila River on May 11 and established Camp Union on its western bank, "about a mile below the depot."[25] It would serve as the base of operations for Miles and his troops, including Lazelle, for the remainder of the campaign. The balance of the southern column, numbering eighty men, had been detached at the Burro Mountains, and their commander, Lieutenant Jackson, led them along the eastern slopes in search of Apaches. This portion of the command did not arrive at Camp Union until May 16, having encountered no Indians on its route.

The second column of troops, under Bonneville's direct command, established their permanent headquarters at a location that became known as the "Gila Depot," which served as the supply base for the entire three-month operation. Overlooking the Gila River, it sat opposite Camp Union, near the mouth of Greenwood Canyon. In correspondence with headquarters in Santa Fe, Bonneville described the site as being "upon a low bluff, about 100 yards from the east bank of the Rio Gila. The country is intersected by mountains in every direction. . . . [T]he depot, under the [supervision] of Major Simonson, R.M.R., is conducted to my perfect satisfaction."[26] Another officer described the depot being "situated upon a very level plateau of the broad prairie bluff; is contiguous to water, wood etc. with excellent grazing. . . . [T]he encampment is well arranged, and contains the usual large and commodious storehouses, the hospital, workshops and quarters for troops which are generally established."[27] With a copious supply of water and forage, the area Bonneville and Miles chose for their bases perfectly suited the campaign's purpose.

On May 1, the same day Colonel Miles departed Fort Thorn, a third column left Albuquerque under the command of one-armed William W. Loring, whose "erect soldierly figure of medium height . . . and imperial, easy courtesy and fine conversational ability . . . made an agreeable and lasting impression."[28] The colonel commanded three companies of riflemen and two companies of the Third Infantry, along with fifty Indians from the pueblos of Acoma and Laguna and sixteen New Mexicans from Cubero and Cebolleta to serve as guides.[29] Both Colonel Bonneville and Governor Meriwether initially directed Loring to employ Navajos as guides, but when attempts to recruit their services failed, the army hired Pueblos instead.[30] Like his colleague Dixon Miles, Loring also followed an indirect route to the rendezvous point on the Gila River. Marching west from Albuquerque, his column utilized a well-established wagon route passing by Cebolleta, Laguna, and Acoma before finally turning southward. Continuing down the Tularosa and San Francisco Rivers, the troops reached Bonneville's headquarters on May 18 after a two-week march. On May 20, while visiting the depot,

Lazelle recalled meeting "at the quarters of this distinguished warrior [Bonneville], Col. Loring and staff. Found them pleasant and agreeable gentlemen."[31] Loring would be among the few officers that Lazelle and his friend DuBois praised during the expedition.

Captain Ewell, a bald-headed and battle-hardened military veteran of the Mexican-American War, commanded the final contingent, en route from Fort Buchanan and comprising approximately 120 men. The column was originally slated to be led by Major Steen, the commanding officer at Fort Buchanan, but he became too ill to make the journey, and Ewell commanded in his stead.[32] Several weeks would pass before Ewell set out and reached the camps along the Gila River.

Not long after the troops began assembling, the few Apaches lingering in the vicinity began committing nightly raids on their camps. Mistakenly believing that these troublesome Indians were camping in a canyon some twenty miles away, Bonneville sent out a detachment of fifty men under Captain Claiborne, whose Pueblo guides assured him that he would find a large encampment there and that a skirmish would doubtless ensue, "all of which but few believe, the general character of our guides being too well known to warrant much faith in their statements."[33]

In response to raids on the depot, Bonneville immediately began sending scouting parties into the surrounding mountains, often for periods exceeding a week at a time. In mid-May Lieutenant Jackson marched south toward the Burro Mountains with a detachment of Company I, Eighth Infantry but encountered no signs of Apache activity. He did, however, experience the harsh terrain in which his troops would be operating for the duration of the campaign. The mounted men had particular difficulty traversing it due to the dense brush and overgrowth, deep ravines, and "rugged nature of the country."[34]

Unknown to Bonneville and his fellow officers, most of the Apaches had abandoned their homes in southwestern New Mexico the moment they realized the soldiers were coming. Scouting parties observed the troops days before they reached the Gila River, whereupon most Indians fled into Mexico. The men realized that with each passing day more Apaches removed to safer regions. "None of us expect to see Indians unless they wish to be seen," proclaimed one of the more realistic officers.[35] The only Apaches remaining behind were a few small subgroups living peaceably along the Mimbres River and several Coyotero bands in southeastern Arizona.[36] Because they remained on amiable terms with Americans, these Indians falsely assumed that they would not be molested by the troops. Ultimately, after weeks of failed attempts to find the Mogollon Apaches responsible for Dodge's murder, the soldiers resorted to attacking other bands instead.

In the process of making their hasty escape into Mexico, the Apaches employed a scorched-earth strategy, utilizing it to their utmost advantage against the army. While en route to the Gila Depot, Colonel Miles and his column observed that the San Vincente Mountains had been set ablaze. "The fires had unquestionably been lighted by the Indians, and seemed a part of their admirable tactics," Lazelle wrote, noting that "as soon as it became dark, I had spread before me one of the grandest sights of the Earth: for a space of at least one hundred miles in diameter, and whose limit was burning mountains, was one gorgeous arena of leaping flames."[37] By May 17 the fires had crept dangerously close to the camps. "The mountain fires approach us rapidly," DuBois recorded, "it is strange how large a fire this short grass makes. One day more may bring it upon us unless the wind should change."[38] Fortunately for the troops, the blaze never reached their camps, otherwise they would have had to remove to a different location. The Apaches started the fires for at least three reasons, all ingenious from a tactical standpoint. The billowing smoke alerted neighboring Indians of the soldiers in the vicinity; the flames destroyed all of the grass, leaving no forage for the troops' horses; and the burned ground masked the Apaches' retreat routes, making it impossible for the soldiers to pursue them.

The end of May fast approached, and the troops, who had been in the field for nearly one month, could boast of little success. Lazelle lamented that the entire command had "neither seen an Indian, nor heard of one having been seen, by any one, since starting [from Fort Thorn]: with the exception of one whom our valiant commander—Col. Bonneville—thinks he saw, from the window of his ambulance, while he was coming out here from Fort Thorn."[39] According to Lazelle, this incident did not benefit the already overly exasperated condition of his aged commander. "Our friend Col. Bonneville is greatly disgusted, and labouring under considerable excitement," the lieutenant fretted, "[and] says that he does not care a damn, whether the Indians burn down the Depot or not! And I am sorry to say, that he is far from being alone in his opinions, so long as he has command . . . so universal is the dislike for him."[40] Within a few days, however, the first contact with Apaches would be made, though Lazelle himself would not be present at the engagement.

Not surprisingly, it was a nonhostile band of Apaches who became the first victims of the campaign. During the final week of May, Bonneville ordered Colonels Miles and Loring to march in two separate columns eastward toward the Mimbres River, where a group of Gila Apaches had purportedly encamped with several hundred stolen sheep. The order, according to one officer, "is, I presume, the offspring of some brilliant reverie, of that acute, gray-headed child, 'Bonne.' . . . [T]hese sheep were stolen about six weeks ago, and the 'trail' which our column of three hundred and fifty men (!!!) are ordered to search for is reported by the guides to be two weeks old!!" Nevertheless, the expedition went ahead as planned with "nearly eight hundred men—to do the work of fifty." Lazelle's journal reveals, in no uncertain terms, the lieutenant's utter astonishment with his commanding officer: "[Bonneville] has caught at the straws of circumstances, floating upon the surface of events, to redeem a flagging reputation, ignominiously won in Mexico; or a notoriety, unenviable, which he obtained in an endeavor at personal aggrandizement, when sent to fight the battles of his country, among the Indians of the western frontier, years ago. . . . [T]hus a head in its dotage, may be a fatal clog to a great enterprise."[41]

Colonel Loring and his riflemen were the first to encounter evidence of Indians, following a trail despite the fact that the Apaches had burned the grass behind them. The route traversed "immense mountains . . . the difficulty of surmounting them was extremely painful to man and horse, many of [the] strongest animals sinking under the intense labor.... [I]t was so difficult in its ascent that many of [the] strongest mules fell backwards with their packs."[42] Loring almost certainly referred to the southern ranges of the Mogollon Mountains, the most precipitous in the vicinity. Passing over this rough terrain, his riflemen located a fresh Indian trail on the morning of May 24, and the colonel immediately ordered his mounted men to be outfitted with three days' rations and dispatched them in pursuit. Later that afternoon they discovered the Indians encamped in a deep canyon, whereupon Loring divided his command and commenced a two-pronged assault on the camp.

The attack caught the Apaches completely by surprise. They no doubt knew of the army's presence on the Gila River but must have thought themselves to be safe because they had not been associated with the hostile Mogollons. This presumption of immunity cost the Apaches dearly. When the smoke cleared, their chief, Cuchillo Negro, lay dead on the field along with five warriors and one woman. Two more Indians were badly injured in the melee, and the troops captured nine women and children, bringing the total Apache casualties to eighteen. The survivors fled in such haste that they abandoned all of their property, including some 1,000 sheep.[43] As the Indians frantically dispersed, Loring's riflemen chased them for as long as possible. Darkness finally inhibited further pursuit, but by that time the men had already covered twenty-six miles through rough mountainous terrain. The trail had been an unusually easy one to follow, owing to the hundreds of stray sheep being abandoned by the Indians along the way. The Apaches discarded every excess item they possessed in order to relieve their horses of weight, allowing them to escape from Loring's riflemen but despoiling themselves of nearly all their possessions.

With the exception of this single camp, Loring had not encountered any evidence of other Indians during his campaign. The colonel correctly surmised that most of them had fled either to the Chiricahua Mountains of southeastern Arizona or to "a little town in Mexico called Janos."[44] Indeed, a report from Agent Steck at Fort Thorn indicated that many of the Apaches had, in fact, gone to Janos while the troops occupied the Gila Depot, some of them at the advice of Steck himself. Ironically, fleeing to Mexico did not save the Indians from disaster. While at Janos, the Mexicans gave them poisoned rations, killing scores of women and children and invoking an animosity among the Indians that never fully dissipated.[45] The Apaches literally had nowhere to run—both the Mexicans and the Americans sought to attack them, through any treacherous means possible. Department headquarters had made certain to notify Mexican officials in both Chihuahua and Sonora in April that the expedition would soon commence, perhaps hoping that authorities there might dispatch troops into the northern reaches of those provinces, thereby making a wholesale Apache escape into Mexico impossible.[46]

Colonel Bonneville was elated when he received news of the attack on the Indian camp. "Colonel Loring has inflicted a blow upon this Mimbres band of Apaches," he gleamed, "which must have a salutary effect upon all others, by convincing them that however secret their hiding place or difficult of access, they can be reached."[47] It apparently did not occur to Bonneville (or if it did, he did not express it) that the Apaches Loring killed were not supposed to be targeted. Although they possessed several hundred stolen sheep, providing partial justification for the assault, Cuchillo Negro and his followers had no involvement with the capture and murder of Agent Dodge. Unfortunately, Bonneville operated upon the same ideology common to many military officers of his day, that one Apache was the same as another. This would not be the only time the colonel and his subordinate officers failed to distinguish between Apache subgroups during the Gila Campaign.

The attack on the Mimbres River camp particularly dismayed Steck, who forewarned many of the passive Indians receiving rations at his agency and advised them to maintain their distance from the Gila River and Mogollon Mountains. If they harbored members of the Mogollon band, the military would consider them enemies merely by association. Steck therefore recommended that they remain encamped either at his Fort Thorn agency or along the Mimbres River in order to ensure their safety, and he urged officers on campaign to exercise caution before attacking any Indians in that vicinity. Cuchillo Negro's band followed Steck's advice, yet the troops still attacked them. Unfortunately for the agent, incidents such as this, though no fault of his own, undermined his hard-earned credibility among the Apaches.

While Colonel Loring busied himself with the Mimbres Apaches, Colonel Miles traversed a different course, one that led him southward from Camp Union to Santa Lucia Springs. Finding no signs of recent activity in that area, Miles continued to San Vincente Spring and then in a southeasterly direction toward the old copper mines at Santa Rita del Cobre, where he arrived on May 24 and found that much of the grass and forage there had already been burned. In the distance could be seen the rising smoke that had become a telltale sign of the Indians' departure from an area. "The whole country is burning or has been burnt," wrote a frustrated Colonel Miles to Bonneville.[48] Upon reaching the Mimbres Valley, the troops were dismayed to discover that much of that region had also been charred by fire.

Colonel Miles's column traveled over a difficult route, causing considerable suffering for soldiers and animals alike. "In following the sinuous, serpentine course," Lazelle wrote, "we frequently ascended and descended the sides of mountains by steep, zig-zag paths, so narrow, and upon such treacherous soil that it seemed but bravado, to follow them. . . . Many of the mules' backs are almost literally skinned, and in some places stripped of their flesh, while others have immense bleeding bruises and raw places upon their sides, three, four, and five inches in diameter. But few of them are sound, and able to go on."[49] On May 25 Colonel Loring's Pueblo guides encountered an advance party from Miles's detachment, led by Lieutenant DuBois of Company K, Mounted Rifles. Thinking the guides to be hostile Apaches, DuBois charged to within 300 yards before recognizing them as the allied Pueblo Indian guides.[50] Upon learning from them of the attack on Cuchillo Negro's camp the previous day, Miles realized that he likely would not encounter any Indians in that vicinity and opted instead to march northward into the Mogollon Mountains.

After returning to Camp Union, Miles admitted the folly in marching his men through the Mogollons, calling it "the most fatiguing march I ever experienced, and at the greatest risk for troops—a dozen Indians on many of the high peaks we were traveling up in a zig-zag manner, could with stones have defeated any body of troops."[51] The men had not discovered a single Indian during the march, and after several days, one participant reported, "remarks prejudicial not only to the capabilities of our Colonel [Miles] but even of his courage are heard everywhere."[52] At this point one officer affectionately dubbed the expedition "The Campaign of Clowns."[53] It is not improbable that every enlisted man and many of the officers involved in the campaign, excepting perhaps Bonneville and Miles, concurred with this slogan.

Colonel Loring returned to the Gila Depot on May 31 (a day after Colonel Miles), toting 400 confiscated sheep and nine Apache prisoners taken during his attack on Cuchillo Negro's camp. Afterward both Loring and Miles remained in camp to rest their men and horses until June 10, at which time the entire garrison, more than 800 men total, planned to probe westward into Coyotero Apache country. Interestingly, the straightforward Lieutenant Lazelle cited a different reason for this lengthy layover at the depot: "By a most culpable but characteristic oversight, Col. Bonneville has neglected to place at the Depot, or, to make any provision for having them placed here, either pack mules for transportation, or horses, for the cavalry.... [T]he various companies of cavalry, have become crippled, and almost useless (except as infantry) by having lost and injured, by long marches, many of their horses. In one company alone, of Col. Loring's Column, no less than six gave out, and were obliged to be shot, in a single day's march, while the troops were in the mountains."[54]

While the troops rested in camp, news arrived from Fort Thorn that Mangas Coloradas had come into the agency and sued for peace. "All this," wrote Lazelle, "is certainly well calculated to discourage, dishearten, and to destroy the ambition of a feeble minded old man, who has staked his present, and his hope for a future reputation upon the success of this Expedition."[55] Despite this information Bonneville remained undaunted, seemingly oblivious to the previous months' shortcomings.

On May 25, with Miles and Loring still in the field harassing the Mimbres Apaches, Lieutenant McCook of the Mounted Rifles departed the depot for the Burro Mountains. Not surprisingly, he returned shortly thereafter without having encountered any signs of Indians. Remarkably, two consecutive fruitless marches (the first under Lieutenant Jackson, the second under McCook) did not convince an obdurate Colonel Bonneville that the Indians had abandoned the Burro Mountains, so he ordered a third campaign in June. This time Lieutenant O'Bannon and his company of the Third Infantry entered the mountains from the north, "proceeding by slow and cautious marches" until reaching the range's southern extremity. From that point, O'Bannon proceeded in a westerly direction until striking the Gila River about forty miles southwest of the depot, where he met Captain Ewell's force from Fort Buchanan. Choosing not to return immediately to Camp Union, O'Bannon instead marched once more through the Burro Mountains. In his final report he stressed, "I have no hesitancy in stating that there are *no Indians* in, or in the vicinity of, the Burro Mountains."[56] It thus took three failed campaigns through that region to convince the senior officers that the Indians had indeed fled elsewhere.

Lieutenant William Dennison of the Third Infantry spent more than three weeks scouting in the Mogollon Mountains but met with much the same results as had Colonel Miles back in May. Much like the situation in the Burro Mountains, senior officers failed to acknowledge that the Indians had abandoned the Mogollon range. No sooner had Dennison returned to the depot than Lieutenants Whipple and Steen marched back into the Mogollons. The two officers left Camp Union on May 23 with Companies C and K, Third Infantry, numbering seventy-six men in all. They were fortunate enough to experience some excitement during their march, although it had nothing to do with the Apaches. According to Whipple's report, one of the enlisted men "very imprudently" shot at and wounded a bear. The shot, however, failed to kill the animal, which instinctively chased the man down the hillside. "It was only by throwing away his musket and running as only a man can do under similar circumstances that he managed to save himself," Whipple recounted.[57] While the officers were not amused by the situation, it no doubt provided a humorous spectacle for the remainder of the men.

Whipple's column experienced further disappointment when they followed the trail of about fifteen Indians that eventually proved to be that of the Pueblo scouts accompanying Colonel Loring. On their return route to the depot, Whipple discovered another Indian trail left by "six or seven" Apaches. On June 2 the soldiers located the Indians' abandoned camp, whose occupants apparently had seen the oncoming soldiers and "[barely] escaped.... [T]hey had dropped everything but their arms and fled for their lives." Their flight had been in extreme haste as evidenced by the fact that they left behind 237 sheep and other belongings.[58]

By the beginning of June, supplies had become scarce at the Gila Depot. With almost 900 men constantly out on strenuous marches, rations and provisions were being consumed at an alarming rate. On June 9 Lieutenant O'Bannon wrote to Fort Thorn requesting that additional supplies be sent as soon as possible. Lieutenant Baker, in temporary command at the fort, replied that he could not fulfill the request: not only did Baker lack surplus provisions at his post, but he scarcely had enough to maintain his own troops there.[59] Despite these shortages, Bonneville and his colleagues continued planning a major expedition into the Coyotero Apache country of present-day southeastern Arizona. The campaign, consisting of every available soldier at the depot, departed on June 13 after finally receiving fresh horses and pack mules for the march; it was the only scout that Colonel Bonneville actually participated in himself.

The combined commands of Bonneville, Miles, and Ewell marched southwest along the Gila River into a region that appeared on maps as "unexplored." Steck had previously informed Bonneville that a large Apache camp might be in that area, intelligence that ultimately proved correct. The campaign thoroughly excited the old commander as it was his first journey away from the depot: "Colonel Bonneville is in a perfect 'tremble of anxiety.' A little smoke frightens him to death and then to hear him explain all his reasons to the cooks, in his 2nd childhood's prattle, is certainly less ludicrous than pathetic."[60]

After his guides discovered an Apache camp nearby, Bonneville divided the column, placing himself and Colonel Miles in command of the rear contingent and Captain Ewell at the helm of the advance guard, consisting of Companies B, G, and K, First Dragoons and Companies C and F, Third Infantry. Miles commanded Companies B and K, Mounted Rifles and Companies B and I, Eighth Infantry. Because they divided their forces and pursued circuitous routes to the Apache camp, the two columns moved more slowly than they might have had they continued on a direct course. Cautiously feeling their way forward, they averaged a mere ten miles per day, considerably less than the daily distance traveled on other campaigns. In a letter to his mother, Ewell lamented the situation at hand and confided: "I am very tired of chasing a parcel of Indians about at orders of men who don't know what to do or how to do it if they knew what they wanted. . . . As we are now starting in a 'solumn' (solid column) of 600 men, we will NOT be apt to see Indians, and mules and horses will be the only sufferers."[61]

On June 27 the most significant episode of the entire Gila Campaign occurred when the troops attacked a Coyotero Apache village along the Gila River near Mount Turnbull. Much like the Mimbres Apaches that Loring attacked in May, the Coyoteros were entirely unsuspecting.[62] Prior to the attack, Ewell captured nine Apache women, who informed him of the precise location of the camp. This intelligence, coupled with his position several miles in advance of Miles and Bonneville, enabled the captain and his troops to arrive first. He ordered his men to charge the camp, despite the fact that Colonel Miles's command remained some two miles behind. Miles and his column proceeded rapidly after hearing the first shots, which occurred around one o'clock in the afternoon. Lieutenant DuBois and Captain Claiborne, with their respective companies, proceeded at full gallop and "passed both our Colonels [Bonneville and Miles], leaving them in rear." DuBois pithily recalled: "Col. Miles had dropped his sabre and stopped to pick it up. As I passed him at a run he said, 'They are fighting like hell just before you.' The remark came to my lips, 'Why are you not there then?'"[63]

The camp was situated in a narrow part of the valley covered by a "thick undergrowth.... [P]ersons within could readily see those outside, but could not be seen within; this gave the enemy a great advantage and it is a miracle how so few of [the] officers and men, exposed as they were, escaped."[64] The Apaches used their surroundings to their advantage, hiding in the bushes to conceal themselves. As a result many of the soldiers fired randomly, with no intended target. This confusing aspect of the battle almost caused a catastrophe for the troops. As DuBois and his company approached, they drove the fleeing Apaches back toward Ewell's men, catching the Indians in a crossfire and forcing them to take cover in the shrubbery along the river. Lieutenants Steen and DuBois, both stationed on the opposite bank across from Miles and Ewell, likewise began firing into the undergrowth. At this juncture one of the officers (probably either Ewell or Miles) ordered a volley to be fired into the bushes. The gunfire was aimed directly at Lieutenant Steen's troops, with many of the rounds landing in their immediate vicinity. "Balls and buckshot now whistled so thick around us that I withdrew my men," DuBois wrote. "We were hidden by the willows and it was unpleasant being shot at by one's friends.... I rallied, and crossing [the river] found Steen and his command under a bank trying also to avoid the shots of the troops on the banks."[65] Precariously trapped in the crossfire, Steen's company had narrowly averted being shot by their own comrades.

As the fight continued, the infantry dealt the finishing blow. One company of riflemen, commanded by DuBois, "got another volley at [the] Indian enemies and the Infantry closed on them from the opposite side [of the river] and they were all killed. It was a perfect stampede."[66] Although the battle lasted less than an hour, it had been intense, contrary to the final misleading statistics that suggest it to have been a relatively effortless victory for the troops. No better example of the desperation and intensity of the fighting can be found than when DuBois removed his hat after the battle and discovered a bullet hole through the top of it.

The troops immediately went into camp near the battlefield, whereupon "all the whiskey was emptied to our success. The pueblo [guides] had a war dance and not before 2 o'clock was our camp quiet."[67] The following day, with the smell of blood fresh in the air, the soldiers scoured the battlefield and found twenty dead warriors and four dead women; they took another twenty-six women and children into custody as prisoners of war. "It was a sad sight," recalled one officer. "I could not avoid asking myself why we had killed these poor harmless savages. It is not pretended that they ever did any harm to us, never coming to the Rio Grande, and robbing only from the Mexicans of Sonora."[68] The battle resulted in an almost total loss for the Coyotero band. Those taken captive informed the officers, through interpreters, that the camp had only consisted of about forty warriors; they thought that only two or three of them might have escaped unscathed. These firsthand reports led Colonel Miles to believe that thirty-seven Indians had been killed in the fighting, although he acknowledged that only twenty-four bodies had actually been recovered. The remainder, he assumed, lay dead in the thick underbrush.[69]

DuBois recorded a disturbing event that never appeared in the official reports. After the fighting subsided, "one fine looking Indian brave was captured and by Col. Bonneville's desire, or express command, was taken out with his hands tied and shot like a dog by a Pueblo Indian—not thirty yards from our camp. Humanity, honor, a soldier's pride, every feeling of good in me was and is shocked by this one act."[70] With this execution, the death toll stood at twenty-five, making this battle the bloodiest confrontation that had yet occurred between U.S. troops and Apache Indians in southern New Mexico.

On the American side only eight persons sustained injuries: two officers and six enlisted men. Lieutenant Steen, whose command was accidentally fired upon by their comrades, received an arrow wound near his eye. All eight casualties suffered arrow wounds, with the sole exception of a Pueblo scout who had been shot three times by troops who apparently had difficulty distinguishing between their guide and the Apaches they were fighting. The fact that no soldiers received gunshot wounds suggests that the Coyoteros had few if any firearms. This single aspect of the skirmish gave a decisive advantage to the Americans, who otherwise would have found themselves in a precarious situation because they held unfortified, open positions during the battle and would have made easy targets for musketry.

While these Coyoteros had not been directly responsible for the killing of Agent Dodge, they apparently did harbor the Mogollon warrior believed to be responsible for the murder. Government officials had ascertained the identity of the guilty Indian; probably, Mangas Coloradas reported his name to Steck during their meetings at Fort Thorn. Among those who lay dead on the battlefield was this very Indian, a fact that Steck later confirmed through several reports from Apaches, indicating that the guilty man in fact had died during the battle.[71] In a strange sense, the campaign might therefore be perceived as a partial success, although it came at the expense of over two dozen innocent Coyoteros who lost their lives in the fighting.

Afterward Captain Claiborne of the Mounted Rifles marched down the Gila River and destroyed all of the Apache cornfields pursuant to Bonneville's orders. The captives taken during the attack would eventually be interred at Forts Thorn and Fillmore until September, at which time the department transferred them to Steck's agency to await orders from higher authority as to their ultimate disposition.[72] The Coyoteros had suffered a tremendous blow, one from which they would struggle to recover. "The chastisement they have received," gleamed General Garland a month later, "will be long remembered by them. The effect . . . will doubtless prove most salutary."[73]

The final report of this incident from Colonel Miles to Colonel Bonneville seems to justify much of the earlier criticism these two men received from their subordinate officers. "I desire to express my sincere thanks to you [Bonneville]," Miles wrote, "who accompanied my column, for many important suggestions and invaluable advice in camping, marching, and guarding my camps, which relieved me from the very many anxieties and perplexities every commander must experience who has not with him an advisor."[74] Clearly, Miles was guilty of ingratiating himself with his commander, and it seems that the officers concerned themselves more with feting one another than with the well-being of their troops. On their return to the Gila Depot, Captain Ewell went in the advance "while our Colonels [Bonneville and Miles] remain safely in rear protected by more than one hundred fighting men."[75]

While returning to the depot, the troops marched in separate columns, each one traversing an alternate course. Several days after the battle, a Coyotero Apache approached Bonneville's column carrying a white flag and requested a prisoner exchange. "He was a noble specimen of humanity, tall, and formed like an Apollo," one officer noted. "He was perfectly naked except a piece of cloth about his loins and a handkerchief of red silk twisted around his head. In his hand he carried his white flag—a piece of cotton three inches square on a short twig."[76] Bonneville did hold several prisoners from the battle, and the bold Apache proposed an even swap for captives the Indians had taken in Mexico some months earlier. The colonel, refusing to cater to such demands, informed the courier that no such transaction would be executed without the presence of the Coyotero chiefs.

It was now July 1, and the troops went into camp awaiting the Apaches' next action. Bonneville flew a white flag in front of his tent all day as Indians appeared in the hills surrounding the camp but did not come in. Here again, DuBois relates an incident indicative of the commanding officer's character:

> Col. Bonneville made me a proposition today that has lowered him still more in my estimation and will probably force me to insult him so that I must jeopardize my commission.... He called me to him and after expressing his satisfaction at my conduct said he had a delicate and dangerous duty for me. He waited a moment and I accepted, thinking it was to go with a small party among the Indians,

or some similar object. But never was I so astonished and dumbfounded as when he said, 'I expect all the big chiefs to meet me in council tomorrow. I wish you to carry concealed arms inside your hunting shirt and bring two of your men around in the same way and when I give the words, seize and tie the chiefs whom I have pointed out to you.' The damned old scoundrel—after the cold-blooded murder of the Indian captive after the fight I might have expected it from him.... I will tell Col. Miles tonight that I will not obey the order and tomorrow in full council will tell his officers of his proposition.[77]

Not long afterward a group of several Apaches appeared on a distant hill, but before any exchange of prisoners or council between the chiefs and officers took place, another approaching column spooked the Indians and caused them to flee. Colonel Loring had been leading a scout along the Tularosa River while the battle on the Gila took place and remained completely unaware of the circumstances. It is questionable whether or not he even realized that Miles and Bonneville had camped in the vicinity. When Loring spotted the Apaches on the hillside, he ordered his riflemen to charge their positions, causing the Indians to disperse. According to Loring, he had been trailing these Indians for over a week, making nighttime marches to avoid being seen. Therefore the Apaches might have been unaware of his presence at the time of the charge. Ironically, Loring's report directly contradicted that of Bonneville, with each officer blaming the other for scaring the Indians away. Loring claimed that his attack would have been successful had it not been for Bonneville's presence, which caused them to flee. Conversely, Bonneville reported that his negotiations would have been successful had Loring not arrived at an inopportune moment.[78]

For Colonel Loring, this proved to be the last service he and his men would see during the Gila Campaign. In mid-July, after returning to the depot, department headquarters reassigned his company to Fort Defiance in the Navajo country. Considering the numerous ill-fated and poorly planned expeditions with which his troops had been involved during the preceding three months, Loring must have been pleased to receive the transfer. Shortly thereafter several other companies serving under Bonneville also received orders to relocate to Fort Defiance.[79] The reassignment of Colonel Loring's riflemen was thus the beginning of the disbandment of the 1857 Gila Campaign.

While Loring prepared his men for the march to Fort Defiance, the remainder of the forces under Colonel Miles and Captain Ewell returned to their headquarters at Camp Union and the Gila Depot. The Coyotero campaign had taken a heavy toll on the troops. Most of the infantrymen returned barefoot, and many of the mounted riflemen, who stayed behind at a grazing camp some four miles from the depot, had not fared much better. The men's suffering did not go unnoticed among the officers, particularly Colonel Miles. "During the march on the Gila," he admitted, "the [troops] resorted to every expedient to protect their feet, making cowhide sandals and moccasins, and some marched barefoot, this without a murmur of complaint." The mules and horses were entirely broken down and beyond hope of recovery, "having sores on their backs and on the sides, some reaching to the bones."[80] Such conditions epitomized the extreme difficulty of operating in Apacheland: it had become obvious that campaigns of this nature could not continue for much longer without taking a heavy toll on the soldiers' health and livelihood.

The expedition's mission had been bluntly stated at the beginning: the army sought to punish the hostile Mogollon Apaches for the death of Indian Agent Dodge. In this they only partially succeeded. Although Dodge's murderer reportedly died during the battle with the Coyoteros (assuming the reports were even true), he was the only Mogollon Apache affected by the campaign. This single fact forces one to question whether the Apaches might have falsified their report of his death in hopes that the military would terminate their operation. The remainder of the Mogollon band, which had been responsible for many of the recent depredations along the Rio Grande, successfully avoided the troops. Not once during the entire campaign did the soldiers encounter any signs of the Mogollons, and the only Indians punished belonged to Gila and Coyotero bands that should have been left unharmed.

Ironically, the troops suffered more than many of the Apaches. They endured long marches across countless miles of rough mountains with inadequate supplies and rations, the triple-digit summer heat all the while bearing down on them. Bonneville's command of nearly nine hundred men proved far more than necessary to carry out the campaign's objectives. The only useful purpose that the large body of troops served was as a show of force. That so many men could be mustered and placed in the midst of their families and homelands caused great concern among the Apaches. Some of them, including Mangas Coloradas, must have realized at that point that the troops would always outnumber them and any resistance would be futile.

The Gila Campaign ended almost as quickly as it began. In reading the dozens of reports from Bonneville, Miles, Ewell, and Loring, one arrives at the conclusion that everything went as planned. In almost every communication, optimism and praise gleamed from their every word. Then suddenly and without much explanation, Bonneville decided to abandon the endeavor altogether. Several minor factors, when considered as a whole, probably brought about this abrupt termination.

During the last week of July 1857, the Coyoteros attacked an immigrant wagon train on the California road near the Chiricahua Mountains. This, coupled with an incident in which Mexican troops crossed the border south of Tucson and attacked a small party of civilians on American soil (see chapter 7), necessitated a strengthening of the garrison at Fort Buchanan. At least one officer, Lieutenant DuBois, reasoned that this might have been why Ewell and his troops hastily returned to their post. Another factor was the resumption of departmental command by Brigadier General Garland, who had been absent on leave for several months, during which time Colonel Bonneville had been acting department commander. Although Garland initially praised Bonneville's efforts, higher command soon began pressuring the colonel to cease his pointless gallivanting along the Gila and return the troops back to their respective posts.[81] Perhaps most importantly, Bonneville had only taken with him to the Gila Depot four months' provisions, which were consumed after less than three months in the field. Owing to scarcity of subsistence stores in Santa Fe, the adjutant general was unable to dispatch additional supplies to the expedition.[82]

All of these occurrences, taking place nearly simultaneously, coalesced in the almost immediate abandonment of the Gila Campaign. On July 12, only a few days after returning from the expedition against the Coyotero Apaches, Bonneville wrote to Major Nichols at headquarters in Santa Fe: "I see now no necessity for the continuance of this depot; the scouting still to be performed may more easily be done from Fort Thorn.... [T]he keeping up of this depot now unnecessarily occupies a body of men, that might otherwise be profitably employed [elsewhere].... I would therefore respectfully recommend its discontinuance, and that the remaining stores be taken to Fort Thorn, from which place Colonel Miles can give the scouting his constant attention."[83]

As the campaign drew to its uneventful close, the two senior colonels remained steadfast in their claims of triumph. "Bonneville and Miles are bragging wonderfully of their exploits," DuBois mused as he returned to Fort Thorn. "One would imagine that they actually proposed and executed the plans which were followed by our massacre [of the Coyotero Apaches], when both remained in rear and notoriously disapproved of Capt. Ewell pushing on.... [W]ell, as they write the reports, everybody will believe that it was so and Ewell will receive no credit for his doing everything. Col. Miles should report of the Gila fight that he 'dropped his sword and while stopping to pick it up the battle was fought.' ... [W]hat a degradation I feel it to be under the command of such imbecility."[84]

The results of Bonneville's expedition failed to impress Superintendent of Indian Affairs James L. Collins, who firmly believed that much more harm than good had come from it. "I am at a loss what to say with regard to the Mogoyon [sic] and Gila Apaches," he summarized in his 1857 annual report. "An expedition, under the command of Colonel Bonneville, has been in the field against those

Indians since May last, and no reliable information can be obtained in reference to them until the report of Colonel Bonneville is received." Collins believed that the attack on the Coyotero Apaches had been a grave mistake, predicting that trouble would inevitably result. "I cannot but regard it as unfortunate that the forces under Colonel Bonneville invaded the country of the Coyotero Apaches," he excoriated. "The attack upon them will doubtless cause them to retaliate upon the Mexican settlements, and may have the effect to add another formidable tribe to the number of those now depredating upon our frontier. Up to the time of this attack it is believed the Coyoteros had not visited our settlements, and were not among the tribes who were committing robberies upon our people."[85] Indeed, the Coyotero Apaches had had little if any contact with the Americans up until that point, and Collins's fear that the attack would have detrimental consequences ultimately proved correct.

Lieutenants Lazelle and DuBois left behind witty assessments of the campaign in their journals. Lazelle, a well-educated man with a talent for expressing his thoughts through the written word, summarized the entire ordeal: "In a campaign of this nature . . . there are three important points to be gained, and which must never be lost sight of, for one instant. . . . Dispatch in organization and arrangements—secrecy—and celerity of movement." In regards to secrecy, Bonneville issued a proclamation months in advance, plainly outlining his plans for the entire expedition. "It [the expedition] became notorious, was the common talk of the common people. . . . The various tribes of Indians against whom it stated the expedition was to be directed, were perfectly informed of it."[86] Concerning celerity of movement, the campaign included far too many troops, more than could possibly be equipped and mounted. Lazelle concluded with a quantification of the Gila Campaign:

> Indeed, it seems that investigations of this problem [the Gila Campaign], as far as developed, may thus be stated:
> Let F = the Force = \$500,000.00 and 800 men
> Let P = the Path passed over by the point of application of the force = 1200 miles

Let Q = the Quantity of effective work performed = the recovery of 500 sheep and 10 Indians.

And we thus have the equation: Q = F x P, or,

500 sheep and 10 Indians = 800 men moving 1200 miles at the expense of $500,000.00[87]

On the surface, Lazelle's equation appears to be little more than a pithy metaphorical analysis of a failed military campaign, intended for humor more than anything else. But whether he intended it or not, his equation is far more than that. If we remove the precise numbers relating to the Gila Campaign, we can insert similar figures from any other military operation that took the field in the 1850s. In so doing, we arrive at a quantification of each one that portrays the successes or failures in easily understandable terms of distance traveled, money spent, and manpower involved. Indeed, Lazelle's equation exemplifies the critical elements in which most antebellum military operations failed.

Colonel Bonneville's ill-fated 1857 Gila Campaign, after only three months in the field, came to a most inglorious finale. The principal accomplishment of Bonneville and Miles had been to incur the anger and contempt of their fellow officers and their men. The outing did, however, perpetuate the militaristic approach toward Indian affairs in New Mexico. The Gila Campaign would forever alter the manner in which the Apaches and the Americans viewed their conflict with one another. Such a large force operating in their homelands overawed the Apaches, who realized that there would be more-severe consequences for their depredations in the future. Accordingly, discourse on Indian policy in the territory took a different direction following this important event.

CHAPTER 9

The Mescaleros

The Mescalero Apaches resided primarily east of the Rio Grande in the rugged Sacramento Mountains, which attain altitudes exceeding 10,000 feet above sea level. "The Mescalero [tribe] of Apaches roam over a vast space of this country," Governor Meriwether explained in 1854, "embracing portions of the State of Texas, the province of Chihuahua, and the Territory of New Mexico." These Indians raided below the Rio Grande into Chihuahua and Coahuila and also targeted portions of Texas both east and west of the Pecos River, but their primary area of residence was the Sacramento and Guadalupe Mountains of southeastern New Mexico. This vast region, according to Meriwether, covered "a space of about fifteen thousand square miles; and as they [the Mescaleros] number about seven hundred and fifty souls, the country occupied by them will average, say twenty square miles to each Indian."[1]

Estimates of Mescalero populations during the antebellum era varied widely, ranging from as few as 750 (as stated by Governor Meriwether) to as many as 6,000.[2] Their social organization also remains obscure. Anthropologist Morris E. Opler noted: "[I]t is impossible to tell whether the Mescalero ever had a well-defined band or moiety system. Their neighbors to the west, the Chiricahua Apache, were divided into named bands, and minor cultural

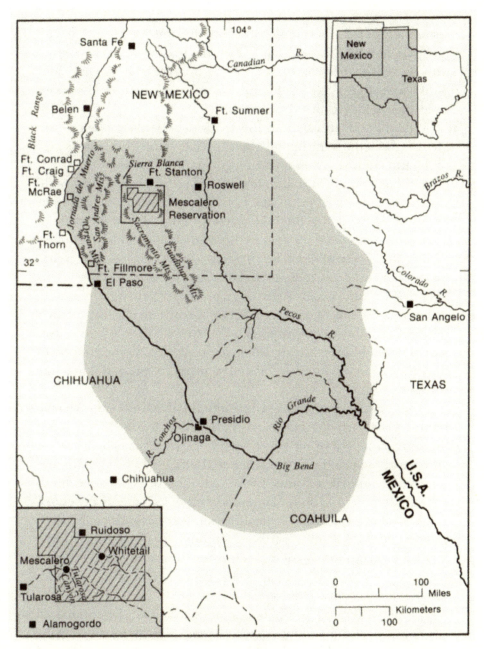

Mescalero Apache country, c. 1830. Reproduced, with permission, from *Handbook of North American Indians*, ed. William C. Sturtevant, vol. 10, *Southwest*, ed. Alfonso Ortiz (Washington, D.C.: Smithsonian Institution, 1983), 419 (fig. 1).

organizations followed along band lines. In contrast, Mescalero culture was uniform throughout."[3] For this reason, military conflict with these Indians took on a different intercultural dynamic and bore some diplomatic distinctions from relations with the more easily identifiable Chiricahua bands.

Indian policy throughout the 1850s necessarily applied to the Mescaleros in the same manner as it applied to the Chiricahuas west of the Rio Grande. Their alternate geographic location did not exempt them from territorial policy objectives, and indeed, throughout the decade civil and military officials continually struggled to devise an appropriate method of controlling Mescalero raiding. The Mescaleros acted independently of the Chiricahuas, although as Meriwether readily acknowledged, the two tribes sometimes formed alliances "as their interest or caprice may dictate."[4] This held true for the Jicarilla Apaches of northern New Mexico as well, with whom the Mescaleros, as a matter of convenience, maintained "a brisk trade in stolen property. . . . [O]ne band will steal horses and mules in its own vicinity, which are driven . . . to the country of the other, to be exchanged for similar property, procured in a like manner."[5]

This tendency represented an important dynamic of the Apache raiding economy; the ability to trade stolen livestock and other property to neighboring tribes significantly influenced the scope and size of their raids. The practice of altering livestock brands and trading the animals to other Indians cloaked the trail of evidence and allowed them to shift blame upon others whenever necessary. For Mescalero Apaches, the Jicarillas and Chiricahuas could often be counted on as trading partners, although long-standing conflict with other neighboring tribes, such as the Comanches and Navajos, typically prevented any similar exchanges of commodified plunder with those respective groups.[6]

Despite a general lack of cohesion that defined the communal relationship of the various Apache bands, Mescaleros bore many similarities to the Chiricahuas both in culture and behavior and raided the Rio Grande settlements with as much frequency as did the Chiricahuas. Northern Mexico had always been a favorite target not only for their plunder but also for their wrath, and much like their relatives west of the Rio Grande, their hatred for the Mexicans burned deep. The army would experience constant difficulties with the Mescaleros throughout the 1850s, and the rough terrain of their homelands would be an object of frustration for troops attempting to pursue and chastise them. "The marauding propensities of these half-starved vagabonds will have to be checked by the strong arm of the military," a frustrated department commander wrote in 1853 in specific reference to the Mescalero Apaches.[7]

The first hostilities between Mescaleros and U.S. troops occurred in the summer of 1849.[8] Responding to recent depredations committed along the Rio Grande, the army established a temporary camp at the mouth of Dog Canyon on the western slopes of the Sacramento Mountains (south of present-day Alamogordo). On July 18 an expedition left the camp with seventy-seven men of Company H, Second Dragoons and Company G, First Dragoons. They reached the summit of the Sacramentos the following morning, having traversed a dangerously steep incline of several thousand feet. An escaped Apache captive named Juan served as guide and traveled in advance of the main column with four dragoons.[9] When they spotted smoke rising in the distance, the troops pressed on at an accelerated pace before finally being spotted, whereupon the Mescaleros immediately dispersed, with the warriors instinctively traveling in opposite directions to draw the attackers away from their families.[10]

A detachment under the command of Lieutenant Harrison followed the Indians, and not long into their pursuit, one of the Mexican guides found a piece of red cloth hanging from a branch. He reasoned that the cloth had been purposely placed there with the expectation that the soldiers would gather around to examine it, at which point the concealed Indians could fire arrows into the clustered men with better chances of hitting them. The guide's foresight may have prevented a massacre. Not long afterward warriors ambushed the troops from a rocky, elevated position and wounded two of them, Private Burke of Company H, Second Dragoons and Private Stanley of Company G, First Dragoons. Harrison's men charged the enemy's hidden positions, whereupon the Indians fled and another rapid pursuit ensued, covering thirty-five miles.[11]

On September 28 a band of Mescaleros traveled to Doña Ana, where they drove off eleven oxen and killed a Mexican herder. Enoch Steen, stationed there with his dragoon company, did not learn of the incident until the following morning. The major immediately dispatched twelve dragoons and ten Mexican volunteers to locate the Indians' trail, which led directly toward the Sacramento Mountains. Continuing to the foot of the range, the sergeant in command saw no reason to advance farther and promptly countermarched to Doña Ana. The twenty-two-man force, only half of them being armed troops, would have been considerably overmatched by the Mescaleros in their own country.

This continued military presence in southern New Mexico prompted a band of twenty-four Mescaleros, including four chiefs, to approach Doña Ana on December 9 with three captive Mexican boys, hoping to exchange prisoners and arrange a compact with the army. Steen wryly ordered that two of the chiefs, Santos and Buffalo, be confined until the Indians returned the captives and the stock stolen in September. In so doing the major sought to uphold article 11 of the Treaty of Guadalupe-Hidalgo mandating the return of Mexican captives to their native country. Steen erroneously believed, however, this to be the same group of Indians who had raided Doña Ana two months earlier. The Mescaleros returned on December 16 and surrendered two of the captives but claimed to know nothing of the stolen livestock, whereupon Steen released Buffalo but retained Santos in confinement. He instructed Buffalo to surrender the third Mexican captive or else Santos would be hanged. The chief quickly returned with the third boy, and Santos was released, but the incident created intense friction between the Mescaleros and Steen's troops. The Indians had come in good faith seeking a peace treaty, yet the major had arrested the chiefs and threatened to execute them.[12]

Remarkably, Steen seems to have met with official approval in his actions, afterward receiving a letter from headquarters expressing the department's "approbation of the course you pursued in recovering from the Apaches the prisoners and property which they had captured."[13] Some months later Colonel Munroe rescinded this initial sentiment, instructing Steen that "when these people visit our posts peaceably it is important that they be received with kindness, excluding from any courtesy those who have by acts evinced a hostile disposition. . . . Assure them that we regard all those who abstain from . . . aggressions . . . as our friends."[14] Munroe's contradictory manner owed partially to a recent treaty negotiation involving Mescalero and Jicarilla Apaches and reflected the department commander's newfound optimism on future Indian relations.

Sensing that trouble might arise from the situation, Steen left Doña Ana on January 3, 1850, with fifty dragoons and twenty infantrymen and marched eastward into Mescalero country. After scouting in the Sacramento Mountains, he concluded that the Indians had moved east to the Pecos River, and he opted not to proceed any farther.[15] After their chiefs' confinement at Doña Ana, the Indians had sensed that troops might be headed their way and indeed relocated themselves accordingly. With even the slightest warning, the Mescaleros could (and usually did) move their camps elsewhere to avoid the soldiers altogether.

Major Steen led another fruitless expedition that summer. A detachment of thirty-two dragoons left Doña Ana in June and marched toward the Sacramentos, where Steen and his guides encountered evidence of recent Apache activity. The major, however, inexplicably believed there to be some 2,000 Mescalero warriors lying in wait and therefore returned immediately to Doña Ana.[16] Interestingly, those familiar with the Indians claimed that the tribe could not muster more than 200 or so warriors at that time. In 1855 Governor Meriwether estimated their population at approximately 150 warriors and 600 women and children.[17] What induced Steen's hyperbolic belief that 2,000 Mescaleros awaited him remains unknown.

Following these two campaigns, the Mescaleros remained quiet for an unusually lengthy period of time, due in part to recent treaty negotiations with civil authorities. The first of these agreements was signed in June 1850 and the second one on April 2, 1851, by

Colonel Munroe and Governor Calhoun at Santa Fe. The latter treaty, a joint negotiation involving chiefs from both the Mescalero and Jicarilla Apaches, stipulated that "the said Apache Indians do hereby declare their unconditional submission to the Government of the United States, and will remove to, and confine themselves to such lands and limits as said Government may assign for their use."[18] Although the terms clearly mandated that a reservation be established, no such reserve would come into existence until many years later, a testament to the meaninglessness of the document.

Regardless of any temporary respite in hostilities that these treaties might have induced, it was only a matter of time before Mescalero uprisings recommenced. On December 14, 1851, a band of Mescaleros struck an army wagon train on the eastern slopes of the Organ Mountains, the only mountain chain between the Rio Grande valley and the Sacramentos. While hauling wood to nearby Fort Fillmore, the dragoons came under attack by an undisclosed number of Apaches. Private Ankle of Company H, First Dragoons was severely wounded in the ensuing affray; an army surgeon later pulled three arrows from his torso. The Indians escaped unscathed with forty-four mules and three horses belonging to the U.S. government. News of the incident reached Fort Fillmore later that evening, and the next morning Lieutenant Abraham Buford of Company H, First Dragoons left there with every available man from his company. The column located the Indians' trail forty miles northeast of the fort and followed it until the fall of darkness inhibited further progress. The dragoons continued their pursuit the next morning but abandoned the chase when the trail reached the Sacramentos. Buford realized the futility of continuing: "They could travel night and day, and I could follow only by daylight. I had only 20 men in the saddle with me . . . raw recruits that I have never had an opportunity to drill or instruct in the least consequence. With such a command as this I knew it would be folly in the extreme to enter the mountains with the view of carrying on war against the Indians."[19] The lieutenant made several important points here, most notably concerning the dragoons' inexperience. The Apaches, whose fighting skills oftentimes exceeded those of even the most well-trained soldiers, would have posed difficulties for Buford's small detachment had they met in battle.

Occasionally, New Mexicans exacted their own revenge on the Apaches without the army's aid. On July 17, 1852, Las Cruces citizens took three Indian ponies they had found tied to a picket post in a nearby cornfield. That night two of the townspeople, a man and a woman, were riddled with Apache arrows. Several armed citizens struck the Indians' trail, overtook them, and managed to kill one in the process.[20] A similar incident occurred several months later, in February 1853, when local residents attacked a Mescalero camp near Doña Ana and killed one woman. The Indians wisely traveled to nearby Fort Fillmore to consult with Colonel Miles before taking any independent action. After being informed of the citizens' unprovoked assault, the colonel devised a solution that he believed would defuse tensions. Hoping to assuage the Indians' bereavement, Miles accompanied them to Doña Ana and held the residents there directly responsible for the attacks, suggesting that they offer the Mescaleros compensatory gifts as a gesture of friendship. To this they reluctantly agreed; while feeling little remorse for the murdered woman, the Mexicans understood the necessity of avoiding Apache vengeance and conceded to Miles's demands.[21]

Despite the colonel's beneficent efforts, retaliation would inevitably occur. In August 1853, several months after the Doña Ana incident, two residents set out for a salt lake eighty miles to the northeast, a foolhardy venture to say the least. The temptation for the Apaches to attack the lone men proved too strong to resist; not surprisingly, the travelers were never seen or heard from again. Rumors circulated around Doña Ana that the men had taken whiskey with them to trade to the Mescaleros, a plausible accusation given the frequency with which unscrupulous citizens attempted to take advantage of Indians through the use of intoxicants.[22]

When a group of ten Mescaleros arrived at Doña Ana two weeks later, Colonel Miles quickly sent a detachment of dragoons from Fort Fillmore to meet them. Wary of another possible attack on their camp, the Indians fled when they noticed the troops approaching. Indian Agent Steck successfully convinced them to return, whereupon they met with several prominent officers, including Major Steen and Lieutenant McFerran. The officers questioned the Mescaleros about the two missing Mexicans, but the Indians maintained their innocence. Finally, two of them agreed to search for Chief Santos, with instructions from McFerran to "tell Santos that if he did not come in at once, we would come out and bring him in, and before starting, would hang those of his tribe we had."[23] Not surprisingly, Santos failed to appear, nor did the dragoons carry out the threat of hangings. An amateur newspaper publisher in El Paso, writing in 1854 about recent Apache hostilities, pithily remarked, "the war that is being carried on with the ... Apaches ... in the magnitude of the campaign[s], and the importance of the results to be anticipated, throws far into the shade the contest between Turkey and Russia."[24] Indeed, ensuing events that year would see a continuing increase in the scale of the army's war with the Mescaleros.

Emboldened by the success of recent raids, the Apaches struck again on March 14, stealing five horses from Keat's Ranch, within a mile of Fort Conrad. Mescaleros rarely ventured so close to a military post when raiding, but they did so in this instance and emerged unscathed. A skirmish occurred the next day, when a small detachment of troops overtook the brash marauders. The fight only augmented the Mescaleros' success, all of whom escaped without injury while killing one of the Mexican scouts. With their horses broken down from the chase, the troops abandoned pursuit and returned to Fort Conrad.[25]

One month later General Garland ordered a column from Fort Fillmore, to be led by Major William B. Johns, to march into Mescalero country. Consisting of three infantry companies and numbering 137 soldiers in all, the men carried rations for thirty days. The column followed an unconventional route to the Sacramento Mountains, traveling south from Fort Fillmore and scouting the Guadalupe Mountains of southeastern New Mexico before striking a path northward. The expedition had not traveled far before scarcity of water became an issue. Arriving at Hueco Tanks (east of El Paso) and finding them dry, the command backtracked to Fort Bliss. Major Electus Backus, commanding at Fort Fillmore, dispatched two water wagons to Fort Bliss for the soldiers to take with them, and when heading back out, Major Johns chose a more direct course. Probing northward toward Dog Canyon, further problems began to plague the campaign: the guide deserted, nobody among the party could profess any knowledge of the country, and the extreme heat prevented them from finding much water, even at traditionally dependable springs. On May 11, three weeks after embarking, Major Johns returned to Fort Fillmore, his infantrymen out of rations and exhausted from the difficult trek.[26] This debacle evidenced the impracticality of detailing foot soldiers in place of dragoons for this type of arduous duty, especially during the hot summers.

Undeterred by recent failures, the army tried another scout a month later. Amid the daunting summer heat, Lieutenant Colonel Chandler left Fort Craig on June 22 with a column of fifty-six dragoons and infantry.[27] Marching toward the White Mountains of east-central New Mexico, Chandler experienced the same problems that Major Johns had on his expedition. By the time the troops reached water, they had already abandoned eleven horses, eighteen mules, and ten oxen that could not keep up due to exhaustion. According to Chandler, these losses owed "entirely to the extreme heat, the desertion of the hired Mexican packmen, and the ignorance and stupidity of the guide."[28]

Despite such burdensome shortcomings, the column pressed onward and eventually reached the Rio Hondo, where a lone Mescalero Apache approached under a white flag. Soon thereafter Chiefs Negrito and Jose came into the camp and met with Chandler, informing him that all recent depredations had been committed by Santa Anna and his followers, known for being among the more bellicose Mescalero contingents.[29] "We [are] going to be at war," Chandler warned the chiefs. "As it is impossible to know what bands commit depredations, war will be carried on against each and every Mescalero and Jicarilla Apache that we can find. . . . [I]n other words, the whole tribe will be held responsible for the misdeeds of individuals."[30] The colonel's admission is telling and reveals the widespread military ambivalence toward guiltless Indians.

Although they seldom admitted it, officers always had difficulty distinguishing between subgroups within the larger tribe and therefore attacked peaceful Indians with regularity. Chandler himself was guilty of this during another expedition against the Mimbres Apaches, during which he ordered an attack on the peaceful camp of Delgadito and Itán (see chapter 7).

Not surprisingly, Negrito and Jose could not convince Santa Anna to meet with Chandler. Realizing that their failure might upset the colonel, they fled and were not heard from again. Following his meetings with the Mescaleros, Chandler continued on an easterly course down the Rio Hondo, where he and his dragoons encountered numerous abandoned Indian camps containing evidence of sheep recently stolen from the Rio Grande settlements. Despite rumors that several large camps could be found at the Bosque Redondo along the Pecos River, Chandler opted not to pursue such a course, partially because his guides had deserted and he knew almost nothing of that area. As the column continued eastward down the Rio Ruidoso and Rio Hondo, the number of deserted Indian camps decreased. Ultimately, the troops left the White Mountains and probed northward until reaching the village of Anton Chico east of Albuquerque. With provisions running low, they sent a rider to Fort Union requesting additional rations to sustain them until they reached Fort Craig.

Although the campaign had been a total failure up to that point, the men's discouragement was temporarily assuaged on the return to Fort Craig when the dragoons stumbled upon a small Mescalero camp near the town of Manzano. The soldiers opened fire but stopped when one of the officers realized that the Indians held several captive Mexican girls. By the time firing ceased, two of the girls had already been shot, though not fatally. Ironically, these two were the only ones in the camp struck by the soldiers' bullets; the Indians themselves did not suffer any casualties. Soon after, with the infantrymen's boots completely worn out and the dragoons' horses broken down, the column was in no condition to further search for Indians. On July 7 Chandler's command returned to Fort Craig from what must have been a truly miserable and fatiguing march under a scorching sun.[31]

Another summer campaign against the Mescaleros departed Albuquerque on July 10 and consisted of thirty-six men belonging to Companies G and K, First Dragoons. Eight days earlier 3,000 sheep, worth an estimated $7,500 and belonging to Mariano Yrisarri, had been run off by raiding Mescaleros.[32] The dragoons struck the Indians' trail on the thirteenth and followed it eastward into the Capitan Mountains, with decaying sheep carcasses along the way making for an easily recognizable path. The expedition never realized its full potential, however, because the Mexican guides continually led the troops in directions where no water could be found. The commanding officer eventually ordered a countermarch toward Albuquerque on July 23, only two weeks after embarking.[33] By this time it must have been obvious to military officials in Santa Fe that the Mescaleros' homelands could not be easily penetrated, and under most circumstances the Indians would be safe from harm as long as they remained there.

Frustration continued to run rampant among both military and civil officials, and after numerous botched operations, General Garland had seen enough. When the Mescaleros stole 2,500 sheep from the vicinity of Anton Chico in December 1854, he ordered a full-scale campaign into the field with instructions to descend upon the Sacramento Mountains from two directions.[34] This would be the largest and most well-organized expedition against the Mescaleros to date, having severe ramifications for both the Indians and the army, resulting in several deaths, and ultimately leading to the establishment of a new post on the Rio Bonito.

The campaign began on December 28 when Captain Ewell left Los Lunas with sixty-one men of Company G and twenty men of Company K, First Dragoons. With nine Mexican guides and one interpreter, his command reached Anton Chico four days later and immediately pivoted southeast to follow the Pecos River toward the Capitan and White Mountains. After discovering recently used Indian trails, he ordered two consecutive night marches in hopes of overtaking the travelers. All efforts failed, and the captain abandoned the pursuit, reverting instead to his originally planned route toward the Capitans. On January 7, 1855, Ewell's column converged with the command of Captain Henry W. Stanton from Fort

Fillmore, consisting of twenty-nine dragoons and fifty infantrymen. The combined force now numbered 160 soldiers, substantially larger than any previous push into Mescalero country.[35]

On the night of January 17, the Apaches raided the troops while they camped along the Peñasco River, stampeding a number of the dragoons' horses and setting fire to the grass to cover their escape. A line of skirmishers immediately formed to protect the camp for the remainder of the night.[36] The soldiers spent the following day randomly chasing individual warriors through the trees and brush without success; indeed, the Apaches seemed to be amusing themselves by toying with the troops at their leisure. Later reports maintained that several of the Indians had been shot during the day and carried off by others, although no physical evidence could be found to substantiate such claims.

The soldiers remained encamped near the Peñasco that night. Unknown to Captain Stanton, he was living his last moments on earth. That evening he led a detachment of twelve dragoons up a steep canyon three-quarters of a mile from the main camp and rode directly into a well-prepared ambush.[37] A musketball slammed into Stanton's forehead, killing him instantly. Two other dragoon privates, Thomas Dwyer and John Hennings, also perished in the attack. One of the privates died when his wounded horse fell, leaving him defenseless and unable to escape; a witness reported seeing the Indians gathered around the man, filling his body with arrows.[38] The sound of gunfire startled the soldiers remaining in camp, and they quickly rode to the aid of their comrades and forced the Indians to flee into the surrounding hills. The soldiers soon discovered the bodies of their two comrades and their slain captain and buried them in shallow graves with the intention of retrieving the remains when returning to Fort Fillmore, where each would receive a formal military burial.[39]

Once the survivors left the canyon, the guides had extreme difficulty following the various Indian trails that criss-crossed each other through the mountains. "No one of our number has ever traveled this country before," admitted one dragoon accompanying the campaign. "It is nothing but snow and ice. We traveled less than four miles before we camped again. . . . [N]o mistake about it, we are living on a light diet. Killed our last beef; flour is gone; we have no shoes. It is hard fare. We have decided to call this Camp Starvation."[40] The command had taken the field in the middle of winter; adding to the hardship, the Indians habitually burned the grass in order to starve the soldiers' animals. When provisions eventually ran out, most of the animals had to be killed for food. By the time Ewell's men returned to Los Lunas, many of them did so barefoot and starving.[41]

Several days later, after aimlessly following any Indian trail their guides could find, the soldiers returned to the fateful canyon where their comrades had died. There they discovered that someone had desecrated the makeshift graves and stolen the blankets wrapping the bodies; their bones lay strewn over the field, picked clean by vultures.[42] Ewell ordered that the three men's remains be burned to remove all remaining flesh, then the column transported the bones back to Fort Fillmore for burial in the post cemetery. Private James Bennett, chronicling the expedition in his diary, recalled the melancholy scene that followed: "Mrs. Stanton, the Captain's wife, stood in the door awaiting her husband. If a person had one drop of pity, here he could use it. Poor woman! She asks for her husband, the answer is evaded. An hour passes. Her smiles are fled. Her merry laugh is turned to sighs, and tears stain her cheek. Him she loved, she never more shall behold."[43]

On February 3, funeral services took place for the three slain dragoons, the more elaborate and formal ceremony being reserved for Captain Stanton.[44] After graduating from West Point in 1842, Stanton had commanded Company B, First Dragoons and transferred to Fort Fillmore in 1854. He had been in New Mexico less than a year at the time of his death. Well liked among his fellow officers as well as those serving under his command, Stanton's passing incited anger throughout the military department and became a prelude to future hard times for the Mescaleros.[45]

The campaign into Mescalero country had an almost immediate psychological effect on at least some members of that tribe. When the expedition commenced in January, Chief Santos took his followers to Steck's agency at Fort Thorn, where he assured the agent that he had "disconnected himself from the main body of his people at the commencement of the war with that tribe and avowed his determination to remain at peace." When Santos visited Fort Fillmore later that month, Colonel Miles promised him military protection provided that his "good conduct merited it." Santos pledged to remain encamped in the Caballo Mountains, about twenty miles northeast of the Fort Thorn agency, so that his whereabouts would be known and his people would not be implicated in any future depredations.[46]

In February 1855 the Mescalero chief Palanquito sent an emissary to meet with Agent Steck and request a peace treaty.[47] Steck informed the courier that the tribe's headmen must visit the governor in Santa Fe to make such a request; according to Steck, "he [the Indian] was afraid to go to Santa Fe, but returned to his own people and called a general council . . . consisting of the following chiefs: Palanquito, Genero, Plumas, Plumas' son, Cosas & Huelta, who are the principal men of the Mescaleros." The council purportedly convened on a mountaintop near Dog Canyon. They jointly asked for peace, whereupon Steck promised to communicate their wishes to the governor, which he did in a letter written on February 6.[48] The recent campaign into the Mescalero country clearly made an indelible impression on several of the chiefs, who did not wish to remain at war with the army and instead sued for peace at the Fort Thorn agency. A month later, having received no reply from Santa Fe, Steck again contacted Governor Meriwether, who informed him that General Garland already planned to lead another expedition into the Sacramento Mountains with the intention of constructing a new military post. Although Meriwether could not halt the operation, he assured Steck that he would ask the commanding officers not to attack the Indians "so long as they remain quiet and peaceable."[49]

While several pacific Mescalero bands continued to hover around Fort Thorn in the spring of 1855 anticipating negotiations, the more bellicose clans continued depredating throughout southern New Mexico. On January 16, while Stanton and Ewell wandered the Sacramento Mountains, a party of nine Mescaleros raided the Eaton Ranch southeast of Santa Fe near Galisteo, a somewhat unusual act due to the fact that most of their raids occurred in the southern and central portions of the territory. Two herders were shot (one killed and the other wounded) as the Indians drove off seventy-five horses and mules, "ransacked the house, and shamefully abused the inmates."[50]

Lieutenant Samuel D. Sturgis, with a meager force of just eighteen dragoons and six volunteer civilian guides, struck out from Santa Fe in rapid pursuit. Three days and 175 miles later, he overtook the Indians "on the opposite side of a deep, stony cañon full of tall pine-trees." In the ensuing skirmish, the dragoons unleashed a volley on the Apache positions before, according to one report, charging them with sabers drawn.[51] Such an action seems highly implausible as the Apaches would have been widely dispersed and concealed behind trees and rocks, making a saber charge incredibly foolhardy. Saber charge or not, the soldiers did kill three Mescaleros and wounded four more, although the Indians inflicted considerable harm upon the troops as well. Three dragoons and the owner of the ranch (Eaton) fell wounded in the affray, all struck by arrows. One of the dragoons, Private Pat Rooney, was "badly wounded, an arrow having gone two and a half inches into his head." Remarkably the wound did not immediately kill the private; after the battle Lieutenant Sturgis "had him carried across the saddle, with a Mexican behind him, for eighty miles."[52] Two weeks later Rooney succumbed to his wound at the hospital in Santa Fe. On January 30 the local Catholic church hosted his funeral, followed by a military ceremony that included a firing party, music, members of the detachment present at the battle, "and nearly all the officers and a great many citizens [bringing] up the rear.... [T]he citizens pronounced it to be the most respectable funeral that ever crossed the Plaza of Santa Fe."[53]

Military action against the Mescaleros continued in the southernmost portions of the territory as well. Major James Longstreet, son-in-law of the department commander, General Garland, and destined to become a famed Confederate general during the Civil

War, left his station at Fort Bliss on January 24, 1855, with a command of fifty-four men. Having been ordered to scout the vicinity of Hueco Tanks east of El Paso, he picked up the trail of Apaches driving a herd of about forty stolen cattle toward the Guadalupe Mountains. Hoping to maintain the element of surprise (assuming he even had one), Longstreet traveled almost exclusively by moonlight.[54] Major John Simonson, commanding a detachment of Fifth Infantry, converged with Longstreet on February 9. Rather than join forces and continue the pursuit, which Longstreet preferred, Simonson opted instead to lead his men south toward Delaware Creek, just north of the Texas–New Mexico boundary. Simonson's unwillingness to aid in capturing the Apaches infuriated Longstreet, who returned to Fort Bliss after his column ran out of provisions. Upon arriving there, Longstreet demanded that a court of inquiry be convened to investigate Major Simonson's actions, citing the poor condition of his own animals and wagons, as well as the major's lack of support, as having directly inhibited the success of his scout.[55] Such a lack of cooperation within the military chain of command continually hamstrung the army's efforts toward enforcing Indian policy and recovering stolen livestock and human captives.

By 1855 nearly six years had passed since Major Steen had led the first military campaigns into the impregnable Mescalero homelands. In that time little of significance had been accomplished. Although the army proved to be an unrelenting antagonist to the Apaches, their raiding continued mostly unabated. The civil government had yet to negotiate any lasting or enforceable treaties with the Mescaleros; indeed, all pacific overtures had been flatly rebuked by Santa Fe officials, allowing hostilities between the two sides to continue without hindrance. If military campaigns had the intention of forcing the Mescaleros into submission, they should have included Indian Bureau officials in their operations in order to negotiate peace treaties and avoid further bloodshed. Six years of campaigning had failed to produce any positive outcome primarily because minimal cooperation occurred between civil and military authorities. Several chiefs earnestly sought peace during those years, but their diplomatic overtures continually went unreciprocated, perhaps in part because officials had to deal simultaneously with several autonomous tribes throughout the entirety of New Mexico and could not direct their full attention to any one Indian group or subgroup. This year, however, would mark a significant turning point in relations between Mescaleros and Anglo-Americans.

In February 1855, just weeks after Captain Stanton's death, Captain Ewell established a grazing camp at the mouth of Comanche Canyon, twenty-five miles east of Los Lunas, with six dragoons detailed to keep permanent watch over the animals.[56] Around midnight on February 23, the camp unexpectedly came under attack by unknown assailants, assumed to be Mescaleros. The initial report from the field claimed that at least five of the six dragoons had been slain, although further investigation proved that information false. Four of the soldiers were sitting in their tent when the perpetrators approached undetected and pulled the canvas down, trapping them inside and riddling it with arrows. The four dragoons somehow made their way outside and managed to fend off their attackers, but in the ensuing fight Privates Ringgold, Culligan, Weaver, and Young were wounded at least four times each by arrows.[57] They obtained medical attention at the military hospital in Albuquerque, and all four later received commendations for bravery. The public also took notice of this event when a Santa Fe newspaper lauded the men as heroes for their "meritorious actions." When Private Ringgold eventually died of his wounds, Captain Ewell sent a personal letter of condolence to his father.[58]

The remaining two dragoons had not been present when the attack occurred—instead they were some two miles distant—and did not arrive in time to aid their comrades; in fact they remained unaware that anything had transpired until they returned to camp the next day. Despite his numerous wounds, Private Culligan crawled to the nearby ranch of Manuel Chavez, who sent a rider to Los Lunas and informed Captain Ewell of the incident. Twenty-five men of Company G, First Dragoons immediately rode to the scene, where a grisly spectacle awaited them. Privates Ringgold, Weaver, and Young lay wounded on the ground, which was littered with over three hundred arrows. Interestingly, the arrows bore several different defining markings, some belonging to the Mescaleros, but others bearing no distinguishing marks at all. The marauders escaped with between forty and fifty head of cattle, although the troops later recovered several of them.[59]

Rather than attempt to follow the culprits, Ewell chose an alternate course of action and made some surprising discoveries. The detachment rode to the town of Manzano, east of the attack site. Here the troops learned that Indians had passed through shortly before them, in the process killing the alcalde's son. According to one report, this was merely a cover story for the town's residents, who likely played a role in the attack. Ewell doubted that the Mescaleros even knew about the grazing camp so soon after its establishment; indeed, the troops had been there only a week when they were assaulted. The captain and his dragoons had been on active duty in the Sacramento Mountains during the previous month, involved in the campaign that claimed the life of Captain Stanton, and the Mescaleros had been preoccupied with those troops that entire time.

Bearing this in mind, officers presumed that the residents at Manzano had discovered the camp and planned the attack so that it would appear as if Indians were responsible. This would also explain the strange arrows found at the site; Apache arrows usually had identifiable markings linking them to a specific group. The fact that many of the recovered arrows had been unmarked caused immediate suspicion.[60] In further support of the theory, Ewell noticed that the people at Torreon, another nearby village, acted suspiciously and seemed disinclined to cooperate with his troops. "When I arrived at Torreon in an instant I saw the unwillingness to say anything," he observed, "and after reflection of a few minutes determined to camp there."[61] The presence of the military, coupled with Ewell's obvious intent to investigate, created a sense of uneasiness among the townspeople and made it appear as though they might have been complicit in the attack.

Such incidents epitomized the impracticality of dispatching small groups of soldiers for any purpose, especially for monitoring the army's grazing camps. Any detachment numbering less than ten men was extremely vulnerable, not only to Apache raiding parties but to conniving residents as well. Mail escorts remained frequent targets because of their small size and isolation. In addition, New Mexico military posts routinely sent out small parties to cut wood and supervise livestock to ensure the Indians did not steal them. But by 1856 the commanding officer at Los Lunas had quit sending soldiers out, to avoid enticing an attack.

The year 1855 would continue to be an eventful one in relations with the Mescalero Apaches. Their continuous raids on the settlements, coupled with the death of Captain Stanton, eventually resulted in serious consequences for the Indians. In March the army established a temporary camp at James Canyon, the site of Stanton's death a month earlier. When General Garland traveled to Mescalero country that same month, he moved the camp to a new site near the confluence of the Rio Bonito and the Rio Hondo. This new location, which he humbly named Camp Garland, served as operational headquarters while he and other officers scoured the countryside searching for a suitable location for a permanent post.[62] "They are here for the purpose of building a fort to be called Fort Stanton in commemoration of the Captain who was killed three months ago," Private Bennett recorded in his diary. "General John Garland selected the site for the fort today. The officers all got drunk."[63]

Built on the grassy southern bank of the Rio Bonito in the shadows of Sierra Blanca and the Capitan Mountains, Fort Stanton was situated in the heart of the Mescaleros' homelands and would prove to be an indispensable deterrent to future hostilities. What had seemed impossible to accomplish during six years of military campaigning was achieved almost overnight with the establishment of Fort Stanton.[64] Coinciding with the construction of the post, and equally influential in stifling Mescalero hostilities, was the death of Chief Santa Anna, whose warlike subgroup claimed responsibility for many of the raids occurring over the previous several years.[65] Immediately after his demise, several different bands visited Agent Steck and reiterated their desire to make treaty arrangements, claiming that Santa Anna's death would enable them to more easily control miscreants within the tribe. Several chiefs, including Marco (brother of the murdered Cuentas Azules), visited Fort Stanton for the first time on February 26, 1856, where they professed "a desire to be on terms of friendship . . . [and] were informed that they would always be kindly received, so long as their conduct was good." Another band of Mescaleros under Palanquito came into the fort a week later and represented "themselves as very poor and hungry."[66]

Several nonrelated events thus coincided in the spring of 1855 that, taken collectively, induced the Mescaleros to seek an alternative path from raiding. The brutal winter months of 1855–56 also took a toll, with many of the malnourished Indians lacking subsistence provisions and becoming overly reliant on government-issued rations. These combined occurrences did not, however, allay the actions of several defiant individuals within the tribe. Much like their Chiricahua neighbors to the west, there remained more than a few rebellious souls among the Mescaleros.

Throughout 1855, troops at Fort Stanton busied themselves constructing the post; it would be many months before the buildings were completed, during which time troops from other stations continued to lead expeditions through Mescalero country. On April 2 Colonel Miles and 300 men of the Third Infantry stumbled upon a camp of several hundred warriors in Dog Canyon. Somehow the Indians failed to notice the soldiers approaching. "What a beautiful chance for a fight," Miles fretted. "The troops will never get such another. But they [the Mescaleros] have met me in faith trusting to my honor." After Miles entered the camp, the Indians pleaded for a peace treaty. Through interpreters he spoke with several of their chiefs but refused to make a compact due to the absence of certain prominent headmen. Accordingly, the colonel promised to take up their cause with Governor Meriwether and Agent Steck.[67]

When news of Colonel Miles's meeting reached Meriwether, he personally traveled to Fort Thorn to speak with members of the tribe. "When I met the Mescaleros at Ft. Thorn for the purpose of negotiating a treaty of peace with them," Meriwether remembered, "I found these Indians in the most destitute condition imaginable."

The Indians were scarcely in any position to refuse whatever terms the governor had to offer. The treaty contained, among other things, a provision calling for the creation of a reservation at Fort Stanton. Although Congress never ratified the treaty, the Mescaleros for the most part kept their word, and the majority of the tribe thereafter refrained from raiding the settlements.[68] The proposed establishment of a reservation, coupled with the issuance of rations at Fort Stanton, had a positive effect overall and prevented many future hostilities. In this sense Indian Bureau diplomacy had achieved a certain degree of success with the Mescaleros that it struggled to attain with the Chiricahua Apaches during these same years.

A passage in Governor Meriwether's memoirs provides an interesting aside to the incident. During his stay at Fort Thorn, he met an Indian who admitted to having been present when Captain Stanton was killed. Meriwether questioned the warrior about Stanton's personal belongings, including his sword and pocket watch, both of which had been stripped from his body before the other dragoons arrived at the scene. While claiming to know nothing of the sword, the Indian understood precisely what Meriwether meant when he asked about the watch. He immediately departed and returned later with Stanton's watch, which had stopped ticking, and according to Meriwether, the Indian thought it had literally "died." Using his own watch key, the governor wound it back up, whereupon the astonished Apache believed that he had magically brought it back to life. Meriwether sent the pocket watch to the captain's widow as a memento of her husband.[69]

By May 1855 the garrison at Fort Stanton consisted of Companies I and K, First Dragoons; Companies A and K, Third Infantry; Company B, Eighth Infantry; and Company C, New Mexico Volunteers.[70] Its troop strength thus exceeded that of any other southern New Mexico post at that time. The wife of an officer stationed there described the fort as it existed in 1858, three years after its establishment: "Fort Stanton was a beautiful post, with the best quarters in the army at the time . . . but it was like being buried alive to stay there. Nothing ever passed that way, and it was seldom a stranger came among us. There was but one mail a month, and on the day it was expected we dropped all work . . . then all was excitement until the post office opened and each had his own letters and papers in his hands."[71]

The permanent presence of so large a body of troops encouraged an immediate influx to the region of both Mexicans and Anglo-Americans, who began farming the fertile valleys and founded the village of Las Placitas del Rio Bonito, later renamed Lincoln. As early as October 1855, a mere five months after Garland established Fort Stanton, U.S. officials made note of settlers arriving near the post but lamented the fact that many of them chose locations within the public domain to establish their farms, necessitating the resurveying of several portions of the Rio Bonito valley and vicinity in order to mitigate land-occupancy concerns and ensure that settlement patterns did not become skewed because of ambiguities in legal title and ownership.[72]

Equally burdensome to territorial officials were the vices of society that inevitably cropped up with so many new settlers, many of whom provided liquor and other contraband items to the Indians on a regular basis. Federal laws dating as far back as 1802 restricted the trade and trafficking of liquor to American Indian tribes, but these regulations went widely ignored on the western frontier.[73] "I find great difficulty in preventing the sale of ardent spirits to the Indians," Governor Meriwether confessed in 1855, "and so long as this practice is continued it will be impracticable to keep them in peace and quietude."[74] When military officers inquired as to where they obtained ardent spirits, tight-lipped Mescaleros commonly replied, "I found a spring."[75] They certainly did not want to reveal their true sources for fear that the army would take action to put a stop to it. Such incidents gave rise to the popular stereotype of Indians as an intoxicated, uncontrollable race with little self-restraint. While drunken intertribal melees did occur on occasion, as evidenced in Steck's 1858 annual report noting that "drunkenness has led to . . . five or six [Mescaleros] being killed . . . in quarrels among themselves," such incidents typically resulted from the unscrupulous actions of American and Mexican traders who provided the intoxicants in the first place.[76] Indeed, one can scarcely blame the Indians alone for such behavior, as they doubtless witnessed a comparable amount of similar debauchery among their Mexican and Anglo-American counterparts.[77]

Almost immediately after Fort Stanton's establishment, an infamous enterprise known as Hacket's Hog Ranch set up shop nearby, and its decadent offerings targeted not only the soldiers but the Apaches as well. In 1859 Major Ruff, the commanding officer at Fort Stanton, became exasperated with the entire situation and wrote headquarters asking whether or not any laws existed prohibiting such practices as those occurring at the Hog Ranch. He must have been distraught when he received a negative response; as a military officer, no laws provided him with the authority to take forceful action against civilian merchants unless he actually caught them in the act of trading contraband to the Indians.[78]

Ironically, the settlers themselves frequently became victims of the contraband-liquor trade near Fort Stanton. Despite being a lucrative business, it oftentimes resulted in unruly drunken behavior among the Apaches. Not surprisingly, in any instance of Indian disorder, the citizens ran to the military for aid. With the Mescaleros finally acting in a somewhat peaceful manner compared to years past, the officers at the fort seemed reluctant to send out any large body of troops. Throughout the winter of 1858, a sizable group of Mescaleros had gathered nearby, anticipating monthly rations from Steck. The Indians "came and went as they pleased, walking into our houses and sitting on our porches without the least hesitation," wrote one observer.[79] With the Apaches living peaceably, dispatching troops could have easily incited them to take up hostilities again. For this reason, many of the more inconsequential Indian uprisings near the post went unchecked by the army. In 1857, for example, headquarters ordered Major J. H. Holmes, commanding at Fort Stanton, to desist from embarking on a planned campaign into Dog Canyon "as it might not be understood by the Indians."[80]

The summer of 1855 also witnessed the advent of artesian wells in Mescalero country near the Pecos River valley southeast of the Sacramento Mountains. A temporary camp consisting of sixty-eight men of Company I, Fifth Infantry, along with dozens of hired civilian laborers, was established on May 26 at the junction of Delaware Creek and the Pecos River, just north of the Texas line. For two months these men dug wells in the desert, an unenviable task if there ever was one. The nearest town was El Paso, 150 miles to the east. Water had to be carried daily from the Pecos River to the wells, a distance of nearly ten miles. On one occasion Mescaleros attacked the men transporting water and killed every one of them. After this incident the size of the escort accompanying the water carriers was increased substantially, which deterred any further attacks. Not long afterward the army wisely abandoned the operation, and the troops returned to Fort Bliss.[81]

On August 6, as a detachment of troops traveled down the Jornada del Muerto toward Fort Fillmore, one of the men went missing. Private Valentine of Company B, Third Infantry left the main column near the southern end of the Jornada to water his mule in the Rio Grande, a few miles to the west. A small band of about a dozen Mescaleros captured Valentine and took him back to their camp in the Organ Mountains. After four days a Mescalero chief arrived and, sensing the trouble that might arise from holding the soldier in confinement, ordered that Valentine be freed. After the man's release, several Indians followed the private as he traveled back across the desert toward Doña Ana, the nearest settlement. Once Valentine passed beyond sight of the chief's camp, the Indians assaulted him again, this time stealing his mule and personal belongings. The soldier now found himself stranded in the desert in the middle of summer without water. Heat exhaustion overcame him, and he lay on the brink of death when a Mexican herder discovered him and carried him to Fort Fillmore, where Valentine eventually recovered in the post hospital.[82]

Despite Private Valentine's unfortunate experience, Colonel Miles wrote to headquarters in October praising the Mescaleros' recent good behavior. No hostilities involving that group had occurred since Valentine's abduction two months earlier. "They should have an agent of their own," Miles suggested, further noting, "Doctor Steck, one of the best I've ever known, being identified by them . . .

Site of Fort Stanton today, viewed from the south. The Rio Bonito Valley passes through the center of the picture, with the Capitan Mountains at right. The buildings on the left mark the location of the fort, though none of the original structures from the 1850s remain. In recent years, the fort has been used as a merchant marine hospital, among other things. Photograph by the author.

can acquire their total confidence or control them."[83] The fact that they requested Steck is not at all surprising. No other agent ever earned the amity and respect of New Mexico's Indians on the same level as the doctor, who eventually did receive the appointment as Mescalero agent, in addition to the position he already held supervising the Gila Apaches.

On October 28, only a week after praising the Mescaleros for their tranquility, Colonel Miles received news that eighteen mules had been driven off from the ranch of Frank Fletcher between Las Cruces and Doña Ana. Miles asked several Mescalero headmen, including Palanquito, to find the stolen mules and return them to Fletcher's ranch. W. W. H. Davis, acting as temporary governor during Meriwether's absence, demanded that Steck inform the Indians that if they failed to retrieve the animals, they could "expect the soldiers among them and in that case we will not bury the hatchet until they are destroyed."[84] Remarkably, Palanquito managed to track down the culprits and recovered all but a couple of the stolen animals.

Miles remained skeptical of this situation from the beginning, believing that Palanquito's Mescaleros in fact had been unaware of the theft until he informed them. Indeed, they had remained quiet for several months, and the colonel had no reason to suspect them of the crime; instead, he believed the incident to be a ruse on the part of the rancher. "I have so little confidence in Fletcher, that I must have the evidence of someone besides himself to believe he ever lost any mules at all—this is my private opinion, which I would thank you to keep to yourself," he confided in a personal message to Steck. "The people of Cruzces [*sic*] and Mesilla have treated these Indians [Palanquito's band] most shamefully and I doubt not Fletcher was [involved in] any outrages committed against them."[85]

Fletcher's testimony exemplifies an issue that occurred frequently, that of citizens making false accusations in hopes of defrauding the government through indemnity claims on stolen animals.[86] The 1834 Indian Intercourse Act allowed stockowners to claim recompense for property lost to Indian raiding. In some instances either the stock had not been stolen at all or the claimants grossly exaggerated the value and the quantity taken. In a claim filed in 1854 by Antonio Constante, for example, he attested to having lost property valued at $7,418 during a raid on his ranch on January 28, 1852. Interior Department investigators, however, discovered that Constante previously filed a claim with Governor Meriwether "under oath, estimating the value of the property at about $5000, and now he swears it was worth $7418." Timothy McGowan, a resident of the Mesilla Valley, submitted a similarly fraudulent claim in 1855. Gila Apaches had purportedly raided his ranch two years earlier and stolen "a large amount of corn, fodder, tobacco, etc." valued at $10,755. "No evidence has been offered in support of this claim," an investigator concluded, "and the statements of the claimant are contradicted by Governor Meriwether."[87]

Fletcher's fraud came in the form of exaggerating the number of animals stolen and falsely attributing blame for the raid. When Palanquito succeeded in locating and returning the animals, Miles reiterated his opinion that the Mescaleros had been innocent of any wrongdoing. "From the direction of the trail and the place found," he concluded, "I believe the [Mexicans] to be guilty. I do not myself believe the Mescaleros stole the mules, or had knowledge of the theft until I informed them. The chiefs deserve credit for the zeal displayed in recapturing them and [this] shows most conclusively their desire to keep unbroken the treaty."[88] Miles displayed a remarkable sense of judgment, recognizing the peculiarities of the situation and conducting an investigation that effectively exonerated the Indians of any wrongdoing. Unfortunately, this type of thorough analysis seldom occurred among military officers and civil officials, causing blame for raids and murders to be falsely attributed to Apaches on many occasions throughout the 1850s.

Only a couple of months earlier, Steck had written to Governor Meriwether informing him that fifty-three mules had been stolen from the Armijo Ranch near Belen. The agent's investigation revealed that this act had likewise been perpetrated by local residents and not the Apaches. Steck had obtained a copy of Armijo's brand and carried it with him to several Apache camps, where he compared it to markings on their own animals. He did not find a single animal marked with Armijo's brand. "I am very confident that they were not stolen by Apaches," Steck concluded in his report to the governor.[89] One cannot help but wonder how much raiding and plundering was perpetrated by non-Indians; after all, whenever any livestock theft occurred in southern New Mexico, the Apaches immediately received the blame. Some of the territory's citizens recognized this and employed it to their advantage, knowing that the Apaches would usually be vilified for any thefts.

Steck and Miles had not been the only officials in the territory to identify this trend. Colonel Thomas T. Fauntleroy, commanding the department in 1860, admitted, "The greatest embarrassment arises from the fact that many of the claims set up against the Indians of New Mexico for plundering, stealing the stock and the like, are either fabricated, or to a considerable degree exaggerated, and if war is to be commenced upon the simple presentation of these claims, the causes for war become interminable or *the Indians must be extirpated.*"[90] Even the territorial newspaper alluded to the frequency with which Mexicans posing as Apaches raided secluded farms and ranches and drove away plunder. Reporting on an 1854 raid near Las Cruces, the *Santa Fe Weekly Gazette* acknowledged that "whether the act was done by Indians, or the Mexicans fleeing to this side of the Rio Grande . . . is not known."[91]

In January 1856 a twelve-year-old drummer boy at Fort Bliss disappeared from the post. A detachment of troops sent to find him met with no luck; the Indians they encountered claimed total ignorance of the situation when questioned. Finally, the colonel commanding the expedition met a Mescalero woman who admitted that the boy had been killed. According to her, he had been unable to keep up, so they "beat his brains out with rocks." The boy's cruel murder would not be the only tragic death emanating from this particular expedition. Private Bennett accompanied the column as it marched into Mescalero country in search of the boy and witnessed a fellow soldier meet with an equally horrific death. The trapper died at the hands of not an Apache, but rather his own commanding officer:

> A corporal belonging to the infantry could not go on any further on account of thirst. Colonel Chandler raised his sword, struck the man across the shoulder, cutting a deep gash 6 inches in length. The man fell, bleeding profusely. We went on and left him. On the road we left 4 other men almost dead. 17 horses and mules died from want of water. . . . I went ahead with 6 men, found a spring; drank copiously, filled a dozen canteens; turned back, picked up the 4 men and gave them water. . . . I found the man wounded by Colonel Chandler just gasping his last breath. Got down from my horse, put the canteen of water to his lips. He opened his eyes, recognized me, and died thanking me for the favor I had done him, a poor victim of an inhuman tyrant. I hope that a day of retribution will surely come.[92]

Military officers, commonly assumed to be the civilized gentlemen of the frontier army, often fell short of that popular perception. Daniel T. Chandler seems to have fit Bennett's description quite well. In several instances the colonel acted in a manner destitute of morality. Indeed, this same officer knowingly ordered the controversial attack on a peaceful Gila Apache camp along the Mimbres River two years earlier (see chapter 7). No report of the soldier's murder ever reached headquarters; Bennett's account appeared in his personal diary, published almost one hundred years after the incident occurred.

Under the diligent guidance of their new agent, Dr. Steck, the Mescaleros' raiding habits gradually waned in the years following the establishment of a subagency at Fort Stanton. Colonel Bonneville praised both Steck and Fort Stanton's commanding officer, Major Holmes, writing in December 1856 that "the good understanding established . . . and since continued by their agent Dr. Steck, is having its beneficial effects—these Indians now visit Fort Stanton with confidence and in large numbers."[93] In the spring of 1857, with the Mescaleros still in a state of starvation, Steck hired several Mexicans to teach the Indians how to farm in hopes that their self-sufficiency might partially relieve their dependence on rations and the government's economic burden in providing them. He allotted seventy acres to the tribe in La Luz Canyon (northeast of present-day Alamogordo), at the foot of the Sacramento Mountains.[94] Steck believed this to be an ideal location since the Mescaleros constantly feared being attacked by the Comanches on New Mexico's southeastern plains. Indeed, Comanches had been the Apaches' traditional enemies for many years, and Mexican officials in Chihuahua had attempted to perpetuate intertribal hostilities beginning in the mid-1830s.[95] Settling on the western slopes of the Sacramentos would allow the mountains to act as a buffer zone, thus reducing the band's vulnerability to Comanche raids. Several Mescalero headmen met Steck at La Luz and approved the location.[96]

The Mescaleros had previously been afforded only two options with the influx of American troops and settlers: either steal or starve. By teaching them to farm, Steck hoped to provide a third alternative, one that would benefit everybody if it succeeded. His continued refusal to issue rations to the Mescaleros until they returned all stolen livestock catapulted them into an urgent predicament. The starving Indians often butchered and ate stolen animals immediately and therefore could not return them. This made it impossible for them to adhere to Steck's conditions, and he therefore minimized their allotment of rations. Governor Meriwether took issue with this strategy, blaming the agent's withholding of provisions for Indian raids throughout southern New Mexico, despite the fact that many of these depredations were attributed to Gila Apaches, not Mescaleros.[97]

Unfortunately, the Apache way of life did not support the Indian Bureau's agrarian plans; since time immemorial they had been a nomadic people who rarely remained in one place long enough to raise crops. One of Morris Opler's Apache informants told him: "My people did not practice farming. The Indians had many plants which were given to them [by nature] and did not have to farm. They moved around too much also."[98] This characteristic of Apache culture contributed to the continued failure of farming experiments throughout the 1850s, although officials often neglected to understand. Mescalero chiefs returned stolen animals whenever they could in hopes that Steck would recommence issuing rations, which he finally did in November 1856. From that point on, the Mescaleros received monthly provisions at Fort Stanton under the stipulation that if raiding resumed, the government would immediately stop feeding them. The policy worked well; a year later Steck happily reported that the group had not perpetrated any depredations during that time, enabling the military department to reduce Fort Stanton's garrison.

By the late 1850s, the Mescaleros began to settle down and desist from raiding north of the international border, although ranches in northern Mexico remained a target. This lull in hostilities provided a perfect opportunity for Mesilla's citizens to recruit their own militia unit and attack the now-peaceful Indians. In February 1858 a sizable contingent of Mescaleros had camped within three miles of Doña Ana and was living there peaceably when a local unincorporated militia, known as the Mesilla Guard, launched a surprise attack. Three Indians perished in the initial assault, whereupon the truculent Mexican militants rode through Doña Ana and began shooting indiscriminately at any Indian they saw. By the time the smoke cleared, nine Mescaleros had been killed, including Chief Shawono. Within a few days a force of over one hundred warriors arrived under Chief Gomez, intent on avenging the murders.[99] Department Commander Garland immediately perceived the severity of the situation at hand, informing his superiors in Washington, D.C., that "this will doubtless give us much trouble" and warning them to expect the worst.[100]

Lieutenant J. W. Alley of the Third Infantry promptly left Fort Fillmore to investigate the incident. His report provides some insight into the mentality of the self-appointed militia. "This Mexican band is held in high esteem by the people of Mesilla," Alley noted. "A party seems to be constantly held in readiness to pursue Indians . . . and when not employed on active service of this nature, [they are] enjoying certain civil privileges in that town."[101] According to Colonel Miles, the Mesilla Guard consisted of about one hundred men, including landholders who volunteered for duty. The majority of the force, however, was comprised of peons who served involuntarily in their master's place. Typically, these destitute men had either run away from ranches in northern Mexico or deserted from the Mexican army and worked as laborers in the fields near Mesilla. In the attack at Doña Ana, only five of the participants were believed to be actual landholders. "Should this independent action of the inhabitants of Mesilla continue," Miles foretold, "the Indians will to a certainty unite . . . by wiping this town out."[102]

Fortunately, Steck learned of the incident and arrived from Fort Thorn in time to defuse the crisis. He successfully deterred Chief Gomez and his war party from going into Mesilla, convincing the Indians to retire to their reservation at Fort Stanton and await the decision of the U.S. district court on the matter. Steck was probably the only man in the territory who could have pacified such a tense situation with the Apaches. Colonel Miles buttressed the agent's authority by threatening to "carry war into their country" if the Mescaleros attacked Mesilla. Anticipating retaliatory action, Miles requested that headquarters reinforce the Fort Fillmore garrison in case of such an assault. "From the numerous signal fires around the mountains... [there is] not a doubt but the Apaches are collecting to take revenge," he observed from within the fort's walls, "and a terrible bloody retribution will follow.... [T]his act will bring the entire Mescalero nation into active hostility."[103]

Miles hurriedly penned a letter to the prefect of Doña Ana County, Rafael Ruelas, warning that every citizen residing in the vicinity, and especially those in Mesilla, faced imminent danger. "It would be well for you to warn the inhabitants of the impending storm... that will break soon over them," the colonel instructed. Perhaps reluctantly, he also offered the assistance of his troops should the need arise: "At any alarm of danger I will come to your assistance with whatever troops I can spare from this fort. You know I have but two [Infantry] companies.... I can defend, but I cannot pursue with any probability of success in overtaking."[104] Without any dragoons or mounted riflemen at Fort Fillmore, an Indian attack would have had a high probability of success. The Apaches would come not only well armed but also well mounted, and the foot soldiers would have had little hope of chasing them down.

The incident infuriated territorial officials in Santa Fe, many of whom viewed the action as debilitating to state power. After years of struggle, the Mescaleros had finally been induced to remain peaceful, and now the brash actions of a few Mesilla citizens jeopardized all previous progress. General Garland threatened to abandon Fort Fillmore and leave the residents to fend for themselves, instructing Colonel Miles that, "as the people of Messilla [*sic*] have taken it upon themselves to protect that region of country against Indian depredation, the garrison of Fort Fillmore will be no longer required, and... the next mail will bring an order for... the evacuation of the remainder of the garrison."[105] Military authorities did not take the situation lightly and clearly sought to make their dissatisfaction known to Mesilla's population.

For area citizens, especially those in Mesilla, removing troops from Fort Fillmore would have been disastrous, and they knew it.

Not only did they rely upon the soldiers for protection from Apache raiding, but local merchants also held lucrative contracts to supply the post with forage and other essential provisions. The withdrawal of the troops would have left the people vulnerable to Indian attacks while simultaneously undermining the local economy.

Mesilla's residents, led by prominent local figures Charles A. Hoppin and James A. Lucas, immediately sent an appeal to Garland, explaining that they believed themselves justified in maintaining the militia unit because there were no mounted troops stationed at Fort Fillmore. They felt an obligation "to pursue and chastise the marauding Indians," and this could not be done with infantry troops. Therefore, they "felt it imperatively necessary to form a company of mounted men."[106] The idea of an armed militia to fight Indians had been suggested and even promoted by former governor James Calhoun as early as 1851, but times had changed, and the Indian Bureau no longer condoned civilians taking matters into their own hands.

The petition, bearing some six hundred signatures, claimed both ignorance of and indifference toward the Doña Ana incident, noting that reports of the attack had been "grossly exaggerated and false." Still, the fact that nine Indians had been slain could not be denied, nor could the conclusive findings of the army's investigation be ignored. The petitioners assumed an overall tone of self-pity and desperation. "There is no county in the territory more exposed, or more in want of military protection than Doña Ana," they pleaded, "[and] if you adhere to your intention of evacuating Fort Fillmore, the result will be disastrous not only to the residents of the county but to the travelers on the roads." If Garland would reinforce the fort with a company of dragoons, the Mesilla citizenry promised to disband their militia. Eventually, Garland withdrew his threat and left the garrison intact, but he refused to send additional troops.[107] Replying directly to the petitioners, he reminded them that Mesilla "is the strongest settlement in New Mexico, and there are two posts with mounted men, each within 40 miles of the town, with every disposition to protect the lives and property of the inhabitants." But if Mesilla residents continued to undertake independent hostile action toward peaceful Apaches, Garland assured them that they would "have no claim to the protection of the military, and will receive none."[108]

"I do not think [we] will ever again hear from the action of their volunteer company," Colonel Miles optimistically predicted after a substantial period of time had passed since the incident.[109] Judging by citizens' pleas to General Garland, it stood to reason that such an attack would not occur again. Unfortunately, Miles spoke prematurely. On April 17, 1858, the Mesilla Guard struck again. Thirty-six heavily armed men made their way up the Rio Grande to Fort Thorn, where a large band of peaceful Mescaleros resided while drawing rations from Steck's agency; many of the Indians even busied themselves with various menial chores at the fort. Nevertheless, the militia attacked, with the result mirroring that of the first incident. Seven Indians died in the ambush (three men, three women, and one boy), and three others sustained wounds. Lieutenant William W. Averell later recalled that "the boy that was killed was a favorite of the garrison, and after killing him the Mexicans had ridden around his body and expended some of their surplus ammunition by shooting his head to pieces."[110] The *Santa Fe Weekly Gazette* corroborated this, noting that the boy "was found and picked up immediately afterwards with his head and body mutilated as if he had been shot with a number of bullets."[111] Initially, some concern arose that more Indians had been killed because many of them fled into the hills during the assault and could not be accounted for, but eventually all of the missing returned.

The seven murdered Apaches were buried behind the Fort Thorn cemetery. "This affair is but a repetition of the horrible massacre perpetrated at Doña Ana," wrote Lieutenant William Henry Wood of the Third Infantry. "These Indians for the last four or five months have been at peace . . . , have been daily in and about this garrison [Fort Thorn], quiet and well behaved and I sincerely believe have given no cause for this cowardly outrage."[112] By all accounts these Apaches were held in high esteem among the troops, who associated with them on an almost daily basis, evidencing the success of Steck's ration program and continuing overtures of friendship.

The militiamen did not get far after their attack. When they congregated atop a hill half a mile from the fort, Lieutenants Wood and Howland of the Regiment of Mounted Rifles promptly overtook and arrested them, at which time Juan Ortega came forward and identified himself as the group's leader.[113] Lieutenant Wood then "brought [them] back into the garrison, disarmed, and placed under a strong guard . . . , [and] was obliged to exercise immediate watchfulness to prevent the soldiers from putting the Mexican fiends to death. . . . [H]ad the enormity of the outrage been fully known to the soldiers when they captured them, there would have been no subsequent proceedings in which these miscreants would have felt any interest, and the government would have been saved some expense."[114] The culprits remained in the guardhouse until a force of forty-four riflemen escorted them to Socorro for trial.

General Garland and his adjutant, Major Nichols, wholeheartedly approved of Lieutenant Wood's action and commended him for his vigilance under pressure, denouncing the militiamen for having "insulted our flag."[115] He also inquired with Judge Kirby Benedict as to the military's authority in the matter and hoped that Benedict might aid in transferring the culprits to civilian authority so that they could be "committed for murder."[116] The antithesis to Garland's sentiment came from his colleague, Governor Abraham Rencher, who heard of the incident and declared it to be "worthy of imitation." Whereas Garland praised his officers for detaining the attackers, Rencher commended the Mesilla Guard, proclaiming, "They have resolved to help themselves; and though upon one occasion, they may have carried their retaliation too far, it is not in human nature always to suffer injustice and wrong, without sometimes being hurried into a fearful, but salutary retribution."[117] As a lifetime politician from the South, Rencher had little prior affiliation with southwestern tribes and therefore espoused the prevailing anti-Indian sentiments of many easterners when making such statements.

Judge Benedict in Santa Fe promptly issued a warrant for the militiamen's arrest, although they had already been confined in the Fort Thorn guardhouse by that time. Their imprisonment had been brief, however, their families having collected the $5,000 necessary to bail them out.[118] Shortly thereafter, all thirty-six men appeared before a jury in a Socorro courtroom. The prosecution had difficulty proving whether or not the Indians had been killed inside or outside the boundaries of the Fort Thorn military reservation. The defense, consisting of attorneys named Smith and Ashurst, contended that the Indians had stolen several oxen from Juan Ortega at Mesilla, and his actions in raising a militia, tracking the stolen animals to the camp, and then attacking the Apaches had therefore been justified. The prosecution, however, satisfactorily proved that none of the stolen animals were in the Indians' possession at the time of the assault.[119]

The trial garnered a significant amount of attention, with "large crowds of spectators collected in and around the court house to witness the proceedings." But from the beginning, the case was never destined to realize any true form of justice. The jury "retired, and immediately returned with a verdict of not guilty," thus acquitting the defendants of all charges.[120] This clemency drew a prompt condemnation from the *Santa Fe Weekly Gazette,* which published a detailed report of the proceedings. "The killing of those Indians was perpetrated within a very short distance of the flag of our country," an editorial lamented, "a fact which adds largely to the aggravation of this bloody deed."[121] Lieutenant Averell later wrote, "There was nothing in the result of the subsequent court proceedings nor in their treatment by the citizens of Socorro to inculcate the idea that they had not done a meritorious deed."[122] It is worth noting that the jury consisted entirely of the defendants' peers—that is, other Hispanic residents. One must not forget the feelings of animosity that most Mexicans felt toward the Apaches, and vice versa. No jury in New Mexico would have convicted Ortega and his men for killing Apaches; indeed, one army officer present at the proceedings commented that "no verdict against a criminal was ever obtained or expected from a Mexican jury."[123]

Remarkably, there is no evidence to suggest that the Mescaleros ever took any retributive measures. Many had come to realize that retaliation would only bring upon them the army's wrath, something that they had grown weary of over the years. With their families starving and dependent on government rations for survival, the

Apaches could hardly carry on such a fight. If they retaliated, Steck would discontinue the government support they so desperately needed.

These legal troubles minimized the Mesilla Guard's activities but did not cause them to disappear from the scene altogether. The unit temporarily disbanded afterward but returned to duty a mere three years later. In May 1861, with a Confederate invasion of the territory imminent and widespread paranoia prevalent throughout southern New Mexico, the citizens held a meeting in which they authorized Captain George Frazier "to raise a company of rangers to chastise the Apaches for their late outrages. The command at Fort Fillmore makes a liberal offer of ammunitions and provisions to the company."[124] With this, the Mesilla Guard was resurrected, although its members never again committed such egregious acts of unmitigated violence.

Several culminating incidents of hostility occurred between the army and the Mescaleros prior to the outbreak of the Civil War. The first took place on March 10, 1857, when a small band of fifteen to twenty warriors under the leadership of Chief Shawono (who was killed in the Mesilla Guard's February 1858 attack at Doña Ana), struck a wagon train north of Fort Thorn. Lieutenant Baker and thirty-five men of Company B, Regiment of Mounted Rifles immediately left the fort in pursuit, following a trail that led northeast across the Jornada del Muerto toward the Sacramento Mountains. At dawn the next morning the lieutenant and his company overtook the Indians east of Laguna de los Muertos. "I attacked their camp completely surprising them," Baker exulted in his report, "so much so as to be able to approach within 35 or 40 yards of them."[125]

The Apaches held their ground as the troops fired but fled to more-concealed locations when bugler Thomas Reed sounded the charge. At the time he blew the signal, Reed had three Apache arrows sticking in him, one in his back and two in his legs; he would later receive a commendation for his meritorious actions during the battle. Another soldier, Private Patrick Sullivan, was killed by an Apache arrow, and three others sustained severe wounds: Sergeant Dugan; Corporal John Brady, struck in the knee by a musket ball;

and Private Dougherty, who sustained an arrow wound in the head. Dougherty's arrow lodged so deep that it could not be extracted at the scene and remained embedded in his head until Dr. T. Charles Henry, post surgeon at Fort Thorn, arrived a few hours later. "[The arrow] required all [my] strength with forceps to extricate it," the physician ominously recalled. On the Apache side, eight men were believed to have been seriously injured, although the soldiers found none dead on the field.[126]

In perhaps the most desperate encounter of this late-antebellum era, men belonging to Company D, Regiment of Mounted Rifles skirmished with Mescaleros camped in Dog Canyon in February 1859. In the ensuing fight three soldiers were killed and seven others wounded, including the commanding officer, Lieutenant Henry M. Lazelle of the Eighth Infantry, who suffered an excruciating gunshot wound through both lungs but survived.[127] The Indians suffered nine killed and an unknown number wounded. When news of the battle reached Fort Fillmore, a detachment of riflemen under Captain Thomas Claiborne rode to the aid of Lazelle's command. The officers accused Chief Gomez of leading the attack, although that charge could not be proven. Not long afterward, Gomez appeared at Fort Thorn to collect the regularly allotted rations for his band and, when questioned about the incident, "denied emphatically" any involvement.[128]

Surprisingly, bureaucrats in Santa Fe did little in response to this action. To his credit, Colonel Bonneville endeavored to properly identify the culprits, ordering investigations throughout the southern portion of the territory. Several Indian informants claimed that the guilty parties had fled to Texas and sought refuge in the vicinity of Fort Davis, but no positive evidence of their identity or whereabouts surfaced.[129] Perhaps in desperation, Bonneville proposed a large campaign against the Mescaleros to mirror the one he had led against the Mogollons and Coyoteros in 1857, but his recommendations went unheeded. Captain William H. Gordon, commanding at Fort Fillmore, fully understood the futility of the situation. In response to the colonel's proposed campaign, Gordon justly claimed that "it would require about 150 men to operate to any advantage . . . , a small force can do nothing in those canyons and mountains." Furthermore, the captain professed to be "totally ignorant of the country east of the Rio Grande" in which he would be operating.[130] Finally, a campaign could not have been led from his post because not enough troops could be mustered. It would have required men from at least four different posts to fill the order for such a large expedition, and the failure of the Gila Campaign two years earlier left most military officials skeptical of the possible outcome.

Since 1849 the army had contended with the Mescalero Apaches, meeting with almost continuous failure until 1855. With the construction of Fort Stanton and the death of the pugnacious chief Santa Anna, depredations began dwindling in the latter half of the decade. But occasional hostile uprisings did occur. Several independent actions on the part of the territory's citizens—especially the Mesilla Guard—incited unnecessary violence by targeting mostly innocent Apaches encamped near their agencies. Likewise, many of the military's campaigns also harmed guiltless subgroups within the larger tribe. Both sides suffered immensely throughout the violence of the decade. On the American side, several dozen troops fell victim to Apache bullets and arrows, while an untold number of Mescaleros died at the hands of the soldiers.

Diplomatic overtures and treaty negotiations on the part of Indian Bureau officials generally failed until the establishment of a reservation at Fort Stanton in 1855, after which time many of the Mescaleros settled nearby and desisted from raiding in exchange for government-issued rations. The Civil War years would prove to be difficult for the entire tribe as the military pursued an alternative strategy that forced them onto a shared reservation with the Navajos and effectively undermined any progress toward peace. In many ways relations with the Mescaleros directly mirrored what occurred between the government and the Chiricahuas during this same period. Neither Apache group benefitted from the lack of cohesion between American civil and military authorities, ultimately resulting in little progress in antebellum Indian affairs.

CHAPTER 10

The Dragoons' Final Years

During the late 1850s, a decline in Apache activity throughout southern New Mexico became noticeable, due in large part to continuous military campaigning but also to several bands drawing rations and living peaceably near posts and agencies, especially at Fort Stanton and Fort Thorn. Another factor was the looming sectional conflict, having now become all but certain. By the waning years of the decade, with Apache raids occurring less frequently, the army began directing its efforts toward thwarting any potential southern invasion of New Mexico. Still, by sheer necessity, troops continued to engage in occasional hostilities with the Apaches, while civil officials sustained their indefatigable quest to formulate an effective and permanent Indian policy. Despite changes in both civil and military leadership, these two governmental authorities generally cooperated in executing a policy whereby the continual implementation of military force encouraged the Apaches to desist from visiting the settlements. Several occurrences between 1857 and 1861 perpetuated this pattern while also signifying a gradual transition away from Indian warfare as the military's attention turned eastward to more demanding threats.

David Meriwether resigned as New Mexico's governor in May 1857, after serving for nearly four years, much longer than either of his two embattled predecessors. Much to his credit, he had generally worked harmoniously with fellow civil officials and cooperated on a professional level with the military. As Meriwether's successor, President Buchanan selected Abraham Rencher, a North Carolina Democrat with proslavery leanings who had almost thirty years of political experience.[1] During Rencher's incumbency, the offices of governor and superintendent of Indian affairs became separate entities for the first time, meaning that he would not have the same level of direct involvement that his three predecessors had. This doubtless came as a relief to Rencher, as he could claim only minimal knowledge of the territory's tribes upon assuming office. Like that of many of his colleagues, Rencher's appointment owed more to his loyalty as a Democrat rather than to any inherent expertise on New Mexico's environment or culture. James L. Collins, a merchant and former editor of the *Santa Fe Weekly Gazette* who had lived in the territory for a number of years, became New Mexico's first non-governor to administer Indian affairs and thus would work closely with Rencher.[2] Unlike those of Calhoun, Lane, and Meriwether, the new governor's term of office would be defined not so much by his handling of Indian uprisings as by the preparations made to ready the territory for the rampant paranoia emanating from the secession crisis.

The Apaches knew little if anything about sectional predicaments, slave debates, secession threats, or the ultimate outbreak in hostilities occurring two thousand miles away. They continued to live and subsist as they had, as yet unaffected by the turmoil occurring in the East. On July 22, 1857, after receiving reports of depredations, Sergeant Hugh McQuade left Fort Craig and followed a southbound Indian trail that led directly to a grisly scene. Indians had attacked a camp of fifteen Mexican herders, killing and scalping every one of them. Pressing on with increased resolve, McQuade and his detachment followed the trail westward into the Mogollon Mountains. With the soldiers in hot pursuit, the marauding Apaches began abandoning the stolen sheep—some 700 of them—along the way and managed to escape. The fifteen victims represented one of the largest civilian death tolls inflicted at one time since before New Mexico came under U.S. control in 1846.[3]

On December 11 the Fort Craig garrison again received reports of livestock thefts, this time at a ranch three miles to the south. Eleven men of Company F, Mounted Rifles, under the command of Lieutenant Averell and Sergeant McQuade, arrived at the scene and discovered the Indians still inside the house. Remarkably the troops approached unnoticed, and almost immediately, according to Averell, "a dozen Indians with their chief came rushing out of the doorway to be held up with the rifles and revolvers of my men who were formed in a semicircle in front of the entrance. We had the dead drop on them and they were silent and quiet." The standoff did not last long. "We had not gone ten yards," Averell continued, "when the chief gave a peculiar yell and the Indians, stooping down, flew out between our horses and scattered like a covey of partridges. I called to my men to fire and hunt them down, and fired at the chief myself, hitting him in the side and back."[4]

McQuade's report differed somewhat in the details of the event. The sergeant stated that the Indians, after being taken prisoner, attempted their flight while en route back to Fort Craig. Averell, however, implied that the escape took place almost immediately after the initial confrontation at the ranch house and prior to their arrest. Chaos inevitably ensued. Following the initial volley, the Indians scattered in all directions, with individual soldiers chasing them to the utmost of their ability. The Apaches suffered three casualties from the opening shots, one killed and two others badly wounded. Three of them attempted to cross the Rio Grande, during which one drowned and was spotted by one of the soldiers floating downriver.[5] Averell vividly recounted being engaged in hand-to-hand combat with the wounded chief:

> The chief ran around the ranch by the north end and I by the south and met him on the river side when I fired again hitting him in the thigh. As I cocked my pistol the fourth time, the lever which revolved the chamber was broken by a protruding bullet preventing movement. Then I ran

to the Indian to strike him with it upon the head. He met me aggressively and seized my uplifted right wrist with his left hand and my left elbow with his right and turned me around into the hollow of his left arm drawing my right arm under my left, all in one quick motion ... [;] we were about the same height, he the heavier. I was young and strong and had never been seriously injured. We tore up about a square rod of the ground in our struggle. I realized that if I ever lost hold of his right wrist my life would go. ... I thought of a great many things: one was, if he was hit in the shooting, why didn't he weaken? He did not pause an instant for breath, as most wrestlers do, while my breath was giving out. He was native to this rarified air and I was unused to it. ... [J]ust then I heard Jackson's voice, "Steady Averell, I'm going to shoot ... ," a revolver was thrust under my right arm, there was a report and the Indian let go and sank to the ground.[6]

Despite this incredible struggle, the chief did not immediately succumb to his wounds. Thinking him to be dead, Averell briefly turned his attention to the other fleeing Apaches. When he returned to collect the body, the chief had disappeared. The wounded leader hid in a small locked room in the ranch house, where the young lieutenant found and detained him, later depositing him in the Fort Craig jail.

By August 1857 the Fort Thorn guardhouse confined thirty-eight captive Apache women and children. Reports did not specify why they had been apprehended, nor is there any evidence of their being guilty of any wrongdoing. After just two weeks there, five had perished, probably victims of the prevalent malarial illnesses that plagued the area. As a gesture of humanity, the post commander recommended that the remaining prisoners be transferred south to Fort Fillmore, hoping that their conditions might improve. A week later the survivors arrived at that post, but the change in location did little to remedy their poor health as they continued to perish at an alarming rate.[7] It therefore came as little surprise to Colonel

Miles when twenty-three of these Indians escaped under cover of darkness. When news spread of their flight the following morning, Miles dispatched three search parties to follow their trails, all leading eastward into the steep defiles and rocky chasms of the Organ Mountains. All of the Apaches successfully evaded recapture, except for one woman who the soldiers discovered dead in the desert, apparently having succumbed to thirst and heat exhaustion. Miles blamed the escape on the negligence of the guards and acknowledged the possibility that the men purposely allowed the prisoners to flee. If true, then the Indians had been blessed by a rare instance in which humanity prevailed, for they all might have perished had they remained in confinement at the post.[8]

By the latter months of 1858, it had become apparent across the department that Fort Thorn should be abandoned "on account of the sickness of the troops."[9] Officers, doctors, and soldiers alike had been pleading for the abandonment of this post for years, and authorities finally took action. On January 6, 1859, Colonel Bonneville received a communication from Secretary of War John B. Floyd informing him that the post's closure had been approved. The department commander promptly wrote to Major Gordon, then commanding at Fort Thorn, ordering that he prepare his troops for removal. All quartermaster stores were freighted south to Fort Fillmore, and by January 18 only a detachment of twelve men and one officer remained. Within two more months the last occupants had departed, marking the end of a post that had played a critical role in southwestern Indian affairs for over five years.[10]

One of the last major antebellum operations directed toward the Gila Apaches took place in the summer of 1859, when on June 27 Colonel Bonneville ordered a campaign into their country. Captain William H. Gordon of the Third Infantry and Lieutenant George W. Howland of Company C, Mounted Rifles left Fort Fillmore with a force of 130 troops: forty-eight dragoons, fifty-two infantrymen, and thirty riflemen. The command was under orders to scout the Gila River valley, and on July 5 it established headquarters at Ojo de Lucero, southeast of the Burro Mountains. Gordon and Howland reported resources to be abundant at that location, going so far as to suggest that a permanent post be constructed there.

Furthermore, the camp at Ojo de Lucero sat in close enough proximity to the copper mines at Santa Rita del Cobre that the soldiers could quickly respond to any threats the Apaches might make to American miners there. As an added incentive, the Ojo de Lucero site lay less than ten miles north of the Butterfield Overland Mail route. This would make a military installation there instrumental in preventing the Apache depredations that continually plagued civilian travelers and mail contractors traversing the region.

Bonneville also had a favorable impression of the site. "The valley of the Mimbres is beginning to be settled," he wrote, "[and] a post located southeast of the Burro Mountains eight or ten miles north of the Overland Mail Station [at Cow Springs], overlooking the valley, would have a moral influence over the surrounding Indians, and would cover the country laid open by the abandonment of Fort Thorn."[11] The favorable attributes of Ojo de Lucero, nestled in a small valley cutting through a grassy prairie that rises gradually toward the mountains farther north, so deeply suited Lieutenant Howland's fancy that he requested permission to begin immediate construction of barracks and officers' quarters. He enlisted the aid of his accompanying surgeon, who penned a letter to department headquarters outlining the location's benefits from his medical perspective. In Steck's 1859 annual report he too represented Ojo de Lucero to be a feasible location for a new fort. "The post would be within twenty-five miles of the Indian planting ground, and between them and the settlements, and within eight miles of the great overland mail route," he wrote. "This post, cooperating with two companies stationed upon the San Pedro [River], and two near Tucson, would induce the settlement of this country, and, in the event of war, would be a sufficient force to chastise the Indians."[12] Ultimately, headquarters denied permission to build the post, and troops never again occupied the site after the column's withdrawal later that summer.[13]

During their two month stay at Ojo de Lucero, the soldiers did not remain inactive. A portion of the command, consisting of approximately fifty troops under Captain Gordon, left on July 10 for an extensive scout of the Santa Lucia Springs region, a favorite camping place for several Apache bands and the same area that

Governor Lane proposed for an Apache reservation during his treaty negotiations at Fort Webster in 1853. Dr. Steck awaited the soldiers' arrival there, intending to inspect the crops being cultivated by some four hundred of Mangas Coloradas's followers. For several weeks the agent resided with the Apaches in their camps while "instructing them how to plant."[14] According to Gordon, the Indians seemed amicably disposed and had begun planting corn, their fields "extending some three miles in length" down the canyon adjoining Santa Lucia Springs to the Gila River. Mangas Coloradas took the captain on a personal tour of his cornfields, of which the aging chief seemed to be very proud.[15] Steck, like Governor Lane, determined that the site would serve well as a reservation for the Apaches, recognizing it as one of their favorite camping places and also as being conducive to farming. Bonneville himself noted that "the mass of them were desirous of being at peace, so much so that they would not allow him [Steck] to travel about for hunting or other purposes without sending two of their people with him for fear some accident might happen and suspicion be thrown upon them."[16] The colonel's observation serves as a testimonial to the high regard in which the Apaches held Steck as their agent.

Despite the officers' high hopes, the entire operation was abandoned by September 19, and Colonel Bonneville ordered the troops permanently withdrawn from Ojo de Lucero. Howland, in a final plea to construct a post there, explained that his men had almost completed a stone corral and had begun gathering building materials for barracks and storehouses. His appeal, however, fell upon deaf ears in Santa Fe. Although they had come in close contact with the friendly followers of Mangas Coloradas, who according to the lieutenant, had visited the military camp almost daily, no hostile Apaches had been encountered by any of the scouting expeditions.[17] In this Howland and Gordon must be commended inasmuch as they properly identified the Apaches in their vicinity as being peaceful and therefore did not attack them. Their prudence represented a stark contrast to the actions of other military officers throughout the 1850s.

Perhaps the most noteworthy accomplishment of the entire operation stemmed from the increased military presence providing an opportunity for Steck to safely conduct his reconnaissance of the Santa Lucia Springs area. The agent immediately began pressuring Congress to establish a permanent fifteen-square-mile reservation there, the first such recommendation since 1855, when Governor Meriwether suggested a site along the Mimbres River. Owing to the rapid influx of white settlers to the Mimbres and Santa Rita del Cobre regions, Steck's proposal for a reservation near secluded Santa Lucia Springs would have been beneficial and might have prevented many of the ensuing Civil War–era hostilities between the Indians and newly arriving prospectors. The region (now known as Mangas Springs for the chief who for many years called the area his home) remained more sparsely populated than the valley of the Mimbres River and the area surrounding the Santa Rita copper mines (where several large mining camps appeared in the 1860s).

In May 1860 Steck traveled to Washington, D.C., to consult with Commissioner of Indian Affairs Alfred B. Greenwood regarding the Santa Lucia Springs site. He proposed removing all bands of the Chiricahua Apaches to this location, leaving the Mescaleros at Fort Stanton east of the Rio Grande. The agent reiterated the importance of the opportunity in a letter to Greenwood: "These Indians complain very much about our permitting the people to settle in their country. They say they are occupying the best portions of it and fast running them out—and every word of their complaints are true." Indeed, by that time, "at least forty settlers [lived] on the Mimbres, most of them with their families, and not less than one thousand souls . . . at or near the Copper Mines." Steck concluded by asking, "If some steps are not taken to set apart a portion of their country as a reserve they will have none worth having left. . . . [C]annot something be done at the present session of Congress?"[18]

Greenwood wrote to General Land Office commissioner Joseph S. Wilson indicating his approbation for the reserve and requesting that his officers acknowledge its boundaries in their reports.[19] Shortly afterward, Congress appropriated $1,500 for Steck to build an agency at Santa Lucia Springs and to erect markers denoting the boundaries; unfortunately, this sum represented only half of the funding Steck projected would be necessary to complete the work.[20] This shortfall effectively undermined his benign intentions. Nevertheless, an optimistic Steck went ahead with his plans, partnering with a government surveyor in September 1860 to demarcate the boundary lines of his proposed reserve. The surveying crew identified each corner with "large stone monuments" and denoted the actual boundary lines with stone mounds at one-mile intervals.[21] Despite Commissioner Greenwood's support, other leading officials dissented, and ultimately Steck's Santa Lucia reservation, much like the Mimbres valley reserve proposed by Governor Meriwether in 1855, fell into obscurity and became another failed Indian-policy objective.[22] The agent could not be blamed for this failure, for he exhibited tremendous zeal and determination in promulgating the creation of a reservation. Rather, differing opinions among higher-ranking officials, coupled with the coming of the Civil War, had the result of marginalizing Steck's proposal in Washington.

On the eve of the Civil War, two significant but unrelated events combined to drive the Chiricahua Apaches to hostilities in southern New Mexico. In an unrelenting flurry of violence, Apaches targeted civilians and military men alike in retribution for two unprovoked attacks that claimed the lives of many Indians. The first incident occurred on December 4, 1860, when a group of approximately thirty miners led by James H. Tevis assaulted a peaceful and unsuspecting Gila Apache camp along the Mimbres River. The assailants killed four Indians, including Chief Elías, and carried away another thirteen women and children as captives.[23] The second event, the Bascom Affair, occurred two months later, on February 4, 1861, and involved the famed Apache chief Cochise. The Bascom Affair is widely considered to be the predominant instigating factor in the widespread Apache hostilities that plagued the region for the duration of the Civil War.[24] By the time the Confederates invaded New Mexico in June 1861, Apache plundering and pillaging in response to these atrocities had become uncontrollable.

In the summer of 1861, southern New Mexico fell under the leadership of Confederate officers. Led by Colonel John R. Baylor and his regiment of Texas volunteers, the Rebel invasion succeeded in wresting the entire southern portion of the territory from Union control and establishing the "Confederate Territory of Arizona." Despite the temporary changes in civil and military jurisdiction, however, the Apache threat remained. The Indians made little distinction between Confederate and Union forces; to them they were one and the same enemy and posed an equal threat to their traditional ways of life. Despite their vast political and ideological differences, both Northerners and Southerners entertained the same imagined disposition for the southwestern landscape when it came to the settlement and economic exploitation of the region.

The *Mesilla Times,* a staunchly pro-South (and short-lived) newspaper, succinctly addressed the Apache threat in July 1861, just days before the Confederates arrived. The newspaper's editor, Robert P. Kelley, observed that raiding had worsened during the preceding months, owing in large part to the fact that Union soldiers had become preoccupied with the Texan invasion and paid little attention to Indian activities. With troops having been withdrawn from the more-secluded military posts in southern New Mexico (Forts Buchanan, Breckenridge, and McLane) and concentrated at Forts Fillmore and Craig along the Rio Grande, the Apaches became bolder in their raids with each passing day. The newspaper painted a gloomy picture of the situation on the eve of the Confederate invasion:

> The rumors of Apache depredations and of Apache murders come to us from all sides and quarters. They ... have been allowed to go on unchecked for so long a space of time, they grow bolder and bolder at each successive stage. They think they have driven off the Overland Mail and compelled the United States troops to abandon their forts and leave the country. They have compelled the abandonment of mines and mining districts, of ranches and whole valleys, and nothing seems to limit their daring. They will soon get some understanding of the war movements now going on amid the whites, and when they once appreciate these difficulties their operations will be incessant and unrestrained,

and a few weeks will wipe out the progress of civilization of years. The situation of Arizona is gloomy in the extreme.[25]

Kelley's editorial exemplified the rapidly changing times in southern New Mexico. The occupying Confederate army had little sympathy for the Apaches. Colonel Baylor despised the Indians more than any prior official in New Mexico. He continually struggled with the problems arising from Apache depredations, and his prior history as an Indian fighter from Texas, coupled with a predetermined personal hatred for all Indians regardless of tribal affiliation, did not help matters. In an infamous letter written to one of his captains, Thomas Helm, he advanced his genocidal ideology, which ultimately catapulted the commander of Confederate Arizona into controversy among his peers.

Most who read Baylor's letter, even those who agreed with him in his malign sentiments toward the Apaches, openly denounced him for it. Baylor ordered Helm, among other things, to "use all means to persuade the Apaches or any tribe to come in for the purpose of making peace, and when you get them together kill all the grown Indians and take the children prisoners and sell them to defray the cost of killing the Indians. Buy whiskey and such other goods as may be necessary for the Indians . . . and have a sufficient number of men around to allow no Indian to escape."[26] Clearly the Confederates cared little for the interests of the Apaches and other Indian tribes in New Mexico and Arizona. The same could be said for the majority of Union officials in New Mexico as well. Only one person, Michael Steck, seemed to hold the best interests of the Indians at heart. When speaking to Congress (and to the entire nation for that matter) in defense of "savage" Apaches, one man simply could not garner enough support. Public sentiment did not play into the favor of the Indians, and indeed it rarely, if ever, had.

As a result of the Civil War and the effect of the Confederate invasion on affairs throughout the territory, Apache relations reverted back to a more hostile nature that had not been seen since prior to 1856. While continued military campaigns in the late 1850s often discouraged large-scale depredations, smaller raids occurred periodically throughout that period. For a brief time it appeared that relations had begun to improve, with Steck fostering beneficent feelings at his Southern Apache Agency and some of the Mescaleros having settled on a reservation. Many Chiricahua and Mescalero Apaches refrained from hostilities, opting instead to draw rations at Fort Thorn and Fort Stanton.

The Civil War reversed all progress that had been made. With opposing American troops pitted against one another in a chaotic series of battles along the Rio Grande, the Apaches seized the opportunity and recommenced raiding practices on a scale unseen for several years. Posts located amid tribal homelands had been completely abandoned, and a military presence no longer protected secluded ranches and settlements. The Indians, unaware of the larger American conflict, perceived this army withdrawal as a complete retreat by Anglo-Americans. The absence of troops from New Mexico's outlying posts continued until 1863, by which time the Confederate threat to New Mexico had entirely dissipated. Accordingly, the Apaches enjoyed almost three years of relative freedom from military persecution, allowing them to raid the small settlements with less probability of being opposed or pursued. This brought about a new dynamic to Anglo-Apache relations, one that completely redefined the nature of the conflict in the post–Civil War years, after the military had once again returned in full force to its outposts in the Apache homelands.

Conclusion

For more than a decade, the Apaches had engaged in a continuous power struggle with the United States, both its government officials and civilian settlers. Dozens of military campaigns into Apache country had returned with little or nothing to show aside from exacerbating an already shaky diplomatic relationship. By the early 1860s, this pattern began to change rapidly. After Abraham Lincoln's election as president, the secession of several southern states became imminent and civil war became not a matter of if, but when. With the nation facing such arduous times, conflict with Indians on the frontier became a distraction and garnered less attention, taking second stage to a struggle that threatened not just the settlers in far-removed western territories but also the very existence of the Republic.

When the troops permanently abandoned posts such as Fort Thorn, Fort Fillmore, and Fort Buchanan in 1861, the Apaches did not understand why. To them the army had finally conceded defeat and was leaving them alone to return to their traditional lifeways. "There came a great war when white men fought white, and their troops were withdrawn from our territory," recounted one Apache, James Kaywaykla. "Mangas Coloradas and Cochise thought that at last the invaders were giving up the attempt at conquest, and they rejoiced."[1] Southern New Mexicans, left to defend themselves in the wake of the military's withdrawal, were ravaged by increased Apache raiding during the Civil War years. This proved especially true in southern Arizona, where Fort Buchanan had once discouraged such forays. Unfortunately, what little progress had been made toward peaceful relations in the late 1850s had dissipated. As the Confederate threat subsided and the war came to a close, "the White Eyes returned in hordes to take our land from us," as one Apache warrior put it many years later.[2]

Much of the southwestern United States experienced a rapid increase in population throughout the 1860s and 1870s. All across the western frontier, mining towns popped up in the heart of traditional Indian landscapes. In the Gila Apache country, Piños Altos became the first such town, settled in 1860 by gold miners several miles northwest of the Santa Rita copper mines.[3] The Apaches reacted in defiant opposition to this permanent settlement in their homelands, and the presence of rowdy, apathetic miners inevitably occasioned violence. Despite threats of Indian vengeance, hundreds of Anglo-American goldseekers flooded into the area, most of whom fostered a sentiment of preconceived contempt toward the Apaches. Sylvester Mowry, a civilian with mining interests in southeastern Arizona, perhaps best reflected contemporary American thought on Indians in general: "My own impression is that the Apaches cannot be tamed; civilization is out of the question.... [T]here is only one way to wage war against the Apaches. A steady, persistent campaign must be made, following them to their haunts.... They must be surrounded, starved into coming in, supervised, or put to death. If these ideas shock any weak-minded individual who thinks himself a philanthropist, I can only say I pity without respecting his mistaken sympathy. A man might as well have sympathy for a rattlesnake."[4]

Writings such as Mowry's, often widely distributed throughout eastern social circles, painted a hyperbolically negative image of the southwestern frontier generally and of the Apaches specifically. Western travel narratives became popular during this time and almost invariably conveyed pessimistic, stereotypical descriptions of frontier Indians. As long as travelogues continued to advance such notions, and as long as eastern newspapers continued carrying stories of Apache atrocities and unabated raiding, settlement and economic development in the Southwest would be slow in materializing. This provided a continuing incentive for the military to take aggressive action. In view of encouraging settlement, many antebellum territorial and federal officials had sought to eliminate unfavorable publicity by eradicating the Apache threat through whatever means necessary. Only with their subjugation could the land truly be made available for American exploitation.

In 1863 friction between the two cultures reached a climax when treacherous white miners at Piños Altos captured Mangas Coloradas and turned him over to troops at nearby Fort McLane. Established on December 1, 1860, by Major Isaac Lynde, that post became the site of one of the greatest wrongdoings ever perpetrated upon the Chiricahuas, a driving force of armed conflict for another twenty years. After receiving custody of Mangas Coloradas, the soldiers promptly locked him in the post guardhouse. At the time of the chief's arrest, Brigadier General Joseph Rodman West instructed: "Men, that old murderer has got away from every soldier command and has left a trail of blood for 500 miles on the old stage line. . . . I want him dead."[5] Before the sun rose the next morning, West's desire had been fulfilled. During the night several soldiers tortured the old chief while he sat in confinement. After heating their bayonets in a campfire, they amused themselves by poking his bare feet with the red-hot steel. When Mangas Coloradas finally offered a verbal retort, the soldiers shot him dead. Afterward, the men decapitated him and shipped his head back east for examination by a phrenologist. The doctor's report stated that the chief had a single bullet hole in his head. It had entered from the back.[6]

Mangas Coloradas had been the single-most-influential Apache leader throughout the 1850s, and countless times he had expressed his good will toward the Anglo-Americans. Virtually every Indian agent and army officer in the territory had become acquainted with him, so great was his importance. Indeed, other Apache leaders frequently explained that no treaty would be taken seriously unless it bore the mark of Mangas Coloradas. Since Kearny's arrival in 1846, the chief had endeavored to maintain peaceful relations, and for all of his trouble, he received only an execution-style death, shot in the back of the head in a prison cell at an isolated frontier fort.

The murder of Mangas Coloradas would not go unpunished by his people. "The killing of an unarmed man who has gone to an enemy under truce was an incomprehensible act, but infinitely worse was the mutilation of his body," one Apache later explained. "Most Apaches believe that the body will go through eternity in the condition in which it leaves the earth, and for that reason they abhor mutilation. Little did the White Eyes know how they would pay when they defiled the body of our great chief!"[7] Revenge came swiftly and in many forms. Countless white settlers were subsequently captured and tortured—the Apache method of evening the score for Mangas Coloradas's decapitation. Many innocent people became victims not only of Apache vengeance but also of the utter ignorance and stupidity displayed by the U.S. soldiers and their officers that fateful night in 1863. The murder of Mangas Coloradas at Fort McLane ranks alongside the 1861 Bascom Affair at Apache Pass and the 1886 surrender of Geronimo as one of the defining moments in the history of the Apache Indian Wars, and his death marked the end of an era in Apache relations with Anglo-Americans.

Commencing with the arrival of American troops in 1846, responsibility for Indian affairs in New Mexico shifted from the Mexican federal government to that of the United States. This propagated a conceptual shift in policy, both at the civil and military levels. Kearny's promise to the citizens that his government would "keep off the Indians, [and] protect you in your persons and property," proved to be an impossible undertaking throughout the antebellum era.[8] The general misgauged the difficulty of the task, perhaps underestimating the motivations driving the Mexican residents and the Apaches in their continuing conflicts. He also misjudged the intensity and determination of American nation-builders seeking economic expansion in the region.

Varying ideologies on the proper method of administering Indian affairs incited turmoil on all fronts. The tradition of bad faith between civil officials, military officers, and Apache communities would take decades to sort out. Competing egos among American officials only exacerbated these difficulties within the federal and territorial governments. In New Mexico very few individuals held office long enough to see their policies firmly enacted and enforced. This held true both nationally and locally and proved especially true in regard to the Interior Department and War Department, respectively. Whether intentionally or not, these two government bureaucracies continually contradicted one another's objectives from the moment they fragmented into separate authorities in 1849.

The rapid influx of settlers into the Southwest Borderlands following the 1848 Mexican Cession instigated inevitable conflict between Anglo-American and American Indian cultures as the two found themselves vying for control of the same landscape. Indeed, violence has traditionally characterized any circumstance in which rival groups—whether they are individual persons, collective tribes, or entire nations—converge in competition for the same resources and space. As territorial populations increased, the Indians' struggle correspondingly became more difficult. For generations the Apaches relied upon a traditional raiding economy supplemented by seasonal mescal harvests, necessitating a nomadic culture in which the people continually moved from one location to another. The hazards of their surrounding desert environment further compelled this continuous movement. The increasing presence of white men in southwestern New Mexico counteracted the Apaches' mobility as miners and merchants bent on exploitation founded settlements at important, sometimes sacred locations within their homelands. This widespread intrusion triggered violent Apache reactions in defense of their own existence and perpetuated a conflict that grew increasingly vicious as years passed.

For the Apaches, armed resistance could only continue for so long. Each man lost was one who could not be immediately replaced, even with the incorporation of young Mexican captives into the tribe as surrogate warriors. Contrarily, the U.S. military suffered no such shortcoming: if a soldier died in battle, a new recruit could quickly replace him. The prophetic Dr. Steck once warned some of the Apaches at his agency: "The [United States] has more soldiers than you can count; they are like the grass on the prairie or the leaves on the trees—you might kill all that are here but [we] would send ten times as many."[9] Another Indian agent, writing in 1854, forlornly observed the futility of the Indians' ability to resist. "That the mountains and plains will, at no distant time, fail to supply [the Indians] with the necessary food, is as certain as that the sun gives light at noonday," he predicted. "This being the case, what is to be done? That the Indians will steal, plunder, rob, and murder, in order to get food, admits of no doubt. If you make war upon and conquer them, the same question arises, what will you do with them? You will have to either take care of them or destroy them. The latter the government will not do, but will be forced to do the former."[10] Indeed, these dilemmas would be the root of internal conflict among government officials and the American public for decades.

A fitting example of these fundamental ideological differences and the pervasive unwillingness to cooperate across bureaucratic lines can be found in the 1852 proclamation of the commissioner of Indian affairs mandating that Indian agents be allowed to accompany military expeditions. This order resulted from several disastrous incidents in which troops mistakenly attacked peaceful bands of Indians; thus the role of the agent on such expeditions, according to the commissioner, would be to identify hostile and peaceful tribes before the soldiers attacked. The department commander at the time, Colonel Sumner, absolutely refused to comply, believing that civil officials had no proper place in military operations. In order to circumvent this order, Sumner began dispatching military expeditions without informing the superintendent of Indian affairs. By the time civil officials learned that troops had taken the field, it was often too late for any Indian agent to join them. In many ways this single example epitomizes the fundamental problems surrounding Indian policy in 1850s New Mexico. How could the Apaches ever be expected to come to any lasting agreements with a group of American officials who could seldom agree among themselves?

Throughout the 1850s, the civil and military authorities found themselves continually at odds with one another over the appropriate policy toward the Apaches. The first half of the decade witnessed two territorial governors, Calhoun and Lane, who sought to negotiate peace treaties in hopes of averting hostilities. They believed that feeding the Indians would eliminate their need to raid settlements and steal livestock for subsistence. The efforts of these men failed, due in large part to the unwillingness of War Department officials to support such diplomatic overtures with a cautious military presence. With army officers leading troops into the field at their own leisure and purposely neglecting to include Indian Bureau officials in their operations, it proved difficult to sustain a long-lasting peace. Indeed, each time civil officials negotiated a treaty, military officers acted autonomously against these very same Indians, often haphazardly attacking peaceful subgroups.

Misperceptions of Apache culture, especially tribal and kinship structures and motivations for conducting raids, led to continuous attempts to implement policies that simply could never work. Some measure of sustainability was achieved when Michael Steck received the appointment as Apache agent in 1853, but he frequently found himself acting alone in his benign efforts and seldom received the full support of his superiors. The arrival of Governor Meriwether and General Garland reversed some of the previous interdepartmental animosity, although the actions of individual officers who failed to distinguish between hostile and peaceful Apaches undermined most efforts at a sustainable peace. Similarly, Meriwether and Garland failed to take into account the uniqueness of Apache culture, instead seeking to force upon the Indians a form of economic capitalism to which they had no prior exposure and that entirely contradicted their communal traditions. Rather than perceive raiding as a necessary form of tribal subsistence, many officials viewed it as an open declaration of hostility and acted accordingly. The majority of Americans—government officials, merchants, and soldiers—acted first and foremost in advancement of imperialist ideologies intended to hasten the economic exploitation of the landscape and to exert social power and authority over cultures viewed as inferior. As an integral component of the southwestern New Mexico landscape, the Apaches fell into this irreversible march of conquest.

Thus, after years of almost ceaseless conflict, relations with the Apaches were worse in 1861 than they had been when the territory came under U.S. control in 1846. American attempts to achieve comprehensive hegemony over the landscape materially failed up to that point, due in large part to continuing Apache resistance. The Civil War served as a turning point in the way the government approached Apache Indian policy, and objectives changed course after the Confederate threat to New Mexico subsided in 1862. Advancements in technology, the enlistment of Apache scouts, increasing numbers of troops, and a drastic rise in the Anglo-American population all had a major influence on the way officials approached Apache relations in the coming decades, making the years from 1846 to 1861 a unique and formative period in the history of Apache-Anglo interaction.

Notes

Abbreviations

AGO	Record Group 94. U.S. War Department, Records of the Office of the Adjutant General. Letters Received. U.S. National Archives.
LR-DNM, M1102	Record Group 393. U.S. War Department, Registers of Letters Received by Headquarters, Department of New Mexico, 1849–1853. Microcopy 1102. U.S. National Archives.
LR-DNM, M1120	Record Group 393. U.S. War Department, Registers of Letters Received by Headquarters, Department of New Mexico, 1854–1865. Microcopy 1120. U.S. National Archives.
LR-OIA	Record Group 75. U.S. Office of Indian Affairs, Letters Received, 1824–80, New Mexico Superintendency, 1849–80. Microcopy 234. U.S. National Archives.
LS-DNM	Record Group 393. U.S. War Department, Letters Sent, Ninth Military Department, Department of New Mexico, and District of New Mexico, 1849–1890. Microcopy 1072. U.S. National Archives.
Steck Papers 1	Inventory of the Michael Steck Papers, Series 1, 1839–53, Microcopy E93. Center for Southwest Research, New Mexico State Archives.
Steck Papers 2	Inventory of the Michael Steck Papers, Series 2, Microcopy E93. Center for Southwest Research, New Mexico State Archives.

Introduction

1. On the role of violence in shaping the West, with an emphasis on indigenous peoples and borderlands, see Blackhawk, *Violence over the Land*; Jacoby, *Shadows at Dawn*; and Hämäläinen and Truett, "On Borderlands," 351.

2. Prucha, *Great Father*, 1:319–23; Ball, *Army Regulars on the Western Frontier*, 14, 16.

3. Wooster, *American Military Frontiers*, 118–19.

4. Turner's Frontier Thesis influenced an entire generation of western historians and remains a reference point to this day, but it has become highly refutable for its oversimplification of westward expansion. See Turner, *Significance of the Frontier in American History*. For Boltonian thought, see Bolton, *Spanish Borderlands;* and Weber, "Turner, the Boltonians, and the Borderlands." For the most recent work tracing the evolution of borderlands studies, see Hämäläinen and Truett, "On Borderlands," 338–61.

5. Bender, Utley, and Frazer are the three early military historians whose works are most often utilized in this book. See Bender, *March of Empire;* Utley, *Frontiersmen in Blue;* Frazer, *Forts and Supplies.* Durwood Ball and Robert Wooster have influenced military historians through their more recent works; see Ball, *Army Regulars on the Western Frontier;* Wooster, *Military and United States Indian Policy;* and Wooster, *American Military Frontiers.*

6. Morris Opler published numerous articles, but most pertinent to this study is his book *An Apache Life-Way.* See also Debo, *Geronimo;* Thrapp, *Victorio and the Mimbres Apaches;* and Sweeney, *Cochise; Mangas Coloradas;* and *From Cochise to Geronimo.*

7. For the new western history, the most frequently consulted sources are White, *It's Your Misfortune and None of My Own;* Limerick, *Legacy of Conquest;* Limerick, Milner, and Rankin, *Trails;* Cronon, Miles, and Gitlin, *Under an Open Sky;* and Hine and Faragher, *American West.* For spatial trilectics, or physical, mental, and social constructs of space, see Lefebvre, *Production of Space.*

8. Blackhawk, DeLay, and Hämäläinen are but three of several scholars who have had a profound influence on southwestern historiography in the past few years. See Blackhawk, *Violence over the Land;* DeLay, *War of a Thousand Deserts;* Hämäläinen, *Comanche Empire,* esp. 6–9; and Hämäläinen and Truett, "On Borderlands," 359.

9. On the new Indian history, see Blackhawk, "Look How Far We've Come," and Fixico, *Rethinking American Indian History.*

10. For nationalism theory emphasizing individual communities, see Anderson, *Imagined Communities,* esp. 5–8.

11. E. Ball, *Indeh,* 62. Apaches called white men "White Eyes," as explained by Ace Daklugie: "*White Eyes* is not the exact meaning of our word for them; a more exact meaning would be *Pale Eyes.* The first white people our people saw looked very queer because Indians have no whites in their eyes: the part around the iris is more nearly coffee-colored." Ibid., 19.

12. For Apache oral histories explaining religion, see ibid., 56–65.

13. Opler, "Myths and Tales of the Chiricahua," 2–11.

14. Geronimo speaking to General George Crook, Mar. 25, 1886, quoted in Brown, *Bury My Heart at Wounded Knee,* 410. The complete transcription of the interview is found in Senate, *Correspondence Regarding the Apache Indians,* 16–17.

15. *Santa Fe Weekly Gazette*, Mar. 14, 1857.

16. Mowry to Denver, Nov. 10, 1857, in *Annual Report of the Commissioner of Indian Affairs* (1857), 298.

17. On Manifest Destiny and westward expansion, see Billington, *America's Frontier Heritage*, esp. 199–217; and Johannsen, "Meaning of Manifest Destiny," 7–21.

18. Calvin, *Lieutenant Emory Reports*, 100.

Prologue

1. Lamar, *Far Southwest*, 52. For the maneuverings of Kearny and his Army of the West, see Clarke, *Stephen Watts Kearny*, 101–45. A firsthand account is found in Cooke, *Conquest of New Mexico and California*, 34–69.

2. Stephen Watts Kearny was born in Newark, New Jersey, on August 30, 1794. He joined the army during the War of 1812 and served with distinction throughout his military career. He was wounded twice at the Battle of San Pasqual on December 6, 1846. In 1848 he served as civil governor of Vera Cruz and Mexico City. Kearny died in St. Louis on October 31, 1848. Heitman, *Historical Register*, 586.

3. Stephen Watts Kearny, General Orders No. 13, Aug. 17, 1846, RG94, Orders Issued . . . to the Army of the West, M-T1115, Roll 1.

4. Calvin, *Lieutenant Emory Reports*, 50; Cooke, *Conquest of New Mexico and California*, 34–38; Twitchell, *Military Occupation of the Territory of New Mexico*, 65–67.

5. Rippy, "Indians of the Southwest," 364. See also Kluger, *Seizing Destiny*, 432–81, esp. 458–61.

6. For recent interpretations of Indian raiding and its effects on the outcome of the Mexican-American War, see DeLay, *War of a Thousand Deserts*, 61–75; and Hämäläinen, *Comanche Empire*, 237.

7. Collins to Mix, Sept. 27, 1858, in *Annual Report of the Commissioner of Indian Affairs* (1858), 188. Collins continued, "When Governor Kearny took possession of New Mexico he found a war existing, and which had existed for many years, between the Mexicans and Navajoes [sic], and, judging from the general's promises to the Mexicans, which were often repeated, he must have considered it an easy matter to relieve them from the war, and to protect them against further depredations from this formidable foe." Ibid.

8. Stephen Watts Kearny, General Orders No. 16, Aug. 25, 1846, RG94, Orders Issued . . . to the Army of the West, M-T1115, Roll 1; General Orders No. 34, Oct. 6, 1846, ibid.; Bender, "Government Explorations in the Territory of New Mexico," 4. See also Twitchell, *Military Occupation of the Territory of New Mexico*, 86–89.

9. Clarke, *Journals of Henry Smith Turner*, 84–85.

10. Calvin, *Lieutenant Emory Reports*, 100; Goetzmann, *Army Exploration in the American West*, 135; Clarke, *Journals of Henry Smith Turner*, 85; Sweeney, *Mangas*

Coloradas, 141–45. In 1851 Boundary Commissioner John Russell Bartlett visited with Mangas Coloradas, and the chief once again "expressed a most earnest desire to be at peace with the Americans and spoke in the highest terms of their bravery and knowledge." Bartlett to Stuart, Feb. 19, 1852, LR-OIA, Roll 546.

11. Calvin, *Lieutenant Emory Reports*, 101. See also Clarke, *Stephen Watts Kearny*, 182–84.

12. Calvin, *Lieutenant Emory Reports*, 100.

13. Sweeney, *From Cochise to Geronimo*, 17.

Chapter 1

1. For a synthesis of antebellum army life for both enlisted men and officers, see D. Ball, *Army Regulars on the Western Frontier*, 56–77.

2. See Coffman, *Old Army*, 42–103. For a comparative study of enlisted men, see ibid., 137–211.

3. Bennett, *Forts and Forays*, 54.

4. Regimental histories of the First and Second Dragoons are found in Rodenbough, *Army of the United States*, 153–92. For general histories of the dragoons in the West, see Herr and Wallace, *Story of the U.S. Cavalry*, 60–87.

5. See Upton, *Military Policy of the United States*, 223–24.

6. Cooper to Scott, Nov. 27, 1855, in *Annual Report of the Secretary of War* (1856), 127.

7. "Table of the 1855 Organization of the Regular Army of the United States," ibid., 126–27. The First Dragoons boasted thirty-six commissioned officers, while the Second Dragoons had thirty-five; the aggregate total of dragoons was 1,301 men. For a statistical table, see D. Ball, *Army Regulars on the Western Frontier*, xxii–xxiii.

8. *Annual Report of the Secretary of War* (1850), 3.

9. In 1845 a dragoon regiment cost $220,292 annually, including equipment and troop salaries. By contrast, the Regiment of Mounted Rifles was projected to cost $203,420 per year, the savings coming from its members' lower pay grade as infantrymen. Towson to Marcy, Jan. 17, 1846, in House, *Regiment of Mounted Riflemen Annual Expenses*. The Mounted Rifles contained an aggregate of 801 men: 640 privates, thirty-six commissioned officers, and 125 noncommissioned officers. *Annual Report of the Secretary of War* (1856), 127.

10. Frazer, *Forts and Supplies*, 122.

11. *Annual Report of the Secretary of War* (1856), 127.

12. For a history of the Third Infantry, see Sawicki, *Infantry Regiments of the U.S. Army*, 52–54.

13. *Annual Report of the Secretary of War* (1850), 4.

14. A sergeant in Company B, First Dragoons wrote of an 1851 expedition: "It was a horrible trip for men so poorly provided for. . . . [O]vershoes, mittens, gloves, leggings or other wraps were not then provided by the Government, nor

kept for sale, and men made for themselves out of old blankets, skins, pieces of old canvas and cast-off clothing, anything that necessity prompted them to invent." Lowe, *Five Years a Dragoon*, 45–46.

15. Illustrations of dragoon equipment and insignia are found in Steffen, *Horse Soldier*, 5–33.

16. For a synopsis of antebellum frontier life for cavalrymen, see Merrill, *Spurs to Glory*, 78–86.

17. Rice, *Cannoneer in Navajo Country*, 47, 54.

18. Quoted in Lamar, *Far Southwest*, 83.

19. Averell, *Ten Years in the Saddle*, 133.

20. Eighth U.S. Census (1860). In 1850 and 1851, immigrants constituted 3,516 of the 5,000 troops recruited. For an analysis of soldier ethnicities in the antebellum army see D. Ball, *Army Regulars on the Western Frontier*, 57.

21. Frazer, *New Mexico in 1850*, 59–61.

22. Sumner to Conrad, May 27, 1852, in *Annual Report of the Secretary of War* (1852), 23–25.

23. *Santa Fe Weekly Gazette*, Mar. 5, 1853.

24. *Annual Report of the Secretary of War* (1852), 5–6.

25. *Santa Fe Weekly Gazette*, Feb. 19, 1853.

26. House, *Official Army Register for the Year Ending 30 June, 1851*.

27. Utley, *Frontiersmen in Blue*, 36.

28. Langley, *To Utah with the Dragoons*, 120–21.

29. Larned to Conrad, Oct. 17, 1850, in *Annual Report of the Secretary of War* (1850), 333.

30. Less than a year after Colonel Miles complained about inadequate funds, Colonel J. K. F. Mansfield reported that the paymaster at Fort Fillmore, Major B. W. Brice, had on hand $35,576 for distribution to the troops. Frazer, *Mansfield on the Condition of the Western Forts*, 57.

31. Steen to Nichols, June 1857, LR-DNM, M1102, Roll 6.

32. Bennett, *Forts and Forays*, 22–23.

33. Bender, "Military Transportation in the Southwest," 124.

34. For expenses and distances to reach western posts with an emphasis on navigation of waterways, see Conrad to Fillmore, Nov. 29, 1851, in *Annual Report of the Secretary of War* (1851), 109–10.

35. Upton, *Military Policy of the United States*, 224.

36. Gibson to Conrad, Oct. 19, 1850, in *Annual Report of the Secretary of War* (1850), 338. See also D. Ball, *Army Regulars on the Western Frontier*, 28–29.

37. Bowman to Brent, Apr. 21, 1850, in *Annual Report of the Secretary of War* (1850), 297.

38. Bender, "Military Transportation in the Southwest," 134.

39. Lane, *I Married a Soldier*, 48.

40. For family life in the army with an emphasis on the role of women, see Coffman, *Old Army*, 104–36.

41. Wadsworth, *Forgotten Fortress*, 119–27.

42. Annual Reports of Regular Army Cavalry Regiments, 1852, RG391, Returns from Regular Army Cavalry Regiments, M744, Rolls 4, 16, National Archives.

43. Frazer, *New Mexico in 1850*, 163. On lack of discipline, see Langley, *To Utah with the Dragoons*, 106–107.

44. Weigley, *History of the United States Army*, 189.

45. Bliss, "Extracts from the Unpublished Memoirs of Major General Z. R. Bliss," 128.

46. Frazer, *Mansfield on the Condition of the Western Forts*, 66.

47. Pfanz, *Richard S. Ewell*, 76. Richard Stoddert Ewell was born on February 8, 1817, and was raised in Virginia. In 1840 he graduated thirteenth in his class from the U.S. Military Academy. During the Mexican-American War, Ewell served under Brigadier General Winfield Scott and was promoted to captain for his actions at Contreras and Churubusco. He resigned on May 7, 1861, and enlisted as a brigadier general in the Confederate army. Ewell died on January 25, 1872. Heitman, *Historical Register*, 410; Altshuler, *Cavalry Yellow and Infantry Blue*, 125.

48. Ewell to Nichols, May 1854, LR-DNM, M1102, Roll 3.

49. Chandler to Nichols, May 1854, ibid.

50. On frontier military weaponry, see Utley, *Frontiersmen in Blue*, 25–28.

51. Ibid., 36.

52. Rice, *Cannonneer in Navajo Country*, 79.

53. Ibid., 66.

54. Bennett, *Forts and Forays*, 42.

55. Ibid., 38.

56. Utley, *Frontiersmen in Blue*, 39; D. Ball, *Army Regulars on the Western Frontier*, 59. On corporal punishment in the army, see Langley, *To Utah with the Dragoons*, 82–84.

57. Fort Bliss, although located in Texas, remained under the jurisdiction of the Ninth Military Department, later the Department of New Mexico. It did not become a part of the Department of Texas until December 8, 1860. Frazer, *Forts of the West*, 143.

58. Annual Reports of Regular Army Cavalry Regiments, 1852, RG391, Returns from Regular Army Cavalry Regiments, M744, Rolls 4, 16, National Archives. The First Dragoons averaged between 650 and 700 total troops in 1853 and recorded a total of ninety-three desertions. Ibid.

59. Morris to McFerran, Oct. 10, 1852, LR-DNM, M1102, Roll 5.

60. Wadsworth, *Forgotten Fortress*, 82.

Chapter 2

1. For the challenges of comparing Apache oral histories to American documentary evidence, see Colwell-Chanthaphonh, *Massacre at Camp Grant*, 6–17.

2. Ibid., 11.
3. See Sweeney, *Mangas Coloradas*, 4–9.
4. See Ferg, "Traditional Western Apache Mescal Harvesting."
5. E. Ball, *In the Days of Victorio*, 45–46.
6. E. Ball, *Indeh*, 15.
7. Sweeney, *Cochise*, 4–5.
8. Goodwin, *Social Organization of the Western Apache*, 2.
9. Opler, "Apachean Culture Pattern and Its Origins," 369. A local group typically consisted of between ten and thirty families. For social organization, see Opler, "Chiricahua Apache," 412.
10. Bartlett, *Personal Narrative*, 2:387. An 1846 population estimate similarly stated "900 lodges, or 5,000 to 6,000 souls." Charles Bent to William Medill, Nov. 10, 1846, in House, *California and New Mexico*, 191.
11. Goodwin, *Western Apache Raiding and Warfare*, 14.
12. Bonneville to Thomas, July 15, 1859, in Walker, "Colonel Bonneville's Report," 359.
13. Debo, *Geronimo*, 18; Opler, *Apache Life-Way*, 5–77.
14. Ogle, *Federal Control of the Western Apaches*, 11–13.
15. The U.S. resident population in 1850 was 23,191,876; by 1860 it had grown to 31,443,321. See Seventh U.S. Census (1850) and Eighth U.S. Census (1860). Population estimates for the Apaches ranged from 2,000 to 6,000. See Meriwether to Manypenny, Sept. 1, 1854, in *Annual Report of the Commissioner of Indian Affairs* (1854), 378–79; and Bartlett, *Personal Narrative*, 2:385. One recent scholar estimates populations as follows: Chiricahua Apaches, 3,000; Mescalero Apaches, 2,500; Western Apaches, 4,500–5,000. DeLay, *War of a Thousand Deserts*, 374n6. Edwin R. Sweeney maintains that the Chiricahua population "never exceeded three thousand during Mangas Coloradas' lifetime." *Mangas Coloradas*, 7.
16. Opler, *Apache Life-Way*, 333. For a study of indigenous raiding economies in northern and southern regions of Mexico prior to the American conquest, see Jones, "Comparative Raiding Economies," 97–114.
17. For analyses of the raiding motivations for Comanches and other tribes, see Hämäläinen, *Comanche Empire*, and DeLay, *War of a Thousand Deserts*.
18. Bartlett, *Personal Narrative*, 2:386.
19. For the Indian Intercourse Act, see House, *An Act Regulating the Indian Department*. Section 17 pertained to Indian depredations and the dispersal of indemnities. It required the claimant to "make application to the proper [authority], who, upon being furnished with the necessary documents or proofs, shall ... make application to the nation or tribe ... for satisfaction." See Prucha, *Documents of United States Indian Policy*, 64–68.
20. Thompson to Breckenridge, May 11, 1858, in Senate, *Claims for Depredations*, 2.

21. Ibid., 9–62.

22. For statistical analyses of Apache raiding in Chihuahua, see Griffen, *Utmost Good Faith*. For similar statistics on Mexico's northern states, see DeLay, *War of a Thousand Deserts*, 317–40.

23. For a firsthand account of raiding in the Spanish colonial period, see Cortés, *Views from the Apache Frontier*, 21–34.

24. Opler, *Apache Life-Way*, 334.

25. Goodwin, *Western Apache Raiding and Warfare*, 16–17; Opler, *Apache Life-Way*, 334–36; Betzinez, *I Fought with Geronimo*, 4–9.

26. Sweeney, *Mangas Coloradas*, 215–19; Griffen, *Apaches at War and Peace*, 237–39.

27. For Spanish policy on deporting Apache prisoners, see Santiago, *Jar of Severed Hands*, 34–36, 43–58.

28. Geronimo's personal recollection of this event is in Barrett, *Geronimo*, 75–83. Geronimo erroneously placed the date of the Janos massacre in 1858. See also Sweeney, "I Had Lost All," 45–49.

29. Steck Papers 1, Roll 1.

30. See DeLay, *War of a Thousand Deserts*, 61–75; and Hämäläinen, *Comanche Empire*, 232–38.

31. Debo, *Geronimo*, 28.

32. See Ruxton, *Adventures in Mexico*, 281–84; Smith, *Borderlander*, 75–171; Hämäläinen, *Comanche Empire*, 228.

33. Griffen, *Utmost Good Faith*, 238–42.

34. *El Sonorense*, Mar. 23, 1849.

35. Graves to Manypenny, June 8, 1854, in *Annual Report of the Commissioner of Indian Affairs* (1854), 180.

36. See Sweeney, *Mangas Coloradas*, 215–19. John Russell Bartlett wrote that "Mangas Colorado [sic], Delgadito, Coleto Amarillo and Ponce have struck terror among the people of Sonora, Chihuahua, and those portions of New Mexico and Texas which border on the Rio Grande." Bartlett to Stuart, Feb. 19, 1852, LR-OIA, Roll 546.

37. Such exaggerations soon led Spanish and Mexican officials to require commanders to cut ears off of slain Apaches as proof of death. See Santiago, *Jar of Severed Hands*, 82–86.

38. A comparative study of difficulties in fighting Indians (in this case Seminoles) during this era is found in Jones, *Elements of Military Strategy*, 19–24. For the reinvention and evolution of military thought, see Weigley, *Towards an American Army*, 38–78.

39. Steck to Meriwether, July 30, 1855, Steck Papers 2, Roll 1.

40. Sumner to Jones, Nov. 20, 1851, LS-DNM, Roll 1.

41. Meriwether to Manypenny, Sept. 1, 1854, in *Annual Report of the Commissioner of Indian Affairs* (1854), 171.

42. Barrett, *Geronimo*, 110.
43. *Santa Fe Weekly Gazette*, Oct. 18, 1856.
44. Steck to Manypenny, Aug. 27, 1856, Steck Papers 2, Roll 2.
45. Senate, *Statistical Report on the Sickness and Mortality in the Army . . . from January 1839 to January 1855*, 416.
46. Frazer, *Forts and Supplies*, 98.
47. Quoted by Keleher, *Turmoil in New Mexico*, 474.
48. E. Ball, *In the Days of Victorio*, 27.

Chapter 3

1. Indian Agent Edmund A. Graves observed: "There are two equal and independent authorities in this Territory, who often have to act upon the same matter. If they differ in opinion, as is frequently the case, the Indian escapes, and the citizen remains without redress." Graves to Meriwether, Aug. 31, 1853, Graves Letters, Center for Southwest Research, New Mexico State Archives.
2. Wooster, *American Military Frontiers*, 118.
3. On conflicting dreams of economic exploitation between Mexicans and Americans, with an emphasis on the transformation of geographic and communal space, see Truett, *Fugitive Landscapes*, 36–51.
4. For the political and economic climate in New Mexico at the time of Kearny's conquest, see Ganaway, *New Mexico and the Sectional Controversy*, 1–13.
5. Griswold del Castillo, *Treaty of Guadalupe Hidalgo*, 3–15.
6. See DeLay, *War of a Thousand Deserts*, 294–303.
7. Miller, *Treaties and Other International Acts*, 5:219–22.
8. House, *California and New Mexico*, 11.
9. House, *Message from the President of the United States*, 18. See also Rippy, "Indians of the Southwest," 363–96.
10. Webster to Fillmore, June 11, 1852, in House, *Rio Grande Frontier*, 2.
11. Conrad to Fillmore, Nov. 29, 1851, in *Annual Report of the Secretary of War* (1851), 106.
12. William Medill to James S. Calhoun, Apr. 7, 1849, in House, *California and New Mexico*, 195. The Bureau of Indian Affairs opposed subsidizing ransoms. In a similar order Medill stated, "it must, if possible, be done without any compensation whatever, as to make compensation would encourage a continuance of the practice of making captives." Medill to Adam Johnston, Apr. 14, 1849, ibid., 188.
13. Bartlett to Stuart, Feb. 19, 1852, LR-OIA, Roll 546.
14. Ibid. Bartlett used Santa Cruz, Sonora, as an example, noting that the town, formerly boasting some 2,000 inhabitants, had diminished to only 300 in 1851 as a result of Apache raiding.
15. Reid, *Reid's Tramp*, 176–77.
16. Radbourne, *Mickey Free*, 2–21, 216–17.

17. On the nature of indigenous captivity in the Southwest, see Brooks, *Captives and Cousins*, 26–40.

18. Miller, *Treaties and Other International Acts*, 6:296.

19. *El Faro* (Chihuahua City), Aug. 12, 1850; Sweeney, *Mangas Coloradas*, 202–204.

20. Almonte to Marcy, Oct. 22, 1853, RG59, New Mexico Territorial Papers, M54, Roll 4, National Archives; Kiser, *Turmoil on the Rio Grande*, 41–44.

21. Bender, "Frontier Defense in the Territory of New Mexico," 258.

22. Brent to Jesup, Oct. 9, 1850, in *Annual Report of the Quartermaster General*, 291.

23. Frazer, *New Mexico in 1850*, 36. The post of Franklin later became Fort Bliss. For an antebellum history of that installation, see Metz, *Desert Army*, 29–45. In 1858 W. W. Mills called Fort Bliss "one of the most desirable posts in the whole country." *Forty Years at El Paso*, 10. For a history of El Paso with an emphasis on military occupation, see Timmons, *El Paso*, 103–33.

24. *Annual Report of the Secretary of War* (1850), 3. For a statistical breakdown of the U.S. Army, see D. Ball, *Army Regulars on the Western Frontier*, xx–xxii. It should be noted that the legislated strength of the army rarely equaled the actual strength. The War Department had difficulty filling quotas, leaving most companies at only partial capacity.

25. *Annual Report of the Secretary of War* (1850), 3.

26. Ibid., 4.

27. Sumner to Jones, Oct. 24, 1851, LS-DNM, Roll 1.

28. Colonel Munroe complained in 1849 that medical staff remained insufficient to treat the high frequency of maladies afflicting the troops, pointing out that "no local physicians [can be] procured." Munroe to Mackall, Nov. 29, 1849, ibid.

29. In 1853 the strength of the U.S. Army was 10,495 men. Four-fifths of that number were stationed west of the Mississippi River. See *Annual Report of the Secretary of War* (1853), 11–12.

30. Senate, *Statistical Report on the Sickness and Mortality in the Army . . . from January 1839 to January 1855*, 493. For similar statistics spanning 1855–60, see Senate, *Statistical Report on the Sickness and Mortality in the United States Army . . . from January 1855 to January 1860*, 225–33.

31. Senate, *Statistical Report on the Sickness and Mortality in the Army . . . from January 1839 to January 1855*, 419.

32. Kiser, *Turmoil on the Rio Grande*, 35–38.

33. Bartlett, *Personal Narrative*, 1:211–12.

34. Woodhouse, *From Texas to San Diego in 1851*, 60.

35. In 1848 the army paid monthly rent of $170 at Doña Ana. Prior to the post's 1851 abandonment, the amount had more than doubled to $362. Swords to Jesup, Oct. 25, 1851, in *Annual Report of the Secretary of War* (1851), 246.

36. Quoted in Sweeney, *Mangas Coloradas*, 177. Born in Harrodsburg, Kentucky, on February 22, 1800, Major Enoch Steen joined the First Dragoons in 1833. He fought in the Mexican-American War and was brevetted major on February 23, 1847, for meritorious conduct at the Battle of Buena Vista. Steen retired as a lieutenant colonel of the Second Cavalry on September 23, 1863, and lived in Missouri until his death on January 22, 1880. Heitman, *Historical Register*, 919; Altshuler, *Cavalry Yellow and Infantry Blue*, 316–17.

37. *Santa Fe Weekly Gazette*, Apr. 5, 1856.

38. Frazer, *New Mexico in 1850*, 166.

39. Ibid.

40. Ibid., 167. Steen sustained the wound in an engagement with Gila Apaches near Santa Rita del Cobre on August 16, 1849. Apache casualties were reportedly twenty-five killed and wounded, while Steen's Company H, First Dragoons suffered one killed (Corporal A. E. Norwood) and two wounded (Steen and Sergeant Snyder). Steen to Dickinson, Sept. 1, 1849, Folder 1548, Schroeder Collection, New Mexico State Records Center and Archives; Sweeney, *Mangas Coloradas*, 177–78.

41. Frazer, *New Mexico in 1850*, 168; Munroe to Jesup, Mar. 31, 1850, LS-DNM, Roll 1. Munroe had previously complained to the adjutant general that "there is none [clothing] in the department . . . except a small supply brought by such of the troops arrived last summer [1849]." Munroe to Mackall, Mar. 1, 1850, ibid.; McLaws to Steen, Apr. 13, 1850, ibid.

42. Abraham Buford graduated from the U.S. Military Academy in 1841. During the Civil War, he played a pivotal role in the Battle of Champion Hill. On June 9, 1884, following his financial ruin and the untimely death of his wife and son, Buford committed suicide at his home in Indiana. New Mexicans referred to him as "hell-roaring Buford." Heitman, *Historical Register*, 260. Captain Ewell described him as "hardly calculated to shine in any ballroom except a Mexican fandango." R. S. Ewell to Ben Ewell, July 21, 1862, in Hamlin, *Making of a Soldier*, 77.

43. Buford to McLaws, Mar. 6, 1849, LR-DNM, M1102, Roll 1.

44. Steen to McLaws, Aug. 10, 1849, ibid.

45. On the Navajo campaigns, see McNitt, *Navajo Wars*, 95–199; and Simpson, *Navaho Expedition*, 5–162.

46. May to McLaws, Dec. 19, 1849, LR-DNM, M1102, Roll 1.

47. Crouch, *Jornada del Muerto*, 43–61.

48. Steen to McLaws, Dec. 1849, LR-DNM, M1102, Roll 1.

49. An indemnity claim in the amount of $450 was filed by Manuel Olona, who lost seven mules and one saddle horse in the raid. He later reported the date as January 22, 1850, but witness affidavits contradicted this and placed the date at the beginning of February. Senate, *Claims for Depredations*, 33.

50. Steen to McLaws, Feb. 5, 1850, LR-DNM, M1102, Roll 2.

51. Ibid.

52. Ibid. Headquarters informed Steen that the Santa Fe storehouse contained a surplus of Colt revolvers, available to him upon request. McLaws to Steen, Aug. 14, 1850, LS-DNM, Roll 1.

53. Steen to McLaws, Feb. 5, 1850, LR-DNM, M1102, Roll 2.

54. Steen to McLaws, Mar. 26, 1850, ibid.

55. For statistics on expenditures at Doña Ana, see Swords to Jesup, Oct. 25, 1851, in *Annual Report of the Secretary of War* (1851), 241–48. For a history of Santa Rita del Cobre in the post-1846 era, see Spude, "Santa Rita del Cobre."

56. D. Ball, "By Right of Conquest," 8–16.

57. May to McLaws, Apr. 16, 1850, LR-DNM, M1102, Roll 2.

58. May to McLaws, July 25, 1850, ibid.

59. Frazer, *New Mexico in 1850*, 180–84; Munroe to Mackall, Mar. 1, 1850, LS-DNM, Roll 1. Colonel Munroe continually cited the necessity of converting infantry companies into cavalry. Ibid.

60. Scott to Munroe, Aug. 6, 1850, in Abel, *Official Correspondence of James S. Calhoun*, 164–65.

61. Bartlett, *Personal Narrative*, 2:212–14.

62. Stegmaier, *Texas, New Mexico, and the Compromise of 1850*, 70–73, 132–33. For the maneuverings of Robert S. Neighbors in southern New Mexico, see Neighbours, *Robert Simpson Neighbors*, 89–93. Neighbors wrote that Major Steen constituted "a perfect Texan in principle, and the strongest advocate of our [land] claims I have found in this territory." Quoted ibid., 91.

63. Munroe to Jones, May 20, 1850, LS-DNM, Roll 1; Stegmaier, "Guadalupe Hidalgo Treaty as a Factor in the New Mexico–Texas Boundary Dispute," 48.

64. Munroe to Steen, Apr. 15, 1850, LS-DNM, Roll 1.

65. McLaws to Steen, Sept. 5, 1850, ibid.

66. For land speculation among military officers, see Coffman, *Old Army*, 84–87.

67. McLaws to Steen, Apr. 13, 1850, LS-DNM, Roll 1.

68. *St. Louis Daily Missouri Republican*, Jan. 16, 1854.

69. Ibid., Jan. 26, 1854. See also *Santa Fe Weekly Gazette*, Feb. 26, 1853.

70. Geck Collection, New Mexico State Records Center and Archives. During the Civil War, Geck conducted business with the occupying Confederate forces. In 1862, when the Union regained possession of the Mesilla Valley, authorities confiscated his store and entire inventory, valued at $21,675, and he was charged with treason. Geck later sued the government to regain his property. Folders 31–32, ibid. The Doña Ana property that Geck obtained through his bounty claim is still in the possession of his descendants in Las Cruces, although his store and house no longer exist.

71. Bieber, *Journal of a Soldier under Kearny*, 48. For competition between infantrymen and dragoons, see Langley, *To Utah with the Dragoons*, 57, 130.

72. McLaws to Steen, Aug. 2, 1850, LS-DNM, Roll 1.

73. Steen to McLaws, Sept. 4, 1850, LR-DNM, M1102, Roll 2.

74. *El Sonorense*, Apr. 23, 1850; Sweeney, *Mangas Coloradas*, 205–206.
75. Steen to McLaws, Sept. 4, 1850, LR-DNM, M1102, Roll 2.
76. Rice, *Cannoneer in Navajo Country*, 80.
77. Steen to McLaws, Sept. 4, 1850, LR-DNM, M1102, Roll 2.
78. McLaws to Steen, Sept. 14, 1850, LS-DNM, Roll 1.

79. Several monographs detail the boundary-commission work. Two classic accounts are Faulk, *Too Far North, Too Far South;* and Hine, *Bartlett's West*. See also Kiser, *Turmoil on the Rio Grande*, 47–69.

80. Goetzmann, *Army Exploration in the American West*, 173.

81. Hine, *Bartlett's West*, 3–4. For thoughtful reinterpretations of the boundary disputes, consult Albuquerque Museum, *Drawing the Borderline;* Werne, *Imaginary Line;* and St. John, *Line in the Sand*, esp. 12–38.

82. McLaws to Van Horn, Sept. 29, 1850, LS-DNM, Roll 1.
83. Bartlett to Stuart, Feb. 19, 1852, LR-OIA, Roll 546.

84. Sweeney, *Mangas Coloradas*, 234–35; Bartlett, *Personal Narrative*, 1:303–12; Cremony, *Life among the Apaches*, 53–61; Bartlett to Stuart, Feb. 19, 1852, LR-OIA, Roll 546.

85. Bartlett, *Personal Narrative*, 1:330–53; Cremony, *Life among the Apaches*, 80–85.

86. Craig to Scott, Sept. 4, 1851, LR-DNM, M1102, Roll 4.
87. Bartlett to Sumner, July 25, 1851, ibid., Roll 3 (emphasis in original).

88. Bartlett to Stuart, Feb. 19, 1852, LR-OIA, Roll 546; Buell to Bartlett, Aug. 3, 1851, LS-DNM, Roll 1.

89. Craig to Sumner, Sept. 1851, LR-DNM, M1102, Roll 3.
90. Giese, *Forts of New Mexico*, 15.
91. Bartlett, *Personal Narrative*, 2:302.
92. Goetzmann, *Army Exploration in the American West*, 186–93.

93. Doña Ana Post Return, June 1850, RG391, Returns from Regular Army Cavalry Regiments, M744, Roll 3, National Archives.

94. For antebellum War Department expenditures, see Upton, *Military Policy of the United States*, 224.

95. Towson to Marcy, Jan. 17, 1846, in House, *Regiment of Mounted Riflemen Annual Expenses*.

96. Swords to Jesup, Oct. 25, 1851, in *Annual Report of the Secretary of War* (1851), 240.

97. Frazer, *New Mexico in 1850*, 164.
98. Ibid. See also Munroe to Mackall, Mar. 1, 1850, LS-DNM, Roll 1.
99. *Annual Report of the Secretary of War* (1850), 4.

100. Greiner, "Private Letters of a Government Official," 549. The equipment carried by a dragoon on campaign weighed seventy-eight pounds. Swords to Jesup, Oct. 25, 1851, in *Annual Report of the Secretary of War* (1851), 253. Greiner's claim that 92,000 Indians inhabited the territory included all of the Pueblos; the number of nomadic Indians was far less. An 1846 estimate placed the Indian population at

36,950 exclusive of Pueblos. Bent to Medill, Nov. 10, 1846, in House, *California and New Mexico*, 193.

101. Fitzpatrick to Cumming, Nov. 19, 1853, in *Annual Report of the Commissioner of Indian Affairs* (1853), 362.

102. Prucha, *Documents of United States Indian Policy*, 83–84; Trennert, *Alternative to Extinction*, 58; Robert A. Trennert, Jr., "Luke Lea," in Kvasnicka and Viola, *Commissioners of Indian Affairs*, 49–54.

Chapter 4

1. See Frazer, *Forts and Supplies*, 61–85; Upton, *Military Policy of the United States*, 224.

2. Rippy, "Indians of the Southwest," 370–74. On freight expenses, see Frazer, "Purveyors of Flour to the Army," 214, 219–20; and Sumner to Thomas, Oct. 22, 1851, LS-DNM, Roll 1.

3. Wooster, *Military and United States Indian Policy*, 10; Trennert, *Alternative to Extinction*, 44.

4. James S. Calhoun was born sometime between 1800 and 1806 in South Carolina, although he claimed Georgia as his home state and was active in Georgia politics from 1828 until 1840. He married Caroline Ann Simmons on December 19, 1822; the couple had two children prior to her death in 1828. See Abel, *Official Correspondence of James S. Calhoun*, xi–xiv; and Green, "James S. Calhoun," 309–47, esp. 310–12. Calhoun found himself in an unenviable situation after taking office: "Without a dollar in our territorial treasury, without munitions of war, without authority to call out our militia, without the cooperation of the military authorities of this territory, and with numberless complaints and calls for protection, do you not perceive I must be sadly embarrassed and disquieted?" Quoted in Twitchell, *Leading Facts of New Mexican History*, 2:284.

5. Calhoun to Medill, Aug. 15, 1849, in House, *California and New Mexico*, 201–202.

6. Calhoun to Medill, Oct. 27, 1849, in Abel, *Official Correspondence of James S. Calhoun*, 62.

7. Calhoun to Marcy, Nov. 25, 1848, ibid., 13.

8. Marcy to Calhoun, Dec. 7, 1848, ibid.

9. *Annual Report of the Secretary of War* (1850), 5.

10. Calhoun Proclamation, Mar. 18, 1851, RG59, New Mexico Territorial Papers, T17, Roll 1, National Archives.

11. Calhoun's Message to the First Territorial Legislature, June 2, 1851, ibid.

12. McNitt, *Navajo Wars*, 174–75.

13. Abel, *Official Correspondence of James S. Calhoun*, 19.

14. On military strategy favoring the annihilation of tribes, see Weigley, *American Way of War*, 153–63.

15. Calhoun to Brown, Feb. 3, 1850, in Abel, *Official Correspondence of James S. Calhoun*, 141; Green, "James S. Calhoun," 334–35.

16. Smith to Brown, Mar. 9, 1850, in *Annual Report of the Commissioner of Indian Affairs* (1850), 142.

17. Espinosa, "Memoir of a Kentuckian in New Mexico," 7.

18. While Munroe generally cooperated with Calhoun on Indian affairs, he wrote in April 1851 that "the appropriations for Indian affairs made by Congress . . . enables the Indian Department to support itself fiscally without assistance from other departments—and that assistance is withdrawn." Munroe to Calhoun, Apr. 9, 1851, LS-DNM, Roll 1; Green, "James S. Calhoun," 342–43.

19. Edwin Vose Sumner was born in Boston, Massachusetts, on June 30, 1797. He entered the army in 1819, served on Kearny's staff during the occupation of New Mexico, and in 1861 became the commander of the Department of the Pacific. He died at Syracuse, New York, on March 21, 1863. Heitman, *Historical Register*, 936. For biographical sketches, see D. Ball, *Army Regulars on the Western Frontier*, 66; and D. Ball, "U.S. Army in New Mexico," 176–79.

20. On the Sumner-Calhoun feud, see D. Ball, *Army Regulars on the Western Frontier*, 20–22.

21. Sumner to Lane, June 15, 1853, LS-DNM, Roll 1.

22. Conrad to Sumner, Apr. 1, 1851, quoted in Abel, *Official Correspondence of James S. Calhoun*, 383. Conrad instructed Sumner: "In the selection of posts, you will be governed mainly by the following considerations . . . : 1st The protection of New Mexico. 2d The defense of the Mexican Territory, which we are bound to protect against the Indians within our borders. 3d Economy and facility in supporting the troops, particularly in regard to forage, fuel and adaptation of the surrounding country to cultivation." Ibid.

23. Frazer, *New Mexico in 1850*, 182.

24. Bartlett, *Personal Narrative*, 2:388.

25. Sumner to Jones, Oct. 24, 1851, LS-DNM, Roll 1.

26. Citizens of Doña Ana to Calhoun, Aug. 8, 1851, quoted in Abel, *Official Correspondence of James S. Calhoun*, 402–403.

27. Timmons, *El Paso*, 109; Sumner to Conrad, Mar. 27, 1852, LS-DNM, Roll 1.

28. Sumner to Jones, Oct. 24, 1851, LS-DNM, Roll 1. For civilian military contracts, see Wooster, *American Military Frontiers*, 121.

29. Swords to Jesup, Oct. 25, 1851, in *Annual Report of the Secretary of War* (1851), 238–39.

30. Brent to Jesup, Oct. 9, 1850, in *Annual Report of the Secretary of War* (1850), 293.

31. Frazer, "Purveyors of Flour to the Army," 213.

32. Brent to Jesup, Oct. 9, 1850, in *Annual Report of the Secretary of War* (1850), 293; Swords to Jesup, Oct. 25, 1851, in *Annual Report of the Secretary of War* (1851), 239. On frontier army farming, see D. Ball, *Army Regulars on the Western Frontier*, 26.

33. Sumner wrote to James Magoffin near El Paso in August 1851: "A post of 3 companies will be established at the Cottonwood midway between Dona Ana and El Paso, and an officer's guard of twenty men will be left near each of those towns. . . . If you feel so inclined to furnish quarters for one of these guards, without rent, at your place 1 1/2 miles below El Paso, I will place it there." Sumner to Magoffin, Aug. 17, 1851, LS-DNM, Roll 1.

34. A history of Stephenson's landholdings in the Mesilla Valley and the litigation surrounding his Brazito land grant is found in House, *Land Claims in the Territory of New Mexico*, 24–95. See also Timmons, *El Paso*, 113–14.

35. In August 1851 Sumner ordered Major Gouverneur Morris to find a location south of Doña Ana suitable for a post. Morris was to "obtain a written consent for the government to occupy a mile square for twenty years *without rent*." Sumner to Morris, Aug. 17, 1851, LS-DNM, Roll 1 (emphasis in original).

When the Confederates took possession of the Mesilla Valley in 1861, Hugh Stephenson leased them Fort Fillmore and its surrounding Brazito land grant. Colonel John R. Baylor, commanding Confederate forces, arranged to pay him $3,000 annually, but Rebel soldiers never occupied Fort Fillmore for any significant period of time. Stephenson and Baylor, Contract for Fort Fillmore Rent, Sept. 1, 1861, Folder 87, Twitchell Collection, New Mexico State Records Center and Archives.

36. Magoffin to Sumner, Aug. 6, 1851, LR-DNM, M1102, Roll 4.

37. Senate, *Statistical Report on the Sickness and Mortality in the Army . . . from January 1839 to January 1855*, 414.

38. Garland to Thomas, Oct. 29, 1853, LS-DNM, Roll 1; Grinstead, *Life and Death of a Frontier Fort*, 3–5.

39. Agnew, *Garrisons of the Regular U.S. Army*, 19, 31–33.

40. Senate, *Statistical Report on the Sickness and Mortality in the Army . . . from January 1839 to January 1855*, 415. This report detailed the diseases in New Mexico for the period 1849–54. In 1850 the Ninth Military Department had a mean troop strength of 880 men and a total of 2,124 cases of illness, with 37 deaths. Four years later the numbers remained much the same: the mean troop strength was 1,175 men, with 2,492 cases of illness and 40 deaths. Ibid., 432–35.

41. Fort Fillmore Post Return, Oct. 1853, RG94, Returns from U.S. Military Posts, M617, Roll 366, National Archives.

42. Frazer, *Mansfield on the Condition of the Western Forts*, 56.

43. Bartlett, *Personal Narrative*, 2:392.

44. Fort Fillmore Post Return, Mar. 1852, RG94, Returns from U.S. Military Posts, M617, Roll 366. Miles received authorization from Sumner to hire ten Mexican laborers in December 1851 as long as the "expense not exceed $175 a month." McFerran to Miles, Dec. 6, 1851, LS-DNM, Roll 1.

45. Miles to Nichols, Aug. 11, 1855, LR-DNM, M1120, Roll 2.

46. Averell, *Ten Years in the Saddle*, 171.

47. Reeve, "Puritan and Apache," 285.

48. Carson, "William Carr Lane Diary," 218–23. Dixon Stansbury Miles was born on May 4, 1804, in Maryland. He graduated from the U.S. Military Academy in 1824 and served with the Seventh Infantry until 1847, when he was transferred to the Third Infantry. In 1859 he was transferred to Kansas. During the Civil War, Miles commanded the federal arsenal at Harper's Ferry, where he was killed on September 16, 1862. Heitman, *Historical Register*, 708.

49. Conrad to Sumner, Apr. 1, 1851, in *Annual Report of the Secretary of War* (1851), 125; General Orders No. 1, Jan. 8, 1851, AGO.

50. Sumner to Miles, Mar. 30, 1852, LS-DNM, Roll 1.

51. Miles to McFerran, Apr. 1852, LR-DNM, M1102, Roll 4.

52. Sumner to Adjutant General, Sept. 24, 1852, in *Annual Report of the Secretary of War* (1852), 26.

53. Sumner to Miles, Sept. 22, 1852, LS-DNM, Roll 1 (emphasis in original).

54. Steen to Sumner, Dec. 13, 1852, LR-DNM, M1102, Roll 4.

55. Frazer, *Mansfield on the Condition of the Western Forts*, 63.

56. Sumner to Cooper, Dec. 17, 1852, LS-DNM, Roll 1. Sumner blamed the failures at Fort Conrad on the post commander, Major Howe, who "made no effort whatever to carry out the farming order." Ibid.

57. Senate, *Statistical Report on the Sickness and Mortality in the Army*, 419.

58. Ibid. For additional data relating to New Mexico posts, see also Senate, *Statistical Report on the Sickness and Mortality in the United States Army*, 438–45.

59. Agnew, *Garrisons of the Regular U.S. Army*, 19, 31–33, 47–49.

60. Sumner to Jones, Oct. 24, 1851, LS-DNM, Roll 1 (emphasis in original).

61. Bartlett, *Personal Narrative*, 2:389.

62. Hatfield, *Chasing Shadows*, 53.

63. The eight claimants recorded a loss of three mules, forty-six oxen, thirty cattle, two horses, and 1,532 sheep with an estimated value of $5,216. One of the claimants was Thomas Biggs, a coproprietor of the land upon which Fort Conrad was built. Senate, *Claims for Depredations*.

64. Twitchell, *Leading Facts of New Mexican History*, 2:292.

65. Buford to McFerran, Dec. 19, 1851, LR-DNM, M1102, Roll 4.

66. Sumner to Morris, Dec. 3, 1851, LS-DNM, Roll 1; Sumner to Jones, Jan. 1, 1852, ibid.

67. Sumner to Jones, Jan. 27, 1852, ibid.

68. Sumner to Jones, Sept. 24, 1852, in *Annual Report of the Secretary of War* (1852), 26. Four years later Secretary of War Jefferson Davis condemned the removal of military posts from the towns: "The expense and embarrassment to the military service resulting from the present policy of locating posts in advance of settlement . . . continue to be seriously felt. . . . It is believed that the efficiency of the troops would be increased proportionally as the expense of supporting them would be diminished [if the troops reoccupied the settlements]." *Annual Report of the Secretary of War* (1856), 5–8.

69. The Gila Apaches were commonly referred to as "Copper Mine Apaches" in early 1850s correspondence. John Russell Bartlett met Chiefs Delgadito and Ponce at Santa Rita in 1851 and observed them to be "men of more than ordinary character, intellect and influence and seem to be reasonable and practicable in their views and expectations. Hitherto, however, they have all been viewed by the inhabitants of this country as cruel, bloodthirsty, implacable enemies." Bartlett to Stuart, Feb. 19, 1852, LR-OIA, Roll 546.

70. Thompson, "With the Third Infantry in New Mexico," 362; Sweeney, *Mangas Coloradas*, 245–47.

71. Howe to McFerran, Jan. 25, 1852, LR-DNM, M1102, Roll 5.

72. Ibid.

73. Sumner to Jones, Feb. 3, 1852, LS-DNM, Roll 1; Sumner to Calhoun, Mar. 21, 1852, ibid.; Sumner to Jones, Mar. 22, 1852, ibid.

74. Sumner to Howe, Feb. 3, 1852, ibid.; Sumner to Jones, Feb. 3, 1852, ibid.; Sumner to Calhoun, Feb. 11, 1852, ibid.

75. Bennett, *Forts and Forays*, 34.

76. Ibid.

77. Morris to McFerran, Mar. 16, 1852, LR-DNM, M1102, Roll 5.

78. Bennett, *Forts and Forays*, 36.

79. Thompson, "With the Third Infantry in New Mexico," 366–68.

80. Bennett, *Forts and Forays*, 37.

81. Morris to Sumner, Feb. 28, 1852, LR-DNM, M1102, Roll 5.

82. Sumner to Morris, Apr. 1, 1852, LS-DNM, Roll 1.

83. Sumner informed Morris that Mangas Coloradas "desires to make peace, and disdains the acts of the hostile band [of Gila Apaches]." Ibid.

84. Smith to Brown, Mar. 9, 1850, in *Annual Report of Commissioner of Indian Affairs* (1850), 142.

85. Lea to Calhoun, Apr. 12, 1851, in *Annual Report of Commissioner of Indian Affairs* (1851), 447.

86. Conrad to Sumner, Apr. 1, 1851, LR-DNM, M1102, Roll 5.

87. Swords to Jesup, Oct. 25, 1851, in *Annual Report of the Secretary of War* (1851), 240.

88. Sumner to Calhoun, Aug. 3, 1851, LS-DNM, Roll 1.

89. Horn, *New Mexico's Troubled Years*, 30.

90. Calhoun to Lea, Aug. 22, 1851, quoted in Abel, *Official Correspondence of James S. Calhoun*, 401. Only weeks before, Sumner had declined to allow Indian Agent Edward H. Wingfield to accompany him on an expedition to the Navajo country. Calhoun wrote: "Col. Sumner, with a command of troops, marched a few days since, in the direction of the Navajo country, and I desired to send out . . . an Agent, but Col. Sumner positively declined affording the 'facilities' which *his* instructions authorized—and therefore, no Agent accompanies him." Ibid. (emphasis in original). He wrote in October 1851: "The Military officers and the executive [Calhoun] can not harmonize, and I am not certain that the public

interests would not be promoted by relieving us all from duty in this Territory." Calhoun to Lea, Oct. 1, 1851, ibid., 433.

91. Greiner, "Private Letters of a Government Official," 546.

92. For early reservation advocacy in the Southwest, see Trennert, *Alternative to Extinction*, 54–60. Years later New Mexicans continued to pressure officials to relegate the territory's Indian tribes to reservations. In 1865, citizens memorialized President Andrew Johnson, asking that he establish several Indian reservations so that residents might "open and develope [*sic*] this rich country." Memorial to Andrew Johnson, 1865, Folder 14, New Mexico Indian Depredation Claims Collection, New Mexico State Records Center and Archives.

93. Abel, *Official Correspondence of James S. Calhoun*, 43.

Chapter 5

1. For Sumner's views on New Mexico, see Keleher, *Turmoil in New Mexico*, 61–66; Wooster, *American Military Frontiers*, 127; and D. Ball, "U.S. Army in New Mexico," 178–79.

2. See *Santa Fe Weekly Gazette*, Feb. 26, Mar. 5, Apr. 9, 1853.

3. On the military's issuance of private contracts, see Frazer, "Purveyors of Flour to the Army," 213–32.

4. Miles to McFerran, Feb. 21, 1852, LR-DNM, M1102, Roll 5.

5. Ibid.; McFerran to Miles, Feb. 27, 1852, LS-DNM, Roll 1.

6. Morris to McFerran, June 16, 1852, LR-DNM, M1102, Roll 5.

7. Green, "James S. Calhoun," 347 (quote); Horn, *New Mexico's Troubled Years*, 33. Indian Agent John Greiner observed one week prior to Calhoun's departure that the governor's health had deteriorated to the extent that he was "unable to stand alone." Greiner to Lea, Apr. 30, 1852, LR-OIA, Roll 546.

8. Abel, *Official Correspondence of James S. Calhoun*, xii–xiii.

9. See *Santa Fe Weekly Gazette*, Apr. 24, Dec. 25, 1852.

10. Sumner to Webster, May 8, 1852, LS-DNM, Roll 1; Sumner to Jones, Apr. 28, 1852, ibid.; Sumner to Jones, May 8, 1852, ibid. The colonel later claimed, "It was with great reluctance that I took charge of the civil government, and nothing but a sense of imperative duty could have induced me to do it." Sumner to Conrad, Oct. 29, 1852, ibid.

11. On the perceived conspiracy among New Mexicans, see Greiner to Lea, Apr. 30, 1852, LR-OIA, Roll 546. Calhoun seemed equally paranoid: "We are not able to fight against the infamous combination that has been so long & so stealthily at work to take this Territory in blood." Calhoun to Dawson, Apr. 12, 1852, ibid. Sumner acknowledged several months later that the "insurrectionary spirit had entirely subsided." Sumner to Lane, Sept. 27, 1852, LS-DNM, Roll 1.

12. Weightman to Lane, Oct. 7, 1852, Lane Papers, Missouri Historical Society; Sumner to Conrad, Oct. 29, 1852, LS-DNM, Roll 1.

13. Morris to McFerran, May 31, 1852, LR-DNM, M1102, Roll 5.

14. Ibid.

15. Sumner to Morris, July 29, 1852, LS-DNM, Roll 1. Wrote Sumner: "In the selection of the particular site for the post, pay no regard whatever, to any present occupation of the land. It is all *Indian Country,* and no whites have any right to settle upon it but the troops." Ibid. (emphasis in original).

16. Miles to McFerran, June 17, 1852, LR-DNM, M1102, Roll 5.

17. Fort Fillmore Post Returns, June, July 1852, RG94, Returns from U.S. Military Posts, M617, Roll 366.

18. Wadsworth, *Forgotten Fortress,* 78.

19. Sweeney, *Mangas Coloradas,* 256–61.

20. Utley, *Indian Frontier,* 43.

21. Prucha, *American Indian Treaties,* 334–45.

22. Weightman to Lane, Oct. 7, 1852, Lane Papers. A Santa Fe newspaper editorialized: "The Indian agents were laid on the shelf, and the Colonel [Sumner] became the great pacificator." *Santa Fe Weekly Gazette,* Nov. 20, 1852.

23. Abel, "Journal of John Greiner," 220.

24. Ibid., 221–22.

25. Ibid., 222.

26. Cuentas Azules was murdered in Mesilla only a few months after signing the treaty. Judge Kirby Benedict issued a warrant for the arrest of Pedro Jose Barule in November 1853 after a grand jury in Las Cruces indicted him of the murder. The alcalde refused to surrender Barule to the U.S. marshal, saying that "the inhabitants of the place have determined he shall not be arrested and have prepared themselves to oppose forcibly any attempt to arrest him." Benedict wrote to Fort Fillmore requesting military aid in apprehending Barule, but Major Electus Backus declined, citing Mexican sovereignty in Mesilla and the potential outbreak of hostilities between the two republics. Benedict to Backus, Nov. 23, 1853, in *Santa Fe Weekly Gazette,* Feb. 4, 1854; Backus to Benedict, Nov. 23, 1853, ibid. See also *St. Louis Daily Missouri Republican,* Jan. 26, 1854; and *Santa Fe Weekly Gazette,* Nov. 19, 1853.

27. Abel, "Journal of John Greiner," 228.

28. Kappler, *Laws and Treaties,* 598–600.

29. Greiner to Lane, Sept. 30, 1852, LR-OIA, Roll 546.

30. Testimony of John Greiner, July 3, 1865, in Senate, *Report on the Condition of the Indian Tribes,* 328.

31. *Santa Fe Weekly Gazette,* Nov. 20, 1852. Colonel Sumner would later write: "Mangus Colorado [*sic*] was not told by me that he could make war upon the Mexicans. He was told that if the Mexicans came into his country, and made war upon his people, that they could defend themselves and that he must immediately report any such occurrence to the nearest post or agent." Sumner to Miles, Aug. 28, 1852, LS-DNM, Roll 1.

32. Kappler, *Laws and Treaties,* 599.

33. Sumner to Jones, July 21, 1852, LS-DNM, Roll 1; Sumner to Stuart, July 21, 1852, Folder 1551, Schroeder Papers, New Mexico State Records Center and Archives. Sumner suggested that annuity payments of $15,000 be issued: "A small annuity has a wonderful effect upon Indians, in repressing all hostile feeling." Ibid.

34. Utley, "Captain John Pope's Plan," 154–55.

35. Greiner to Lea, Aug. 30, 1852, Folder 1551, Schroeder Papers.

36. Greiner, "Private Letters of a Government Official," 550. Sumner assured Lane that he would not furnish supplies to civil officials without orders from higher authority. Sumner to Lane, Sept. 27, 1852, LS-DNM, Roll 1. Ironically, in a letter to the governor two months later, he stated, "I am fully aware how indispensible it is, in all interactions with Indians, that the civil and military authorities should harmonize." Sumner to Lane, Nov. 3, 1852, ibid.

37. Sumner justified his relocation by claiming that the garrison was no longer needed from a tactical standpoint. Sumner to Cooper, Oct. 25, 1852, LS-DNM, Roll 1.

38. Weightman to Lane, Nov. 18, 1852, Lane Papers; *Santa Fe Weekly Gazette*, Feb. 12, 1853.

39. See, for example, two tersely worded letters between Sumner and Lane in which they chide one another over the colonel's assumption of civil authority during Calhoun's absence: Lane to Sumner, Oct. 22, 1852, LR-DNM, M1120, Roll 3; and Sumner to Lane, Oct. 24, 1852, LS-DNM, Roll 1.

40. On Lane's controversy with Mexico, see Kiser, *Turmoil on the Rio Grande*, 72–80.

41. Miles to McFerran, Aug. 16, 1852, LR-DNM, M1102, Roll 5.

42. Sumner to Morris, July 29, 1852, LS-DNM, Roll 1.

43. Sweeney, *Mangas Coloradas*, 268; Sumner to Cooper, Dec. 17, 1852, LS-DNM, Roll 1.

44. Agnew, *Garrisons of the Regular U.S. Army*, 31–32.

45. Miles to McFerran, Mar. 15, 1852, LR-DNM, M1102, Roll 5.

46. Indian Agent Edmund A. Graves reiterated this notion later: "You cannot make the Indian understand the action of Congress, either its necessity or its importance." Graves to Meriwether, Aug. 31, 1853, Graves Letters, Center for Southwest Research, New Mexico State Archives.

47. Morris to McFerran, Oct. 12, 1852, LR-DNM, M1102, Roll 5.

48. Senate, *Claims for Depredations*, 51. Morris noted that stock thefts had occurred at the post on September 22, 29, and October 4.

49. Morris to McFerran, Oct. 12, 1852, LR-DNM, M1102, Roll 5.

50. Fort Webster Post Returns, Jan.–Mar. 1853, RG94, Returns from U.S. Military Posts, M617.

51. Miles to McFerran, Aug. 16, 1852, LR-DNM, M1102, Roll 6.

52. Thrapp, *Victorio and the Mimbres Apaches*, 29.

53. Sweeney, *Mangas Coloradas*, 268–69.
54. Steele to Howe, Feb. 1, 1853, LR-DNM, M1102, Roll 6.
55. Lane to Lea, Dec. 31, 1852, LR-OIA, M-T21, Roll 546.
56. Four claims were filed for stock stolen on February 15, 1853. Claimants were José María Padilla (three oxen, two cows), Antonio Montoya (six oxen, two mules), William J. Conner (one ox, three cows), and Juan N. López (two oxen), for a total value of $605. Senate, *Claims for Depredations*.
57. Steen to Lane, Jan. 10, 1853, Lane Papers.
58. Thrapp, *Victorio and the Mimbres Apaches*, 29.
59. *Santa Fe Weekly Gazette*, Dec. 18, 1852.
60. Carson, "William Carr Lane Diary," 218–23. For Apache religion, see Opler, *Apache Life-Way*, 186–200.
61. Provisional Compact, Apr. 7, 1853, LR-DNM, M1102, Roll 6.
62. Steen to Lane, May 20, 1852, ibid.
63. Sweeney, *Mangas Coloradas*, 280.
64. On the authority to issue rations to Indians at military posts, see Cohen, *Handbook of Federal Indian Law*, 73–75.
65. Lane to Steck, July 11, 1853, Steck Papers 1, Roll 2.
66. Wingfield to Lane, May 28, 1853, LR-DNM, M1102, Roll 6.
67. Steen to Miles, June 1, 1853, ibid.
68. Sweeney, *Mangas Coloradas*, 273.
69. Carson, "William Carr Lane Diary," 222–23.
70. Dr. Michael Steck was born in Hughesville, Pennsylvania, in 1818. He graduated from Jefferson Medical College in Philadelphia in 1842 and came to New Mexico in 1849 at an annual salary of $1,550. He was eventually appointed superintendent of Indian affairs by President Abraham Lincoln. Steck married twice during his lifetime. His first wife and child died in Santa Fe sometime in the 1850s. He later married Elizabeth Wood, and the couple had three children together: Rachel, John Michael, and Thomas Wood. After resigning his position, he returned to Pennsylvania, where he "built the finest house" in Hughesville. Steck died of a cerebral hemorrhage while fishing near the Shenandoah River in Virginia in 1880. T. Kenneth Wood to William A. Keleher, n.d., Folder 25, Michael Steck Biographical Sketch, Box 7, Keleher Papers, Center for Southwest Research, New Mexico State Archives. See also Steck Papers 1, Roll 1.
71. Miles to Nichols, May 24, 1855, LR-DNM, M1102, Roll 4.
72. Sumner to Cooper, Dec. 19, 1852, LS-DNM, Roll 1.
73. Bender, *March of Empire*, 155.
74. *Santa Fe Weekly Gazette*, Aug. 13, 1853.

Chapter 6

1. Steck to Biddle, Dec. 11, 1852, Steck Papers 1, Roll 1.
2. Steck to Wingfield, May 28, 1853, ibid.

3. Horn, *New Mexico's Troubled Years*, 53.

4. Meriwether to Manypenny, Sept. 1, 1854, in *Annual Report of the Commissioner of Indian Affairs* (1854), 166.

5. *Santa Fe Weekly Gazette*, Dec. 31, 1853.

6. Meriwether to Manypenny, Sept. 1, 1854, in *Annual Report of the Commissioner of Indian Affairs* (1854), 166–67.

7. Meriwether to Manypenny, Aug. 31, 1853, in *Annual Report of the Commissioner of Indian Affairs* (1853), 429–33.

8. Ibid.

9. Graves to Manypenny, June 8, 1854, in *Annual Report of the Commissioner of Indian Affairs* (1854), 181. Graves also noted: "To exterminate the aborigines . . . is a policy that no enlightened citizen or statesman will propose or advocate. That this race . . . are destined to a speedy and final extinction, according to the laws now in force, either civil or divine, or both, seems to admit of no doubt. . . . [A]ll that can be expected from an enlightened and Christian government, such as ours is, is to graduate and smooth the pass-way of their final exit from the stage of human existence." Ibid.

10. John Garland was born in Virginia and joined the U.S. Army as a first lieutenant during the War of 1812. During the Mexican-American War, he fought under Zachary Taylor and was severely wounded at Mexico City. In 1848 his daughter married James Longstreet, who later became a Confederate general during the Civil War. Heitman, *Historical Register*, 447; D. Ball, *Army Regulars on the Western Frontier*, 68.

11. *Santa Fe Weekly Gazette*, Feb. 4, 1854.

12. Ibid., Oct. 11, 1856.

13. Garland to Cooper, Oct. 28, 1853, LS-DNM, Roll 1.

14. Garland to Cooper, Nov. 27, 1853, ibid.

15. Frazer, *Mansfield on the Condition of the Western Forts*, 25–26.

16. Garland to Thomas, Oct. 29, 1853, LS-DNM, Roll 1.

17. Garland to Steen, Nov. 7, 1853, ibid.

18. Frazer, *Forts of the West*, 104. Captain Thorn had once been an aide-de-camp to General Garland, explaining why Garland ordered that the new fort be named for him. Thorn, in command of a company of dragoons, "got drowned by being capsized in crossing the Gila [River] with two Mexicans and one dragoon; it seems that Capt. Thorn was quite a good swimmer but the two Mexicans who were drowning also got hold of him—one by the leg the other by his arm—and carried him under." George Clinton Gardner to his Father, Oct. 28, 1849, in Weber and Elder, *Fiasco*, 65–66. Gardner erred in stating that Thorn drowned in the Gila; the incident actually occurred in the Colorado River.

19. Garland to Cooper, Jan. 27, 1854, LS-DNM, Roll 1.

20. Reid, *Reid's Tramp*, 171.

21. Garland to Thomas, Oct. 29, 1853, LS-DNM, Roll 1.

23. Evans and Pleasonton to Pierce, Feb. 24, 1854, LR-OIA, Roll 547.

22. Thrapp, *Victorio and the Mimbres Apaches*, 37.
24. Meriwether to Steck, July 23, 1854, Steck Papers 2, Roll 1.
25. Steck to Meriwether, Oct. 1854, ibid.
26. Giese, *Forts of New Mexico*, 22.
27. Frazer, *Mansfield on the Condition of the Western Forts*, 51.
28. Quoted in Ruhlen, "Fort Thorn," 127.
29. Averell, *Ten Years in the Saddle*, 123.
30. Frazer, *Forts of the West*, 98; Garland to Cooper, May 11, 1854, LS-DNM, Roll 1.
31. Miles to McFerran, Aug. 20, 1852, LR-DNM, M1102, Roll 5.
32. Socorro citizens to Garland, Mar. 8, 1854, LR-DNM, M1120, Roll 1.
33. Chandler to Nichols, June 5, 1855, ibid., Roll 4.
34. Meriwether to Steck, Apr. 28, 1855, Steck Papers 2, Roll 2.
35. Meriwether to Steck, May 15, 1855, ibid.
36. Thrapp, *Victorio and the Mimbres Apaches*, 43.
37. Miles to Steck, Aug. 12, 1855, Steck Papers 2, Roll 2.
38. Meriwether to Steck, Aug. 28, 1855, ibid.
39. Sweeney, *Mangas Coloradas*, 314.
40. *Santa Fe Weekly Gazette*, Oct. 18, 1856.
41. Pelham to Steck, Oct. 3, 1855, Steck Papers 2, Roll 2. Lt. W. H. Emory also reported in 1857 on mining operations in the Gadsden Purchase lands. See Emory, *United States and Mexican Boundary Survey*, 1:94–96.
42. Steck to Pelham, Oct. 1855, Steck Papers 2, Roll 2. Indian Agent Edmund A. Graves likewise mentioned creating an Apache reservation: "The attempt should be made, at as early a day as practicable, of inducing them to till and cultivate the soil. . . . In order to bring about a consummation of this policy it will be necessary to concentrate and to bring together the several tribes (that is, the members of each tribe should be drawn together, and not the tribes, because the different tribes would not harmonize, whilst individuals of the same tribe would) into a smaller area." Graves to Manypenny, June 8, 1854, in *Annual Report of the Commissioner of Indian Affairs* (1854), 182.
43. Eaton to Nichols, Nov. 1855, LR-DNM, M1120, Roll 2.
44. Moore to Nichols, Nov. 1, 1855, ibid.
45. Davis to Manypenny, Nov. 15, 1855, LR-OIA, M-T21, Roll 548.
46. Crittenden to Garland, Oct. 1, 1856, LR-DNM, M1120, Roll 3.
47. Steck to Manypenny, Dec. 22, 1855, Steck Papers 2, Roll 2.
48. Steck to Davis, Jan. 9, 1856, ibid.
49. Ibid.
50. Eaton to Nichols, Dec. 23, 1855, LR-DNM, M1120, Roll 4.
51. Ibid.; Sweeney, *Mangas Coloradas*, 323.
52. Steck to Garland, Jan. 7, 1856, Steck Papers 2, Roll 2.
53. Steck to Eaton, Dec. 6, 1855, LR-DNM, M1120, Roll 4.

Chapter 7

1. Steck to Eaton, Mar. 12, 1856, LR-DNM, M1120, Roll 5; Sweeney, *Mangas Coloradas*, 325–26.

2. Delgadito had previously been poorly regarded by military commanders. Writing in 1852, Colonel Miles warned, "he is suspicious and fearful, besides being hostile." Years of warfare with U.S. troops, coupled with treaty negotiations, eventually induced the chief to remain on peaceful terms. Miles to Sumner, Aug. 28, 1852, LS-DNM, Roll 2.

3. Steck to Davis, Apr. 6, 1856, LR-OIA, M-T21, Roll 550.

4. Sweeney, *Mangas Coloradas*, 325–27.

5. Steck to Davis, Apr. 6, 1856, LR-OIA, M-T21, Roll 550.

6. Steck to Manypenny, Apr. 10, 1856, Steck Papers 2, Roll 2.

7. Sweeney, *Mangas Coloradas*, 327.

8. "Costelles [*sic*] was a *Mexican*, then thirty years old, of medium size, had been stolen, when a child, from his parents whilst journeying in their country (Chihuahua), by a party of Indians, headed by Delgareta [Delgadito]. . . . [I]n due time [he] acquired a fondness for his captors and their mode of living; showed himself active and efficient in their forays . . . and by his deeds of daring and cunning became a 'head man.'" Reid, *Reid's Tramp*, 175 (emphasis in original).

9. McClelland to Davis, Sept. 25, 1856, LR-DNM, M1120, Roll 4.

10. Steck received no official word that an investigation occurred but heard from Governor Meriwether and Captain Steen that Garland had conducted his own private investigation. The general found Chandler's report satisfactory and dismissed Steck's account as unreliable. Steck to Manypenny, Oct. 18, 1856, Steck Papers 2, Roll 2.

11. Steck to Meriwether, June 16, 1856, ibid.

12. Thrapp, *Victorio and the Mimbres Apaches*, 51.

13. Davis to Steck, July 9, 1856, Steck Papers 2, Roll 2.

14. Bennett, *Forts and Forays*, 80–81.

15. Miles to Nichols, Mar. 1856, LR-DNM, M1120, Roll 5.

16. Eaton to Grier, May 15, 1856, ibid.

17. Eaton to Nichols, May 31, 1856, ibid.

18. Miles to Nichols, Jan. 1857, LR-DNM, M1120, Roll 6.

19. Richardson to Nichols, June 27, 1854, ibid., Roll 1.

20. Garland to Cooper, Jan. 31, 1855, LS-DNM, Roll 2.

21. Blake to Nichols, Aug. 23, 1856, LR-DNM, M1120, Roll 5.

22. Nichols to Steen, Sept. 10, 1856, LS-DNM, Roll 2; Rathbun and Alexander, *New Mexico Frontier Military Place Names*, 18. Steen commanded Companies B, D, G, and K, First Dragoons and had orders to establish a new post near Tucson. Bonneville to Thomas, Oct. 31, 1856, LS-DNM, Roll 2.

23. Senate, *Statistical Report on the Sickness and Mortality in the United States Army . . . from January 1855 to January 1860*, 223.

24. Blake to Nichols, Sept. 14, 1856, LR-DNM, M1120, Roll 5; Nichols to Blake, Sept. 24, 1856, LS-DNM, Roll 2.

25. Senate, *Statistical Report on the Sickness and Mortality in the United States Army . . . from January 1855 to January 1860*, 224.

26. Ibid., 223–24; Kraemer, "Sickliest Post in the Territory of New Mexico," 222–23.

27. Senate, *Statistical Report on the Sickness and Mortality in the United States Army . . . from January 1855 to January 1860*, 223. In August 1857 fifteen of eighty-one men at Fort Thorn were sick; a month later, of one hundred soldiers, nineteen were confined to the post hospital. During the summer months, as much as 20 percent of the garrison was bedridden with illness. Fort Thorn Post Returns, Aug., Sept. 1857, RG94, Returns from U.S. Military Posts, M617, Roll 1271.

28. Henry to Nichols, Aug. 1857, LR-DNM, M1120, Roll 6.

29. Henry to Nichols, Aug. 1858, ibid.

30. Senate, *Statistical Report on the Sickness and Mortality in the United States Army . . . from January 1855 to January 1860*, 224–25.

31. See Bonneville to Thomas, Oct. 31, 1856, LS-DNM, Roll 2.

32. Roberts to Nichols, Oct. 1856, LR-DNM, M1120, Roll 5.

33. Garland to Thomas, Jan. 28, 1854, LS-DNM, Roll 1.

34. Nichols to Steen, Aug. 31, 1856, ibid., Roll 2. For antebellum military activity in southern Arizona, see Altshuler, *Chains of Command*, 1–15.

35. Quoted in Sacks, "Origins of Fort Buchanan," 210.

36. Bonneville to Thomas, Oct. 31, 1856, LS-DNM, Roll 2.

37. Frazer, *Forts and Supplies*, 122.

38. For campaigns targeting Western Apaches, see House, *Indian Hostilities in New Mexico*, 19–36. Writing in 1852, John Russell Bartlett observed that "the Pinalenos and Coyoteros . . . never cross the country of the Copper Mine Indians to trade with the Americans on the Rio Grande, nor with the New Mexicans." Bartlett to Stuart, Feb. 19, 1852, LR-OIA, Roll 546.

39. Alexander, *Arizona Frontier Military Place Names*, 89.

40. Nichols to Steen, Dec. 26, 1856, LS-DNM, Roll 2. Major Nichols informed Steen, "the site selected by you, some sixty miles south of Tuczon [*sic*], is too far from Tuczon [*sic*] and the settlements within our line, to afford them any protection." Ibid.

41. Petition from Tucson Citizens to Garland, n.d., LR-DNM, M1120, Roll 6.

42. Mowry to Denver, Nov. 10, 1857, in *Annual Report of the Commissioner of Indian Affairs* (1857), 303.

43. A description of Mowry's mine is found in Browne, *Adventures in the Apache Country*, 203–11. For Mowry's political role in southern New Mexico and Arizona, see Ganaway, *New Mexico and the Sectional Controversy*, 106–108.

44. Mowry, *Arizona and Sonora*, 15–55. See also Poston, *Building a State in Apache Land*, 66–98.

45. R. S. Ewell to Elizabeth Ewell, Aug. 10, 1858, in Hamlin, *Making of a Soldier*, 86. Ewell sold his share in the enterprise before leaving Fort Buchanan on the eve of the Civil War. For his activities while commanding Fort Buchanan, see Casdorph, *Confederate General R. S. Ewell*, 53–99, esp. 83. On his speculation in the Patagonia Mine, see Pfanz, *Richard S. Ewell*, 100–21, esp. 103–105 and 111–13.

46. For a transnational history of early mining pursuits and the role of Fort Buchanan in sustaining these endeavors, see Truett, *Fugitive Landscapes*, 38–51, esp. 47–49.

47. Steen to Nichols, June 1857, LR-DNM, M1120, Roll 6.

48. Sacks, *Be It Enacted*, 11.

49. Steen to Nichols, June 4, 1857, LR-DNM, M1120, Roll 6; Nichols to Steen, June 20, 1857, LS-DNM, Roll 2. Nichols instructed Steen that "should the Mexican troops again invade our territory, they must be repelled by force of arms." Ibid. He also warned that trouble with Mexican authorities might ensue owing to "the perfect anarchy existing there [in Sonora]" and ordered Steen to uphold neutrality at all costs. Nichols to Steen, Jan. 28, 1857, ibid.

50. General Orders No. 3, Apr. 3, 1858, LS-DNM, Roll 2.

51. Sacks, "Origins of Fort Buchanan," 210, 225n68.

52. Kiser, *Turmoil on the Rio Grande*, 172, 179–80. For the commanding officer's report of Fort Buchanan's abandonment, see Wilson, "Retreat to the Rio Grande," 4–8.

53. Bonneville to Thomas, July 15, 1859, in Walker, "Colonel Bonneville's Report," 358. An excellent physical description of Fort Buchanan and surrounding environs is found in Senate, *Statistical Report on the Sickness and Mortality in the United States Army . . . from January 1855 to January 1860*, 207–20.

54. Bonneville to Thomas, Dec. 31, 1856, LS-DNM, Roll 2.

55. Roberts to Nichols, Nov. 29, 1856, LR-DNM, M1120, Roll 5.

56. Randall to Nichols, Dec. 4, 1856, ibid.

57. Ibid.

58. Ibid.

59. Smith to Brown, Mar. 9, 1850, in *Annual Report of the Commissioner of Indian Affairs* (1850), 141.

60. McLaws to John Buford, June 1850, LS-DNM, Roll 1. Colonel Munroe wrote, "the proper regulation of Trade and Intercourse between the people of New Mexico and the Indian Tribes on its Borders, is so intimately connected with whatever relates to military operations," and he suggested that his command would be benefitted by "the extension over New Mexico of the present Laws regulating Trade and Intercourse with the Indian Tribes, with such modification as may adapt them to this new sphere of operation." Munroe to Jones, June 11, 1850, ibid.

61. Steen to Lane, Jan. 10, 1853, Lane Papers, Missouri Historical Society.

62. *El Sonorense,* July 16, 1849.

63. Calhoun to Dawson, Oct. 31, 1849, Folder 9, Box 5, James S. Calhoun File, Keleher Papers, Center for Southwest Research, New Mexico State Archives.

64. Swords to Jesup, Oct. 25, 1851, in *Annual Report of the Secretary of War* (1851), 240.

65. Howe to McFerran, Sept. 1851, LR-DNM, M1102, Roll 4.

66. Sumner to Jones, Feb. 3, 1852, LS-DNM, Roll 1. Wrote Sumner: "The Indians came in the next day and demanded that the [Mexican] should be confined for trial. This was done, and the Indians left satisfied, but as soon as they were gone, the murderer was permitted to go at large . . . and when the Indians heard of it, they became furious." Ibid.

67. Sweeney, *Mangas Coloradas,* 347–48.

68. Bonneville to Thomas, Jan. 31, 1857, LS-DNM, Roll 2. Colonel Bonneville noted that the two Mexicans killed the Apaches "while lying asleep" and that they did so "in revenge for relatives killed or captured."

69. Steen to Claiborne, Jan. 1, 1857, LR-DNM, M1120, Roll 5.

70. Reid, *Reid's Tramp,* 175.

71. Ibid., 175–76.

72. Steck to Meriwether, Jan. 3, 1857, Steck Papers 1, Roll 3.

73. Meriwether to Steck, Mar. 24, 1857, ibid.

74. Miles to Nichols, Jan. 1857, LR-DNM, M1120, Roll 6.

75. Crittenden to Nichols, Jan. 1857, ibid.; Miles to Nichols, Jan. 1857, ibid.

76. Gibbs to Whipple, Feb. 23, 1857, ibid.

77. Garretson to Editor, Mar. 11, 1857, in *Santa Fe Weekly Gazette,* Mar. 28, 1857.

78. Gibbs to Whipple, Mar. 11, 1857, LR-DNM, M1120, Roll 6.

79. Morris to Nichols, Mar. 28, 1857, ibid.

Chapter 8

1. Kendrick to Nichols, Nov. 26, 1856, LR-DNM, M1120, Roll 3.

2. See McNitt, *Navajo Wars,* 287–89.

3. Meriwether to Steck, Nov. 28, 1856, Steck Papers 2, Roll 2. Military commanders quickly reiterated that ransom money must be paid using Indian Bureau funds and that War Department coffers could not be drawn upon. Nichols to Claiborne, Jan. 16, 1857, LS-DNM, Roll 2.

4. Unlike the Gila and Mimbres bands, the army knew very little about the Mogollon band in the 1850s due to their secluded homelands and unwillingness to negotiate with Americans. Of these Indians Steck wrote in 1855 that they "have never visited the agency, nor do they seem disposed to be friendly." Several Mexican traders, with the agent's permission, had ventured into the Mogollon Mountains and promptly had most of their provisions stolen and several of their animals shot before returning. Steck recommended that an agent be sent to the Mogollon

country "with a view of correcting their evils and bringing about a better state of feeling." He estimated the band to number not more than 400 Indians total. Steck to Manypenny, Feb. 28, 1855, Steck Papers 2, Roll 3.

5. Bonneville to Thomas, Jan. 31, 1857, LS-DNM, Roll 1.
6. Steck to Nichols, Dec. 18, 1856, LR-DNM, M1120, Roll 5; Steck to Meriwether, Dec. 17, 1856, Steck Papers 2, Roll 3.
7. Claiborne to Nichols, Dec. 18, 1856, LR-DNM, M1120, Roll 5.
8. Bonneville to Thomas, Jan. 31, 1857, LS-DNM, Roll 2.
9. McNitt, *Navajo Wars*, 293–95.
10. Bonneville to Thomas, Jan. 31, 1857, LS-DNM, Roll 2.
11. Nichols to Steen, Feb. 17, 1857, ibid.
12. Averell, *Ten Years in the Saddle*, 146.
13. Reeve, "Puritan and Apache," 285–87.
14. Hammond, *Campaigns in the West*, 7.
15. Reeve, "Puritan and Apache," 288.
16. Ibid., 289; Nichols to Miles, Feb. 17, 1857, LS-DNM, Roll 2.
17. Reeve, "Puritan and Apache," 291.
18. Hammond, *Campaigns in the West*, 9.
19. Reeve, "Puritan and Apache," 290–91.
20. Hammond, *Campaigns in the West*, 11.
21. Reeve, "Puritan and Apache," 297.
22. Ibid.
23. Ibid., 296.
24. Ibid., 12.
25. Ibid., 46.
26. Bonneville to Nichols, May 24, 1857, LR-DNM, M1120, Roll 6.
27. Reeve, "Puritan and Apache," 22.
28. Averell, *Ten Years in the Saddle*, 110. Loring lost his arm during the Mexican-American War at Chapultepec. See Herr and Wallace, *Story of the U.S. Cavalry*, 63–64.
29. McNitt, *Navajo Wars*, 300; Bonneville to Loring, Apr. 20, 1857, LS-DNM, Roll 2. The column from Fort Buchanan received authorization to employ a number of Pima Indians as guides, many of whom, as traditional Apache enemies, asked permission to join the campaign. Nichols to Steen, Feb. 17, 1857, ibid. These men knew Apache country well from previous decades of intermittent trade and warfare.
30. McNitt, *Navajo Wars*, 299.
31. Reeve, "Puritan and Apache," 26–27.
32. Nichols to Steen, Feb. 17, 1857, LS-DNM, Roll 2; Steen to Nichols, May 3, 1857, LR-DNM, M1120, Roll 6; Nichols to Bonneville, June 22, 1857, LS-DNM, Roll 2.
33. Reeve, "Puritan and Apache," 23.

34. Jackson to Bonneville, May 1857, LR-DNM, M1120, Roll 6.
35. Reeve, "Puritan and Apache," 25.
36. Sweeney, *Mangas Coloradas*, 351.
37. Reeve, "Puritan and Apache," 18.
38. Hammond, *Campaigns in the West*, 13.
39. Reeve, "Puritan and Apache," 24.
40. Ibid., 25.
41. Ibid., 28–29.
42. Loring to Bonneville, May 1857, LR-DNM, M1120, Roll 6.
43. Ibid.
44. Ibid.
45. Steck to Collins, Nov. 25, 1857, Steck Papers 2, Roll 3. Indian Agent John Greiner alluded to this incident several years later, writing, "I . . . have since learned from the agent of the tribe, Dr. Steck, that sixty Indians of the same tribe [Mimbres Apaches] were poisoned by strychnine." Testimony of John Greiner, July 3, 1865, in Senate, *Report on the Condition of the Indian Tribes*, 328. See also Sweeney, *Mangas Coloradas*, 358.
46. Nichols to Thomas, Apr. 28, 1857, LS-DNM, Roll 2.
47. Bonneville to Nichols, May 1857, LR-DNM, M1120, Roll 6.
48. Miles to Bonneville, May 30, 1857, ibid.
49. Reeve, "Puritan and Apache," 34–42.
50. Hammond, *Campaigns in the West*, 16. Officers sought to avoid such confusion by ordering that Indian guides wear red sashes for identification. They were also instructed to call out "Acomas! Pimas!" whenever troops approached "so as to prevent mistakes." Nichols to Steen, Feb. 17, 1857, LS-DNM, Roll 2.
51. Miles to Bonneville, May 30, 1857, LR-DNM, M1120, Roll 6.
52. Hammond, *Campaigns in the West*, 15.
53. Quoted by Thrapp, *Victorio and the Mimbres Apaches*, 55.
54. Reeve, "Puritan and Apache," 48–50.
55. Ibid.
56. O'Bannon to Bonneville, June 1857, LR-DNM, M1120, Roll 6 (emphasis in original).
57. Whipple to Bonneville, June 4, 1857, ibid.
58. Ibid.
59. Baker to O'Bannon, June 9, 1857, ibid.
60. Hammond, *Campaigns in the West*, 22.
61. Ewell to his mother, June 10, 1857, in Hamlin, *Making of a Soldier*, 83.
62. Steck to Bonneville, June 1857, LR-DNM, M1120, Roll 6.
63. Hammond, *Campaigns in the West*, 29.
64. Ewell to Bonneville, June 27, 1857, LR-DNM, M1120, Roll 6.
65. Hammond, *Campaigns in the West*, 29.
66. Ibid.

67. Ibid.
68. Ibid., 30.
69. Miles to Bonneville, June 1857, LR-DNM, M1120, Roll 6. A San Francisco newspaper reported the incident four months later but grossly exaggerated the events. See "Slaughter of Apaches," *Golden Era*, Oct. 18, 1857.
70. Hammond, *Campaigns in the West*, 29–30.
71. Steck to Collins, Sept. 4, 1857, Steck Papers 2, Roll 2.
72. Garland to Thomas, Aug.1, 1857, LS-DNM, Roll 2; Nichols to Bonneville, July 26, 1857, ibid.; Nichols to Miles, Sept. 20, 1857, ibid. Colonel Miles returned to Fort Thorn with the Apache captives on July 30. Fort Thorn Post Return, July 1857, RG94, Returns from U.S. Military Posts, M617, Roll 1271.
73. Garland to Thomas, Aug. 1, 1857, LS-DNM, Roll 2.
74. Miles to Bonneville, July 13, 1857, LR-DNM, M1120, Roll 6.
75. Hammond, *Campaigns in the West*, 31.
76. Ibid.
77. Ibid., 32.
78. Loring to Bonneville, July 1857, LR-DNM, M1120, Roll 6.
79. See McNitt, *Navajo Wars*, 298–309.
80. Miles to Bonneville, July 1857, LR-DNM, M1120, Roll 6.
81. Garland to Thomas, Aug. 1, 1857, LS-DNM, Roll 2.
82. Nichols to Bonneville, June 22, 1857, ibid.
83. Bonneville to Nichols, July 12, 1857, LR-DNM, M1120, Roll 6.
84. Hammond, *Campaigns in the West*, 35–40.
85. Collins to Denver, Aug. 30, 1857, in *Annual Report of the Commissioner of Indian Affairs* (1857), 275. Colonel Bonneville's report provided few details of the expedition other than to describe the topography of the region. Ibid., 294–96.
86. Reeve, "Puritan and Apache," 50–51.
87. Ibid., 52–53.

Chapter 9

1. Meriwether to Manypenny, Sept. 1, 1854, in *Annual Report of the Commissioner of Indian Affairs* (1854), 378–79; Connell-Szasz, "Cultural Encounters," 198.
2. Estimates of the 1850s Mescalero population range from as few as 1,000 to as many as 3,000. Some resided in the trans-Pecos region of Texas and thus did not come into contact with troops stationed in New Mexico. See DeLay, *War of a Thousand Deserts*, 374n6.
3. Opler, "Mescalero Apache," 427–29. For Mescalero tribal organization, see Basehart, *Mescalero Apache Subsistence Patterns and Socio-Political Organization*, 104–39; and Basehart, "Mescalero Apache Band Organization," 35–47.
4. Meriwether to Manypenny, Sept. 1, 1854, in *Annual Report of the Commissioner of Indian Affairs* (1854), 378–79.

5. Ibid.
6. For intertribal trade in stolen plunder, see DeLay, *War of a Thousand Deserts*.
7. Garland to Thomas, Nov. 27, 1853, LS-DNM, Roll 1.
8. Julian Lucero filed a claim for thirty-six mules, valued at $720, stolen from his ranch by Apaches on July 7, 1849. Senate, *Claims for Depredations*, 9.
9. This same man, Juan, served as a guide for Company H on an expedition a month earlier that took the dragoons from Santa Fe southward to Doña Ana, skirting the Manzano Mountains. See D. Ball, "U.S. Army in New Mexico," 173–75.
10. Harrison to McLaws, July 18, 1849, LR-DNM, M1102, Roll 3.
11. Ibid.
12. Steen to McLaws, Dec. 9, 1849, ibid., Roll 2.
13. McLaws to Steen, Jan. 28, 1850, LS-DNM, Roll 1.
14. Munroe to Steen, June 15, 1850, ibid.
15. Steen to McLaws, Jan. 3, 1850, LR-DNM, M1102, Roll 2.
16. Steen to McLaws, July 8, 1850, ibid.
17. Thrapp, *Victorio and the Mimbres Apaches*, 46.
18. The complete text of the treaty is contained in Abel, *Official Correspondence of James S. Calhoun*, 314–16. Chacon represented the Jicarillas; Lobo and Josecito were the Mescalero emissaries. In a letter dated April 5, 1851, McLaws stated: "Governor Calhoun has made a treaty of peace with Chacon, Chief of the Jacarillas [*sic*] and Lobo, Chief of the Muscaleros [*sic*]—Chacon, I believe, has been made—if he is not—Chief of all the Apaches east of the Rio Grande." Thus, it seems that even those associated with Chacon were not positive of the extent of his authority among the Apache tribes. McLaws to Howe, Apr. 5, 1851, ibid., 317; Munroe to Jones, Apr. 28, 1851, LS-DNM, Roll 1; Sonnichsen, *Mescalero Apaches*, 70–73.
19. Buford to McFerran, Dec. 20, 1851, LR-DNM, M1102, Roll 4.
20. Miles to McFerran, July 17, 1852, ibid., Roll 5.
21. Miles to AAG, Feb. 1853, ibid.
22. This salt lake was located near Dog Canyon at the foot of the Sacramento Mountains. An 1854 description noted: "This lake has obtained considerable celebrity from having been the 'casus belli' between the Doñanians and the Pasonians.... The lake is one of the finest in the country and affords an inexhaustible yield of the 1st quality of salt." *El Sabio Sembrador*, June 1854, in Strickland, *El Paso in 1854*, 8.
23. McFerran to Sturges, Aug. 1853, LR-DNM, M1102, Roll 7.
24. *El Sabio Sembrador* (El Paso), 1, no. 3, June 1854, in Strickland, *El Paso in 1854*, 2.
25. Chandler to Nichols, Mar. 14, 1854, LR-DNM, M1120, Roll 3.
26. Alexander to Nichols, May 7, 1854, ibid.
27. Nichols to Chandler, Dec. 11, 1853, LS-DNM, Roll 1.
28. Chandler to Nichols, July 7, 1854, LR-DNM, M1120, Roll 3.
29. Many Mescalero subgroups avoided Santa Anna altogether: "Two chiefs of the Mescalero Apaches, Palanquito and Santos . . . , [gave] me the information

of their location with about forty warriors together with all their women and children. They . . . have separated themselves from that part of their nation engaged in murder and robbery." Garland to Thomas, July 30, 1854, LS-DNM, Roll 1.

30. Chandler to Nichols, July 7, 1854, LR-DNM, M1120, Roll 3; Garland to Thomas, July 30, 1854, LS-DNM, Roll 1.

31. Chandler to Nichols, July 7, 1854, LR-DNM, M1120, Roll 3.

32. Senate, *Claims for Depredations*, 46–47.

33. Moore to Nichols, July 23, 1854, ibid.

34. Nichols to Miles, Dec. 26, 1854, LS-DNM, Roll 1; Ryan, *Fort Stanton and Its Community*, 1. The Mescaleros were blamed for two additional raids in December 1854 that resulted in claims amounting to $6,231. Senate, *Claims for Depredations*.

35. Ewell to Nichols, Feb. 10, 1855, LR-DNM, M1120, Roll 4.

36. Sonnichsen, *Mescalero Apaches*, 84.

37. Ewell to Nichols, Feb. 10, 1855, LR-DNM, M1120, Roll 4.

38. Ryan, *Fort Stanton and its Community*, 2–3; Garland to Cooper, Feb. 2, 1855, LS-DNM, Roll 1; Garland to Thomas, Feb. 28, 1855, ibid. Garland claimed at least twelve Mescaleros were killed in the skirmish, an exaggerated number.

39. Bennett, *Forts and Forays*, 60–62; Sonnichsen, *Mescalero Apaches*, 85–87.

40. Bennett, *Forts and Forays*, 61–62.

41. Ewell to Nichols, Feb. 10, 1855, LR-DNM, M1120, Roll 4.

42. Bennett, *Forts and Forays*, 61–62.

43. Ibid., 63.

44. Captain Stanton's grave was the only one in the Fort Fillmore cemetery that ever had a permanent marker. In 1868 his remains were exhumed and moved to nearby Fort Selden. See Wadsworth, "Fort Fillmore Cemetery."

45. Garland to Thomas, Feb. 28, 1855, LS-DNM, Roll 1; Wadsworth, *Forgotten Fortress*, 110.

46. Steck to Manypenny, Jan. 31, 1855, Steck Papers 2, Roll 1.

47. Steck was particularly fond of Palanquito, who proved to be a cooperative Mescalero leader. Steck to Meriwether, June 16, 1856, ibid. Palanquito died in September 1856 and was succeeded as chief by his son, Cadete.

48. Steck to Meriwether, Feb. 6, 1855, ibid.

49. Meriwether to Steck, Mar. 14, 1855, ibid.

50. Sturgis to Thomas, Jan. 17, 1855, LR-DNM, M1120, Roll 4; Garland to Thomas, Jan. 31, 1855, LS-DNM, Roll 1.

51. Rodenbough, *From Everglade to Cañon*, 200–201. William Drown, who provided this description, served as a trumpeter in the First Dragoons at the time. His dates and basic information are corroborated by official reports, but he offers a highly exaggerated account.

52. Sturgis to Thomas, Jan. 17, 1855, LR-DNM, M1120, Roll 4.

53. Rodenbough, *From Everglade to Cañon*, 203.

54. Hays, "General Garland's War," 263–64.

55. Ibid., 264–65.

56. Ewell to Nichols, Feb. 28, 1855, LR-DNM, M1120, Roll 4.
57. Garland to Thomas, Feb. 28, 1855, LS-DNM, Roll 1.
58. *Santa Fe Weekly Gazette*, Mar. 10, 1855; Pfanz, *Richard S. Ewell*, 79.
59. Ewell to Nichols, Feb. 28, 1855, LR-DNM, M1120, Roll 4.
60. Moore to Nichols, Feb. 23, 1855, ibid.
61. Ewell to Nichols, Feb. 28, 1855, ibid.
62. Garland to Thomas, May 31, 1855, LS-DNM, Roll 1.
63. Bennett, *Forts and Forays*, 66.
64. On Fort Stanton's role in antebellum Indian affairs, see Ryan, *Fort Stanton and Its Community*, 1–32.
65. Santa Anna's death was first reported in a letter from Garland dated February 28, 1855: "I am gratified to say, that I have positive information, that their great War Chief *Santa Anna* and one of his sons were killed." Garland to Thomas, Feb. 28, 1855, LS-DNM, Roll 1 (emphasis in original).
66. *Santa Fe Weekly Gazette*, Mar. 29, 1856.
67. Ryan, *Fort Stanton and Its Community*, 5; Miles to Steck, Apr. 3, 1855, Steck Papers 2, Roll 1.
68. Meriwether, *My Life in the Mountains and on the Plains*, 211–18.
69. Ibid., 215–16.
70. Ryan, *Fort Stanton and Its Community*, 7–8.
71. Lane, *I Married a Soldier*, 65.
72. Wilson to Pelham, Oct. 12, 1855, RG49, M1288, LR, SGNM, Roll 1.
73. For a legal history of Indian liquor laws, see Cohen, *Handbook of Federal Indian Law*, 352–57. See also *Trade and Intercourse Act*, Mar. 30, 1802 (2 Stat. 139–46), in Prucha, *Documents of United States Indian Policy*, 17–21. The *Santa Fe Weekly Gazette* mentions these laws and the inability to enforce them in the western territories in its issues of November 27, 1852, and January 21, 1854.
74. Meriwether to Manypenny, Sept. 1855, in *Annual Report of the Commissioner of Indian Affairs* (1855), 189.
75. Meriwether to Steck, May 26, 1856, Steck Papers 2, Roll 2.
76. Steck to Collins, Aug. 10, 1858, in *Annual Report of the Commissioner of Indian Affairs* (1858), 196.
77. Utley, *Indian Frontier*, 17.
78. Ruff to Wilkins, Sept. 16, 1859, LR-DNM, M1120, Roll 10; Wilkins to Ruff, Oct. 5, 1859, ibid.
79. Lane, *I Married a Soldier*, 65.
80. Nichols to Holmes, May 29, 1857, LS-DNM, Roll 2; Ryan, *Fort Stanton and Its Community*, 28–30.
81. Simonson to Nichols, Aug. 1855, LR-DNM, M1120, Roll 4.
82. Miles to Nichols, Aug. 1855, ibid.
83. Miles to Nichols, Oct. 11, 1855, ibid.
84. Davis to Steck, Nov. 16, 1855, Steck Papers 2, Roll 2.

85. Miles to Steck, Nov. 29, 1855, ibid.
86. Colonel Munroe warned about civilian indemnity claims and the nefarious nature of many of them. See Munroe to Jones, Mar. 30, 1851, LS-DNM, Roll 1.
87. Senate, *Claims for Depredations*, 46–50.
88. Miles to Nichols, Oct. 28, 1855, LR-DNM, M1120, Roll 4.
89. Steck to Meriwether, Jan. 23, 1855, Steck Papers 2, Roll 1.
90. Fauntleroy to Scott, May 21, 1860, in House, *Memorial of the New Mexican Railway Company*, 6 (emphasis in original).
91. *Santa Fe Weekly Gazette*, Feb. 18, 1854.
92. Bennett, *Forts and Forays*, 80–81.
93. Bonneville to Thomas, Dec. 31, 1857, LS-DNM, Roll 2.
94. Julyan, *Place Names of New Mexico*, 191.
95. See DeLay, *War of a Thousand Deserts*, 63–64.
96. Steck to Meriwether, Apr. 7, 1857, Steck Papers 2, Roll 3.
97. Meriwether to Manypenny, Sept. 30, 1856, in *Annual Report of the Commissioner of Indian Affairs* (1856), 181; Sonnichsen, *Mescalero Apaches*, 90–96.
98. Opler, *Apache Life-Way*, 372.
99. Kiser, *Turmoil on the Rio Grande*, 119–26; Sonnichsen, *Mescalero Apaches*, 96–97; Barrick and Taylor, *Mesilla Guard*, 29–30.
100. Garland to Thomas, Mar. 14, 1858, LS-DNM, Roll 2.
101. Alley to Hildt, Feb. 8, 1858, LR-DNM, M1120, Roll 7. Two years earlier Charles D. Poston, a prominent southern New Mexican, pointed out that a local militia was necessary to guard the California trail, protect immigrants, and prevent Indian depredations between the Rio Grande and Colorado River. Poston to Meriwether, July 10, 1856, Meriwether Papers, Roll 98, New Mexico State Records Center and Archives.
102. Miles to Nichols, Mar. 4, 1858, LR-DNM, M1120, Roll 7. General Garland dispatched a detachment of twenty troops to Santa Rita del Cobre to protect a group of men mining there, fearing that Apaches might attack them to avenge the Mesilla Guard murders. Nichols to Miles, May 2, 1858, LS-DNM, Roll 2.
103. Miles to Nichols, Mar. 4, 1858, LR-DNM, M1120, Roll 7.
104. Miles to Ruelas, Feb. 9, 1858, ibid; Ruelas to Steck, Aug. 1857, quoted in Taylor, *A Place as Wild as the West Ever Was*, 58.
105. Nichols to Miles, Mar. 15, 1858, LS-DNM, Roll 2.
106. Mesilla Citizens to Garland, Mar. 24, 1858, LR-DNM, M1120, Roll 7.
107. Ibid. The territorial legislature simultaneously requested that Garland establish two new posts in the lower Rio Grande valley, one in Valencia County and the other in Socorro County. Garland never acted on this. *1855–1856 Laws of the Territory of New Mexico*, 132.
108. Garland to Hoppin and Lucas, Apr. 7, 1858, LS-DNM, Roll 2.
109. Miles to Nichols, Mar. 1858, LR-DNM, M1120, Roll 7.
110. Averell, *Ten Years in the Saddle*, 139.

111. *Santa Fe Weekly Gazette,* July 24, 1858.
112. Wood to Nichols, Apr. 17, 1858, LR-DNM, M1120, Roll 8.
113. *Santa Fe Weekly Gazette,* July 24, 1858.
114. Averell, *Ten Years in the Saddle,* 139–40.
115. Nichols to Wood, Apr. 22, 1858, LS-DNM, Roll 2.
116. Garland to Benedict, Apr. 22, 1858, ibid.
117. Message of Governor Abraham Rencher, Dec. 7, 1859, RG59, New Mexico Territorial Papers, T17, Roll 1, National Archives.
118. Barrick and Taylor, *Mesilla Guard,* 33.
119. *Santa Fe Weekly Gazette,* July 24, 1858.
120. Ibid.
121. Ibid.
122. Averell, *Ten Years in the Saddle,* 142.
123. Ibid., 133–42.
124. *San Francisco Herald,* June 16, 1861.
125. Baker to Nichols, Mar. 11, 1857, LR-DNM, M1120, Roll 6.
126. Henry to Nichols, Mar. 1857, ibid.
127. Unknown to Wilkins, Feb. 11, 1859, ibid., Roll 9.
128. Ibid.
129. Bonneville to Thomas, Mar. 31, 1859, LS-DNM, Roll 2.
130. Gordon to Wilkins, Feb. 11, 1859, LR-DNM, M1120, Roll 9.

Chapter 10

1. Horn, *New Mexico's Troubled Years,* 73.
2. Lamar, *Far Southwest,* 86.
3. McQuade to Porter, July 25, 1857, LR-DNM, M1120, Roll 6.
4. Averell, *Ten Years in the Saddle,* 127.
5. McQuade to Nichols, Dec. 7, 1857, LR-DNM, M1120, Roll 7.
6. Averell, *Ten Years in the Saddle,* 127–28.
7. Miles to Nichols, Aug. 16, 1857, LR-DNM, M1120, Roll 7.
8. Miles to Nichols, Aug. 24, 1857, ibid.
9. Wilkins to Gordon, Oct. 15, 1858, LS-DNM, Roll 2.
10. Wilkins to Gordon, Jan. 6, 1859, ibid.; Ruhlen, "Fort Thorn," 134.
11. Walker, "Colonel Bonneville's Report," 359.
12. Steck Annual Report of 1859, Steck Papers 2, Roll 3.
13. Howland to AAG, June 27, 1859, LR-DNM, M1120, Roll 9; Bonneville to Gordon, Aug. 6, 1859, LS-DNM, Roll 2.
14. Walker, "Colonel Bonneville's Report," 358.
15. Gordon to Wilkins, July 28, 1859, LR-DNM, M1120, Roll 9.
16. Walker, "Colonel Bonneville's Report," 358.
17. Howland to Wilkins, Aug. 16, 1859, LR-DNM, M1120, Roll 9.

18. Steck to Greenwood, May 11, 1860, LR-OIA, M-T21, Roll 550.
19. Greenwood to Wilson, May 14, 1860, in Kappler, *Laws and Treaties*, 1:873.
20. Steck to Greenwood, May 10, 1860, Steck Papers 2, Roll 3.
21. Steck to Greenwood, Oct. 1860, ibid.
22. Steck to Greenwood, Mar. 20, 1860, ibid.
23. Tevis, *Arizona in the '50s*, 206–16; Sweeney, *Mangas Coloradas*, 395.
24. Sweeney, *Cochise*, 142–65.
25. *Mesilla Times*, July 20, 1861.
26. Baylor to Helm, Mar. 20, 1862, in *War of the Rebellion*, 50(1):942; Baylor to Magruder, Dec. 29, 1862, in ibid., 15:918.

Conclusion

1. E. Ball, *In the Days of Victorio*, 45.
2. Ibid.
3. Julyan, *Place Names of New Mexico*, 268.
4. Mowry to Denver, Nov. 10, 1857, in *Annual Report of the Commissioner of Indian Affairs* (1857), 584–93.
5. Quoted in Sweeney, *Mangas Coloradas*, 455.
6. Ibid., 455–57.
7. E. Ball, *In the Days of Victorio*, 48; E. Ball, *Indeh*, 20.
8. Calvin, *Lieutenant Emory Reports*, 50.
9. Steck Papers 1, Roll 1.
10. Graves to Manypenny, June 8, 1854, in *Annual Report of the Commissioner of Indian Affairs* (1854), 183.

Bibliography

Archival Sources

Missouri Historical Society. St. Louis.
    William Carr Lane Papers.
New Mexico State Archives. Center for Southwest Research. University of New Mexico, Albuquerque.
    Edmund A. Graves Letters.
    William A. Keleher Papers.
    Inventory of the Michael Steck Papers, Series 1, 1839–53, Microcopy E93; Series 2, Microcopy E93.
New Mexico State Records Center and Archives. Santa Fe.
    Louis William Geck Collection.
    David Meriwether Papers.
    New Mexico Indian Depredation Claims Collection.
    Albert H. Schroeder Collection.
    Ralph Emerson Twitchell Collection.
U.S. National Archives. Microfilm Publications. Washington, D.C.
    Record Group 49. U.S. Department of the Interior, Bureau of Land Management, Letters Received, Surveyor General of New Mexico, 1854–1907. Microcopy 1288.
    Record Group 59. U.S. Department of State, New Mexico Territorial Papers. Microcopy T17; Microcopy 54.
    Record Group 75. U.S. Office of Indian Affairs, Letters Received, 1824–80, New Mexico Superintendency, 1849–80. Microcopy 234.
    Record Group 94. U.S. War Department, Records of the Office of the Adjutant General. Letters Received.
    ———. U.S. War Department, Orders Issued by Brigadier General Stephen Watts Kearny and Brigadier General Sterling Price to the Army of the West, 1846–48. Microcopy T1115.
    ———. U.S. War Department, Returns from United States Military Posts, 1800–1916. Microcopy 617.

Record Group 391. U.S. War Department, Returns from Regular Army Cavalry Regiments, 1833–1916. Microcopy 744.

Record Group 393. U.S. War Department, Registers of Letters Received by Headquarters, Department of New Mexico, 1849–1853. Microcopy 1102.

———. U.S. War Department, Registers of Letters Received by Headquarters, Department of New Mexico, 1854–1865. Microcopy 1120.

———. U.S. War Department, Letters Sent, Ninth Military Department, Department of New Mexico, and District of New Mexico, 1849–1890. Microcopy 1072.

U.S. Government Documents and Publications

Abel, Annie Heloise, ed. *The Official Correspondence of James S. Calhoun while Indian Agent at Santa Fe and Superintendent of Indian Affairs in New Mexico, 1849–1852.* Washington: Government Printing Office, 1915.

Annual Report of the Quartermaster General. Washington: Government Printing Office, 1850.

Annual Report of the Secretary of the Interior. Washington: Government Printing Office, 1854.

Annual Reports of the Commissioner of Indian Affairs. Washington: Government Printing Office, 1850–61.

Annual Reports of the Secretary of War. Washington: Government Printing Office, 1850–61.

Cohen, Felix S. *Handbook of Federal Indian Law.* Washington: Government Printing Office, 1941.

Heitman, Francis B. *Historical Register and Dictionary of the United States Army, From Its' Organization, September 29, 1789, to March 2, 1903.* 2 vols. Washington: Government Printing Office, 1903.

Kappler, Charles J. *Indian Affairs: Laws and Treaties.* 7 vols. Washington: Government Printing Office, 1904.

Laws of the Territory of New Mexico Passed by the Legislative Assembly, 1855–1856. Santa Fe: Santa Fe Weekly Gazette Printing Office, 1856.

Miller, Hunter, ed. *Treaties and Other International Acts of the United States of America.* 8 vols. Washington: Government Printing Office, 1931–48.

Upton, Bvt. Maj. Gen. Emory. *The Military Policy of the United States.* Washington: Government Printing Office, 1907.

U.S. Congress. House. *An Act Regulating the Indian Department, May 20, 1834.* 23rd Cong., 1st sess. H. Exec. Doc. 474.

———. *California and New Mexico: Message from the President of the United States.* 31st Cong., 1st sess. H. Exec. Doc. 17.

———. *Indian Hostilities in New Mexico.* 36th Cong., 1st sess. H. Exec. Doc. 69.

———. *Land Claims in the Territory of New Mexico.* 35th Cong., 1st sess. H. Rep. 457.

———. *Memorial of the New Mexican Railway Company.* 36th Cong., 1st sess. H. Misc. Doc. 85.

———. *Message from the President of the United States, December 2, 1851.* 32nd Cong., 1st Sess. H. Exec. Doc. 2.

———. *Official Army Register for the Year Ending 30 June, 1851.* 32nd Cong., 2nd sess. H. Exec. Doc. 48.

———. *Regiment of Mounted Riflemen Annual Expenses.* 29th Cong., 1st sess. H. Exec. Doc. 82.

———. *Rio Grande Frontier.* 32nd Cong., 1st sess. H. Exec. Doc. 112.

U.S. Congress. Senate. *Claims for Depredations by Indians in the Territory of New Mexico.* 35th Cong., 1st sess. S. Exec. Doc. 55.

———. *Correspondence of Col. Edwin V. Sumner.* 32nd Cong., 2nd sess. S. Exec. Doc. 1.

———. *Correspondence Regarding the Apache Indians.* 51st Cong., 1st sess. S. Exec. Doc. 88.

———. *Report on the Condition of the Indian Tribes.* 39th Cong., 2nd sess. S. Report 156. Serial 1279.

———. *Statistical Report on the Sickness and Mortality in the Army of the United States . . . from January 1839 to January 1855,* prepared by Richard H. Coolidge. 34th Cong., 1st sess. S. Exec. Doc. 96.

———. *Statistical Report on the Sickness and Mortality in the United States Army . . . from January 1855 to January 1860,* prepared by Richard H. Coolidge. 36th Cong., 1st sess. S. Exec. Doc. 52.

———. *Treaties, Conventions, International Acts, Protocols and Agreements between the United States of America and Other Powers,* prepared by William M. Malloy. 61st Cong., 2nd sess. S. Exec. Doc. 357.

Seventh U.S. Census (1850). Washington: National Archives.

Eighth U.S. Census (1860). Washington: National Archives.

The War of the Rebellion: A Compilation of the Official Records of the Union and Confederate Armies. Series 1, 53 vols. Washington: Government Printing Office, 1880–1901.

Newspapers

El Faro (Chihuahua City, Chihuahua)
El Sonorense (Ures, Sonora)
Golden Era (San Francisco)
Mesilla Times
Santa Fe Weekly Gazette
San Francisco Herald
St. Louis Daily Missouri Republican

Published Primary Sources

Averell, William Woods. *Ten Years in the Saddle: The Memoir of William Woods Averell, 1851–1862*. Edited by Edward K. Eckert and Nicholas J. Amato. San Rafael, CA: Presidio Press, 1978.

Ball, Eve. *In The Days of Victorio: Recollections of a Warm Springs Apache*. Tucson: University of Arizona Press, 1970.

———, with Nora Henn and Lynda Sánchez. *Indeh: An Apache Odyssey*. Provo, Utah: Brigham Young University Press, 1980.

Barrett, S. M., ed. *Geronimo's Story of His Life*. New York: Duffield, 1906.

Bartlett, John Russell. *Personal Narrative of Explorations and Incidents in Texas, New Mexico, California, Sonora, and Chihuahua, 1850–1853*. 2 vols. New York: D. Appleton, 1854.

Bennett, James A. *Forts and Forays: A Dragoon in New Mexico, 1850–1856*. Albuquerque: University of New Mexico Press, 1948.

Betzinez, Jason, and Nye, W.S. *I Fought with Geronimo*. New York: Bonanza Books, 1959.

Bieber, Ralph P., ed. *Journal of a Soldier under Kearny and Doniphan*. Glendale, Calif.: Arthur H. Clarke, 1935.

Browne, J. Ross. *Adventures in the Apache Country: A Tour through Arizona and Sonora, with Notes on the Silver Regions of Nevada*. New York: Harper & Brothers, 1871.

Calvin, Ross, ed. *Lieutenant Emory Reports: Notes of a Military Reconnaissance*. Albuquerque: University of New Mexico Press, 1951.

Clarke, Dwight L., ed. *The Original Journals of Henry Smith Turner: With Stephen Watts Kearny to New Mexico and California, 1846–1847*. Norman: University of Oklahoma Press, 1966.

Cooke, Philip St. George. *The Conquest of New Mexico and California: An Historical and Personal Narrative*. 1878. Reprint, Albuquerque: Horn and Wallace, 1964.

Cortés, José. *Views from the Apache Frontier: Report on the Northern Provinces of New Spain*. Edited by Elizabeth A. H. John. Translated by John Wheat. Norman: University of Oklahoma Press, 1989.

Cremony, John C. *Life among the Apaches*. San Francisco: A. Roman, 1868.

Emory, William H. *Report on the United States and Mexican Boundary Survey*. 3 vols. Austin: Texas State Historical Association, 1987.

Frazer, Robert W., ed. *Mansfield on the Condition of the Western Forts, 1853–54*. Norman: University of Oklahoma Press, 1963.

———. *New Mexico in 1850: A Military View*. Norman: University of Oklahoma Press, 1968.

Hamlin, Captain Percy Gatling, ed. *The Making of a Soldier: Letters of General R. S. Ewell*. Richmond, Va.: Whittet & Shepperson, 1935.

Hammond, George P., ed. *Campaigns in the West, 1856–1861: The Original Journal and Letters of Colonel John Van Deusen DuBois.* Tucson: Arizona Pioneers Historical Society, 1949.

Lane, Lydia Spencer. *I Married a Soldier; or, Old Days in the Old Army.* Albuquerque: Horn & Wallace, 1964.

Langley, Harold D., ed. *To Utah with the Dragoons and Glimpses of Life in Arizona and California, 1858–1859.* Salt Lake City: University of Utah Press, 1974.

Lowe, Percival G. *Five Years a Dragoon, and other Adventures on the Great Plains.* Kansas City, Mo.: Franklin Hudson, 1906.

Meriwether, David. *My Life in the Mountains and on the Plains: The Newly Discovered Autobiography.* Edited by Robert A. Griffen. Norman: University of Oklahoma Press, 1965.

Mills, W. W. *Forty Years at El Paso, 1858–1898.* Edited by Rex W. Strickland. El Paso: Carl Hertzog, 1962.

Mowry, Sylvester. *Arizona and Sonora: The Geography, History, and Resources of the Silver Region of North America.* New York: Harper & Brothers, 1864.

Poston, Charles D. *Building a State in Apache Land: The Story of Arizona's Founding Told by Arizona's Founder.* Edited by John Myers Myers. Tempe, AZ: Aztec, 1963.

Prucha, Francis Paul. *Documents of United States Indian Policy.* Lincoln: University of Nebraska Press, 1975.

Reid, John C. *Reid's Tramp, or a Journal of the Incidents of Ten Months Travel through Texas, New Mexico, Arizona, Sonora, and California.* Austin, TX: Steck, 1935.

Rice, Josiah M. *A Cannoneer in Navajo Country.* Edited by Richard H. Dillon. Denver: Denver Public Library, 1970.

Rodenbough, Theophilus F. *From Everglade to Cañon with the Second Dragoons.* New York: D. Van Nostrand, 1875.

Ruxton, George F. *Adventures in Mexico and the Rocky Mountains.* 1848. Reprint, Glorieta, N.M.: Rio Grande, 1973.

Simpson, James H. *Navaho Expedition: Journal of a Military Reconnaissance from Santa Fe, New Mexico, to the Navaho Country, Made in 1849 by Lieutenant James H. Simpson.* Edited by Frank McNitt. Norman: University of Oklahoma Press, 1964.

Strickland, Rex. *El Paso in 1854, with a 30-page Handwritten Newsletter by Frederic Augustus Percy Entitled* El Sabio Sembrador. Edited by E. H. Antone and Carl Hertzog. El Paso: Texas Western, 1969.

Tevis, James H. *Arizona in the '50s.* Albuquerque: University of New Mexico Press, 1954.

Weber, David J., and Jane Lenz Elder, eds. *Fiasco: George Clinton Gardner's Correspondence from the U.S.-Mexico Boundary Survey, 1849–1854.* Dallas: Southern Methodist University Press, 2010.

Woodhouse, S. W. *From Texas to San Diego in 1851: The Overland Journal of Dr. S. W. Woodhouse, Surgeon-Naturalist of the Sitgreaves Expedition.* Edited by Andrew Wallace and Richard H. Hevly. Lubbock: Texas Tech University Press, 2007.

Books

Agnew, S. C. *Garrisons of the Regular U.S. Army, New Mexico, 1846–1899.* Santa Fe: Press of the Territorian, 1971.

Albuquerque Museum. *Drawing the Borderline: Artist-Explorers of the U.S.-Mexico Boundary Survey.* Albuquerque, 1996.

Alexander, David V. *Arizona Frontier Military Place Names.* Las Cruces, N.M.: Yucca Tree, 1998.

Altshuler, Constance Wynn. *Chains of Command: Arizona and the Army, 1856–1875.* Tucson: Arizona Historical Society, 1981.

———. *Cavalry Yellow and Infantry Blue: Army Officers in Arizona between 1851 and 1886.* Tucson: Arizona Historical Society, 1991.

Anderson, Benedict. *Imagined Communities: Reflections on the Origin and Spread of Nationalism.* New York: Verso, 1991.

Ball, Durwood. *Army Regulars on the Western Frontier, 1846–1861.* Norman: University of Oklahoma Press, 2001.

Barrick, Norma, and Mary Taylor. *The Mesilla Guard, 1851–1861.* El Paso: Texas Western, 1976.

Basehart, Harry W. *Mescalero Apache Subsistence Patterns and Socio-Political Organization.* University of New Mexico: Mescalero-Chiricahua Land Claims Project, 1960.

Bender, Averam B. *The March of Empire: Frontier Defense in the Southwest, 1848–1860.* Lawrence: University of Kansas Press, 1952.

Billington, Ray Allen. *America's Frontier Heritage.* New York: Holt, Rinehart, & Winston, 1966.

Blackhawk, Ned. *Violence over the Land: Indians and Empires in the Early American West.* Cambridge, Mass.: Harvard University Press, 2006.

Bolton, Herbert Eugene. *The Spanish Borderlands: A Chronicle of Old Florida and the Southwest.* New Haven, Conn.: Yale University Press, 1921.

Brooks, James F. *Captives and Cousins: Slavery, Kinship, and Community in the Southwest Borderlands.* Chapel Hill: University of North Carolina Press, 2002.

Brown, Dee. *Bury My Heart at Wounded Knee: An Indian History of the American West.* New York: Holt, Rinehart, & Winston, 1970.

Casdorph, Paul D. *Confederate General R. S. Ewell: Robert E. Lee's Hesitant Commander.* Lexington: University Press of Kentucky, 2004.

Clarke, Dwight L. *Stephen Watts Kearny: Soldier of the West.* Norman: University of Oklahoma Press, 1961.

Coffman, Edward M. *The Old Army: A Portrait of the American Army in Peacetime, 1784–1898.* New York: Oxford University Press, 1986.

Colwell-Chanthaphonh, Chip. *Massacre at Camp Grant: Forgetting and Remembering Apache History.* Tucson: University of Arizona Press, 2007.

Cronon, William, George Miles, and Jay Gitlin, eds. *Under an Open Sky: Rethinking America's Western Past*. New York: W. W. Norton, 1992.

Crouch, Brodie. *Jornada del Muerto: A Pageant of the Desert*. Spokane, Wash.: Arthur H. Clark, 1989.

Debo, Angie. *Geronimo: The Man, His Time, His Place*. Norman: University of Oklahoma Press, 1976.

DeLay, Brian. *War of a Thousand Deserts: Indian Raids and the U.S.-Mexican War*. New Haven, Conn.: Yale University Press, 2008.

Faulk, Odie. *Too Far North, Too Far South*. Los Angeles: Westernlore, 1967.

Fixico, Donald Lee, ed. *Rethinking American Indian History*. Albuquerque: University of New Mexico Press, 1997.

Frazer, Robert W. *Forts and Supplies: The Role of the Army in the Economy of the Southwest, 1846–1861*. Albuquerque: University of New Mexico Press, 1983.

———. *Forts of the West: Military Forts and Presidios and Posts Commonly Called Forts West of the Mississippi River to 1898*. Norman: University of Oklahoma Press, 1965.

Ganaway, Loomis M. *New Mexico and the Sectional Controversy, 1846–1861*. Albuquerque: University of New Mexico Press, 1944.

Giese, Dale F. *Forts of New Mexico*. Published by the author, 1995.

Goetzmann, William H. *Army Exploration in the American West, 1803–1863*. Lincoln: University of Nebraska Press, 1959.

Goodwin, Grenville. *The Social Organization of the Western Apache*. Chicago: University of Chicago Press, 1942.

———. *Western Apache Raiding and Warfare*. Edited by Keith H. Basso. Tucson: University of Arizona Press, 1971.

Griffen, William B. *Utmost Good Faith: Patterns of Apache-Mexican Hostilities in Northern Chihuahua Border Warfare, 1821–1848*. Albuquerque: University of New Mexico Press, 1988.

———. *Apaches at War and Peace: The Janos Presidio, 1759–1858*. Norman: University of Oklahoma Press, 1988.

Grinstead, Marion C. *Life and Death of a Frontier Fort: Ft. Craig, New Mexico, 1854–1885*. Socorro, N.M.: Socorro County Historical Society, 1973.

Griswold del Castillo, Richard. *The Treaty of Guadalupe Hidalgo: A Legacy of Conflict*. Norman: University of Oklahoma Press, 1990.

Hämäläinen, Pekka. *The Comanche Empire*. New Haven, Conn.: Yale University Press, 2008.

Hatfield, Shelley Bowen. *Chasing Shadows: Apaches and Yaquis along the United States–Mexican Border, 1876–1911*. Albuquerque: University of New Mexico Press, 1998.

Herr, Maj. Gen. John K., and Edward S. Wallace. *The Story of the U.S. Cavalry, 1775–1942*. New York: Bonanza, 1984.

Hine, Robert V. *Bartlett's West: Drawing the Mexican Boundary.* New Haven, Conn.: Yale University Press, 1986.

———, and John Mack Faragher. *The American West: A New Interpretive History.* New Haven, Conn.: Yale University Press, 2000.

Horn, Calvin. *New Mexico's Troubled Years: The Story of the Early Territorial Governors.* Albuquerque: Horn & Wallace, 1963.

Jacoby, Karl. *Shadows at Dawn: A Borderlands Massacre and the Violence of History.* New York: Penguin Books, 2008.

Jones, Archer. *Elements of Military Strategy: An Historical Approach.* Westport, Conn.: Praeger, 1996.

Julyan, Robert. *The Place Names of New Mexico.* Albuquerque: University of New Mexico Press, 1996.

Keleher, William A. *Turmoil in New Mexico, 1846–1868.* Albuquerque: University of New Mexico Press, 1952.

Kiser, William S. *Turmoil on the Rio Grande: The Territorial History of the Mesilla Valley, 1846–1865.* College Station: Texas A&M University Press, 2011.

Kluger, Richard. *Seizing Destiny: How America Grew from Sea to Shining Sea.* New York: Alfred A. Knopf, 2007.

Kvasnicka, Robert M., and Herman J. Viola, eds. *The Commissioners of Indian Affairs, 1824–1977.* Lincoln: University of Nebraska Press, 1979.

Lamar, Howard R. *The Far Southwest, 1846–1912: A Territorial History.* Albuquerque: University of New Mexico Press, 2000.

Lefebvre, Henri. *The Production of Space.* Translated by Donald Nicholson-Smith. Oxford, UK: Basil-Blackwell, 1991.

Limerick, Patricia Nelson. *The Legacy of Conquest: The Unbroken Past of the American West.* New York: Norton, 1987.

———, Clyde A. Milner II, and Charles E. Rankin, eds. *Trails: Toward a New Western History.* Lawrence: University Press of Kansas, 1991.

McNitt, Frank. *Navajo Wars: Military Campaigns, Slave Raids, and Reprisals.* Albuquerque: University of New Mexico Press, 1972.

Merrill, James M. *Spurs to Glory: The Story of the United States Cavalry.* Chicago: Rand McNally, 1966.

Metz, Leon C. *Desert Army: Fort Bliss on the Texas Border.* El Paso: Mangan Books, 1988.

Neighbours, Kenneth Franklin. *Robert Simpson Neighbors and the Texas Frontier, 1836–1859.* Waco, Tex.: Texian, 1975.

Ogle, Ralph H. *Federal Control of the Western Apaches, 1848–1886.* Albuquerque: University of New Mexico Press, 1970.

Opler, Morris E. *An Apache Life-Way: The Economic, Social, and Religious Institutions of the Chiricahua Indians.* New York: Cooper Square, 1965.

Pfanz, David C. *Richard S. Ewell: A Soldier's Life.* Chapel Hill: University of North Carolina Press, 1998.

Prucha, Francis Paul. *American Indian Treaties: The History of a Political Anomaly.* Berkeley, Calif.: University of California Press, 1994.

———. *The Great Father: The United States Government and the American Indians.* 2 vols. Lincoln: University of Nebraska Press, 1984.

Radbourne, Allan. *Mickey Free: Apache Captive, Interpreter, and Indian Scout.* Tucson: Arizona Historical Society, 2005.

Rathbun, Daniel C. B., and David V. Alexander. *New Mexico Frontier Military Place Names.* Las Cruces, N.M.: Yucca Tree, 2003.

Rodenbough, Theophilus F. *The Army of the United States: Historical Sketches of Staff and Line with Portraits of Generals-In-Chief.* New York: Maynard, Merrill, 1896.

Ryan, John P. *Fort Stanton and Its Community.* Las Cruces, N.M.: Yucca Tree, 1998.

Sacks, Benjamin. *Be It Enacted: The Creation of the Territory of Arizona.* Phoenix: Arizona Historical Foundation, 1964.

Santiago, Mark. *The Jar of Severed Hands: Spanish Deportation of Apache Prisoners of War, 1770–1810.* Norman: University of Oklahoma Press, 2011.

Sawicki, James S. *Infantry Regiments of the U.S. Army.* Dumfries, Va.: Wyvern, 1981.

Smith, Ralph A. *Borderlander: The Life of James Kirker, 1793–1862.* Norman: University of Oklahoma Press, 1999.

Sonnichsen, C. L. *The Mescalero Apaches.* Norman: University of Oklahoma Press, 1958.

St. John, Rachel. *Line in the Sand: A History of the Western U.S.-Mexico Border.* Princeton, N.J.: Princeton University Press, 2011.

Steffen, Randy. *The Horse Soldier, 1776–1943: Volume II, The Frontier, the Mexican War, the Civil War, the Indian Wars, 1851–1880.* Norman: University of Oklahoma Press, 1978.

Stegmaier, Mark J. *Texas, New Mexico, and the Compromise of 1850.* Kent, Ohio: Kent State University Press, 1996.

Sweeney, Edwin R. *Cochise: Chiricahua Apache Chief.* Norman: University of Oklahoma Press, 1991.

———. *Mangas Coloradas: Chief of the Chiricahua Apaches.* Norman: University of Oklahoma Press, 1998.

———. *From Cochise to Geronimo: The Chiricahua Apaches, 1874–1886.* Norman: University of Oklahoma Press, 2010.

Taylor, Mary Daniels. *A Place as Wild as the West Ever Was: Mesilla, New Mexico, 1848–1872.* Las Cruces: New Mexico State University Museum, 2004.

Thrapp, Dan L. *Victorio and the Mimbres Apaches.* Norman: University of Oklahoma Press, 1974.

Timmons, W. H. *El Paso: A Borderlands History.* El Paso: Texas Western Press, 1990.

Trennert, Robert A., Jr. *Alternative to Extinction: Federal Indian Policy and the Beginnings of the Reservation System, 1846–1851.* Philadelphia: Temple University Press, 1975.

Truett, Samuel. *Fugitive Landscapes: The Forgotten History of the U.S.-Mexico Borderlands*. New Haven, Conn.: Yale University Press, 2006.

Turner, Frederick Jackson. *The Significance of the Frontier in American History*. 1893. Edited by Harold P. Simonson. New York: Ungar, 1963.

Twitchell, Ralph Emerson. *The History of the Military Occupation of the Territory of New Mexico from 1846 to 1851 by the Government of the United States*. Chicago: Rio Grande, 1963.

———. *Leading Facts of New Mexican History*. 2 vols. Cedar Rapids, Iowa: Torch, 1911.

———. *Old Santa Fe: The Story of New Mexico's Ancient Capital*. Chicago: Rio Grande, 1963.

Utley, Robert M. *Frontiersmen in Blue: The United States Army and the Indian, 1848–1865*. Lincoln: University of Nebraska Press, 1967.

———. *The Indian Frontier of the American West: 1846–1890*. Albuquerque: University of New Mexico Press, 1984.

Wadsworth, Richard. *Forgotten Fortress: Ft. Millard Fillmore and Antebellum New Mexico*. Las Cruces, N.M.: Yucca Tree, 2002.

Weigley, Russell F. *Towards an American Army: Military Thought from Washington to Marshall*. New York: Columbia University Press, 1962.

———. *The American Way of War: A History of United States Military Strategy and Policy*. New York: MacMillan, 1973.

———. *History of the United States Army*. Enlarged edition. Bloomington: Indiana University Press, 1984.

Werne, Richard. *The Imaginary Line: A History of the United States and Mexican Boundary Survey, 1848–1857*. Fort Worth: Texas Christian University Press, 2007.

White, Richard. *It's Your Misfortune and None of My Own: A New History of the American West*. Norman: University of Oklahoma Press, 1991.

Wooster, Robert. *The Military and United States Indian Policy, 1865–1903*. New Haven, Conn.: Yale University Press, 1988.

———. *The American Military Frontiers: The United States Army in the West, 1783–1900*. Norman: University of Oklahoma Press, 2009.

Articles and Book Chapters

Abel, Annie Heloise, ed. "Indian Affairs in New Mexico under the Administration of William Carr Lane, from the Journal of John Ward." *New Mexico Historical Review* 16, no. 2 (April/August 1941): 206–31.

———, ed. "The Journal of John Greiner." *Old Santa Fe* 3, no. 11 (July 1916): 189–243.

Ball, Durwood. "By Right of Conquest: Military Government in New Mexico and California, 1846–1851." *Journal of the West* 41, no. 3 (Summer 2002): 8–16.

———. "Fort Craig, New Mexico, and the Southwest Indian Wars, 1854–1884." *New Mexico Historical Review* 73, no. 2 (April 1998): 153–73.

———. "The U.S. Army in New Mexico, 1846–1886." In *Telling New Mexico: A New History*, edited by Marta Weigle, 173–89. Santa Fe: Museum of New Mexico Press, 2009.

Basehart, Harry W. "Mescalero Apache Band Organization and Leadership." In *Apachean Culture History and Ethnology*, edited by Keith H. Basso and Morris E. Opler, 35–49. Anthropological Papers of the University of Arizona No. 21. Tucson: University of Arizona Press, 1971.

Bender, A. B. "Frontier Defense in the Territory of New Mexico, 1848–1853." *New Mexico Historical Review* 9, no. 3 (July 1934): 249–72.

———. "Government Explorations in the Territory of New Mexico, 1846–1859." *New Mexico Historical Review* 9, no. 1 (January 1934): 1–33.

———. "Military Transportation in the Southwest, 1846–1860." *New Mexico Historical Review* 32, no. 2 (April 1957): 123–50.

Blackhawk, Ned. "Look How Far We've Come: How American Indian History Changed the Study of American History in the 1990s." *OAH Magazine of History* 19 (November 2005): 13–17.

Bliss, Zenas R. "Extracts from the Unpublished Memoirs of Maj. Gen. Z. R. Bliss." *Journal of the Military Science Institution of the United States* 38 (1906): 120–34.

Carson, William G. B., ed. "William Carr Lane Diary." *New Mexico Historical Review* 39, no. 3 (July 1964): 181–234.

Connell-Szasz, Margaret. "Cultural Encounters: Native People, New Mexico, and the United States, 1848–1948." In *Telling New Mexico: A New History*, edited by Marta Weigle, 195–207. Santa Fe: Museum of New Mexico Press, 2009.

Espinosa, J. Manuel. "Memoir of a Kentuckian in New Mexico, 1848–1884." *New Mexico Historical Review* 13, no. 1 (January 1938): 1–13.

Ferg, Alan. "Traditional Western Apache Mescal Harvesting as Recorded by Historical Photographs and Museum Collections." *Desert Plants* 19 (December 2003): 1–56.

Frazer, Robert W. "Purveyors of Flour to the Army: Department of New Mexico, 1849–1861." *New Mexico Historical Review* 47 (July 1972): 213–38.

Green, Fletcher M. "James S. Calhoun: Pioneer Georgia Leader and First Governor of New Mexico." *Georgia Historical Quarterly* 39 (December 1955): 309–47.

Greiner, John. "Private Letters of a Government Official in the Southwest." Edited by Tod B. Galloway. *Journal of American History* 3, no. 4 (October 1909).

Hays, Kelly R. "General Garland's War: The Mescalero Apache Campaigns, 1854–1855." *New Mexico Historical Review* 67, no. 3 (July 1992): 251–68.

Johannsen, Robert W. "The Meaning of Manifest Destiny." In *Manifest Destiny and Empire: American Antebellum Expansionism*. Edited by Sam W. Haynes and Christopher Morris, 7–20. College Station: Texas A&M University Press, 1997.

Hämäläinen, Pekka, and Samuel Truett. "On Borderlands." *Journal of American History* 98 (September 2011): 338–61.

Jones, Kristine L. "Comparative Raiding Economies: North and South." In *Contested Ground: Comparative Frontiers on the Northern and Southern Edges of the Spanish Empire*. Edited by Donna J. Guy and Thomas E. Sheridan, 97–114. Tucson: University of Arizona Press, 1998.

Kraemer, Paul. "Sickliest Post in the Territory of New Mexico: Fort Thorn and Malaria, 1853–1860." *New Mexico Historical Review* 71, no. 3 (July 1996): 221–35.

Myers, Lee. "Military Establishments in Southwestern New Mexico: Stepping Stones to Settlement." *New Mexico Historical Review* 43, no. 1 (January 1968): 5–48.

Opler, Morris E. "The Apachean Culture Pattern and Its Origins." In *Handbook of North American Indians*, 10:368–92. Washington: Smithsonian Institution, 1983.

———. "Chiricahua Apache." In *Handbook of North American Indians*, 10:401–418. Washington: Smithsonian Institution, 1983.

———. "Mescalero Apache." In *Handbook of North American Indians*, 10:419–39. Washington: Smithsonian Institution, 1983.

———. "Myths and Tales of the Chiricahua Apache Indians." *Memoirs of the American Folk-lore Society* 37 (1942): 1–114.

Park, Joseph F. "The Apaches in Mexican-American Relations, 1848–1861: A Footnote to the Gadsden Treaty." *Arizona and the West* 3, no. 2 (Summer 1961): 129–46.

Reeve, Frank D., ed. "Puritan and Apache: A Diary." *New Mexico Historical Review* 23 (October 1948): 269–301; and 24 (January 1949): 12–53.

Rippy, J. Fred. "The Indians of the Southwest in the Diplomacy of the United States." *Hispanic-American Historical Review* 2 (August 1919): 363–96.

Ruhlen, George. "Fort Thorn: An Historical Vignette." *Password* 5, no. 4 (October 1960).

Sacks, Benjamin. "The Origins of Fort Buchanan." *Arizona and the West* 7 (Autumn 1965): 207–26.

Spude, Robert L. "The Santa Rita del Cobre, New Mexico: The Early American Period, 1846–1886." *Mining History Journal* 6 (1999): 8–38.

Stegmaier, Mark J. "The Guadalupe Hidalgo Treaty as a Factor in the New Mexico–Texas Boundary Dispute." In *The Treaty of Guadalupe Hidalgo, 1848: Papers of the Sesquicentennial Symposium, 1848–1998*. Edited by John Porter Bloom, 27–48. Las Cruces, N.M.: Doña Ana County Historical Society, 1999.

Sweeney, Edwin R. "I Had Lost All: Geronimo and the Carrasco Massacre of 1851." *Journal of Arizona History* 27 (Spring 1986): 35–52.

Thompson, Jerry D., ed. "With the Third Infantry in New Mexico, 1851–1853: The Lost Diary of Private Sylvester M. Matson." *Journal of Arizona History* 31 (Winter 1990): 349–404.

Utley, Robert M. "Captain John Pope's Plan of 1853 for the Frontier Defense of New Mexico." *Arizona and the West* 5, no. 2 (Summer 1963): 149–63.

Wadsworth, Richard. "The Fort Fillmore Cemetery." *Southern New Mexico Historical Review* 8, no. 1 (January 2001).

Walker, Henry P. "Colonel Bonneville's Report: The Department of New Mexico in 1859." *Arizona and the West* 22 (Autumn 1980): 343–62.

Weber, David J. "Turner, the Boltonians, and the Borderlands." *American Historical Review* 91 (February 1986): 66–81.

Wilson, John P. "Retreat to the Rio Grande: The Report of Captain Isaiah N. Moore." *Rio Grande History* 2 (1975): 4–8.

Index

Acoma Treaty, 132–38, 140, 142, 146, 164
Albuquerque, N.Mex., 34–35, 62, 63, 139, 161, 181, 186, 207, 211, 243, 249
Alexander, Lt. Col. Edmund B., 61
Alley, Lt. J. W., 263
Almonte, Juan N., 60
Anglo-Americans: anti-Indian ideology, 38; cope with environment, 19; ethnocentrism, 38, 73, 105, 133, 145; imagined landscape of, 10–12, 55, 281; land speculation, 76; population, 299n15; relations with Mexicans, 24; settlement patterns, 39, 254. *See also* Captives
Anton Chico, N.Mex., 242–43
Apaches, 14, 98, 110–11, 133, 155, 167–68, 209; acculturation, 58; Acoma Treaty, 132–38; attack mail escorts, 114–15, 125–26, 144, 251; burn Fort Webster, 159; described, 16; disease, 49, 183–84, 186; endurance, 44; engagements with troops, 20, 70, 113–14, 144, 175–77, 191, 193–94, 200–201, 215, 221–24, 274–75, 303n30; farming, 158, 166, 261–62, 278; flee into Mexico, 171, 203, 209, 212–13, 215–16; homelands, 39, 52; imagined landscape of, 9–10, 37, 39–40, 53, 111, 137; innocents attacked, 43–44, 96, 115, 137–38, 175–77, 214–16, 241–42; internal tensions, 181; kinship, 42, 58–59, 83; language, 51–52, 70; meet with Greiner, 198–99; nationalism, 9; oral history, 37–38; population, 42, 45, 49–50, 299n10, 299n15; as prisoners, 221, 223–25, 275–76; raiding, 14, 16, 39, 42, 45–46, 48–49, 50, 57, 94, 110–11, 115–16, 123, 135–36, 144, 173, 174, 179, 190, 234, 281, 288; relations with Anglo-Americans, 82–85; relations with Mexicans, 17, 39, 46–47, 48–50, 57–58, 80, 136, 194–97, 216, 239, 268; scouts, 52, 58; specific raids, 65–66, 69–71, 83, 125–26, 142–43, 168, 169–70, 192–93, 207, 212, 273–74; spirituality, 9–10, 39–40, 49, 51, 145; tribal structure, 38–39, 41–43, 137–38, 299n9; women, 46, 50, 73, 170, 221. *See also* Captives; Reservation proposals; Treaties; Western Apaches; *names of Apache bands*
Arizona, 10; as Apache homelands, 38–39; as Confederate Territory, 281; military affairs in, 186–92
Armendariz, Pedro, 102
Armijo Ranch, N.Mex., 259
Army of the West, 13, 15
Artillery, 61, 205. *See also* U.S. troops
Averell, Lt. William W., 206, 266, 274–75

Backus, Maj. Electus, 240–41, 312n26
Bacoachi, Sonora, 83
Baker, Lieut., 220
Bartlett, John Russell, 45, 57, 63, 97, 105, 111, 163, 296n10, 310n69; with boundary commission, 82–85; describes Apaches, 42

345

Barule, Pedro Jose, 312n26
Bascom Affair, 280, 287
Baylor, Col. John R., 280–81, 308n35
Bee, Capt. Barnard E., 126
Benedict, Kirby, 267, 312n26
Bennett, James A., 20, 34, 117–18, 245, 260
Biggs, Thomas, 102, 309n63
Blake, Maj. George A. H., 116, 183, 187
Blancito (Apache chief), 134
Bolton, Herbert Eugene, 6–7
Bonneville, Col. Benjamin L. E., 43, 185–86, 191, 261, 270, 276–78; background, 205–206; on Gila Campaign, 212, 214, 216, 218–19, 220–21, 223–26, 228–29, 231
Bosque Redondo, N.Mex., 68, 242
Brady, Cpl. John, 269
Brent, Robert T., 112
Brent, Thomas L., 100–101
Brice, Maj. B. W., 297n30
Brown, Orlando, 94, 194
Buchanan, James, 188, 273
Buffalo (Apache chief), 236
Buford, Lt. Abraham, 66, 68, 85, 104, 110–11, 238–39; background, 303n42
Bureau of Indian Affairs, 5, 51, 81, 89, 91, 262, 265, 290, 301n12, 320n3
Burro Mountains, N.Mex., 209, 210, 212, 219, 276–77
Butterfield Overland Mail Route, 277, 281

Cadete (Apache chief), 325n47
Calabasas Ranch, Ariz., 188
Calhoun, James S., 56–57, 81, 88–95, 99, 112, 120–23, 132, 148, 155, 195, 202, 238, 265, 273, 290, 324n18; background, 306n4; death of, 127–28, 311n7. *See also* Civil-military contention
Camino Real, 108, 161. *See also* Jornada del Muerto, N.Mex.
Campbell, Capt. Reuben, 31, 74
Camp Blake, N.Mex., 182–83
Camp Garland, N.Mex., 251
Camp Moore, Ariz., 188

Camp Union, N.Mex., 210, 211, 217–19
Cantonment Dawson, N.Mex., 84, 112
Capitan Simon (Apache chief), 134
Capitan Vuelta (Apache chief), 134
Captives, 48, 52, 57–59, 136, 192–93, 195, 197–98, 225, 235, 288, 301n12; Anglo-American, 204–205; Apache, 46, 275–76, 280, 323n72; Mexican, 56, 69, 79–80, 83, 116, 236, 242. *See also* Treaty of Guadalupe Hidalgo (Article 11)
Carleton, Maj. James H., 6
Carlisle, Lt. J. Howard, 205
Carrasco, Col. José María, 46, 47
Carrizalillo Springs, N.Mex., 209
Chacon (Apache chief), 324n18
Chandler, Col. Daniel T., 32–33, 199; leads Apache campaign, 175–78, 317n10; kills soldier, 178–79, 260–61; meets with Mescaleros, 241–42
Chaves, Jose, 169
Chavez, Manuel, 249
Chihuahua, Mexico, 14, 17, 39, 46, 48, 49, 57, 111, 136, 148, 190, 197, 198, 216, 232, 261
Chiricahua Apaches, 16, 53, 148, 181, 191, 195, 232, 234, 252, 279, 280, 283, 286; negotiate treaties, 133–38, 164–67; tribal structure, 38–43. *See also* Apaches
Civil-military contention, 54, 73, 88, 91, 95, 120–23, 128–29, 134, 139–40, 148–49, 151, 155, 168, 173, 174, 195, 202, 248–49, 272, 287–90, 301n1, 310n90, 313n36
Claiborne, Capt., 209–10, 212, 221, 224, 270
Coahuila, Mexico, 49, 232
Cochise (Apache chief), 6, 191, 280, 284
Cockburn, William, 76
Collins, James L., 15, 51, 166, 229–30, 273
Colorado River, 159, 187, 315n18
Comanche Canyon, N.Mex., 249–50
Comanche Indians, 14, 21, 45–47, 94, 261
Compromise of 1850, 75, 90
Conner, William J., 314n56

INDEX 347

Conrad, Charles M., 21, 26, 56, 61, 87, 92, 96, 106, 120
Constante, Antonio, 66, 258
Contraband trade, 41, 68, 74, 166, 194–96, 239, 254–55
Cooke's Spring, N.Mex., 171, 201, 208, 209
Corps of Topographical Engineers, 15, 138
Corrales, Martín, 197
Cosas (Apache chief), 246
Costales (Apache), 177, 197–99, 317n8
Cow Springs, N.Mex., 201, 209, 277
Coyotero Apaches, 57, 83, 146–47, 188, 192, 204, 213, 218, 220, 225, 270, 318n38; attacked by troops, 191, 221–24, 227–28, 230. *See also* Apaches
Craig, Capt. Louis S., 82–84, 162–63
Crook, Gen. George, 6
Croty, John, 113
Cuchillo Negro (Apache chief), 126–27, 131, 142, 180, 215–18
Cuentas Azules (Apache chief), 134, 252, 312n26
Culligan, Private, 249–50

Daklugie, Ace, 9, 41, 294n11
Davis, Jefferson, 178, 309n68
Davis, Lt. Matthew L., 177, 178
Davis, William W. H., 257–58
Delaware Creek, 248, 256
Delgadito (Apache chief), 79–80, 113, 175–76, 181, 197, 198, 201–202, 242, 300n36, 310n69, 317n2, 317n8
Dennison, Lt. William, 219
Department of the Interior, 81, 120, 129, 146, 154, 155, 258, 288
Dodge, Henry L., 175, 203–205, 216, 224, 227
Dog Canyon, 235, 241, 252, 255, 270, 324n22
Doña Ana, N.Mex., 29, 59, 67, 69–73, 77–78, 83, 97, 101, 108, 126, 141, 161, 189, 237, 256, 257, 266, 304n70; abandonment by troops, 97–99, 104; described, 63–64; land grant at, 63, 76–77; Mescalero Apaches at, 165–66, 179–80, 262–63; military post at, 64–65, 302n35; raids at, 79, 236
Doniphan, Alexander W., 15, 67
Dragoons, 11, 15, 19, 31, 57, 72, 74, 79, 87, 92, 108, 110, 113, 132, 147, 159, 163, 169, 180, 190, 192, 236–39, 241, 264, 265, 276; armaments, 31–33, 304n52; described, 22–23; engagements with Apaches, 32–33, 113–15, 144; 175–77, 193–94, 244, 247, 249–50; horses, 65, 69–70, 85–87, 116, 143, 218, 242; salaries, 27; transfer to California, 182–83. *See also* First U.S. Regiment of Dragoons; Second U.S. Regiment of Dragoons; U.S. troops
Drown, William, 325n51
DuBois, Lt. John V. D., 208, 209, 212, 217, 221–23, 228, 230
Dugan, Sgt., 269
Dunbar, Edward E., 191
Duran, Francisco, 195
Durango, Mexico, 17, 49
Duvall, Alexander, 182
Dwyer, Thomas, 244

Eaton, Capt. Joseph H., 168–69, 171–72, 179–80
Eaton Ranch, N.Mex., 247
Eighth U.S. Infantry Regiment, 208, 212, 221, 253, 270
El Cautívo (Apache chief), 175
Elías (Apache chief), 280
El Paso, Texas, 61, 63, 81, 82, 85, 99, 101, 104, 132, 161, 179, 192, 256. *See also* Fort Bliss, Texas; Paso del Norte, Mexico
Emory, William H., 15–16
Evans, Lt. Nathan G., 115, 141
Ewell, Capt. Richard S., 191; background, 298n47; at Fort Buchanan, 189–90, 319n45; on Gila Campaign, 212, 219–22, 228; at Los Lunas, 32, 116; on Mescalero campaigns, 243–44, 249–50

Fandangos, 34–35, 303n42
Fauntleroy, Col. Thomas T., 259

Fifth U.S. Infantry Regiment, 248, 256
Fillmore, Millard, 56, 93, 129
First U.S. Regiment of Dragoons, 20–21, 31, 75, 182–83, 191, 238, 245, 249–50, 253, 296n7, 298n58, 317n22, 325n51; on campaign, 79–80, 110–11, 116–19, 169, 171–72, 201, 221, 235–36, 243–45, 303n40, 324n9; desertion, 35; at Doña Ana, 64–65, 69, 78, 85; ethnicity of troops, 25; at Fort Buchanan, 187–91; at Fort Conrad, 102; at Fort Fillmore, 108, 132; at Fort Webster, 141, 158. *See also* Dragoons; U.S. troops
Fitzgerald, Maj. Edward H., 191
Fitzpatrick, Thomas, 87–88
Fletcher, Frank, 182, 257–59
Florida Mountains, 171, 208–209
Floyd, John B., 276
Fort Apache, Ariz., 58
Fort Bliss, Texas, 35, 161, 240–41, 248, 256, 260, 298n57, 302n23
Fort Breckenridge, Ariz., 189, 281
Fort Buchanan, Ariz., 25, 28, 188–92, 204, 219, 228, 281, 284–85, 318n45, 321n29
Fort Conrad, N.Mex., 32, 108, 110, 113–16, 118, 125, 126, 131, 144, 158, 161; 196, 240, 309n56, 309n63; abandoned, 162; established, 102–104
Fort Craig, N.Mex., 30, 162–63, 175, 181, 199, 241, 242, 273–75, 281
Fort Davis, Texas, 270
Fort Defiance, Ariz., 67, 203–206, 226–27
Fort Fillmore, N.Mex., 30, 59, 99, 110, 112, 113, 126, 131, 140, 141, 144, 158, 161, 165, 179, 224, 238, 244, 256, 269, 275, 276, 281, 284, 308n35, 312n26; abandonment threatened, 264–65; desertion at, 35, 132; established, 101–102, 105–106; farming at, 106–108; payment of troops at, 27–28, 297n30; post garrison, 132, 149; Captain Stanton's funeral at, 245, 325n44
Fort Leavenworth, Kans., 13, 28, 101
Fort McLane, N.Mex., 281, 286, 287
Fort Selden, N.Mex., 325n44
Fort Sill, Okla., 50
Fort Stanton, N.Mex., 181, 182, 263, 271, 272, 279, 283; contraband trade at, 255; described, 253–54; established, 251; Mescaleros at, 252, 261, 262. *See also* Reservation proposals
Fort Thorn, N.Mex., 47, 175, 177, 180–82, 187, 197–99, 208, 209, 215, 224, 229, 263, 269, 272, 275, 284, 323n72; abandoned, 186, 276; Apache Agency, 152, 161, 163–64, 170, 171, 173, 176, 200, 204, 216, 218, 246, 283; described, 185; established, 159–60; health problems at, 182–86, 276, 318n27; Mescalero Apaches at, 51, 164–66, 252–53, 270; Mesilla Guard attack at, 266–67; raids at, 168, 207
Fort Union, N.Mex., 28–29, 183, 242
Fort Webster, N.Mex. (first), 51, 116–18, 120, 121, 126–27, 138–39; abandoned, 131–32, 141; contraband trade at, 140–41; desertion at, 35; established, 112; skirmish at, 113–14
Fort Webster, N.Mex. (second), 152, 154, 161, 165, 181, 184, 195, 278; abandoned, 158–59; Apache Agency, 147, 159; Apache raids at, 142–43; described, 158; engagements at, 144; established, 132, 141, 149, 312n15
Fort Yuma, Ariz., 163
Franklin, Texas *See* El Paso, Texas.
Frazier, Capt. George, 269
Free, Mickey (Apache scout), 58
Fronteras, Sonora, 46, 83

Gadsden Purchase, 59, 104, 148, 187, 188, 193
García Conde, Alejo, 59–60
García Conde, Pedro, 82
Garland, Gen. John, 151, 156–57, 161, 162, 174–75, 182, 187, 188, 202, 203, 224, 228, 240, 254, 263, 267, 290, 327n102, 327n107; background,

315n10; on Mescalero campaigns, 243–45, 251; threatens to abandon Fort Fillmore, 264–66
Garretson, John W., 200
Geck, Louis William, 77–78, 304n70
Genero (Apache chief), 246
Geronimo, 6, 10, 12, 46–47, 50, 287
Gibbs, Lt. Alfred, 200–201
Gibson, George, 29, 79
Gila Apaches, 42–43, 51, 71, 85, 97, 112, 121, 127, 134, 140, 142, 145, 148, 170, 178, 180, 197, 201, 214, 228, 229, 257, 258, 261, 262, 276, 280, 303n40, 310n69; annuities, 166; meet with Steen, 79–80; raiding, 115–16, 144, 163, 168; skirmish at Fort Webster, 113–14; treaty at Fort Thorn, 164–67. *See also* Apaches; Mimbres Apaches
Gila Campaign, 206–207, 271; disbanded, 227–29; Southern Column, 207–10
Gila Depot, N.Mex., 211, 213, 216, 218, 220, 225, 229
Gila River, 16, 17, 65, 72, 77, 79, 117–18, 137, 147–48, 158–59, 166, 171, 175–76, 187, 188, 193–94, 206, 215, 220–22, 278. *See also* Reservation proposals
Gomez (Apache chief), 263, 270
González, Inez, 83
Gordon, Capt. William H., 270–71, 276–78
Goyahkla. *See* Geronimo
Graham, Maj. Lawrence P., 126
Graves, Edmund A., 48–49, 155
Gray, Andrew B., 82
Greenwood, Alfred B., 279
Greiner, John, 87, 121, 132, 146; feuds with Sumner, 134–36; meets with Apaches, 138–39
Guadalupe Mountains, 232, 240, 248
Guerrero, Vicente, 47

Hackett's Hog Ranch, N.Mex., 255
Harrison, Lieut., 235–36
Hart, Simeon, 99
Helm, Capt. Thomas, 282

Hennings, John, 244
Henry, Dr. T. Charles, 183–85, 270
Heradia, Saverro, 83
Holmes, Maj. J. J., 255, 261
Homestead Act, 78
Hoppin, Charles A., 265
Howe, Maj. Marshall S., 102, 125, 126, 309n56; leads Apache campaign, 115–19
Howland, Lt. George W., 267, 276–78
Hueco Tanks, Texas, 240, 248
Huelta (Apache chief), 246

Indemnity claims, 45, 258–60, 299n19, 303n49, 314n56, 324n8, 325n34, 327n86
Indian agencies. *See* Fort Thorn, N.Mex.; Fort Webster, N.Mex. (second)
Indian Appropriation Act, 88
Indian Bureau. *See* Bureau of Indian Affairs
Indian Intercourse Act, 45, 258
Infantry, 19, 21, 31, 34, 60, 74–75, 79, 84, 87, 91, 98, 108, 113, 116, 132, 175–76, 180, 190, 237, 240–42, 265; armaments, 32; on Gila Campaign, 211, 222; salaries, 27. *See also* Eighth U.S. Infantry Regiment; Fifth U.S. Infantry Regiment; Second U.S. Infantry Regiment; Seventh U.S. Infantry Regiment; Third U.S Infantry Regiment; U.S. troops
Interior Department. *See* Department of the Interior
International boundary disputes, 81–82, 104, 139, 187
Itán (Apache chief), 139, 175–76, 201, 242
Iturbide, Agustín de, 47

James Canyon, 251
Janos, Chihuahua, 46, 84, 215–16, 300n28
Jaramillo, Teofilo and Mateo, 79–80
Jicarilla Apaches, 20, 46, 234, 237, 241, 324n18. *See also* Apaches

Johns, Maj. William B., 240–41
Jornada del Muerto, 69, 162, 256, 269; raids on, 112, 114–15, 125–26. *See also* Camino Real
Jose (Apache chief), 241–42
Josecito (Apache chief), 79–80, 324n18

Kaywaykla, James, 39–40, 52, 284
Kearny, Gen. Stephen W., 10, 12, 67, 80, 112, 287; background, 13, 295n2, 295n7; marches to California, 15–16; meets with Apaches, 16–18, 137; pledges protection to citizens, 14
Keat's Ranch, N.Mex., 240
Kelley, Robert P., 281
Kendrick, Capt. Henry Lane, 203–204
Ker, Capt. Kroghan, 60
Kirker, James, 48

La Luz Canyon, 261
Land grants, 63, 76, 78, 102, 308n35
Lane, Lydia Spencer, 30
Lane, William Carr, 106, 128, 131, 136, 138, 143, 147–48, 150–52, 155, 195, 202, 273, 278, 290; background, 129; feuds with Sumner, 139–40; treaty with Apaches, 50–51, 133, 144–46, 153–54, 166, 172. *See also* Civil-military contention
Las Cruces, N.Mex., 63, 64, 108, 182, 239, 257, 258, 312n26; mines at, 77; raids at, 260
Las Placitas del Rio Bonito, 254
Las Vegas, N.Mex., 14, 17
Lazelle, Lt. Henry, 106, 210, 212, 213, 230, 270
Lea, Luke, 88, 120
Lemitar, N.Mex., 68, 194
Liquor. *See* Contraband trade
Lobo (Apache chief), 324n18
Longstreet, Maj. James, 247–48
Longworthy, E. P., 52, 103, 162
López, Juan N., 314n56
Loring, Col. William W., 207, 211–12, 214–18, 220–21, 226–27, 321n28
Los Amoles, N.Mex., 200

Los Lunas, N.Mex., 32, 63, 161, 169, 186, 192–94, 243, 245, 246
Lucas, James A., 265
Lucero, Julian, 324n8
Lynde, Maj. Isaac, 286

Magoffin, James W., 101–102, 308n33
Magoffin, Samuel, 85
Magoffinsville, Texas, 132
Malaria, 182–86, 199, 275. *See also under* U.S. troops
Mangas Coloradas (Apache chief), 127, 138–39, 143, 148, 164, 171, 191, 204–205, 218, 224, 228, 278, 284, 296n10, 300n36, 310n83, 312n31; killed, 286–87; meets with Kearny, 16–17, 137; meets with Steen, 79–80, 146; signs Acoma Treaty, 134–37
Manifest Destiny, 11, 13, 55
Mansfield, Col. Joseph K. F., 32, 104, 107, 158–59, 162, 170
Manypenny, George W., 152, 177
Manzano, N.Mex., 242, 250
Marcy, William L., 60, 92
Matson, Sylvester M., 114
May, Col. Charles A., 31, 68, 74
McCall, George A., 64–65, 74, 87, 96–97
McFerran, Lieutenant, 240
McGowan, Timothy, 258
McQuade, Sgt. Hugh, 273–74
Medical Department, 62
Medill, William, 91
Meriwether, David, 50, 51, 138, 151, 156, 173, 174, 177, 198, 202, 203, 211, 232, 246, 258, 272–73, 279, 290; background, 152–53; Indian policy, 155, 262; treaty with Gila and Mescalero Apaches, 164–67, 172, 252–53
Mesa del Contadero, 162
Mescal, 9, 39, 138, 288
Mescalero Apaches, 20, 32, 85, 179–81, 279, 283; at Doña Ana, 165–66, 239–40, 262–63; engagements with troops, 235–36, 240–42, 244, 247, 249–50, 269–70, 325n38; at Fort

INDEX   351

Stanton, 255, 262; at Fort Thorn, 51, 266–67; negotiate treaties, 164–67, 237–38, 246, 252–53, 324n18; population, 232, 237, 323n2; raids, 236, 238, 257–59, 325n34; threaten attack on Mesilla, 263–64; tribal structure, 232. *See also* Apaches

Mesilla, N.Mex., 63, 77, 78, 104, 106, 108, 168, 182, 198, 200, 258, 263–64, 268, 312n26

Mesilla Guard, 262–69, 271, 327n102

Mesilla Valley, 63, 69, 76–78, 102, 107, 126, 192, 197, 258, 304n70, 308n35

Mestizos, 27

Mexican-American War, 3–4, 14–15, 21, 26, 29, 31, 45, 55, 59, 95, 111, 140

Mexican Cession, 29, 61, 288

Mexicans/New Mexicans, 169; described by Anglo-Americans, 24–25; as guides for military, 53, 66, 116, 175, 208, 211, 235, 240, 241, 243, 247, 324n9; as laborers at army posts, 25, 105–107, 159, 182, 308n44; merchants/traders, 41, 62, 194–96, 254; nationalism, 13–15, 73; petition government, 97–99, 163, 264–65; posing as Apaches, 250, 259–60; relations with Apaches, 39, 48–50, 57–58, 194–97, 239, 268; relations with troops, 24–25, 73; supply contracts for posts, 29–30, 62, 125, 150, 265; threaten rebellion, 129–30, 311n11. *See also* Captives

Mexico: boundary commission, 82; diplomacy with U.S., 55–56, 59–60, 104, 111–12, 191, 312n26, 319n49; government, 14, 26, 47–48, 61–62, 167

Meztas, Manuel, 197

Miles, Col. Dixon S., 27–28, 126, 132, 140–41, 143, 149, 165, 179, 191, 263; background, 105–106, 309n48; at Fort Fillmore, 30, 31, 35, 104, 106–108, 239, 246, 275–76; at Fort Thorn, 199–200; during Gila Campaign, 207–10, 213, 214, 217–18, 220–25; meets with Mescaleros, 252, 257–59

Miles, Gen. Nelson A., 6

Military strategy, 31, 49, 66–67, 71–73, 95, 108, 110, 119–20, 173, 203

Militia units, 41, 92–93, 112, 327n101. *See also* Mesilla Guard; New Mexico Volunteers

Mimbres Apaches, 42–43, 144–46, 161, 199, 242, 322n45; attacked by troops, 216–21; treaty at Fort Thorn, 164–67. *See also* Apaches; Gila Apaches

Mimbres River (valley), 117, 127, 131–32, 142, 147, 158, 165, 167, 176–77, 188, 201, 213, 261, 279, 280. *See also* Reservation proposals

Minié, Claude Etienne, 33

Mining, 77, 84, 167, 189, 279, 281. *See also* Santa Rita del Cobre, N.Mex.

Missouri Volunteers, 67

Mogollon Apaches, 41–43, 146–47, 158, 169–70, 175–78, 181, 192, 216, 229, 270, 320n4; murder of agent Dodge, 203–205, 213, 224. *See also* Apaches

Mogollon Mountains, 66, 72, 163, 169, 174–75, 193, 215–19, 273, 320n4

Montoya, Antonio, 314n56

Moore, Lt. Isaiah N., 169, 177

Morris, Maj. Gouverneur, 117–20, 126–27, 131–32, 140–42, 158, 308n35

Mowry, Sylvester, 10, 188–89, 285

Mt. Turnbull, Ariz., 191, 221

Munroe, Col. John, 74–76, 79, 93, 95, 194–95, 237, 238, 304n59, 307n18, 317n86

Navajo Indians, 14, 20, 21, 45, 46, 67–68, 72, 94, 96, 133, 170, 203, 204, 211, 271, 295n7

Negrito (Apache chief), 134, 241–42

Neighbors, Robert S., 76

New Mexico: climate, 30, 33–34, 39, 108; Indian population, 154–55; surrendered to U.S., 15

New Mexico Volunteers, 63, 253

Ninth Military Department, 26, 60, 62, 67, 74, 85, 87, 88, 93, 95, 96, 124, 129, 150, 298n57, 308n40

Norwood, Cpl. A. E., 303n40

O'Bannon, Lt. Laurence, 64, 69, 70, 142, 182, 219, 220
O'Daugherty, Bernard, 113
Ojo del Lucero, N.Mex., 276–78
Ojo del Oso, N.Mex., 67
Olona, Manuel, 303n49
Organ Mountains, 105, 238, 256
Ortega, Juan, 267, 268

Padilla, José María, 314n56
Padilla, Juan, 169
Palanquito (Apache chief), 246, 252, 257–58, 324n29, 325n47
Paso del Norte, Mexico, 29, 65
Pecos River, 232, 237, 242, 243, 255–56
Pelham, William, 167
Peñasco River, 244
Pierce, Franklin, 27, 137, 161
Pima Indians, 188, 321n29, 322n50
Pinal Apaches, 43, 57, 83, 188, 318n38. *See also* Apaches
Piños Altos, 285, 286
Plumas (Apache chief), 246
Polk, James K., 14, 17
Point of Rocks, N.Mex., 126
Ponce (Apache chief), 113, 139, 142–44, 300n36, 310n69
Pope, Capt. John, 138
Poston, Charles D., 327n101
Pueblo Indians, 25, 79; as military guides, 116, 211, 212, 217, 220, 223, 322n50
Puerco River, 170

Quinan, Dr. P. A., 185

Ratón (Apache), 197–98
Reed, Thomas, 269
Regiment of Mounted Rifles, 19, 30, 60, 185, 187, 264, 276, 296n9; engagements with Apaches, 200–201, 269–70, 274–75; on Gila Campaign, 208, 211, 214–15, 217, 219, 221, 222, 226; organization, 21–22. *See also* U.S. troops
Reid, John, 58, 197–98
Rencher, Abraham, 267, 273

Reservation proposals, 50, 94, 122–23, 127, 128, 173, 238, 271, 278, 311n92, 316n42; at Fort Stanton, 253; at Gila River, 51, 166; at Mimbres River, 145, 165–67; at Santa Lucia Springs, 147–48, 279–80
Rice, Josiah M., 24, 33–34
Richardson, Maj. Israel B., 112, 117, 182
Riflemen. *See* Regiment of Mounted Rifles
Ringgold, Private, 249–50
Rio Bonito, 164, 243, 251, 254
Rio Grande (valley), 62–63, 108, 159, 162, 184, 208, 223, 256, 274, 283
Rio Hondo, 241–42, 251
Roberts, Lt. Col. Benjamin S., 186, 193
Robledo Mountains, 110, 200
Rooney, Pat, 247
Ruelas, Rafael, 264
Ruff, Maj., 255

Sackett, Lt. Delos B., 64
Sacramento Mountains, 181, 236, 237, 240, 243, 246–47, 250, 269
San Antonio, N.Mex., 115–16, 196
Sanches, Dolores, 197
San Diego Crossing (Rio Grande), N.Mex., 69, 171; Apaches killed at, 197–99
San Elizario, Texas, 99, 104
San Pedro River, Ariz., 187, 188, 277
Santa Anna (Apache chief), 241–42, 251–52, 271, 324n29, 326n65
Santa Anna, Antonio Lopez de, 47
Santa Barbara, N.Mex., 159
Santa Cruz, Sonora, 83, 301n14
Santa Cruz River, Ariz., 187–89
Santa Fe, N.Mex., 14, 15, 17, 20, 62, 63, 127, 128, 139, 152, 153, 186, 238, 246, 247
Santa Fe Trail, 13, 77, 86, 127, 129
Santa Lucia Springs, N.Mex., 147–48, 171, 217, 277–78. *See also* Reservation proposals
Santa Rita del Cobre, N.Mex., 71–72, 77, 97, 127, 131, 159, 161, 167, 175,

217, 277, 279, 285, 303n40, 310n69, 327n102; Bartlett visits, 82–85; military post at, 112–14; Steen visits, 79–80
Santos (Apache chief), 236, 240, 245–46, 324n29
San Vincente Spring, 217
Scalp hunters, 48–49, 136
Scott, Gen. Winfield, 75, 79, 83, 187, 298n47
Second U.S. Infantry Regiment, 159
Second U.S. Regiment of Dragoons, 20–21, 31, 60, 118, 127, 196, 296n7; desertion, 35; engagements, 115, 126, 235–36; at Fort Fillmore, 108, 132; at Fort Webster, 141–43; at Socorro, 63, 66, 74. *See also* Dragoons; U.S. troops
Sectionalism, 26, 56, 90, 273
Seminole Indians, 61, 86
Seventh U.S. Infantry Regiment, 75
Sharps carbine, 32–33
Shawono (Apache chief), 263, 269
Shepherd, Maj. Oliver L., 64, 175
Simonson, Maj. John, 211, 248
Skeleton Canyon, 12
Smith, Hugh N., 94, 102, 120, 194
Smith, James, 161
Socorro, N.Mex., 67–68, 73–74, 115, 169, 196; abandoned by troops, 102, 163; described, 63; Mesilla Guard trial at, 267–68; military post at, 31, 65–66, 86
Soledad Canyon, N. Mex., 105
Sonoita Valley, Ariz., 58, 189
Sonora, Mexico, 14, 17, 39, 46–49, 57, 80, 111, 136, 148, 187, 188, 190, 216, 223
Southern Apache Agency. *See* Fort Thorn, N.Mex.
Stanton, Capt. Henry W., 243–45, 249–51, 253, 325n44
Steck, Dr. Michael, 47, 50, 51, 147, 151, 152, 155, 156, 158, 170–72, 179–80, 197, 198, 200, 204, 215–16, 220, 224, 277–78, 282–83, 290; background, 149, 314n70; dispute with Chandler, 176–78, 317n10; Indian policy, 161–62, 164, 168; as Mescalero agent,
239–40, 246, 251–52, 256–57, 259, 261–63, 266
Steele, Capt. William, 144
Steen, Lt. Alexander E., 172, 175, 176, 180, 197, 198, 219–20, 222–23
Steen, Maj. Enoch, 83, 84, 97, 125, 183, 248, 304n62; background, 303n36; at Doña Ana, 64–67, 69–73, 172, 237; at Fort Buchanan, 28, 187–91, 317n22; at Fort Webster, 141, 144, 147, 158, 195; land claim at Doña Ana, 76–77; meets with Apaches, 79–80, 236–37, 240; military strategy, 71–73; recommends post at Santa Rita, 72–73; wounded, 303n40
Stephenson, Hugh, 101–102, 308n35
Sturgis, Lt. Samuel D., 247
Sullivan, Patrick, 269
Sumner, Col. Edwin V., 22, 50, 67, 87, 88, 112, 116, 119–23, 128, 141, 145, 289, 308n44, 310n90; angers citizens, 124–25, 131, 150; background, 95, 307n19; criticized by Garland, 156–58; farming program, 101, 106–108, 159, 309n56; feuds with Lane, 139–40; as governor of New Mexico, 129–32, 138, 311n10, 317n39; Indian policy, 95–96, 313n33; leaves New Mexico, 149–51; military strategy, 95–97, 100–102, 110, 113, 116; negotiates Acoma Treaty, 132–38; opinion of New Mexico, 24–27; reorganizes military department, 72–73, 96–98, 125, 313n37. *See also* Civil-military contention
Swords, Maj. Thomas, 99, 196

Taylor, Zachary, 56, 82
Tevis, James H., 280
Texas, 48, 61, 85, 187, 232; claims to New Mexico, 75–79; troops invade New Mexico during Civil War, 280–82
Third U.S. Infantry Regiment, 60, 206, 252, 253, 256, 263, 276; at Albuquerque, 149; on campaign, 171–72; at Doña Ana, 64, 69, 70;

Third U.S. Infantry Regiment (*continued*) at Fort Fillmore, 104, 108, 132; at Fort Thorn, 185; at Fort Webster, 112, 117–18, 142, 158; on Gila Campaign, 198, 211, 219, 221; organization, 22; at Santa Rita de Cobre, 82. *See also* U.S. troops
Thompson, Jacob, 45
Thorn, Capt. Herman, 159, 315n18
Torreon, N.Mex., 250
Treaties, 50–52, 59, 66, 67, 112, 127, 138, 144–46, 150, 153, 164–67, 237–38, 246, 252–53, 324n18. *See also* Acoma Treaty
Treaty of Guadalupe Hidalgo, 76, 80, 111, 148; Article 11, 55–60, 79, 81, 135–36, 192–93, 236
Trinfan, José, 83
Tubac, Ariz., 187
Tucson, Ariz., 183, 187–92, 228, 277, 317n22, 318n40
Tularosa River, 175, 181, 211, 226
Turner, Frederick Jackson, 6–7, 294n4

Ussen (Apache god), 9–10, 41
U.S. troops, 19; accoutrements, 22–23; armaments, 31–33, 70; attack innocent Apache subgroups, 43–44; campaigning, 33–34; daily life, 20, 24–26, 30, 35–36; desertion, 34–35, 132, 163, 298n58; discipline, 30–31, 34–35, 62, 102–103; engagements with Apaches, 20, 32–33, 70, 113–14, 144, 191, 193–94, 200–201, 215, 221–24, 235–36, 240, 242, 244, 247, 249–50, 269–70, 274–75, 303n40, 325n38; family life, 30; farming at posts, 101; gambling, 28, 159; illness among, 20, 62, 103–104, 302n28, 318n27; killed by Apaches, 113–15, 126, 144, 247, 249, 256, 269–70; linguistic difficulties, 25, 51–52; morale, 34, 36, 73; mortality rate, 62; numerical strength, 21–22, 60–61, 64–65, 74–75, 79, 296n7, 297n20, 298n58, 302n29, 308n40; officers, 11, 19–20, 30, 36; relations with Mexicans, 24, 73; salaries, 27; supplies and provisions, 28–29, 34; supply contracts, 29–30, 99, 125, 150. *See also* Artillery; Dragoons; First U.S. Regiment of Dragoons; Infantry; Regiment of Mounted Rifles; Second U.S. Regiment of Dragoons; Third U.S. Infantry Regiment
Ute Indians, 20, 21, 45, 46, 94

Valentine, Private, 256
Valverde, N.Mex., 162
Van Horne, Maj. Jefferson, 61, 85, 86
Vera Cruz, Mexico, 13
Victorio (Apache Chief), 6, 52

Wade, Nicholas, 113–14
Ward, John, 52
War Department, 5, 17, 25, 31, 89–91, 96, 129, 155, 158, 173, 178, 187, 199, 288, 290, 302n24, 320n3; expenditures, 22, 29, 86, 100–101, 106, 296n9; issues bounty land, 78; issues supply contracts, 29–30
Washington, John M., 60, 67
Weaver, Private, 249–50
Webster, Daniel, 112, 129
Weightman, Richard H., 133, 139
Weller, John B., 82, 85
West, Brig. Gen. Joseph Rodman, 286
Western Apaches, 41–42, 57, 83, 187, 188
Whipple, Lieut., 219–20
Wilson, Joseph S., 279
Wingfield, Edward H., 143, 147, 152, 153, 158, 310n90
Wood, Lt. William Henry, 266–67
Woodhouse, Dr. S. W., 64

Young, Private, 249–50
Yrisarri, Mariano, 243